SOCIOLOGICAL REVIEW MONOGRAPH 27

On the Margins of Science: The Social Construction of Rejected Knowledge

Issue Editor: Roy Wallis

D1613425

Managing Editors: W. M. Williams and R. J. Frankenberg
University of Keele
March 1979

On the Margins of Science:
The Social Construction of Rejected Knowledge
Monograph 27
Editor: Roy Wallis

Contents

University of Keele, Keele, Staffordshire

Notes on Contributors

Paul D. Allison PhD
Assistant Professor, Department of Sociology, Cornell University

Eileen Barker BSc (Soc)
Lecturer, Department of Sociology, London School of Economics and Political Science

Barry Barnes MA, MSc
Lecturer, Science Studies Unit, University of Edinburgh

Joseph A. Blake MA, PhD
Assistant Professor, Department of Sociology, Virginia Polytechnic Institute and State University

H. M. Collins BSc (Econ), MA
Lecturer, School of Humanities and Social Sciences, University of Bath

R. G. A. Dolby MA, MSc
Senior Lecturer, Unit for History, Philosophy and Social Relations of Science, University of Kent at Canterbury

Donald MacKenzie BSc, PhD
Lecturer, Department of Sociology, University of Edinburgh

Jon Palfreman BSc, MSc
Producer of Science Features, B.B.C. Television

Terry M. Parssinen MA, PhD
Associate Professor, Department of History, Temple University, Philadelphia

T. J. Pinch BSc, MSc
Graduate Research Student, School of Humanities and Social Sciences, University of Bath

Steven Shapin BA, MA, PhD
Lecturer, Science Studies Unit, University of Edinburgh

Roy Wallis BA, D.Phil
Professor of Sociology, Department of Social Studies, The Queen's University of Belfast

A. J. Webster BSc (Soc.Sci)
Lecturer in Sociology, Department of Management and Business Studies, Cambridgeshire College of Art and Technology

Ron Westrum AB, MA, PhD
Associate Professor, Department of Sociology, Eastern Michigan University

Peter W. G. Wright BSc (Econ), MSc (Econ)
Principal Lecturer, Department of Applied Social Studies, Sheffield City Polytechnic

Brian Wynne MA, PhD, M.Phil
Lecturer, Department of Independent Studies, University of Lancaster

Cover Design by Cal Swann FSIAD

Editorial Board

Note

Manuscripts to be considered for publication in the form of *Monographs of the Sociological Review* and contributions to be considered for inclusion in *The Sociological Review* should be sent to Professor Ronald Frankenberg, Managing Editor.

ISBN 0 904425 06 1

Printed and bound in Great Britain
by J. H. Brookes (Printers) Limited, Hanley, Stoke-on-Trent, Staffs.

INTRODUCTION

Roy Wallis

UNTIL quite recently, the acceptance or rejection of ideas within and at the boundaries of science has rarely been considered a matter of sociological concern. Sociologists maintained a deferential attitude towards prevailing scientific orthodoxy, accepting that in respect of the esoteric content of science, scientists knew best.[1] For some sociologists this meant that the corpus of currently accepted knowledge constituted the 'truth', arrived at by unimpeachable means through the 'scientific method'. Logic and the technical procedures of the substantive scientific field were believed to provide not only a complete *justification* but also a sufficient *explanation,* for the current content of scientific knowledge.

The sociologist's role was thus a highly limited one, permitting enquiry into the social relations involved in the production of that content; the origins and differential productivity of the scientists concerned; the political economy of greater or lesser increments to that content by one nation or another; or the ideological biases, social influences, or 'irrational' commitments which led to *departures* from that content, or from the allegedly consensually agreed rules and procedures for its production. There was, on this account, simply no room for the addition of a sociological component in the explanation of the *content itself*. Hence, while there could be sociological explanation of false or 'irrational' belief,[2] or the 'irrational' behaviour of scientists in contravention of the norms supposedly governing their behaviour as in the notorious case of Velikovsky[3] there could be none of true or 'rational' belief.[4] To suggest otherwise was said to lead to a vicious relativism. To question the 'scientific method' was to undermine the foundation upon which one's own argument was built. If the 'scientific method' provided no firm foundation for knowledge then what could provide a basis for the debunking claim of the sociological sceptic?

More recently—particularly under the liberating impact of Thomas Kuhn's[5] bold challenge to this complacent view of scientific knowledge—sociologists and historians have adopted a more method-

5

ologically 'agnostic' view of the truth claims of scientists. Despite his objections to the sociology of knowledge, Popper's critique of induction and verificationism eliminated one barrier to it. If the truth of scientific propositions could never be established with absolute certainty, criteria for distinguishing truth and error in order to allocate them to distinctive explanatory modes disappeared. There yet remained the claim that what was at issue was not the truth status of the proposition, but the means by which it had been derived. The critique of falsificationism more recently has shown that *in principle* there are no logically water-tight grounds for belief, and that those grounds which are employed are at many important points crucially *conventional* matters on which decisions are taken in the context of professional colleagues on the basis of the intuitions of practising scientists.[6]

Lakatos, while still retaining a commitment to the rationality of science, has clearly shown the conventional character of the grounds upon which decisions are taken at crucial points in the scientific enterprise.[7] Logic and 'fact' simply do not provide sufficient grounds upon which such decisions can be made. Sociologists of science, like Collins,[8] have shown the negotiated character of essential methodological issues such as what is to *count* as a replication of an experiment. These assaults on the bastion of 'naive falsificationism' have convinced many historians and sociologists of science that distinctive modes of explanation for allegedly rationally-held and allegedly irrationally-held beliefs are unnecessary. A major sociological protagonist of this view is Barry Barnes[9] who has argued that the only salient distinction is one in terms of *normal* practice.

> 'Certain institutionalised beliefs and actions are normally associated with an actor through consideration of the position he occupies within the social structure. A causal account of their acquisition must be sought in the theory of socialization. Their persistence can be causally related to a normal patten of influences surrounding the actor. Beliefs and actions departing from this normality are causally attributable to the idiosyncratic experience of the actors holding them. Here is the formal scheme which must organise causal analyses of the social distribution and variation of beliefs and actions.'[10]

Some have also concluded that the esoteric content of scientific belief and its production can now legitimately be explored to elucidate the role of social factors in the decision-procedures and strategies of practising scientists.[11] Such an approach is not new, of course. Hessen's account of the sources of Newton's *Principia*[12] is notorious

Introduction

as an early economic determinist attempt to explain the esoteric content of science. Forman's recent work[13] exhibits a more subtle approach to the influence of social milieux on the detailed technical cognitive content of science, in which he seeks to show that an acausal quantum mechanics was particularly welcomed by physicists in Post-First World War Germany because it provided an opportunity for practitioners of this branch of science to adapt to an environment dominated by a profound romantic reaction to deterministic science, and to recover some of its lost public esteem. Forman's work appears to signal a major emerging trend in sociological studies of science, which is exemplified by some of the accounts that follow in this volume.

The generally changing ethos, the shift away from an earlier deferentialism, provides an opportunity for a broad re-examination of 'rejected knowledge'. The undermining of 'the crucial experiment' as final arbiter in the long-run evaluation of a 'research programme', or 'paradigm', provokes a re-consideration of the historical, social and cognitive circumstances surrounding and embedded in the success or failure of particular knowledge-claims. The purpose of the present collection is to provide the beginnings of such a reassessment. A number of major historical and contemporary controversies within and at the margins of science are examined by scholars who have secured an intimate acquaintance with the detail of these controversies. Several essays are addressed to the illumination of the role played in such controversies by the social and intellectual milieux within which they took place; and by the role of social interests deriving from these milieux. Others focus on the processes involved in the social construction of deviant ideas; in their management and presentation *as deviant;* and in the organisational and intellectual strategies deployed and implemented by those so labelled, in their effort to shed the label and secure a hearing, funding, and the status of respectable knowledge.

The Queens University, Belfast.

Notes

[1] Such a view is characteristic of Merton, Storer and the functionalist approach to science. See R. K. Merton: *The Sociology of Science,* University of Chicago Press, London, 1973; N. W. Storer: *The Social System of Science,* Holt, Rinehart and Winston, New York, 1966. Also M. D. King: 'Reason, Tradition and the Progressiveness of Science', *History and Theory,* Vol. 10, No. 3, 1971, pp. 3-32.

[2] For example, B. Barber: 'Resistance by Scientists to Scientific Discovery', *Science*, Vol. 134, 1961, pp. 596-602.

[3] A. de Grazia: *The Velikovsky Affair*, Sidgwick and Jackson, London, 1966.

[4] King: op. cit., p. 15.

[5] T. S. Kuhn: *The Structure of Scientific Revolutions*, University of Chicago Press, London, 1962.

[6] See the chapters by I. Lakatos, T. S. Kuhn and P. K. Feyerabend in I. Lakatos and A. Musgrave: *Criticism and the Growth of Knowledge*, Cambridge University Press, London, 1970.

[7] Lakatos and Musgrave: op. cit.; I. Lakatos: 'History of Science and its Rational Reconstructions', in R. Buck and R. Cohen: *Boston Studies in the Philosophy of Science*, Vol. 8, Dordrecht, Reidel, 1971.

[8] Collins: 'The Seven Sexes: A Study in the Sociology of a Phenomenon, or the Replication of Experiments in Physics', *Sociology*, Vol. 9, No. 2, 1975, pp. 205-224.

[9] S. B. Barnes: 'Sociological Explanation and Natural Science: A Kuhnian Reappraisal', *European Journal of Sociology*, Vol. 13, No. 2, 1972, pp. 373-391; and S. B. Barnes: 'On the Reception of Scientific Beliefs', in S. B. Barnes (ed.): *Sociology of Science*, Penguin, Harmondsworth, 1972.

[10] Barnes: op. cit., 1972, p. 376.

[11] For example, P. Forman: 'Weimar Culture, Causality, and Quantum Theory, 1918-1927: Adaptation by German Physicists and Mathematicians to a Hostile Intellectual Environment' in R. McCormmach (ed.): *Historical Studies in the Physical Sciences*, Vol. III, University of Pennsylvania Press, Philadelphia, 1971.

[12] B. M. Hessen: 'The Social and Economic Roots of Newton's "Principia"' in *Science at the Cross Roads* (collected papers of the Delegation of Soviet Scientists, Second International Congress of the History of Science and Technology, London June-July 1931). Reprinted in G. Basalla (ed.): *The Rise of Modern Science*, Heath, Lexington, Massachusetts, 1968.

[13] Forman: op. cit.

REFLECTIONS ON DEVIANT SCIENCE

R. G. A. Dolby

1. *Introduction. Deviant Science as an Issue Arising out of Philosophical Discussion of the Demarcation of Science and Pseudo-Science*

PHILOSOPHERS of science have long been interested in characterising modern science in such a way that its striking success over the last three or four centuries may be explained and distinguished from activities which have made less progress. Although such philosophical discussions have usually been conducted at a high level of philosophical abstraction, they have had immediate relevance to those criticising or defending new or marginal scientific enterprises. In the twentieth century, the demarcation of science from non-scientific and especially from pseudo-scientific forms of belief or investigation has attracted special attention. Such proposals for the demarcation of science as those contained in Percy Bridgman's operationism,[1] The Vienna Circle's logical positivism,[2] or Karl Popper's method of conjecture and refutation,[3] initially provided sharp, simple and rational demarcation principles. But the elaboration required to defend the proposals has led in each case to a much more complex and diffuse division between the scientific and the non-scientific than was originally put forward. This has meant that the revised demarcation principles lost much of their utility as practical debating tools in the assessment of marginal scientific activities. For example, Popper orginally proposed that science could be demarcated from metaphysics by the rule that only the former could be falsified by empirical test. The falsifiability criterion was applied to the demarcation of scientific from pseudo-scientific inquiry by requiring that scientific investigators should employ falsifiable conjectures, they should agree in advance of empirical testing what observations would count as falsifications, and they should not attempt to save the theory from falsification by adding to it *ad hoc* hypotheses which reduced its testable content. However, even this more complex demarcation is inadequate. For example, it fails to recognise that scientists *may* be rationally justified in keeping their theory alive by *ad hoc* means if

9

they believe that it will soon lead to discoveries which will significantly increase its empirical content. In an influential paper, Imre Lakatos produced his own version of Popperian methodology which took account of such difficulties.[4] But Lakatosian methodology does not offer a sharp demarcation between science and pseudo-science; it merely distinguishes progressive and degenerative problem shifts in scientific research programmes, and stresses that in the very long term we may regard as unscientific a researcher who refuses to abandon a degenerating research programme.

Part of the difficulty in dealing with the demarcation between science and pseudo-science is that the more rationally defended examples of the latter tend to present their ideas within the rational framework of current established science. It is trivially easy to dismiss ancient astrology as failing to meet some modern criterion of scientific method; it is harder to show its inadequacies by the rational standards of its own time. Modern rejected sciences are often presented in terms of modern methodology. In the mid-1960s, for example, Velikovsky was defended as having made a number of predictions about the objects and forces in the solar system which had subsequently been found to be true rather than false. Surely, it was argued, this justified serious consideration of his theories.[5]

The difficulties in providing explicit rational principles of demarcation have increased the attractiveness of the view that in the present state of philosophy of science, the most reliable immediate indication of what is scientific is provided by the mature judgement of the relevant expert scientists.[6] This *social* criterion does, of course, introduce difficulties. For example, provided the orthodoxy is satisfied with its own work, the criterion implies that it is always doing the best science and that any alternative approach should be rejected. But at least in principle, orthodox science has no right to a monopoly of research. Since deviant science can be defended in principle, this gives a reason for examining deviant systems of belief in society, to see what significance they should be allowed to have as alternatives to orthodox science.

A social criterion of good science can, however, be applied in practice whether or not a fully rational demarcation criterion is ultimately produced. Thus it has special value for empirical studies of science. The distinction between orthodox and deviant science is especially useful for such a purpose. Orthodox science is that which commands the approval of all the leading scientific experts of the time. It includes all the historically successful sciences. Deviant science is that which is rejected by the orthodox scientific experts, and which they may label 'pseudo-science'; however, it has it own body of supporters, who claim it to be a science. The terms 'orthodox science' and 'deviant science' are not purely descriptive, for they involve a social evaluation, as is clear when there is disagreement about who the experts really are. But in most cases of modern *natural* science, the distinction between orthodox and deviant science is unproblematic.

If we are to understand why some forms of science have been so successful, it is helpful to know more about why other forms of science survive but have been less successful. To identify them as pseudo-sciences is to prejudge their quality, so that less can be learned from their descriptive study. Indeed, if we admit that philosophy of science has not yet provided a decisive rational criterion of demarcation suitable for distinguishing actual (rather than idealised) cases of science, we must accept that to label a form of activity as pseudo-scientific is to make a controversial evaluation which tends to reflect our prejudices rather than the unambiguous application of universally accepted rational principles. The term 'deviant science' in contrast does not oblige empirical study to presuppose that the activity is inadequate, merely that it has been rejected by a certain orthodoxy.

The subject of this paper is systems of belief in conflict with orthodox views, but which have some supporters who are sufficiently committed to ideals of rationality to claim them to be scientific. If one is to study deviant belief systems, there is a special interest in looking at those which claim to be sciences, because in them sufficient argumentation and evidence is produced to make it easier to understand the nature of the rationality involved. However, the term 'deviant science' is relatively unfamiliar and may be applied to a range of belief systems and activities in society. We shall begin, therefore with a discussion of types of deviant sciences in terms of their differing social bases. This will lead into a discussion of the rationality of deviant sciences. The paper will end by considering how the belief system of a deviant science can develop and the extent to which it can come to affect orthodox science.

R. G. A. Dolby

2. The Social Basis of Deviant Science

2.1 Orthodoxy and Deviance in Science

Modern natural science seems to involve very little explicit cognitive conflict. Is this high degree of consensus simply a consequence of effective rational procedures forcing all scientific knowledge into a close correspondence with natural phenomena? If so, what are the rational procedures? Many philosophers of science claim to have characterised such procedures, but their arguments are normally idealised, and it is not clear to what extent they apply to the actual interactions of scientists. Other philosophers of science have argued that there are *no* decisive rational principles adequate for the whole of scientific practice. Michael Polanyi, for example has argued that the process of scientific evaluation requires learned tacit skills as well as the application of rational principles.[7] But those who have accepted the limits to explicit rationality have still usually insisted that science normally proceeds in relative internal harmony. For example, Thomas Kuhn's influential account of normal science describes how scientists proceed according to routines accepted throughout a paradigm-sharing community.[8]

The identification of the scientific orthodoxy is simple on such views. It shares rational principles and tacit skills which it applies in an orderly manner to the advancement of knowledge. The institutional structure of science aids the avoidance of controversy and promotes research as a harmoniously run co-operative enterprise. Knowledge-seeking activity which attempted to depart from this admirable consensus could be condemned as irrational, conflicting with tacit scientific knowledge, and would be expected to be outside the institutionalised structure of science.

Not everybody is convinced by the image of scientists proceeding in such harmony, however. There have been, for example, theoretical accounts of scientific change in which an important place has been given to dissent and controversy, a process in which the relative merits of rival ideas are argued out.[9] In such accounts, it is usually assumed that scientific advance occurs through the resolution of disagreements, so that for practical purposes, scientific knowledge is that which the scientists have come to agree about (and which they regard as knowledge). More recently, some sociologists of science have become more interested in the manner in which controversies are produced in science.[10]

It is possible to argue that our presumption of the extent of consensus in the scientific orthodoxy is idealised. It is not just the human
sciences in which controversies are endemic. If one looks for them,
the history of science is rich in heated arguments, often over important divergencies of scientific belief. The rare but spectacular
major scientific revolution is merely an extreme case of a common
process in which rival ways of engaging in further research are
in competition.

In addition to highly visible explicit controversy, scientists may
hide their disagreements from sight for a number of reasons. Scientists
often follow a theory of scientific method in which controversies are
regarded as signs of irrational commitment to unsubstantiated
opinions. Then they try to conceal any disagreements which become
visible. The same tendency encourages the common disposition of
scientists to regard issues as unscientific if they turn out not to be
resolvable by immediate empirical test. Thus, when it became clear
that comparison of rival interpretations of the new quantum mechanics
of the 1920s required philosophical argument rather than empirical
investigation, it became customary to regard the interpretation of
quantum theory as a non-scientific issue. The published literature
of science may be a poor guide to the extent of consensus, unless
studied with great care. Scientists often ignore work with which they
disagree, rather than openly challenge it.[11] This is especially true of
bad work by lesser scientists which every scientist in a specialism
can reasonably be expected to have learned to treat cautiously. A
study made of a controversy over the theory of solutions in physical
chemistry at the end of the nineteenth century, revealed that residual
disagreements from the dispute could be detected many decades
later. For example, the intellectual descendents of the rival protaganists
tended to give contradictory reviews of the significance and outcome
of the original arguments.[12] Such divergent opinions did not tend to
erupt into further controversy because the people holding them
did not think it worth their while to resurrect them, especially as there
was no new material which might have encouraged people to change
their minds.

The main processes of scientific change depend disproportionately
on a relatively small number of elite scientists.[13] A small proportion
of the most productive scientists produce a large proportion of the
work, and leading scientists often form informal communication net-

works (invisible colleges) which give them a competitive advantage in rapidly changing fields. The work of eminent scientists is more visible and hence more influential, and such scientists are often in the best position to see what is worth rapid exploitation in the work of lesser scientists. As I shall explain later, the dominance of each science by a relatively small number of the most expert tends to inhibit other scientists from expressing contrary views if they accept that they are less expert or would not be regarded by fellow scientists as experts on the issue in question. It may be argued, therefore, that science is very far from being democratic, and widespread apparent agreement is due to submission to the shared views of a small proportion of elite scientists. In a social system in which dissent is discouraged and in which the expert is always deferred to, the views of the elite naturally have a disproportionate influence.

The discussion so far has suggested that the appearance of consensus in science is not due to the universal agreement of scientists. Rather, commentators on science have tended to pay more attention to signs of agreement than to signs of disagreement, and scientists themselves usually try to minimise visible controversy. The actual consensus is not produced by universal use of completely effective methods or rational assessment of scientific ideas, but rather by the general tendency to defer judgement about most of science to a relatively small proportion of elite scientists who interact fully with one another. This is the nature of the scientific orthodoxy. Each orthodox scientist builds upon the apparent consensus and his original contributions offer arguments which extend it further.

2.2 *Deviant Science in the Scientific Elite*

We will consider deviant science first as it involves the scientific elite, and then in the lower ranks of institutionalised science, before going on to look outside the institutionalised activity of orthodox science. The scientific elite so completely determines the nature of the orthodox consensus that the possibility of institutionalised deviant elite science is almost a conceptual contradiction.[14] If there is no consensus among the scientific elite, then there is no simply identifiable scientific orthodoxy of belief. Thus, in fields such as those human sciences in which there are deep divisions even in the elite about the optimum form of inquiry, the identification of elite deviant science becomes problematic. In mature natural sciences, in contrast, it is rare for the elite to disagree over fundamental issues. According to Kuhn, it is only when a field is in a state of crisis that the leading scientists become receptive to radically new approaches.[15] Thus, in revolutionary science, alternative approaches which at other times would be thought to be deviant, may be developed and defended by some members of the scientific elite, and may even, under suitable conditions, develop into the new paradigm for the science. Kuhn's account should be qualified by the observation that the social perception of crisis may not occur at the same time throughout the international scientific elite of a field if its members are unable to influence one another strongly, as when there are barriers to rapid and full communication. Thus, one group of scientists may consider that a radically new approach is required, while others with whom they are not in full contact, may reject their revolutionary efforts as deviant science. Many scientific controversies in the history of science have occurred when a theory, developed in one area, was introduced into a new geographical region or a new domain of subject matter, which was not receptive to it.[16]

In a mature science there is always a tension between the need for new research to build directly on the great achievements of the recent past,[17] and the elite scientist's aim to make original and productive contributions. In most fields the basic standards must often be reinterpreted or modified if research is to remain fruitful. There can be disagreement over the extent to which modification is justified. Disagreements are especially likely over what constitutes a significant initial step when a new line of investigation is just beginning. William Crookes, for example, regarded a number of his late nineteenth century discoveries in physics as opening up new fields of science, an opinion that his fellow scientists rejected. For example, he made extravagant claims for a fourth state of radiant matter.[18]

In general, however, disagreements among the elite in a phase of scientific investigation which is regarded as preliminary and provisional do little to upset the prevailing consensus. For example, if a scientist considers that some unusual area of investigation is suitable for intensive study by the accepted methods of his science, intellectual (but perhaps not social) considerations would suggest that his colleagues should allow him to get on with the project, suspending most of their criticism until they saw what he managed to do. Thus, although in many fields the elite may show a marked preference for pure science investigation, they would usually tolerate one of their number who attempted to apply the orthodox theory to an area of practical application—and would applaud whatever successes he managed to produce. The same degree of toleration is not to be expected for a leading scientist whose work was in conflict with some standard landmark of his specialism. Unless he managed to attract an influential following, his eminence would be reduced by such a sign of deviation from orthodoxy.

Elite scientists may also deviate from orthodoxy by taking up a novel theme which is not closely related to their earlier expertise and success. A leading scientist who is already successful in his own field may be prepared to take risks of this kind. The new venture is given publicity by the fame of the scientist, even if it is highly unorthodox. Crookes's investigation of spiritualism in the 1870s may be regarded in this way.[19] Similarly, a recent well known example of deviant science was publicised by the Nobel Prize winning chemist Linus Pauling, who took an eccentric view of the benefits of taking large doses of Vitamin C, as in his claim that this gave resistance to colds.[20]

The problems of characterising deviant elite science are, in summary, tied closely to conceptual issues. We can describe (and find) examples of well known individual scientists who have had a phase of enthusiasm for deviant ideas. A temporary or local preoccupation of a group of elite scientists with deviant ideas is to be expected if that group differ from other scientists in believing that their science is in crisis. But the conceptual possibility of a sustained interest in deviant ideas by a portion of the scientific elite would imply that the orthodox consensus against which deviance could be judged had broken down. We would be less inclined to describe such cases as deviant elite science than to wonder if the orthodox and deviant groups were merely rival factions in a controversy.

2.3 *Deviant Science at Lower Levels of Institutionalised Science*

While examples of deviant science from the scientific elite are rare but reasonably well publicised, deviant beliefs in the lower ranks of science are much more common and much less publicised. Those lower ranking scientists who disagree with the orthodox viewpoint tend to keep quiet about their disagreement, and if they do speak out, those around them have every incentive to ignore them.

In spite of the image provided by empiricist philosophies of science dominant in science since the seventeenth century, the knowledge-producing activity of the individual modern scientist is *not* mainly a matter of reasoning solely from a limited range of independent and well-attested evidence. The generation of reliable data and the production of more general insights depends essentially on the acceptance of a vast amount of background knowledge. This is gained by the individual scientist from the rest of the scientific community and from its literature. The scientific beliefs which guide research form an interdependent network of ideas of which a sceptical scientist could only ever check a tiny fraction, and then only by presupposing the rest. Thus, the conclusions a scientist reaches always depend on his evaluation as to which of the relevant ideas that he has acquired from other scientists are trustworthy. This evaluation is guided by his assessment of the expertise of the sources of knowledge. On each issue, it is the *most* expert scientists whose judgement the scientists defer to. The moment a scientist begins to question orthodox beliefs in his science, he finds that he is challenging expert opinion. If he speaks out, he is in effect proclaiming himself as more expert than the experts. In the normal process of science, a low ranking scientist who manages to keep his challenge restricted to a specific issue may be able to convince other scientists that he *is* expert on this issue, that the evidence he has assembled and the thought he has given the matter are to be preferred to earlier beliefs. But very often, other scientists remain unimpressed, and the deviant ideas are ignored or rejected after brief criticism. A scientist who doubts whether he can make an impressive case on behalf of his deviant belief may not make the effort, and turn to other scientific matters, or even leave scientific research.

Because there are such strong pressures in the lower ranks of science discouraging the expression of deviant belief and preventing the growth of disagreements into deviant intellectual movements, it is easiest to find indirect evidence for the nature and extent of deviant belief in this social context.

One indirect source of evidence is provided by the prehistory of the forms of belief which rose to orthodoxy in a scientific revolution. A scientific community tends to remember and honour its own intellectual ancestry. It is quite common for a revolutionary approach to science to have developed as an unorthodox alternative to established science before the revolutionary phase which brought it to dominance. Thus, those cases in which the revolutionary approach had been developed in the lower ranks of science before the period of crisis in which it was taken up by members of the scientific elite, provide us with examples of deviant science. The arguments for continental drift by Alfred Wegener in the early twentieth century, which were scorned by virtually all of his contemporaries were suddenly to become highly relevant to a new intellectual movement in geology in the 1960s. Wegener's name was then restrospectively extracted from scientific obscurity, though in his own time he was clearly a deviant scientist from the lower ranks of institutionalised science.[21] The long neglected work on genetics by the Augustinian monk Gregor Mendel, provides a similar example.[22]

Another indirect source of evidence for deviant beliefs is well known to teachers of history, philosophy or social studies of science. They find that their subjects attract many students and young researchers, often of high intellectual calibre with unorthodox ideas, who have decided that they are powerless to force change from within their science, have become disillusioned with it, and so have moved to a discipline studying the nature of science in general.

Another indication of deviant belief in the lower ranks of science may be found from the study of extra-scientific causes which are in conflict with scientific orthodoxy. The anti-fluoridation movement, for example, in spite of its denunciation by large numbers of orthodox dental researchers, has been able to recruit some lower ranking scientists to its banner. A movement more closely linked to scientific issues which has exposed deviant beliefs among scientists is environmentalism. Even in its early phases, scientists from many fields were prepared to express their disagreement with the opinion of major institutions and their leading scientific advisors on the environmental risks associated with particular sciences and science-based technologies.

However, in spite of this evidence for the existence of deviant belief among the lower ranks of scientists, it is very difficult for such beliefs to escalate into sustained intellectual movements within orthodox science expressing a deviant scientific viewpoint. Unless a deviant approach can gain support from among the scientific elite, it must find its social basis outside the institutionalised orthodoxy of science, or it will die away. There have, however, been a very few transient cases of deviant science which were argued to be 'democratic' in contrast to the exclusive elitism of the established science, and which gained considerable support from the lower scientific ranks. Phrenology was once presented in this way, for example.[23] But although phrenologists never gained complete respectability for their science, and although they managed to attract a significant following from among lower ranking scientists, it is noticeable that the social basis of phrenology tended to change; it appealed more to the general public and less to those earnestly seeking to advance knowledge.

The few exceptions of deviant science which have been incorporated into the lower ranks of institutionalised science show the limits to the control of institutionalised scientific activity from the top. For example, private sources of funds for academic research can be taken up by a researcher provided his own institution does not disapprove. Experimental research on parapsychology by American psychologists in the early twentieth century was often supported by grants from private sources. The work of Joseph Rhine in the Psychology Department at Duke University, which was funded in this way, was sufficiently impressive to grow into the Duke Parapsychology Laboratory with Rhine as its director. This degree of respectability was achieved for parapsychology in spite of widespread criticism from orthodox scientists.

2.4 *Popular Deviant Science*

The most widely known examples of deviant science are those to which popular or fashionable attention has been given. Popular journalism plays an important part in the emergence and growth of this kind of deviant science. At the earliest stages, the claim to have established a new kind of phenomenon, or a new technique with practical benefits, has news value, and thus newspapers tend to be eager to report it. Periods of widespread interest in flying saucer observations, for example, were brought about by press coverage of a few stories.[24] In cases in which there is a strong favourable public response, the eagerness of journalists to cater to the new interest may aid in the generation of a craze. Whether or not the increase of reported flying saucer sightings was directly produced by the positive feedback of interest generated by newspaper reports, by the time that interest was stimulating popular books and Hollywood movies on UFOs, the topic had clearly become a popular fashion. Cases in which the interested individual could directly involve himself in the

R. G. A. Dolby

phenomenon have produced the most pronounced deviant science crazes. Table turning in the mid-nineteenth century was an example of a popular craze that built on the early interest in spiritualist phenomena.

Popular fashions in deviant science may also be spread by enthusiasts who publicise their activities themselves. A charismatic leader of deviant science may be able to attract a popular following by his impact on a particular section of local society. Mesmer, for example, managed to gain enthusiastic support from among the higher social classes in late eighteenth century Paris.[25] In the nineteenth century, popular interest in Mesmerism was diffused by travelling mesmerists, who lectured on and demonstrated mesmeric phenomena. Similarly, a founder of a deviant science may gather a popular following through his writing. Erich von Däniken's books on extra-terrestrial beings who visited Earth 10,000 years ago and created man in their own image from monkeys have generated an immense popular interest.[26]

But widespread popular interest in a deviant science is difficult to maintain. Once the issue is no longer novel it loses newsworthiness unless it can continue to produce new and varied achievements. Thus, it is common for popular deviant sciences to die away rapidly as fashionable discussion turns to other things. However, in the wake of a phase of fashionable interest, a proportion of those exposed may acquire a more lasting interest. For example, deviant theories of human races have tended to retain strongest support among right wing political movements, especially in countries with conflict between culturally discrete groups.[27] Similarly, the interest in Velikovsky, which was at first fashionable, has subsequently tended to be concentrated in a more limited special interest group.[28] In such groups, the most active enthusiasts continue to elaborate and to publicise the deviant science. Their work is disseminated to a wider more passive group, from which further enthusiasts are drawn. If the active heart of the group fails to generate sufficient interest to keep up recruitment, the deviant science will die away. In more successful cases, however, those with a mild and passive interest in the deviant science are sufficient in number to provide a market for further journalistic activity. They buy books and read popular articles on the subject. As their critical standards are usually not very high, the commercial pressures of writing for as large a market as possible encourage professional writers to write at a low intellectual level and discourage the display of the apparatus of scholarship. Popular literary traditions in deviant science therefore may be of low quality, as in von Däniken's case, and tend to show degenerative tendencies.[29] The total literature of a sustained popular deviant science is compounded out of the publications of professional writers and the more literate enthusiasts. It is therefore the latter who determine whether or not the published literature of the deviant science degenerates into a sterile tradition in which each author embroiders the presentation of his predecessors with minimal checking on their sources.

In order that a passing fashion for a set of deviant ideas should generate a segment of the population whose interest is captured and held, it is necessary that claims should be made which are in some way important to that segment. Those whose interest and involvement is most superficial may be satisfied by being entertained by popular presentations of the ideas; more active and more committed involvement generally requires that the deviant beliefs offer solutions to some kind of problem.[30] The best known examples of popular deviant belief systems all fit within a fairly simple classification in terms of the nature of their main appeal. This appeal can be practical, in particular medical, or offering some ability to anticipate or cope with the future; religious, including the mystical and occult; political; or scientific, and especially relating to the widespread disposition to take seriously marvellous explanations, often of enigmatic phenomena, as part of a meaningful and satisfying view of the universe. Although many deviant belief systems exploit a number of such appeals, so that the categories appear to overlap, very often one kind of appeal is dominant. For example, the Scientology movement founded by L. Ron Hubbard developed out of Hubbard's earlier Dianetics, which offered a route to mental health. Although making therapeutic, scientific and political claims, Scientology is now proclaimed primarily as a religion. In part, this transition has been because of the greater social toleration of deviant religions than of deviant medical therapy.[31]

The nature of the appeal of the deviant belief system affects the extent to which it attempts to display the rational features of a science and to employ critical standards. A mystical religion may present itself as anti-rational rather than as deviant science. Since established religions appeal to faith as much as to reason, such a stance is socially acceptable. In contrast, a deviant form of medicine must compete with orthodox medicine, which claims to be science-based. In our culture, deviant medicine normally requires some kind of justificatory theory and evidence that it can indeed prevent or cure ill health as it claims. In general, those deviant systems of belief which compete with orthodoxies appealing to the authority of science, thrive best if they also claim to have their own scientific basis.

2.5 *Popular Deviant Science Involving Leading Intellectuals: The Case of Mid-Nineteenth Century Britain*

Among the most interesting popular deviant sciences are those which have succeeded in attracting sustained social support from the more intellectual strata of society. Avant garde artistic and literary culture has often provided a refuge for beliefs in conflict with those of established society, but avant garde culture has often been anti-scientific and even anti-rational rather than a form of deviant science.[32] When intellectuals do support deviant science, they tend to work strenuously for acceptance of their ideas. An especially interesting group of examples is to be found in mid-nineteenth century British thought. There was a strong interaction between a number of intellectual radicals, who were prepared to challenge religious, political and social orthodoxy and to take up and popularise new causes which attracted their enthusiasm. In addition to social and political issues, these intellectuals often seized upon *potential* new sciences. Some of their causes attained orthodoxy as revolutionary new sciences, others never overcame strenuous opposition from scientists and are now remembered only as deviant science. Among the most prominent of these intellectual movements on the borders of science were positivism (a philosophy of science rather than a new science), new natural sciences of human and social phenomena, evolutionary theory, mesmerism, phrenology, and spiritualism and its investigation as psychic research. Evolutionary theory in the period immediately before Darwin is a clear example of a deviant science which only achieved respectability with Darwin. Evolutionary ideas had been introduced into social and scientific speculation especially since the late eighteenth century.[33] But by the 1830s, considered scientific opinion, especially as represented by such influential men of science as Cuvier and Lyell, rejected the evolution of species.[34] But evolutionary ideas were not completely dead. They could be related to an increasing range of observations, and undermined so many of the complacent assumptions of religious, social and scientific orthodoxy that they were well suited to titillate the imagination of daring intellectuals. It was in this context that Robert Chambers, a successful Edinburgh publisher of informative and educational literature, published anonymously *Vestiges of the Natural History of Creation* (1844). His book applied a law of progressive development to the geological and the organic world and to the human species. It generated indignant condemnation from a number of leading scientists,[35] but nevertheless had sold 20,000 copies in eleven editions by 1860.[36] In its first edition, the book displayed the kind of scientific naivety common among those with wide but unguided reading in the scientific literature. It drew as enthusiastically on phrenology and the idea that galvanic electricity has life-creating powers as it did on reputable geology and natural history. It was clearly not respectable science, and Charles Darwin, who had already sketched out but had not yet published his theory of evolution by natural selection, did not regard Chambers as having anticipated him. Nevertheless, there was a clear sense in which Chambers's work led naturally into orthodox evolutionary theory. One of his readers was Alfred Russell Wallace, then a young man. Wallace was convinced by *Vestiges* that species evolve in accordance with natural law.[37] He engaged in a series of expeditions beginning in 1848, seeking information on the evolution of species. In 1858, he sent to Darwin his independently developed theory of natural selection as the mechanism of evolution. His letter, which Darwin presented to the Linnaean Society with some of his own work on evolution, was published in 1858. Under this stimulus Darwin hurriedly completed a booklength version of his argument, the famous *Origin of Species* (1859). It was Darwin's work which made evolutionary theory scientifically orthodox, but the alternative route to respectability through Wallace makes it clear that a popular deviant science which can attract dedicated intellectuals may move towards scientific orthodoxy. It is worth noting that Wallace was also an enthusiastic supporter of a number of other deviant sciences of his day. These included mesmerism and phrenology, their composite phreno-mesmerism, and, later, spiritualism.[38]

The deviant and pioneering science supported in the intellectual milieu of mid-nineteenth-century British radical thought does not fit social characterisations of orthodox science such as that offered by Polanyi and Kuhn. This context was one in which non-conformist intellectuals were prepared to speculate and then to try to build a science on the basis of their speculations. Such a process involved taking intellectual risks, and was not always successful. It is suggested by John Palfreman in his article in this volume that many of the scientist supporters of the psychic research movement were members of the tradition of (affluent) amateurs which was opposed by a rising trend towards professional science in nineteenth century Britain. An amateur, who does not have a career at stake, may be more prepared to take intellectual risks than a career-oriented professional. This intellectually adventurous milieu may have been one of the factors affecting the different quality distribution of British and German science in the mid-nineteenth century. The successful British risk takers added greatly to the reputation of British science, while the caution encouraged by the German professional career pattern produced large numbers of diligent second rank scientists.[39]

2.6 Deviant Science in Cults and the Cultic Milieu

We have already noted that popular deviant sciences may reach a more stable form than that of a transient newsworthy social fashion if a segment of the population acquires a lasting interest in the deviant beliefs. This section of the population may not have any special social organisation, beyond the popular journalism which presents its issues in a form attractive to the widest market. However, it is common for those who have a high degree of commitment to unusual interests to organise themselves to some extent. The most secretive may form small and exclusive groups which can only be joined by those prepared to go through a process of initiation; in other cases, more open groupings may be formed as those with a high degree of commitment to the unusual interests seek each other out, correspond, distribute written material, and hold meetings. Such groups may be formalised further. For example, if the belief system is directly modelled on orthodox science or scientific medicine, institutions may be founded which offer quasi-educational facilities for training and research.[40]

Sometimes the culture from which cohesive groups defending deviant beliefs emerge is indistinguishable from the general culture in which news of the deviant ideas was given publicity. But more commonly, we can distinguish subcultures in our society which attract and provide a home for deviant systems of belief. We have noted how a series of mid-nineteenth century fringe sciences were taken up enthusiastically by British radical intellectuals, and have mentioned that the artistic and literary avant garde has often been a seedbed for unorthodox systems of ideas. Similarly, it has been argued that the countercultures of modern youth have provided havens for such unorthodox beliefs as astrology, witchcraft, parapsychology and Eastern religious thought.[41] Although there has often been only slight overlap in the youth countercultures which embraced these separate systems of unorthodox belief,[42] there does seem to have been a special fascination for the unothodox within special segments of the population in the late 1960s.

Sociologists of religion have used the concept 'cultic milieu' to characterise the subculture in which religious cults seem to thrive.[43] The cultic milieu is characterised by an ideology of 'seekership', for a significant part of its population consists of individuals who have some problem or are in some way dissatisfied with their lives so far, and have failed to find satisfaction within the framework of more orthodox institutions. They seek resolution of their difficulties by trying a succession of deviant forms of belief. Within the milieu, cultic groups are always being formed around new constellations of deviant belief and new charismatic leaders. The milieu contains large numbers of loosely structured cults, most of which are either ephemeral or become sufficiently successful to organise themselves into more permanent sects. In spite of the multiplicity of belief systems in the milieu, the whole is held together in a number of ways. The cults are united in challenging orthodoxy. Seekers tend to move from one transient cult to another, and this encourages each cult to adopt or at least to tolerate many of the claims made by its neighbours. Furthermore, the organs of communication of the cultic world tend to cover several cults, so that they help to draw cultic ideas together. Campbell has suggested that the cultic milieu applies not merely to alien and heretical religion, but also to unorthodox science and to deviant medicine; it is, in fact, the 'cultural underground of society'.[44] Therefore, the idea of a cultic milieu appears very promising for the investigation of the social basis of deviant science. However, there are problems in its application. Although the idea of the 'seeker' applies just as plausibly to the dedicated patron of fringe medicine as it does to religious cultists, the cohesiveness of the cultic milieu is gradually lost as the concept is widened beyond its original religious context. Although deviant religious, medical, scientific and political forms of belief are often united in a single cult, a rather different population of seekers seems to be involved when considering cults which are *primarily* religious, *primarily* medical, *or primarily* political. Furthermore, the religious analogy does not make clear that most of those involved in many systems of deviant belief treat them as casual entertainment rather than as a chance of solving a major problem in the life pattern of the seeker. The idea of a generalised cultic milieu is thus not simply a description; rather it is an idealisation of the social basis of deviant belief, building on analogy with the sociology of religious cults.

But though problematic, the idea of the cultic milieu can be valuable. We may regard it as a repository of rejected knowledge in which alternatives to current orthodoxy are kept alive, perhaps to re-emerge when the demands of orthodoxy have changed. For example, after Mesmerism had declined as a popular craze in Pre-Revolutionary France, there were periods in which it dropped from public attention. The segments of society in which it was kept alive can be regarded as the cultic milieu. Cultists, popular entertainers and other enthusiasts periodically emerged who sought to demonstrate mesmeric effects. The continuing interest occasionally attracted a few doctors and scientists to its serious study. But because of the general rejection by the orthodoxy, mesmerism and hypnotism remained on the fringes of medical science, vital to a succession of cults and the subject of a succession of popular books and demonstrations, as scientific and medical orthodoxy gradually came to appreciate its nature and significance.[45] One can also usefully regard the cultic milieu as a seedbed for new constellations of belief, which combine orthodox and unorthodox features. For example, the period of the emergence of modern science in the sixteenth and early seventeenth century was one in which a rich variety of alternative systems of belief thrived within a section of intellectual society. Explanation of the rise of natural philosophy, which grew into modern science, requires a full understanding of the social milieu of the sixteenth and seventeenth centuries in which a number of intellectual movements interacted, combining mystical, millenarian, rational and empirical features. This milieu has recently been much discussed, especially by historians of science concerned with the role of Hermeticism in the rise of modern science.[46]

26

2.7 Deviant Science in Sects

If we understand sects to be groups sharing a common ideology which have erected some kind of barrier between themselves and the rest of society, it is easy to see how they may defend a deviant belief system. There is considerable sociological evidence that our beliefs and standards are gained primarily by personal interactions.[47] For example, although a few individuals in a community may be externally oriented 'cosmopolites', who are interested in learning about and applying the ideas of the wider society, most individuals identify with and conform to the standards and attitudes of their immediate contacts. For such 'localites', personal interactions fill their social horizons. Although they may be exposed to the mass media and to casual contacts with people outside their own group, they are primarily affected only by what is in accord with their existing attitudes.[48] The organisation of a sect typically 'protects' its members from the most disruptive influences of the rest of society. It can thus maintain a system of beliefs in conflict with social orthodoxy. A number of defensive stratagems are immediately available to explain to members why the rest of society should fail to appreciate the 'true' beliefs of the sect. For example, it is only those who have been fully introduced to the inner complexities of the sect's beliefs who can be expected to appreciate them fully. The introduction may be a dramatic process of conversion or an extended programme of training, as in the hierarchy of Scientology courses.[49] From the outsider's point of view, such processes may be criticised as 'brainwashing', in which the state of heightened suggestibility produced by severe emotional stress, accentuated by such physical factors as fatigue or even sensory deprivation is exploited in the conversion. But the insider can proudly point to the high degree of rational commitment which the fully inducted sect members show. Another defensive stratagem open to the sect is to present itself to its members as subject to unfair persecution—viewed by critics as a kind of collective paranoia. 'It is not our group which is pig-headed and unreasonable', the sect argues, 'but the ignorant public, who persist in attacking us when they don't really understand what we are trying to say.' Examples of this kind of argument can be found in a wide variety of sects.[50]

A considerable amount of general and case study discussion has been given of the processes by which sects can be formed and of

27

how individuals can be recruited into cults and sects.[51] Thus, provided that the wider society is prepared to tolerate the sect, it is easy to see how it can survive and even flourish as a social basis for deviant beliefs.

The extent to which the deviant belief systems of such sects can be *science* is more problematic. In our society the idea of science is especially associated with open knowledge-seeking systems, rather than with the closed knowledge-conserving systems characteristic of most sects. However, a number of sects do claim their beliefs to be a science. This may be a residue of an earlier more open cultic phase of the movement, or it may be a debased use of 'science', which merely underscores the sect's insistence that its beliefs are true, or that they 'work', as when applied in therapy.

3. Deviant Sciences as Alternative Forms of Rationality

The problems of understanding people with dramatically different beliefs and standards of reasoning from our own have been much discussed in the context of the study of other cultures and also in the study of earlier phases of our own culture, especially in the history of science. Many modern anthropologists and philosophers have argued that to understand other cultures we must avoid prejudging the issue by assuming that what seems irrational or silly to us *is* irrational or silly.[52] Similarly, philosophers of the history of ideas, and especially of scientific ideas, have argued that if an obviously capable historical actor reasons and makes judgements in ways which seem foolish or mistaken to us, we should try to see if he is in fact employing standards and methods of reasoning which were perfectly acceptable in his own time but which we no longer accept.[53] But if fringe groups can occur in *our* culture at the *present* time, which defend deviant beliefs to their own standards of rationality, are we to dismiss their reasoning without attempting to understand it, merely because it seems silly to us? Does the fact that such people have had some exposure to the rational standards of our general culture but have nevertheless chosen other standards mean that they must be irrational? Or can they be defended as having a different rationality or as applying rationality differently? The problem of the relativity of rationality may thus apply not merely to independent cultural systems and to different historical periods, but also to forms of reasoning in open competition.

Such a view seems at first to be rather extreme. Surely, it will be
argued, there are forms of rational evaluation available in our present
culture accessible to the proponents of deviant science and by which
orthodox science is far superior to any deviant science? Such a
view is not as decisive as it at first appears. The available standards
turn out either not to be universally accepted in our culture or to be
highly idealised and to involve assumptions in their application which
are interpreted by defenders of deviant science in their own favour.
Typically, where orthodox science claims superiority over deviant
science by one rational criterion, such as the logical rigour of the
reasoning, or the quantitative precision of the explanation, the deviant
scientists can claim that *his* account is superior in terms of some other
rational criterion, such as comprehensiveness of explanation, qualit-
ative plausibility, or immediacy of application to important practical
cases. The problem of the apparent relativism of rationality within our
own culture can be given some substance and plausibility by considering a number of general arguments by which defenders of deviant
science can show that their position is perfectly rational in their own
terms and by *their* interpretation of the rational standards of the
society as a whole.

One very general argument supporting almost all deviant science
has its greatest appeal among those people and in those contexts in
which it is doubted whether the current orthodox science is close
to the ultimate truth. Under these circumstances a fallibilist view of
knowledge is attractive. It can be argued, as Popper does, that we
can *never* be sure that we have reached the ultimate truth, for further
empirical inquiry could always reveal new failures of our theories.[54]
It becomes plausible to argue that there may be many mutually incompatible ways of approaching closer to the truth. The orthodox
position is not necessarily vastly superior to all others. It may even
be inferior, especially if its methodological preoccupations have led
it systematically to ignore especially important but problematic
sources of evidence, such as myths, legends, anecdotes, craft traditions, non-expert testimony of unreproducible events, and so on.
Thus, a deviant science which contradicts the orthodoxy, may still
contain important aspects of the ultimate truth, which the seeker
after full understanding is not entitled to ignore. This argument
could be used as a defence of a limited form of relativism. But at the
level of social practice rather than philosophical principle, scientists

have often been convinced that a particular theory gives a complete and exact understanding of a realm of phenomena. For this reason, the defenders of successful mature orthodox sciences are often disinclined even to look at deviant alternatives, because they could not possibly explain as much as the orthodox theory.

While there are relatively few contexts within orthodox science in which it is openly conceded that the best available theory is still a long way from the ultimate truth, deviant scientists tend to stress the limits of large parts of orthodox theory. Thus, for them, the fallibilist argument is very strong. Since we cannot prove conclusively the certain truth of any part of empirical science, our judgement of whether there is room for alternative and incompatible scientific approaches is essentially intuitive and unreasoned. As long as this is the case, the judgement of the deviant scientist need be no less rational than that of the orthodox scientist.

There are some contexts in which the practitioners of orthodox science readily admit the limits and fallibility of current theory. If they have some sense of crisis over the failure of their theory to cope with anomalies, they may become responsive to deviant approaches which they would otherwise have ignored. This process as been explained clearly by Kuhn.[55] Another context in which orthodox science becomes more tolerant of alternatives is when a new field is first being opened up, and it is clear that no single theory is yet adequate to explore or explain it. Under these circumstances, theories are evaluated less by realist criteria than by more conventional and pragmatic considerations, such as whether a coherent and sensible form of systematic description is possible, and how effectively new discoveries are being generated.

Outside orthodox science, the fallibilist sense of the limits of scientific orthodoxy is more important. Defenders of popular deviant sciences often claim that the current topic of popular enthusiasm has not yet been adequately investigated by scientists, so that there is still value in a variety of less disciplined, more speculative approaches. Many of the fringe sciences taken up by radical intellectuals of the nineteenth century were in fields not previously reduced to successful science. The situation in such areas was comparable to many of the social sciences today—in which no single approach has yet become sufficiently successful for all the practitioners to agree that it would be more productive to try to develop it further than to start anew from a different set of assumptions. The advocates of the many fringe medicine movements argue strongly for the limited nature of orthodox medicine, and insist that alternative approaches can be more effective in particular cases. The fallibilist argument for methodological pluralism applies most fully to the cultic milieu. A common attitude in that context is to regard *every* alternative approach as having the same epistemological status. It is only after the cultist has investigated an approach for himself, studying it as its proponents want it to be studied, that he is in a position to make a critical evaluation. Until then, he refuses to criticise or reject what might well be a part of the greater truth. The fallibilist argument has less application in the closed sect. For there, it is claimed that the sect *has* found the ultimate truth; it is the rest of society that, through ignorance and prejudice, refuses to appreciate this.

Fallibilist pluralism can also be applied to philosophical theories of how science should be done so as to justify deviant science. I have suggested that no definitive account of what differentiates effective science from inferior imitations has yet been produced. Thus, when a group of orthodox scientists appeals to a given methodology to show why what they do is scientific and what the deviant scientists do is not, it is always possible for the deviant scientists to set up their *own* theory of scientific method, and to criticise the orthodox scientists for failing to match up to that. Marxist theories, for example, have been criticised by Karl Popper as pseudo-scientific because Marxists do not proceed by trying to falsify their ideas.[56] But Marxists have their own dialectical conception of the nature of scientific inquiry.[57] By their standards, much of modern orthodox Western social science is in fact unscientific. So in this case approaches which are orthodox in one political system may be deviant in another. Deviant sciences which import non-European rational traditions also have available an alternative theory of knowledge. Acupuncture, for example, can be defended on the basis of its original Chinese tradition. Although the advocates of most deviant sciences have not developed such a full philosophical elaboration of their position, it is usually possible to fill out a rival philosophical version of the nature of science. For example, an alternative conception of science can be extracted from the writings of Velikovsky and his supporters.

R. G. A. Dolby

Paul Feyerabend's philosophy of science can be construed as a defence of fallibilist pluralism, both at the level of scientific theory and of scientific method. For example, Feyerabend has argued vociferously that no one approach to the pursuit of knowledge can be allowed to dominate all others. Rival and even incommensurable theoretical approaches are to be encouraged, and at the level of methodology, 'anything goes'.[58] Thus Feyerabend's philosophy encourages full toleration of deviant science.

It is not merely in the conception of what it is to be scientific that deviant sciences can display an alternative form of rationality; because scientific arguments from empirical evidence to general conclusions are never logically impeccable, each science tends to have its own style and standards in the presentation of argument and evidence. Even within orthodox science, the standards of different specialisms vary considerably. Deviant sciences show even further variation. A common feature of deviant sciences is that, following a tradition of medical science rather than natural science, they argue from the outcome of a few individual detailed cases rather than from a large statistical sample. The astrologer expects you to be convinced by the success of the forecast he gives *you*. The same is true of the claims of deviant medical sects to have effective methods of cure—particular cases or testimonials are invoked. Although this form of argument may not meet the standards of statistical method in modern social and applied sciences, it is clear that statistical arguments do not give certainty, and arguments from individual cases *do* give added reason for entertaining or accepting a general idea. They may have greater psychological appeal to counter their lesser statistical force. It should be noted, moreover that even in orthodox science, there is no simple resolution of the disagreement between those who believe that one should collect as much statistical evidence as possible to support a conclusion and those who argue that a few cases *thoroughly* studied are more informative than masses of cases superficially treated.[59]

There is another group of arguments for the rational defensibility of deviant science which depend on the fact that science is a social rather than an individual activity in which the scientist must often depend on the judgements of others. I have already suggested that the conclusions a scientist reaches always depend on his judgment that the ideas and observations he has acquired from other scientists are trustworthy. Within orthodox science, it is the views of those who are thought to be most expert on any question which are accepted, and contradictory suggestions by the less expert are rejected. Deviant scientists are often aggrieved at the way a hurried rejection of their pet ideas by a few leading scientists can produce a consensus in which the deviant ideas are generally rejected as foolish and irrational by those with no first hand knowledge.[60] David Jacobs has described in detail how the orthodox scientific image of UFOlogy built up through deliberate campaigns by the US Airforce and others to discredit the issue without having made the careful and unprejudiced studies they claimed.[61] Thus, deviant sciences are often rejected because most scientists tend to trust their leaders and other sources rather than to check for themselves.

The problem of who to trust is most intuitive when one is considering which observational reports are to be accepted in a piece of scientific reasoning. One has to assess on the basis of reputation and a verbal presentation whether an individual had sufficient experimental and observational skill to be without error in his account of what he did and what he saw. The skills involved are partly tacit, and are much too complex to be written out fully in a scientific report. It may seem that it is only in rare cases of fraudulent misconduct that the observations of physical scientists are not to be trusted. But the situation seems quite different if one considers psychic research or parapsychology. A nineteenth century physicist such as William Crookes investigating a seance may have insisted that he had taken adequate precautions against trickery. But his sceptical colleagues, even though they were perfectly prepared to trust his observations in physics, were not prepared to take his word as to what went on in the seances. Many were so sceptical that they did not think it worth the effort to look for themselves. In this case, it was sometimes argued that a physicist does not in fact have the right kind of observational expertise. He is too easily deceived. A conjurer can do better. But the same problem arises in twentieth-century parapsychological experimentation. Many orthodox scientists are not prepared to trust the claims of parapsychologists to have carried out the work competently, even though it is admitted that the precautions required are so sophisticated that no one other than parapsychologists *could* have sufficient expertise.

The problems of who can be trusted are especially striking in deviant sciences which use observational evidence not under the direct control of the scientific expert. Modern UFOlogy, for example, is primarily a matter of investigating observational reports from people who were unable to explain what they saw in the sky (or on the ground) in terms of normal and known phenomena. Although some such reports come from people who may be considered untrustworthy, especially cult leaders who have something to gain from inventing a dramatic story, restrained defenders of UFOlogy such as J. Allen Hynek[62] point out that it is possible to restrict UFOlogical study to reports which experts cannot explain away in detail in terms of known phenomena, and which involve a number of independent observers who are all sufficiently respectable to have their word accepted in a court of law. Hynek is prepared to *trust* such reports, especially as the people who make them risk unpleasant public ridicule, and to use them as the basis of an argument that orthodox explanations of UFO phenomena are inadequate. Hynek and other defenders of the middle ground of UFOlogy argue strongly that it is unreasonable to reject *all* unexplained UFO reports as has been done by some of the scientific orthodoxy,[63] but he does reject those reports by UFO cultists in which they claim to have met alien intelligences and to have travelled in their flying saucers. There is an interesting parallel between orthodox scientific attitudes to UFO reports and the sceptical attitude of the French Academy of Sciences to tales of stones that fell from the sky in the early nineteenth century. One scientist who was important in reviving scientific interest in meteorites was Ernst Chladni, who had had a legal training which encouraged him to regard some eyewitness reports as trustworthy.[64]

If you are prepared to trust the claims of a group of people who have evidence that you yourself are not in a position to gain, while the orthodoxy of science or of society as a whole reject them, it is easy to see that beliefs may be rationally defended which are dismissed by others as unreasonable or irrational. An important factor in orthodox science is that in general it is *only* the most expert who are trusted in any conflict of opinion, while many deviant sciences take a much more open approach on whose word is acceptable. This contrast is *not* an objectively rational one; each attitude may be perfectly acceptable in the appropriate community. For example, it might seem that deviant scientists who seek to reconstruct the full knowledge they believe was held by the ancients, are credulous in their trust in the reliability of alchemical and other mystical traditions. Yet a major proportion of the manuscript material of Sir Isaac Newton, arguably the greatest scientist ever, was devoted to recovering ancient knowledge from such traditions.[65]

Special criteria of who to trust are taken even further in more highly organised movements of deviant science, especially those with sect-like features. These often claim that the kind of expertise possessed by the leaders of the sect (and perhaps those that they have trained) gives them a far greater authority than that of any individual in the rest of society. Many deviant science movements claim that only those who have been through a full programme of training can possibly appreciate the full force and appeal of the claims made. Thus outsiders are not entitled to criticise the movement, for they would be doing so with inadequate understanding. This argument is interesting in that it shows an analogy between 'irrational' sects, and elite specialisms of orthodox science. In both cases, it is only the word of the expert that should be trusted, and his word should always be trusted by the non-expert.

One of the commonest arguments employed by defenders of scientific orthodoxy against the claims of deviant sciences is that modern science has led to so many applications that it must be substantially true. This may be conceded by the deviant scientist (though he may point out that many applications of science have turned out to be less beneficial than was first thought), who goes on to make the counter-claim that his own deviant science also leads to valuable applications. Most deviant sciences flourish *because* they produce applications needed and appreciated by a segment of society and, in particular, the seekers in the counter-culture. Deviant sciences thrive which offer guidance for the future, character analysis and advice, methods of retaining health or of curing an ailment which orthodox medicine has done little to help, or solving psychological or social difficulties, or of giving satisfying religious guidance. By the standards of the supporters of the deviant science such applications are as secure as those of orthodox natural science. A sceptic can point out that a false theory may underlie an application which is *socially* regarded as successful. But the same scepticism can be applied to orthodox science. There too, the successes of the applications do not *prove* the truth of the science which led to them.[66] In practice, in both cases, believers *do* rely on the existence of applications as a justification for accepting their theories, or at least for taking them seriously.

The fact that a system of deviant science has immediate practical significance provides another argument for its support, at least in the short term, by exploiting the excessive idealisation of the proposals for the demarcation of science of Karl Popper. In practice, there are inevitable delays between the time any theory is proposed and that at which the significance of searching tests becomes clear. The deviant scientist may not have the resources to carry out such tests on his ideas, while the orthodox are too scornful to bother. Thus the deviant scientist can argue that his ideas are worth implementing immediately by his followers, while pointing out the narrowness of the scientific orthodoxy which ignores them. This may encourage a social following from those individuals who feel similarly helpless before social authorities. Similarly, theories which are of immediate practical significance but which can only be tested directly at some future time, are especially common in deviant science. Millenarian movements (sometimes involving deviant science, as in flying saucer cults) which predict dramatic changes in the near (or even remote) future are successful in every culture at encouraging people to change their behaviour immediately so as to be ready for the millennium. In situations in which the immediate practical need is vital enough, people may think that they may as well guide their actions by a plausible untested (but testable) deviant science. A deviant movement which manages to change its claims in an acceptable way so that the negative evidence against past claims is never relevant and new claims are always attracting attention, may be able to flourish for an extended period. It has been suggested that Lysenko was able to remain influential for so long in Soviet agricultural science because he changed his ground in this way.[67]

The critics of a deviant science naturally remind their opponents of the leading scientists who have spoken out against the deviant science. However, the deviant scientists have a ready response. They point to the strong opposition which has accompanied many revolutionary new scientific developments, and insist that that is all that is involved in their own case.

It is common for those who wish to debunk a deviant science to dismiss all its supporters as belonging to the idiot fringe of society. Those who are seriously committed to a deviant science take a quite different view. UFOlogists, for example, often distinguish their own scientific work very sharply from that of flying saucer cults, which they also dismiss as foolish and credulous.[68]

These general arguments show that deviant sciences can and do have their own rational basis. Although arguments can be found which would dismiss most deviant sciences as pseudo-science, those arguments are never conclusive, and there are frequently counter-arguments which suggest just as forcibly that some of successful orthodox science should be rejected as pseudo-science. Unless some definitive rational criterion were to be found which displays the complete superiority of orthodox science and which also commands universal assent, we must accept that preference for orthodox science is based on biased application of rational principles, or depends on intuition. The best argument for orthodox science must remain that it is preferred by most of those who seek scientific knowledge. But if we are to depend on social rather than rational criteria we must understand more fully what the inherent limits are to deviant science.

4. *The Problems and Prospects of Deviant Science*

Deviant sciences flourish if they have sufficient social support to recruit followers at least as fast as they lose them. Although rejected or ignored by most people, those who do accept them find them plausible and helpful in their problems. However, the social success of a deviant belief system in a particular social milieu is not simply related to the extent to which the people who consider it regard it as scientific, or even as true. For example, those with terminal cancer may not actually believe the claims of a healing cult, but they still reason that when everything else has failed the small but finite chance that the cult can help makes it worth trying. This kind of reasoning can enable a deviant movement to thrive if it can capitalise on an urgent need of some individuals, while avoiding excessive restrictions by the wider society. A discussion of the conditions under which social movements flourish is not, therefore, closely connected with the more central problems of this paper: the nature and significance of deviant constellations of rationally supported belief. However, given that a system of deviant science does have an adequate social basis for its perpetuation, a number of interesting questions arise about the character of its ideas.

One of the characteristic features of modern orthodox science is

37

the extent to which cognitive change is actively sought. The individual scientist does not merely seek to understand, and then to pass on
his understanding to new generations, even more important to his
occupational role is the aim of improving and extending knowledge.
Indeed, the institutionalised activity of science is such that if a field is
not perceived by its participants as rapidly growing, they regard it
as being in decline, a prospect they find distressing. This feature is so
fundamental to modern science that one can develop arguments that
if the proponents of a system of belief in competition to orthodox
science do not seek improvement in this way, then their ideas deserve
far less to be called 'science'. In an open society in which many systems
of belief may compete, and in which it is widely accepted that no
system of empirical understanding can be shown to be both true and
complete, it is anti-scientific dogmatism to claim to have reached the
ultimate certainty about empirical matters.

In many ways, therefore, the most interesting cases of deviant
science are those which are open to improvement, and which have
proponents who actively seek to develop their ideas in a manner
analogous to the evolution of orthodox sciences. Those examples in
which development actually occurs allow the fullest comparisons of
orthodoxy and deviance in science. However, many deviant sciences
remain static, or change in a less analogous way. I will say something
about these latter cases, before going on to the former.

Static systems of deviant belief are clearly different from living
sciences, which are being revised and extended by the scientists who
support them. The defenders of a static system of belief will generally
defend it as both true and complete, so that the task of a believer is
merely to appreciate and apply it. Such a view is unattractive to outsiders. For example, none of the arguments offered in the last section
support the extreme view that a certain set of deviant beliefs represents the ultimate truth and are incapable of improvement. The outsider is more likely to take the view that a static system of deviant
belief merely has no supporters who are acting as scientists. Some
modern concepts of science, such as that of Karl Popper, exclude
static or fossilized sciences, which cannot be developed through
criticism. Sectarian movements often succeed in freezing their basic
theory, especially if authoritarian in structure and with leaders who
prefer to keep the central insights unchanged. Any potential in-
novators in the movement can be treated as heretics and excom-

municated. But many non-sectarian movements also resist change in their guiding ideas. The beliefs claimed to be scientific by a deviant group function as an ideology, to be changed only in response to social circumstances, such as a new internal or external threat. The unity of a movement might depend, for example, on the pronouncements of a founder. Once he has ceased to develop his ideas, any further innovation would risk losing the distinguishing feature of the movement.

Deviant sciences typically change in three different ways. The first is defensive changes designed primarily to retain the central features of the movement. The theory may be elaborated so as to evade challenges offered by its critics. For example, those nineteenth century investigators studying the psychic phenomena of seances who believed in the unexplained powers of the medium, were obliged to say that a medium did not display her psychic power on every occasion. Since the power was beyond her conscious control a medium who had built up a reputation had a strong incentive to use trickery when it was needed. Thus, the argument developed that the exposure of a medium as a fraud on any one occasion did not automatically disqualify all her earlier seances at which trickery was not detected. Defensive arguments are used in orthodox science too, particularly those which complicate a bold and useful theory in order that it may avoid apparent falsification. Their use must be allowed in at least some cases, and the judgement of when they have been used to excess can never be decisive and final while the theory is still developing.[69] Developments designed to avoid criticism in orthodox and deviant science are not always purely defensive, however, for new claims with new implications may often be made. For example. Velikovsky has used his ideas of geologically recent planetary catastrophes to claim that rocks on the moon's surface have been melted in the last three thousand years. As radioactive dating methods have established an immensely older date for the moon's scars, Velikovsky has been obliged to question the assumptions used in those methods. His counter arguments have testable implications (should any orthodox scientist ever wish to bother).[70]

A second form of change in deviant science is change primarily designed to meet social rather than cognitive requirements. The changes from Dianetics to Scientology, for example, seem to have been mainly connected with the founder's desire to increase central control of the movement. Many movements acquire characteristics which increase their acceptability to potential recruits. It is easy to see that in the cultic milieu conditions would favour natural selection of those variants of cults which offer the greatest appeal to client 'seekers'.

The third type of change in deviant science is more analogous to the development of orthodox science. Changes are made in order to improve and extend the basic insights of the system. This third type of change is more limited in deviant than in orthodox science, because a smaller proportion of individual effort and material resources tends to be devoted to improving rather than conserving and applying the belief system. Nevertheless, it does go on. Consider the activity of successive generations of Pyramidologists, who believe that the ancient Egyptians constructed the shape and internal passages of the pyramids according to mystically significant numerical ratios. Pyramidology developed with the discovery of new ratios and new kinds of significance. From within the approach, these developments appear as progressive science. From outside, they may be dismissed as a series of purely subjective projections on to data which support no such conclusions.[71] Many other deviant sciences involve continuing development of the basic approach in a manner that seems progressive to insiders, but is regarded as an escalation in the ridiculousness of the activity by critics. There seems to be an interesting kind of relativism in such cases in that judgements of progress turn out to depend on whether a favourable or unfavourable attitude to underlying presuppositions of the activity has been taken. One common argument for denying that deviant sciences which develop in this way are progressive is to say that the standards of the deviant sciences are so low that apparent achievements have no objective significance. However, in the absence of universally accepted rational principles by which such achievements can be decisively assessed, this appeal to differing standards is merely an insistence that orthodox scientists are the most expert, and should therefore be deferred to. Such an appeal to experts is, of course, relative to who is regarded as most expert—that is, who is to be trusted the most—an intuitive judgment over which the orthodox and the deviant disagree.

One of the most interesting questions about deviant sciences is that of the circumstances under which their claims can become accepted by the bulk of society, and in particular by the expert elite of orthodox science. The most sceptical view of deviant science can be extracted from the work of Polanyi.[72] That is that unless an idea develops as a natural extension of the orthodox consensus, then it is not worth considering at all. Even though it may in retrospect have approached close to the truth, it is orthodox science which progresses most reliably and orthodox science can only produce or assimilate new ideas which are natural extensions of its current activity. This view encourages the conclusion that there is never any point in even looking at rejected knowledge. That conclusion should not, however, be accepted without critical evaluation. Once accepted, it would be self-fulfilling; it would be even more difficult for a deviant science to have any influence if orthodox scientists invariably refused to consider it. Furthermore, it is contrary to a number of interesting historical cases in which deviant sciences *have* had influence.

There are three distinct patterns by which the claims of a deviant science can become respected science. The only one allowed by Polanyi's argument is for the same ideas to be developed independently by orthodox scientists. Thus, it might be argued that the theory of evolution became a part of the consensus of orthodox science only as a result of the definitive contribution of Charles Darwin. The deviant evolutionary science which preceded and paralleled Darwin's career could not transform the orthodox consensus by itself. Darwin regarded his own detailed argumentation as independent of the deviant evolutionary science, and he was right to do so. However, the significance of Wallace's contribution poses special problems for this interpretation.

A second pattern is for scientific orthodoxy to take up an idea from deviant science in its own way, and having found value in it, to keep it and develop it in its own terms. Thus orthodox medical science has at times examined herbal and other remedies of unorthodox medicine, and has sometimes found useful medicines in this way. Orthodox medicine has, however, retained its illness-oriented therapy and has continued to ignore the patient-oriented therapy of the deviant medicine from which the treatment was obtained. The history of mesmerism in the nineteenth century may be viewed as another example of this kind of vindication.

A third pattern for the claims of a deviant science to become accepted is for the deviant movement itself to become orthodox. Thus

R. G. A. Dolby

osteopathy has striven for assimilation into orthodox American medicine.[73] The degree of success achieved has required sacrifice of many of the more deviant claims of the original movement. But enough remains to make osteopathy an interesting example of respectable but fringe medicine. Many religious cults have gone through a comparable evolution to relative respectability. In the process, however, they have tended to weaken the testable empirical content of their deviant scientific claims. Perhaps the most spectacular examples of the route from deviance to a form of orthodoxy are provided by Marxism and Freudian psychoanalysis. Both started as intellectual movements on the fringes of respectability and rose to prominence by acquiring a popular following rather than by converting some orthodox scientific elite. Both have now become respectable for whole societies or major sectors of society and the associated orthodox science, although their claims to be knowledge are still fundamentally criticised. As they have moved towards greater respectability, Marxism and Psychoanalysis have lost the appearance of discrete sectarian movements. Versions of the original systems are supported in a plurality of movements and basic insights have been extracted by increasing numbers of orthodox (human) sciences.

University of Kent at Canterbury.

[1] The classic statement of operationism is by P. W. Bridgman: *The Logic of Modern Physics*, Macmillan, New York, 1927. Bridgman developed and qualified his ideas in a series of later works. The original operational criterion was applied by behavioural psychologists, especially in criticism of the opposing introspectionist school. See, for example, E. C. Tolman: *Purposive Behavior in Animals and Men*, Century, London, 1931; S. S. Stevens: 'The Operational Definition of Psychological Concepts', *Psychological Review*, Vol. 42, 1935, pp. 517-527 and 'Psychology and the Science of Science', *Psychological Bulletin*, Vol. 36, 1939, pp. 221-263; and, E. G. Boring, P. W. Bridgman, H. Feigl, H. E. Israel, C. C. Pratt and B. F. Skinner: 'Symposium on Operationism', *Psychological Review*, Vol. 25, 1945, pp. 241-294. Bridgman came to insist that he intended to include mental operations, but this reduced the polemical use of operationism, and was resisted by behaviourists. One influential critique of operationism is C. G. Hempel: 'A Logical Appraisal of Operationism', *Scientific Monthly*, Vol. 79, 1954, pp. 215-220.

[2] Logical positivists proposed to distinguish the meaningful from the meaningless by using the Verifiability Principle. A classic discussion of the problem in English is A. J. Ayer: *Language, Truth and Logic*, Gollancz, London, 1946. See also A. J. Ayer (ed.): *Logical Positivism*, The Free Press, Glencoe, 1959.

[3] K. R. Popper: *The Logic of Scientific Discovery*, Hutchinson, London, 1959.

[4] I. Lakatos: 'Falsification and the Methodology of Scientific Research Programmes' in I. Lakatos and A. Musgrave (eds.): *Criticism and the Growth of Knowledge,* Cambridge University Press, London, 1970, pp. 90-195.

[5] See, for example, *American Behavioral Scientist,* Vol. 7, No. 1, 1963, which led in turn to the publication of A. de Grazia (ed.): *The Velikovsky Affair,* University Books, New York, 1966.

[6] See, for example, M. Polanyi's justification for the inadequately reasoned rejection by orthodox scientists of Velikovsky's theories in M. Polanyi: 'The Growth of Science in Society', *Minerva,* Vol. 5, 1967b, pp. 533-545, reprinted in M. Polanyi: *Knowing and Being,* Routledge & Kegan Paul, London, 1969. I have discussed the problems the criterion raises in R. G. A. Dolby: 'What Can We Usefully Learn from the Velikovsky Affair?', *Social Studies of Science,* Vol. 5, 1975, pp. 165-175.

[7] See M. Polanyi: *Personal Knowledge,* Routledge & Kegan Paul, London, 1958; M. Polanyi: *The Tacit Dimension,* Routledge & Kegan Paul, London, 1967a; and, M. Polanyi: op. cit. 1967b, 1969.

[8] T. S. Kuhn: *The Structure of Scientific Revolutions,* University of Chicago Press, Chicago, 1970.

[9] E. G. Boring: 'The Psychology of Controversy' in Boring: *History, Psychology and Science: Selected Papers,* Wiley, New York, 1963, pp. 67-84.

[10] H. Nowotny: 'Controversies in Science: Remarks on the Different Modes of Production of Knowledge and their Use', *Zeitschrift für Soziologie,* Vol. 4, 1974, pp. 34-45.

[11] J. Ziman: *Public Knowledge: The Social Dimension of Science,* Cambridge University Press, London, 1968, p. 115.

[12] R. G. A. Dolby: 'Debates over the Theory of Solution: A Study of Dissent in Physical Chemistry in the English-Speaking World in the Late Nineteenth and Early Twentieth Centuries', *Historical Studies in the Physical Sciences,* Vol. 7, 1976, pp. 297-404.

[13] Recent studies of the disproportionate significance of the scientific elite stem in particular from the work of D. J. de S. Price: *Little Science, Big Science,* Columbia University Press, London, 1963. Among more recent works, see for example. D. Crane: *Invisible Colleges: Diffusion of Knowledge in Scientific Communities,* University of Chicago Press, Chicago, 1972; and S. Cole and J. Cole: *Social Stratification in Science,* Chicago University Press, Chicago, 1973. A useful summary discussion of recent ideas on the nature and significance of the scientific elite is given in the first part of M. Mulkay: 'The Mediating Role of the Scientific Elite', *Social Studies of Science,* Vol. 6, 1976, pp. 445-470.

[14] R. Wallis and P. Morley (eds.): *Marginal Medicine,* Peter Owen, London, 1976, pp. 13-14.

[15] Kuhn: op. cit., chapter 7.

[16] R. G. A. Dolby: 'The Transmission of Science', *History of Science,* Vol. 15, 1977, pp. 1-43.

[17] Kuhn: op. cit.

[18] W. H. Brock: 'William Crookes', in C. C. Gillispie (ed.): *Dictionary of Scientific Biography,* Vol. 3, Scribners, New York, 1971, pp. 474-482.

R. G. A. Dolby

[19] W. Crookes: *Crookes and the Spirit World,* Taplinger, New York, 1972.

[20] L. Pauling: *Vitamin C, the Common Cold and the Flu,* Freeman, San Francisco, 1976.

[21] Wegener developed his ideas after 1915 in successive editions of *Die Entstehung der Kontinente und Ozeane,* see A. Wegener: *The Origin of Continents and Oceans,* Dover, New York, 1966.

[22] On Mendel and his rediscovery, see for example, H. Iltis: *Life of Mendel,* Allen and Unwin, London, 1932; R. A. Fisher: 'Has Mendel's Work been Rediscovered?' *Annals of Science,* Vol. 1, 1936, pp. 115-137; R. C. Olby: *The Origins of Mendelism,* Constable, London, 1966.

[23] 'Any man of ordinary understanding may, in a single day, qualify himself as thoroughly for entering upon the study of phrenology, as the profoundest physician who ever lived.' Anon., as quoted by G. N. Cantor: 'The Edinburgh Phrenology Debate, 1803-1828', *Annals of Science,* Vol. 32, 1975, p. 216.

[24] D. M. Jacobs: *The UFO Controversy in America,* Indiana University Press, London, 1975.

[25] See for example, A. Binet and C. Féré: *Animal Magnetism,* Kegan Paul, London, 1905; R. Darnton: *Mesmerism and the End of the Enlightenment in France,* Harvard University Press, Cambridge, Massachusetts, 1968.

[26] See, for example, the article by the Editors of *Der Spiegel:* 'Anatomy of a World Best Seller: Erich von Däniken's Message from the Unknown', *Encounter,* Vol. 41, 1973, pp. 8-17. See also, *Encounter,* 1977, pp. 44-46.

[27] For example, such 'scientific' racists writing for a general public as A. de Gobineau and H. S. Chamberlain, retained a following in right wing movements, including the German Nazi party as in the writings of Hitler and Rosenberg. See, for example, A. Rosenberg: *Selected Political Writings,* Cape, London, 1970.

[28] Groups supporting Velikovsky have collected around the journal *Pensée,* the editors of which have recently republished articles from their issues on Velikovsky: *Velikovsky Reconsidered,* Sidgwick and Jackson, London, 1976. In Britain the *Society for Interdisciplinary Studies Review* is especially concerned with Velikovsky.

[29] This is a general feature of popular science, orthodox or deviant. On the degeneration of encyclopaedic traditions, see, for example, H. Einbinder: *The Myth of the Britannica,* McGibbon and Kee, London, 1964.

[30] In a discussion of levels of involvement in modern astrology and modern witchcraft, M. Truzzi makes a similar distinction between the leisure-time fad and the preoccupation of the true believer. See M. Truzzi: 'The Occult Revival as Popular Culture: Some Random Observations on the Old and Nouveau Witch', *The Sociological Quarterly,* Vol. 13, 1972, pp. 16-36.

[31] For a general sociological account of the Scientology movement, see R. Wallis: *The Road to Total Freedom: A Sociological Analysis of Scientology,* Heinemann, London, 1976.

[32] For suggestions of connections between avant-garde and anti-rational culture, see, for example, E. A. Tiryakian: 'Towards the Sociology of Esoteric Culture', *American Journal of Sociology,* Vol. 78, 1972-3, pp. 491-512.

Reflections on Deviant Science

33 For example, B. Glass *et al* (eds.): *Forerunners of Darwin, 1745-1859,* Johns Hopkins Press, Baltimore, 1959.

34 C. Cuvier: 'Eloge de M. Lamarck', *Memoires de l'Académie Royale des Sciences de l'Institut de France,* 2nd series, Vol. 13, 1831, i-xxxi; C. Lyell: *Principles of Geology,* 3 vols., London, 1830-3, Book III.

35 For historical accounts of the impact of *Vestiges,* see, for example, C. C. Gillispie: *Genesis and Geology,* Harvard University Press, Cambridge, Massachusetts, 1951, especially chapter 6; and M. Millhauser: *Just Before Darwin: Robert Chambers and Vestiges,* Weslyan University Press, Middletown, Connecticut, 1959.

36 W. C. Williams: 'Robert Chambers' in C. C. Gillispie (ed.): *Dictionary of Scientific Biography,* Vol. 3, Scribners, New York, 1971, pp. 191-193.

37 A. R. Wallace: *My Life,* Chapman and Hall, London, 1905, Vol. 1, p. 254.

38 See in particular, A. R. Wallace: *Miracles and Modern Spiritualism,* Trübner, London, 1881, especially 'Notes of Personal Evidence'; Wallace: op. cit., 1905, chapters 20, 21.

39 On the contrast between British and German science in the nineteenth century, see, for example, J. T. Merz: *A History of European Thought in the Nineteenth Century,* 4 Vols., Blackwood and Sons, Edinburgh, 1896-1914, Vol. 1, chapters 2 and 3.

40 Osteopathy and chiropractic provide clear examples. See, for example, P. K. New: 'The Osteopathic Students: A Study in Dilemma' in E. G. Jaco (ed.): *Patients, Physicians and Illness,* Free Press, New York, 1958, pp. 413-421; and, W. I. Wardwell: 'A Marginal Professional Role: The Chiropractor' in E. G. Jaco: op. cit; and, W. I. Wardwell: 'Orthodox and Unorthodox Practitioners: Changing Relationships and the Future Status of Chiropractors' in Wallis and Morley: op. cit., pp. 61-73.

41 T. Roszack: *The Making of a Counter-Culture,* Faber & Faber, London, 1970; Truzzi: op. cit.,; and, K. Leech: *Youthquake: The Growth of a Counter-Culture Through Two Decades,* Sheldon Press, London, 1973.

42 Truzzi: op. cit.

43 For example, C. Campbell: 'The Cult, the Cultic Milieu and Secularization', *A Sociological Yearbook of Religion in Britain,* Vol. 5, 1972, pp. 119-130.

44 ibid., p. 122.

45 On the history of Mesmerism, see, for example, Binet and Féré: op. cit.; H. F. Ellenberger: *The Discovery of the Unconscious,* Allen Lane, London, 1972, especially chapters 2-4.

46 On Hermeticism and the rise of modern science, see, for example, F. A. Yates: *Giordano Bruno and the Hermetic Tradition,* Routledge & Kegan Paul, London, 1964; F. A. Yates: 'The Hermetic Tradition in Renaissance Science', in C. S. Singleton (ed): *Art, Science and History in the Renaissance,* Johns Hopkins, Baltimore, 1967; and, F. A. Yates: *The Rosicrucian Enlightenment,* Routledge and Kegan Paul, London, 1972. For a recent collection of papers discussing the issue, see M. L. Righini Bonelli and W. R. Shea (eds.): *Reason, Experiment and Mysticism in the Scientific Revolution,* Science History Publications, New York, 1975.

47 E. Katz and P. F. Lazarsfeld: *Personal Influence: The Part Played by People in the Flow of Mass Communications,* Free Press, New York, 1955.

R. G. A. Dolby

[48] On the localite-cosmopolite distinction, see R. K. Merton: *Social Theory and Social Structure*, Free Press, New York, 1957, pp. 387-420.

[49] An interesting account of how the hierarchy of Scientology courses is experienced by prospective Scientologists is given by R. Kaufman: *Inside Scientology*, Olympia, London, 1972.

[50] Wallis: op. cit., 1976, chapter 7.

[51] See, for example, Campbell: op. cit.; W. R. Catton, Jr.: 'What Kind of People Does a Religious Cult Attract?' in M. Truzzi (ed.): *Sociology and Everyday Life*, Prentice-Hall, Englewood Cliffs, 1968, pp. 235-242; J. Lofland and R. Stark: 'Becoming a World-Saver: A Theory of Conversion to Deviant Perspective', *American Sociological Review*, Vol. 30, 1965, pp. 862-875; R. Wallis: 'Ideology, Authority and the Development of Cultic Movements', *Social Research*, Vol. 41, 1974, pp. 299-327; R. Wallis (ed.): *Sectarianism: Analyses of Religious and Non-Religious Sects*, Peter Owen, London, 1975; B. R. Wilson: 'An Analysis of Sect Development', *American Sociological Review*, Vol. 24, 1959, pp. 3-15.

[52] For example, B. R. Wilson (ed.): *Rationality*, Blackwell, Oxford, 1970.

[53] See, for example, R. G. Collingwood: *The Idea of History*, Oxford University Press, London, 1946; P. K. Feyerabend: *Against Method: Outline of an Anarchistic Theory of Knowledge*, New Left Books, London, 1975; Kuhn: op. cit.; and, S. E. Toulmin: *Foresight and Understanding*, Huchinson, London, 1961.

[54] K. R. Popper: *Conjectures and Refutations*, Routledge & Kegan Paul, London, 1972, 4th edn., chapter 10.

[55] Kuhn: op. cit., chapter 7.

[56] See, for example, K. R. Popper: *The Open Society and its Enemies*, Routledge & Kegan Paul, London, 1966, 5th edn.; Popper: op. cit., 1972, especially chapters 1 and 15; K. R. Popper: 'Autobiography' in P. A. Schilpp (ed.): *The Philosophy of Karl Popper*, Open Court, La Salle, Illinois, 1974, pp. 23-33.

[57] See, for example, M. A. Cornforth: *The Open Philosophy and the Open Society: A Reply to Dr. Karl Popper's Refutations of Marxism*, Lawrence & Wishart, London, 1968; E. Conze: *The Scientific Method of Thinking: An Introduction to Dialectical Materialism*, Chapman and Hall, London, 1935.

[58] Feyerabend: op. cit.

[59] B. F. Skinner: 'A Case History in Scientific Method', in S. Koch (ed.): *Psychology: A Study of a Science*, Vol. 2, McGraw-Hill, New York, 1959, pp. 359-379.

[60] See, for example, de Grazia: op. cit., on the opposition to Velikovsky; a charming discussion of the unfair opposition to nineteenth century astrology is given by P. Powley (ed.): *The Astrologer*, Vol. 1, Foulsham, London, 1887, pp. 73-77.

[61] Jacobs: op. cit.

[62] J. A. Hynek: *The UFO Experience: A Scientific Enquiry*, Abelard Schuman, London, 1972.

[63] D. H. Menzell: *Flying Saucers*, Harvard University Press, Cambridge, Massachusetts, 1953.

Reflections on Deviant Science

[64] F. A. Paneth: 'The Origin of Meteorites' in H. Dingle, G. R. Martin and E. Paneth (eds.): *Chemistry and Beyond*, Interscience, New York, 1964, pp. 127-153. See also, R. Westrum: 'Science and Social Intelligence about Anomalies: The Case of Meteorites', unpublished paper submitted for presentation at 1977 meeting of the American Sociological Association.

[65] B. J. T. Dobbs: *Newton and Alchemy*, Cambridge University Press, London, 1975.

[66] M. Bunge: 'Technology as Applied Science' in C. Mitcham and R. Mackey (eds.): *Philosophy and Technology*, Free Press, New York, 1972, pp. 329-347.

[67] D. Joravsky: *The Lysenko Affair*, Harvard University Press, Cambridge, Massachusetts, 1970.

[68] Jacobs: op. cit.; Hynek: op. cit.

[69] Lakatos: op. cit.

[70] *Pensée*, Editors of: op. cit., part V.

[71] For example, M. Gardner: *Fads and Fallacies in the Name of Science*, Dover, New York, 1957.

[72] Polanyi: op. cit., 1958, 1967a, 1969.

[73] New op. cit.

ON THE ROLE OF INTERESTS IN SCIENTIFIC CHANGE

Barry Barnes and Donald MacKenzie

IN our society, knowledge claims which fail to achieve or sustain general legitimacy are usually those which are rejected by the professional community of scientists. Intriguingly, most such claims are made by scientists themselves. And, if history is any guide, most currently accepted scientific knowledge can expect eventually to be rejected in favour of some alternative, or more precise, conceptualisation. Science is both a major source of rejected knowledge and the main instrument of its rejection. Hence the generally acknowledged importance of understanding how evaluation proceeds in science, and what constitutes the inadequacy of the knowledge it rejects.

Unfortunately, however, study of this topic has been unduly influenced by the very fact of its importance, and by anxiety lest anything other than ideally 'rational' procedures might thereby be uncovered. Consequently, idealised accounts of the evaluation process, constructed by philosophers of science, have been assumed actually to be operative within the institution of science itself; and concrete naturalistic study of how far this is in fact the case has been avoided, or prejudiced by prior conviction.

Thus it was particularly disturbing when Thomas Kuhn demonstrated[1] that, in general, the successive paradigms within any particular tradition of scientific research are formally incommensurable with each other. This meant that, at key points in the development of science, logic and experiment did not and could not have sufficed as justifications for major conceptual and procedural transitions, and that debate at these times could not have generated sufficient reason for the transitions but at best only 'persuasive argumentation'.[2] The responses of philosophers and historians to this disconcerting finding remain tentative and confused; yet it has valuable positive implications for the concerns of both groups. It highlights intriguing formal problems concerning the nature and possibility of translation, the character

49

of universals, and the problem of reference. And it re-emphasises the pressing need for historical studies which are focused entirely upon how evaluation actually proceeds in science, and unconcerned with how it 'ought' to proceed.[3]

Unfortunately many historians remain wedded to a conception of their craft which obliges them to produce findings suitable for a defence of the 'rationality' of science. Thus, Darden[4] organises interesting historical materials about a monumental non-sequitur, in attempting to refute Kuhn's view that 'no conclusive argument' can be given for the adoption of a new paradigm.[5] She proceeds as though relating scientific changes to 'good reasons' refutes Kuhn's claims about 'conclusive argument' or sufficient reason, and thus she by-passes important questions concerning the actual historical role of reasons, in pursuit of a misconceived objective.[6] Other historians, more willing to recognise 'imperfection' and 'insufficiency' in scientific argumentation, have organised their material to display the (limited) extent to which it is consistent with this or that philosophical conception of rationality. Much otherwise admirably concrete and detailed historical study is restricted by this kind of presentation.[7]

Surely, the historical question is not how evaluation didn't proceed, but how it did. Where a scientific community makes a major shift of paradigm the factors which actually brought about that shift are what need to be elucidated. Familiarity with such factors, and their relevance in different contexts, could lead to genuine insight into the actual nature of cultural change in science and into the character of our cognitive processes. Similarly, historical study of incommensurability should not address itself to formal problems of translation, of what can properly and 'rationally' be rendered as what, of what meanings in two systems are 'logically' identical. What should be asked is how far incommensurability presents a *practical* barrier to communication, how far discourse and effective communication is actually established between exponents of different paradigms, and what in fact are the characteristics of such discourse. Given their apparent historical significance, what are the properties of 'imperfect communications' and 'persuasive argumentation' as phenomena in their own right?[8]

At present, we lack any general scheme of interpretation which makes the relationship of competing scientific paradigms intelligible naturalistically. One possible but obviously implausible account is often erroneously attributed to Kuhn himself, and then attacked as his position. On this account, incommensurability functions as an insuperable obstacle to verbally articulated cognitively based judgements, and the scientist who moves from one paradigm to another must, like some latter-day Saint Paul, undergo some mystical process of conversion.

We would question any general account which laid such weight on the alleged empirical consequences of incommensurability.[9] Clearly, the existence of incommensurable paradigms and modes of discourse may present actors on the two sides with technical problems of communication and mutual understanding. But the evidence suggests that, in practice, such technical problems can be overcome, given only a minimum of incentive such as usually exists among communities of scientists. Translation may pose massive philosophical problems, but it does not pose equivalent practical problems.[10] Anthropology has proved to be practically possible, as has real communication and interaction between participants in radically diverse cultures and sub-cultures; all of us appear to possess the competences requisite to constructing meanings and shared understanding with others, however alien. Moreover, the comparison of competing paradigms does not in any case necessitate translation. Scientists may separately develop competence within two paradigmatic frameworks, or practise one but imaginatively rehearse the processes of the other, and thus be properly and directly cognisant of the methods of both. Since the time of Galileo, scientists have demonstrated their capacity thus to understand a competing position. There is little evidence to suggest that tensions between competing paradigms have ever been predominantly sustained by problems of intelligibility as such.[11]

How then are we to understand the tension between competing paradigms and/or the transition from one to another? As we see it, what general insights are to be gained here will only become apparent if we insist upon treating the problem as more than a clash of ideas or alternative modes of discourse. Kuhn provides us with an important indication of how we should proceed when he writes:

> Like the choice between competing political institutions, that between paradigms proves to be a choice between incompatible modes of community life.[12]

The way to exploit this insight is to remember that 'modes of community life', whether of overall cultures or of particular sub-cultures, are typically goal-oriented. Their organised activities must generally be related to purposes, aims, goals, objectives, interests, or some such categories, if they are to be made intelligible. Thus it is plausible to hypothesise that when a sub-culture evaluates knowledge the process should be understood to some extent in terms of the goal-oriented character of its thought and activity, rather than in totally abstract contemplative terms.

Since there is no generally accepted vocabulary with which to frame an hypothesis of this kind, we shall adopt a variant of that of Habermas,[13] recognising that it might eventually prove expedient to move to some alternative mode of expression.[14] We shall say that paradigms are evaluated against each other in relation to some set of context-dependent (situated) instrumental interests, or, as Habermas says, interests in prediction and control. We should avoid thinking of paradigms as abstract theories or modes of discourse, and instead emphasise their character as resources or instruments. Essentially, they are clusters of calculative and interpretative procedures exhibited in concrete problem solutions. Scientists compare such clusters in terms of what can be *done* with them, that is, by considering their perceived achievements and potential achievements rather than their formal characteristics. [This does not, however, eliminate the difficulties of those who wish to see transitions between paradigms as necessarily 'progressive' and 'rational'. Rarely, if at all, will a paradigm solve all the puzzles resolved by its rival and more, at a time of transition. Typically, in any decision between paradigms based upon accomplishments, the relative success of one alternative in one context has to be balanced against relative failure in another. And any attempt to rationalise such a decision by verbally formulated criteria merely leads back to the formal problems of incommensurability.]

Paradigms, then, are to be regarded as resources. Scientists can imaginatively rehearse the potential procedures, activities and accomplishments which paradigms represent, and relate these directly to their instrumental interests. They can thereby separately assess their potential as resources in the pursuit of such interests, rather than comparing them directly with each other in terms of their formal properties. Where scientists disagree in their choice of paradigms one should hence always check whether they do not differ also in the instrumental interests which pre-structure their evaluations.[15]

On the Role of Interests in Scientific Change

The situated patterns of instrumental interests in terms of which scientists construct and evaluate knowledge-claims, and from time to time, compare paradigms, are generally in turn related to the fact that their activity is socially structured, and related to a set of social interests. Often this structure and set of social interests is simply part of the esoteric social organisation of science itself, the consequence of the ongoing activity of some group of scientific specialists. This may generate certain shared esoteric social interests: interests in the resolution of a certain particular set of puzzles and problems; in the continuance-in-use of central techniques, competences and theoretical structures; in the uncovering of areas of applicability for such techniques, competences and structures; perhaps in the maintenance of the group's image as a specialism with notable existing achievements; certainly in the availability of continuing opportunity for activity and the exercise of skills by members of the group. Such social interests serve to particularise the instrumental interests which pre-structure the evaluations of the group, linking them to the improvement of one particular kind of prediction rather than another, the enlargement of the scope of particular kinds of competence and not others, the sustenance and articulation of some problem solutions and not others. Or, more profoundly, social interests may modulate the conceptions of what counts as prediction or problem solution which partially define the situated instrumental knowledge—constituting interests of the scientists.

Good discussions of episodes which can be understood in these terms are Dolby[16] and Frankel.[17] Dolby's work considers the reception of the theories of solution of Arrhenius and van't Hoff. These theories, enthusiastically advocated by a coherent group of German physical chemists (the Ostwald school), were extensively criticised when introduced into Great Britain late in the nineteenth century. In an extensive concrete discussion which demands direct examination, Dolby reveals how these critical evaluations were a function of the scientific situations and interests of those who made them. J. J. Thomson, and later Oliver Lodge, assessed the theories in relation to their concerns as physicists. H. E. Armstrong sustained a prolonged opposition to the theories, of which he gained a detailed understanding, on the grounds of their incompatibility with his general experience as a chemist. He was able to draw a good deal of sympathy and support from his professional colleagues, who were

53

presumably able to see his point when he characterised the views of the Germans as incompatible with 'chemists' common sense'.[18] Overall, the conflicting evaluations manifested in the debate are revealed to be structured and sustained by diverse professional interests. As Dolby says, 'Only after the death of the main opponents of the Ostwald school, the emergence of new theories, and changes in the major interests of physical chemists, did the debate finally end'.[19]

The instrumental interests which inform scientific evaluation need not however be related solely to social interests established entirely by esoteric professional activity and thus completely 'internal to science'. They may relate to more general social interests, either directly, or indirectly in the sense that the social interests of some esoteric scientific sub-culture may themselves be expressions of more general social interests. Indeed, we are unsure whether a role for general social interests is usual or exceptional at times of paradigm conflict or change; certainly their importance in some instances is evident, c.f. MacKenzie and Barnes,[20] and more tentatively Forman.[21] This is not however central to our present concerns. What we wish to show is that opposed paradigms and hence opposed evaluations may be sustained, and probably are in general sustained, by divergent sets of instrumental interests usually related in turn to divergent social interests. The form of our argument is not affected by whether the social interests are esoteric or general, 'internal' or 'external' to 'science'. Although, intuitively, evaluation structured by 'external' social interests might seem undesirable and inferior, it is difficult to see how a general argument in support of this might be constructed. How can we be sure that one mode of particularisation of instrumental interests is better than another in all circumstances? If we could contrast a narrow basis of evaluation produced by social interests with a properly scientific context-independent basis involving only a completely general interest in prediction and control, then things would be different. But such a conception of scientific evaluation is utopian; interests in prediction and control can only inform scientific judgement if they are to some extent defined and made specific by reference to pre-existing particular exemplary instances.

Let us then consider in some detail an instance where interests arguably did pre-structure scientific judgements, and where they sustained a major conflict between incompatible modes of discourse and patterns of procedure and inference. As it happens, the example chosen does involve reference to general social interests as well as narrow professional ones, but nothing hangs upon the point.

We shall consider the controversy within the small community of British statisticians early in this century, concerning the measurement of association. This is an episode which should prove readily intelligible to sociologists, and of which we ourselves have detailed knowledge. Thus it is particularly suitable for illustrative purposes. It does, however, assume an essential similarity between mathematical and scientific practice; this is an assumption which we believe we can justify, but which we cannot address ourselves to here.

The controversy was centred upon the merits of two alternative kinds of solution to the association problem, those of Karl Pearson on the one hand,[22] and of George Udny Yule[23] on the other. It does however deserve to be accorded a broader significance as an indication of the existence of alternative overall conceptual frameworks for the practice of statistics.[24]

Association in nominal-type data[25] may be usefully considered in terms of the simplest possible case, which will doubtless be familiar to sociologists. Consider a set of N objects, classified according to two nominal variables A and B, so that every object must either be A_1 or A_2, and either B_1 or B_2. Such a classification can always be presented as a contingency table. The problem is to compute the extent that A and B are associated variables [i.e. the degree of their dependence] given a, b, c, d :

TABLE I

	B_1	B_2	Total
A_1	a	b	a + b
A_2	c	d	c + d
Total	a + c	b + d	N

When British statisticians turned to this problem they did so as a professional community possessing, as well as a shared general mathematical culture, specifically statistical techniques and concrete problem solutions for the treatment of interval level data. In particular, they accepted as valid a theory of regression and correlation which had been generalised to n variables; and they took Pearson's product-moment formula as the means for the numerical calculation of coefficients of correlation.

In Pearson's attempts to deal with nominal data we note a persistent attempt to maximise the analogy between it and interval data: he treated association as a kind of correlation. Given a table like 1 above, we might loosely say that he proceeded as though, for example, A was height and B weight—both of which are normally distributed interval variables. A_1 might be $> 6'$ and $A_2 \leq 6'$; $B_1 > 100$ lb and $B_2 \leq 100$ lb. By thus assuming underlying normal distributions, Pearson was able to calculate a 'tetrachoric coefficient of correlation' r_T analogous to the product-moment correlation coefficient for interval level data. The calculation, however, depended only upon a, b, c, d, and thus could be computed for, and was held by Pearson to apply to, any nominal data in the form of Table 1. Pearson was willing to conceive of all nominal variables—brown-eyed/blue-eyed, alive/dead, male/female as the product of our perception and categorisation of continuous phenomena which were normally distributed. r_T measured the real correlation of the normally distributed interval variables which underlay nominal level data.

Pearson's production and evaluation of measures of association was pre-structured by an interest in prediction and technical control defined by existing work on interval level data. His very specification of association as the correlation between underlying variables reflected his situated instrumental interests.

Yule, on the other hand, made no attempt to treat nominal and interval level data as analogous, and disregarded appeals to the analogy in evaluating attempts to measure association. Essentially, what Yule did was to take existing mathematical intuitions about the dependence and independence of variables, and construct, ad hoc, a coefficient which would express them in quantitative idiom. His argument was that such a coefficient should be zero when A and B were independent, $+1$ when they were completely associated and -1 when they were completely negatively associated. That is, the coefficient should be O when being A_1 rather than A_2 implied nothing about the chances of being B_1 or B_2; it should be $+1$ if being A_1 implied B_1, or being B_1 implied A_1; and it should be -1 if being

A_1 implied B_2, or being B_1 implied A_2.[26] Yule suggested that a convenient coefficient Q was

$$Q = \frac{ad - bc}{ad + bc}$$

and he showed that it was in conformity with the three formal requirements he had set out. He acknowledged that any number of other coefficients existed in accord with these requirements, and was aware that different coefficients of this kind could contradict each other in their rank orderings of the degree of association of different sets of data. But this did not disturb him. Evidently Yule was content to allow investigators of different practical problems to use his coefficient in a way which made sense in context. He himself treated it as a convenient accessory to a range of problems in which he had a particular involvement. Most importantly, he used it to deal with medical survey data on the efficacy of vaccination.

Thus, Yule's evaluation of measures of association was pre-structured by an instrumental interest in nominal data as distinct separate phenomena. The possible modes of prediction and control appropriate to them were defined in his thinking by traditional mathematical perspectives and by direct consideration of particular problems involving nominal data. His evaluations proceeded independently of the recent statistical accomplishments in the treatment of interval level data.

Although both Pearson and Yule did further work on association, the polarisation of their instrumental interests continued, and they and their followers remained in a state of controversy for many years. The controversy is one of several which indicate that Karl Pearson and his followers sustained their own particular paradigm for the practice and extension of statistics.[27] Hence it is a controversy exhibiting the familiar features of paradigm clash as detailed by Kuhn. The two sides used existing problem solutions differently and held different views concerning their scope or applicability. And they defined what was to count as a statistical problem differently, to the extent that their concepts of 'association' were incompatible the one with the other.

Consequently, although doubtless there were 'reasonable men' on both sides of the controversy, abstract argument could not hope to provide sufficient reason for choosing one or other side. Thus,

Pearson regarded it as a defect of Yule's coefficients that they could indicate complete association between sets of data generated from incompletely associated underlying variables; for Pearson this indicated a failure in measurement. Yule, however, did not accept the notion of association which was used to define the failure of his coefficient here. He continued to define perfect association in his own way (as described earlier), which vindicated his own practice and in turn cast doubt on aspects of Pearson's work.

To take another example, it was not disputed by either side that applied to genuinely continuous, binormal data, such as tables of the inheritance of height, the value of Yule's Q differed according to where the division (into tall/short) was taken, and that the agreement of Q with the coefficient of correlation for the full data was poor, and indeed very poor for extreme divisions. For Pearson this invalidated Q: no valid comparisons could be made from one table to another using it, nor could it be compared with ordinary coefficients of correlation. For Yule this property that Q had when applied to continuous data did not affect its use for dichotomous categories, because he rejected the basic Pearsonian model of underlying binormal variables. For Yule, the given categories were all one had to work with, and to attempt to go beneath them was to stray into dangerous areas of theoretical assumption. For Pearson, not to go beyond them was to make impossible the measurement of association in his sense.[28] These, and many other instances of their particular disagreements, indicate that the positions of Pearson and Yule can reasonably be characterised as incommensurable. They were, if one wishes to put it so, arguing as if they lived in different worlds.[29]

But precisely what makes this controversy so significant as far as our present interests are concerned is that the incommensurability clearly manifest between the two opposed positions cannot plausibly be invoked to explain the tension between them. The protagonists in the controversy, and Yule and Pearson particularly, well understood each other's positions. They competently expounded and carried out each other's procedures in the course of criticising them. And they recognised that they could enhance their own credibility if they could overcome the objections of the opposition in its own terms: Pearson, for example, sought justifications of r_T and analogous estimates of 'real' correlation which could be accepted even by those who did not accept the existence of underlying normally distributed variables. The decisive point, however, is that for a time Pearson's work was almost definitive of what had been accomplished as mathematical statistics in Britain, and during that time Yule had learned his statistics from Pearson. The two men started from shared assumptions, meanings and competences, and diverged. The subsequent formal incommensurability of their discourse must be taken as a puzzle; we should treat it as a correlate of diverging instrumental interests within the small statistical community, and accordingly we should seek to understand why that divergence occurred. The most likely answer would seem to be that it was generated and sustained by contrasting social interests.

When Mackenzie attempted to define who was actively involved in the development of statistical theory in Britain between 1900 and 1914, he was able to identify a core of 26 individuals, 12 of whom could be clearly placed in the 'biometric school' dominated by Karl Pearson, and based upon the biometric and eugenic laboratories at University College London. At least 10 of these 12 either advocated or employed Pearson's measures of association, whereas only one of the 13 individuals clearly separate from the school employed them, and he was clearly in partial sympathy with the social aims and interests of the biometric movement. In contrast, Yule drew what support he had from this group of 13 very loosely connected individuals, probably via his participation in the Royal Statistical Society. (One supporter, Major Greenwood, had like Yule, left the biometric school during this period. He had employed r_T when a member of the school, but ceased to use it upon leaving, and indeed then began to criticise the biometrical approach to the measurement of association. This is further evidence that favourable evaluation of r_T was entailed by the distinctive characteristics of the biometric school's approach to statistical theory.)

Biometry was the research programme within which modern mathematical statistics initially arose in Britain. Initiated by Francis Galton's mathematical study of human heredity for eugenic ends, it was continued by a larger group of researchers built up and dominated by Karl Pearson. It can be regarded as a project aimed at providing a scientific basis for eugenic policy and ideology, and thus as an enterprise wherein objectives and evaluations were preconstrained by general social interests; for as has been shown elsewhere eugenic ideas were, at this time and place, shaped and sustained by the interests of a rising professional class.[30]

It is evident that these same social interests shaped and particularised the instrumental interests assumed in the biometricians' evaluations, and hence their approach to the problem of association. To see how this occurred we must look back to Pearson's work on interval level statistics, including his work on correlation. This work was presented as a series of 'Mathematical Contributions to the Theory of Evolution' and this is exactly how it was regarded. Like Galton, Pearson conceived of correlation specifically as a measure of the association between properties of successive generations in a population. And like Galton he tended to assume that such association must be entirely a function of heredity. The measure of heredity of characteristics from parents to offspring was *defined* as the correlation of the characteristics between the two generations. Thus, Pearson's scientific work built the characteristic hereditarian assumptions of eugenics into its basic structure by definition, and circumvented any systematic consideration of the influence of environment on the phenomena he studied. And this same definition made correlation a key concept in all Pearson's thinking. Correlation was simply the measure of heredity. At times indeed Pearson would refer to the product-moment correlation coefficient simply as 'the coefficient of heredity'. It was his representation of 'the strength of heredity', and *its actual numerical values in particular instances were facts about nature* of real significance in the understanding of inheritance, and thus in the formulation of eugenic policy.

Unfortunately, as Pearson wrote in 1900, 'many characters are such that it is very difficult if not impossible to form either a discrete or a continuous numerical scale of their intensity'. These characters lay without the scope of his statistical techniques and thus of his methods of assessing the 'strength of heredity'. Hence Pearson's desire to extend the scope of these techniques and methods to nominal data: 'if the theory of correlation can be extended so as to readily apply to such cases, we shall have much widened the field within which we can make numerical investigations into the intensity of heredity . . .'[31]

It should be noted that among 'such cases' at this time were the eugenically crucial 'mental and intellectual characters'.[32] To measure the 'strength of heredity' of these characters was essential to any scientifically based eugenic programme, and advantageous as an adjunct to eugenic polemic. Pearson was eventually to show that the 'strength of heredity' of intelligence as measured by r_T was very close to that of physical characters like eye-colour (by r_T), or height (by product-moment correlation). From this, he argued that as these physical characters were indubitably determined in their intensity by heredity and not environment, the same had to be true of intelligence. Hence the lack of intelligence central to British failure in imperialist competition with Germany and the U. S. could only be remedied by the eugenic prescription of 'altering the relative fertility of the good and the bad stocks in the community'.

We can now see how social interests shaped and particularised the instrumental interests which pre-organised the evaluations of the biometricians. Possible modes of prediction and control in the realm of nominal data were taken as analogous to these in the realm of interval data because this analogy facilitated computations and permitted inferences which in their general form were potentially applicable to eugenically significant problems, and which could help to justify the hereditarian presuppositions of the eugenists.[33] The analogy with the interval level both legitimated the notion of 'strength of heredity' for nominal data, and indicated possible techniques by which it could be computed and employed in calculating the effects of eugenically oriented intervention.

Eugenic problems and concerns were in turn significant foci of scientific activity, and central to the biometrical enterprise, because they were sustained by general social interests. Eugenics was at this time an important ideological strand in a body of thought closely associated with the rising professional middle class.[34]

In contrast, the work of Yule reveals no concern with eugenic programmes or problems, just as it reveals no disposition to model the study of nominal data upon existing accomplishments at the interval level. Indeed, it is perhaps the case that Yule and his supporters found eugenics and biometry uncongenial to their basically conservative social and political views, and that this is why Yule moved away from the biometric laboratory where Pearson had taught him, into the more conservative context provided by the Royal Statistical Society. In any case, the objectives, social and technical, proper to statistical work as conceived within the R. S. S. seem to have provided what coherent particular structure there was in Yule's statistical judgements. His ideas on correlation mainly developed in connection with problems of pauperism and poor relief, those on association in connection with vaccination and its efficacy. These favourite topics for discussion and controversy in the R. S. S. were of technical interest within that body because of their bearing upon the possibilities of social amelioration. But framed in this way disputes over the potency of vaccination would not have been one whit advanced by all the excess labour of calculating r_T rather than Q, whereas the very character of the data tended to prejudice one against underlying variables: as Yule put it, 'all those who have died of small-pox are all equally dead'.[35]

In this example then, statistical judgement should be understood as it was situated in particular contexts of goal-oriented research activity. And the controversy outlined should be taken to reflect a divergence of orientation, albeit at a highly general and not necessarily fully perceived level. Incommensurability should be taken as a symptom of this divergence. Perhaps the particular way employed here of describing the goal-oriented character of scientific judgements will eventually prove to be unsatisfactory; the role and relationship of social and instrumental interests postulated here may prove to be significantly misconceived. We would remain convinced, nonetheless, that some constitutively goal-linked notion of evaluation was essential in understanding scientific change, and particularly in throwing light upon those episodes where alternative paradigms stand in opposition.

Traditionally, there has been great reluctance to characterise scientific evaluation other than in terms of entirely abstract, contemplative notions of rational inference. Goals, objectives, or especially interests,[36] have seemed too diverse and variable to be part of the evaluative structure that produced the coherent, generally accepted and in many ways enduring body of knowledge that is our science. But this difficulty is illusory and arises out of a misconceived individualistic conception of scientific evaluation. The value and utility of our present scientific knowledge is not dependent upon single acts of evaluation wherein knowledge-claims are permanently endowed with the status of science. Rather the growth of science should be seen as an historical development, wherein, over a period, systems of knowledge may be evaluated and re-evaluated, and consequently refined and modified, in many ways—if not with respect to all possible kinds of prediction and control as Habermas says, at least with regard to many particular kinds. The overall effects of such a historical process have to be conceptualised in a very different way from those of a series of unconnected, once and for all, individual judgements.

University of Edinburgh.

[1] T. S. Kuhn: *The Structure of Scientific Revolutions*, Chicago University Press, Chicago, 1970, 2nd. edn.

[2] ibid., p. 94.

[3] For a detailed argument in favour of such dissociation see S. B. Barnes: 'Natural Rationality: A Neglected Concept in the Social Sciences', *Philosophy of the Social Sciences*, Vol. 6, 1976, pp. 115-126. It should be added that although Kuhn's work clearly illustrates the inadequacy of any current ideal model of rationality at points of paradigm change, there has never been any firm demonstration of the relevance of such a model *at any point* in ongoing scientific work; indeed Kuhn's work implicitly questions their relevance to 'normal science' also. Perusal of such realistic, concrete historical accounts of 'normal science' as we possess lends further weight to this point (see W. Provine: *The Origins of Theoretical Population Genetics*, Chicago University Press, Chicago, 1971; R. Fox: *The Caloric Theory of Gases*, Clarendon Press, Oxford, 1971; N. W. Fisher: 'Organic Classification before Kekule', *Ambix*, Vol. 20, no. 1, 1973, pp. 106-131; Vol. 20, no. 3, 1973, pp. 297-404; and N. W. Fisher: 'Kekule and Organic Classification' *Ambix*, Vol. 21, no. 1, 1974, pp. 29-52, among others, although none of these authors deals wholly with 'normal science').

[4] L. Darden: 'Reasoning in Scientific Change', *Studies in the History and Philosophy of Science*, Vol. 7, no. 2, 1976, pp. 127-170.

[5] ibid., p. 128.

[6] For analogous misconceptions set in a broader framework see, I. Lakatos and A. Musgrave (eds.): *Criticism and the Growth of Knowledge*, Cambridge University Press, London, 1970; and J. D. Rabb: 'Incommensurable Paradigms and critical idealism', *Studies in the History & Philosophy of Science*, Vol. 6, no. 4, 1975, pp. 343-346.

[7] A good example, precisely because of its real historical value is H. Gay: 'Radicals and Types: A Critical Comparison of the Methodologies of Popper and Lakatos and their Use in the Reconstruction of Some Nineteenth Century Chemistry', *Studies in the History and Philosophy of Science*, Vol. 7, no. 1, 1976, pp. 1-51.

[8] We apologise if it seems that excessive stress is being given to an obvious point, but the stress is needed. Relatively little historical work has emulated Kuhn's naturalistic orientation to paradigm change or conflict. For work which comes close to this orientation see E. Frankel: 'Corpuscular Optics and the Wave Theory of Light: The Science and Politics of a Revolution in Physics', *Social Studies in Science*, Vol. 6, no. 2, 1976, pp. 141-184; M. J. S. Rudwick: *The Meaning of Fossils*, London, 1972; R. G. A. Dolby: 'Disputes Over the Theory of Solution', *Historical Studies in the Physical Sciences*, Vol. 7, 1976, pp.297-404.

[9] For a statement of the opposed point of view see G. N. Cantor: 'The Edinburgh Phrenology Debate: 1803-1828', *Annals of Science*, Vol. 32, 1975, pp. 195-218, who writes: —
    'Many case-studies suggest that frequently there exists a degree of incommensurability between the views held by the two groups of protagonists

which prevents a constructive outcome of the debate through means of dialogue' (p. 196, our italics).
Kuhn too ascribes considerable weight to incommensurability as a practical barrier to communication and the resolution of disagreements. See Kuhn: op. cit., pp. 198-204.

[10] When Popper wrote 'The fact is that even totally different languages . . . are not untranslatable', he highlighted the importance of this point. See Lakatos and Musgrave: op. cit., p. 56. How one evaluates his statement depends upon whether one's interests are formal or naturalistic, and hence upon what one regards as proper translation.

[11] With more space, we would have offered an argument to the effect that chronic problems of intelligibility are *always* phenomena requiring explanation in terms of divergent interests. The citation of intelligibility problems as explanations for associated social phenomena stems, like many other misconceptions, from a faulty understanding of the general relationship of people and their ideas.

[12] Kuhn: op. cit., p. 94.

[13] J. Habermas: *Knowledge and Human Interests*, Heinemann, London, 1972.

[14] The interesting speculations of Habermas: op. cit., appear likely to prove an invaluable resource in the future investigation of problems in this field. See also the treatment of knowledge and interest in S. B. Barnes: *Interests and the Growth of Knowledge*, Routledge & Kegan Paul, London, 1977.

[15] Emphatically, this should not be taken as claiming that scientific evaluation is always, or even usually, related to immediate short term aims or interests, or shaped by specific concerns with practical application. The immediate uses to which knowledge is put must be distinguished from the less specific, but never completely context-independent, instrumental interests which pre-structure its evaluation.

[16] Dolby: op. cit.

[17] Frankel: op. cit.

[18] That the phrase correctly characterised Armstrong's detailed and longstanding assessments of the German work, and was not merely an isolated locution, is at once apparent when Dolby's account is read in detail.

[19] Dolby: op. cit., p. 298. In view of what has already been suggested with reference to the practical significance of incommensurability, it is worth citing another of the general conclusions which Dolby draws from his work:
'As the present study illustrates, even though the *initial* confrontation appears incommensurable, the two sides soon came to understand one another more fully, though they continued to disagree. Although methods of rational persuasion had very little effect, the two sides came to be separated less by misunderstanding than by contrasting commitments' (op. cit., p. 404).

[20] D. A. Mackenzie and S. B. Barnes: 'Biometrician v. Mendelian: A Controversy and its Explanation', *Kölner Zeitschrift für Soziologie*, Special issue, Vol. 18, 1975, pp. 165-196.

[21] P. Forman: 'Weimar Culture, Causality and the Quantum Theory', *Historical Studies in the Physical Sciences*, Vol. 3, 1971, pp. 1-115.

On the Role of Interests in Scientific Change

[22] K. Pearson: 'Mathematical Contributions to the Theory of Evolution VII: On the Correlation of Characters not Quantitatively Measurable', *Philosophical Transactions of the Royal Society of London*, Series A, Vol. 195, 1900, pp. 1-47.

[23] G. U. Yule: *The Statistical Papers of G. U. Yule*, Griffin, London, 1971, edited by Kendall and Stuart.

[24] This is made clear in Mackenzie's Ph.D. thesis, University of Edinburgh, 1977.

[25] The use of nominal/interval nomenclature is anachronistic but useful in an abbreviated exposition.

[26] Thus if vaccination (A_1) implies survival of epidemic (B_1), or if survival (B_1) is only manifested by the vaccinated (A_1), then A and B, vaccination status and survival status, are treated as fully associated. Whereas where vaccination guarantees death, or where death only occurs among the vaccinated, a complete negative association is indicated.

[27] One can cite also Pearson's evaluation of Gosset's work on small samples; his adverse judgement of the early work of R. A. Fisher and his subsequent rejection of Fisher's general theory of statistics; and his general methodological position concerning Mendelism. Indeed the biometrician-Mendelian controversy is another excellent example by reference to which our argument concerning the roles of interests and incommensurability could be substantiated.

[28] Pearson's position on association, depending as it does on assumptions concerning ubiquitous normally distributed underlying variables, makes an interesting contrast with his strongly positivistic philosophical prescriptions. Needless to say, the explicit methodological pronouncements of practising scientists rarely provide any insight into their actual modes of procedure.

[29] Although there is no necessity here, scientists do often elaborate explicit cosmologies out of their practice and their paradigmatic frameworks. Norton suggests that Pearson did indeed elaborate such a cosmology—a 'statistical Weltbild' which denied that any two physical entities could ever be exactly alike and constituted all of reality out of entities with normally distributed properties. See B. Norton: 'Metaphysics and Population Genetics: Karl Pearson and the Background to Fisher's Multi-factorial Theory of Inheritance', *Annals of Science*, Vol. 32, 1975, pp. 537-553. In terms of this cosmology, Yule's position appears as a contrasting world view which either assumes the real identity of the physical entities we call 'the same', or makes the nominalist assumption that valid knowledge can be produced by treating that which we call 'the same' as being indeed 'the same' (Intriguingly, Pearson made these points against Yule by accusing him of illegitimate realism whilst presenting himself, for all his faith in underlying variables, as a nominalist.)

[30] MacKenzie and Barnes: op. cit.; D. A. MacKenzie: 'Eugenics in Britain', *Social Studies of Science*, Vol. 6, no. 3-4, 1976, pp. 219 ff; D. A. Mackenzie: 'Statistical Theory and Social Interests: A Case Study', *Social Studies of Science*, Vol. 8, 1978, pp. 35-83. This last describes the present controversy in much more detail than is possible here.

[31] K. Pearson: 'On the Application of Certain Formulae in the Theory of Correlation to the Inheritance of Characters not Capable of Quantitative Measurement', *Proceedings of the Royal Society*, Vol. 66, 1900, pp. 324-325. It is also relevant here to note that Pearson held to a 'blending' conception of inheritance, and that although he had himself no explicit theory concerning the mechanism of inheritance, his informal thinking on the subject was certainly incompatible with any theory, like Mendelism, which involved

Barry Barnes and Donald MacKenzie

discontinuities. Thus, the treatment of discrete nominal data as the product of underlying continuous variables was not only expedient in mathematical calculation, but was also an important reinforcement of his (Darwinist) biological thinking. See Mackenzie and Barnes: op. cit.
It is unfortunate that by considering only one episode in a restricted space the coherent integrated quality of Pearson's thought and work as a whole has to remain unexamined. Pearson's writings in mathematics, in biology, and for that matter in history and philosophy too, are strongly interconnected and alike related to identical social interests.

[32] An alternative 'solution' to this difficulty with mental characteristics was soon to be developed. They were simply equated with the interval level data obtained by the use of 'intelligence tests'.

[33] This is not to say that work done from such a perspective was utilisable only in the context of eugenic problems. The product-moment correlation coefficient was itself initially conceived and evaluated from the same perspective but is evidently of use in the context of a vast range of problems. Similarly, referring back to earlier themes, the production and evaluation of knowledge with prior regard to its predictive and instrumental potential in the context of say academic chemistry does not necessarily restrict its applicability to chemical problems.

[34] We shall deliberately avoid here the complex matter of the detailed relationship between general social interests, associated beliefs or ideologies, and the distribution of such beliefs among individuals. Suffice it to say that nothing here is intended to account for Pearson's or Yule's individual actions or preferred beliefs. For an attempt to deal with some of the problems in this area see Barnes: op. cit., 1977; for a specific discussion of what made eugenics an appropriate form of ideological expression see MacKenzie: op. cit. 1976.

[35] Yule: op. cit., p. 139. It might be argued that Yule's evaluative framework is to be preferred because it is more general and less 'narrowed' by interests than Pearson's. But the narrow professionally based interests that structure the evaluation of highly productive normal science should suffice to cast doubt upon this thesis. Again, it might be argued that the role of interests 'external to science' is a basis for criticism of biometry; but since such work as Forman: op. cit. it is difficult to see how to press this position home. (Interestingly, both r_T and Q continue sporadically to be used in modern academic contexts, and no single 'best' solution to the problem of the measurement of association has yet been agreed upon.)

[36] Habermas: op. cit., p. 311 has diagnosed the basis of the prejudice against interests:
'Because science must secure the objectivity of its statements against the pressure and seduction of particular interests, it deludes itself about the fundamental interest to which it owes not only its impetus but *the conditions of possible objectivity* themselves.'

66

BETWEEN ORTHODOXY AND OBLIVION:
THE NORMALISATION OF DEVIANCE IN SCIENCE

Brian Wynne

1 Introduction

SCIENTIFIC controversies have justifiably enjoyed a great deal of attention from sociologists and historians of science, especially in the recent
past.[1] Not only have they been regarded as the usual medium of
scientific change and development, but also the implicit social
premises and precepts of different schools of thought are often more
clearly exposed under conditions of substantial conflict than in more
peaceful times.

The notion of scientific conflict implies a sustained exchange with
the antagonists more or less equally balanced in terms of resources
and power. The conflict may arise out of, or contribute further impetus
to differentiation of separate sub-cultures in science, with more or less
independent (but overlapping in the area of conflict) spheres of
legitimation.

Scientific mistakes or deviance on the other hand, tend to be
associated with individuals or groups which are categorically rejected
by a (supposedly) solid consensus. The 'deviant' is usually dispatched
rapidly, has little or no following nor institutional power with which
to cultivate a divergent route,[2] and the 'mistake' is consigned to
oblivion, even if in some cases it later undergoes reincarnation.

However there is of course no absolute boundary between 'controversies' and mere 'mistakes', and there are cases which lie some-
where in the middle-range of the continuum. Bohm's 'hidden variables'
school of quantum theorists may be one. The case I shall examine in
this paper is also middle-range in this sense. It involves the eminent
physicist C. G. Barkla and his Edinburgh Department of Natural
Philosophy between the mid- 1920s and 1945. Barkla's advocacy of
the widely discredited 'J phenomenon' and the form of his relations
with the rest of British physics raises some interesting and I think
important points about cognitive and technical diversity in science;
about power and the nature of social control; and about the wider
social constraints—going beyond the immediate confines of the

Brian Wynne

research area—which themselves influence the forms of social control that are exercised.

The more general issue within which I shall locate this discussion is—what factors cause the very different responses which are to be found in science, to diversification of beliefs and practices in the same field? Why is it that divergence, or an attempt at it, is treated in some cases as a major threat and calls forth violent reaction, whilst in other situations an apparently roughly equivalent degree of divergence is accepted routinely, perhaps hardly even recognised as such? Defining divergence as 'deviance' is of course one index of this sense of threat. I shall not at all claim to answer this question fully, but would like to propose it as a framework for research, and to make some relevant observations. In adopting a broadly interpretive approach to the issue, I discard the positivistic idea that the sharpness of the reaction against diversification is simply proportional to the degree of 'deviation' from 'the truth'. We must find other co-ordinates by which to plot the strength of reaction to divergence, and other criteria by which to analyse it as a social *process* of interaction, as opposed to a set of social-cognitive acts in themselves. Sociologists of knowledge will naturally look to the social and intellectual structure of the relevant scientific research field, and ask what it is in that social environment which causes differentness to be regarded in different cases as benign, neutral, or malignant, and what factors amplify or diminish the strength of response.

Clearly this would demand systematic, detailed comparative studies; it would also I contend, demand a thoroughgoing anthropological treatment examining the social-structural co-ordinates of the qualitatively different scientific cosmologies which generate different reactions to 'internal' divergence.[3] In the case which I shall examine, Barkla's divergence was recognised and rejected by orthodox physics,[4] yet for a divergence which so radically contradicted fundamental tenets of orthodoxy, it was granted a remarkable degree of toleration and even legitimacy in terms of the formal currency of scientific recognition. Given Barkla's stubborn refusal to yield to the orthodox view of his J phenomenon, and his refusal either to repudiate the J phenomenon or quietly to drop it for an alternative line of research, it is surprising that he was allowed to thrust 14 Ph.Ds and two D.Sc.s in favour of the J phenomenon, through the gates of 'quality-control' in science, during the period of his rejection, 1924-1945. It is valuable to picture this situation as one in which Barkla and mainstream physics managed tacitly to establish a mutual accomodation whereby the 'official' norms of quality-control in physics were in practice re-interpreted in a relaxed fashion, so as to allow Barkla even in his 'deviance', a viable degree of scientific self-respect and thus avoid an open (and because of Barkla's eminence, undoubtedly highly visible) conflict. In a sense, orthodoxy took the risk of giving official licence to dubious entrants (Barkla's Ph.D.s) to avoid the arguably greater risk of direct confrontation with a powerful scientist. It is not that they would have been afraid of losing the ensuing fight-to-the-death; rather it is my suggestion that such manifest conflict itself, especially with someone on whom science's highest international honour (the Nobel Prize) had just been conferred, would have been (and is in general) a major threat to science's public identity and authority. A delicate balance was struck in that, had orthodoxy exerted its powers of control in respect of Barkla's 'deviant' Ph.Ds, and failed them, then Barkla may have felt this to have been impossible to accept for his own self-respect, and it may therefore have provoked him into a more aggressively open and direct confrontation with orthodoxy. A 'softly, softly' approach was therefore adopted in which Barkla was unofficially granted some scientific recognition and legitimacy, whilst being 'officially' in total error. This unofficial generosity was extended in exchange for Barkla's not upsetting the situation by aggressively publicising his views and their radical incompatibility with orthodox scientific beliefs and practices. As long as Barkla confined his un-orthodox paradigm to his own sphere of control, namely Edinburgh, then it seemed that he was legitimate, albeit in a diminished universe of status compared to his previous standing. A strategy of 'silent' witness to his alternative paradigm was adopted by Barkla. He was allowed to culivate it, but only within the limits of his own survival and minimal self-respect. After the brief encounter of the mid-1920s, the J phenomenon was not allowed to become an 'official'conflict, and some important aspects of social control were suspended so as to ensure this.[5]

To generalise therefore, I am suggesting that it is important to treat the patterns of social control in science as flexible from situation to situation, and to be sensitive to wider contextual factors which influence social control as a process of interaction between groups or individuals. Each party has its own (albeit mutually overlapping) constellation of reference groups and needs, and the process of social control is negotiated within this framework. Before going on to describe the case of Barkla and his research school in detail, a very brief digression is in order, to outline the significance of an interpretive sociological approach (which I shall broadly adopt) in relation to uniformity and diversity in science.[6]

Normative sociological perspectives tend to regard uniformity within identified normative patterns as natural and taken for granted. The factors of explanation are those norms, and they are thus taken to be internally homogeneous themselves. It is implied that all actors see and follow the rules, in exactly the same way. Deviance, or generally centrifugal tendencies are thereby clearly defined, and can be explained in terms of the deviant's having assimilated and thus followed, a different overall constellation of cognitive and technical rules. A normative approach therefore, although it does not necessarily entail it, tends to imply that uniformity under identified normative frameworks is natural, and diversity of beliefs is not. An interpretive approach on the other hand, regards diversity of beliefs and practices as natural, and uniformity or orthodoxy as a social achievement which employs all the usual social paraphernalia of control and consensus-maintenance. Even then according to an interpretive approach, the apparently consensually held and uniformly interpreted norms conceal an unofficial reality of differing interpretations of the same norms. Since in this view a general rule or norm never contains the rules of its own practical enactment in particular real circumstances, there will always be informal diversity beneath formal uniformity. Indeed scientific development can be regarded as the constant attempt to eradicate by elaboration and proliferation of concepts, the ambiguity which is essentially ineradicable in all scientific definitions, no matter how precisely refined they are.[7]

Furthermore, the appreciation of an extra dimension of social interaction given by an interpretive approach allows us to treat 'public' or official norms with some caution. They may be less the real rules of action and interaction, and more the focus of ritualised obeisance—a collectively accepted self-deception, to which lip-service is paid as if in the creation of an identity for the consumption of an invisible reference group. Becker gives a good example of this in the widespread acceptance of the flaunting of the 'official' social norms of sexual propriety. The only time that such 'deviance' is negatively sanctioned is when someone does something contrary to the official rules (e.g. becoming pregnant out of marriage) which cannot be *pretended* not to have happened.[8] There may be an illuminating analogy here with Barkla's case, but I shall discuss this after entering into the details of Barkla's research school from 1924-1945.

II C. G. Barkla and Edinburgh Physics, 1920-1944

In a paper such as this only an extremely condensed account of the relevant history can be given.[9] Barkla had taken the Chair and Headship of the Department of Natural Philosophy at Edinburgh University in 1913. After a scientific apprenticeship under J. J. Thomson and Oliver Lodge, Barkla had already established himself as one of the world's leading experimental X ray physicists and was awarded a Nobel Prize in 1917 for work carried out between 1905 and 1912 on X ray scattering, polarisation, etc. His work threw light upon both the nature of electromagnetic radiation, and the structure of the atom. Barkla's discovery and elucidation of the K and L characteristic series of secondary X ray emissions led quickly to the fundamentally important insight that the atom was composed of concentric electron shells around the central high density nucleus. By 1920 therefore, when Barkla went to Sweden to receive his Nobel Prize, he went in a blaze of publicity as the sole representative of British physics, to meet his counterparts from German physics in a residual atmosphere of great hostility following the bitter patriotic conflicts within science during the First World War. Through radio broadcasts, meetings with the King of Sweden, etc., Barkla was very much in the limelight as a leader of British science. Not only his material power in a very well-endowed Universiy Department but also his personal prestige, gave him the springboard to lasting fame and even wider honours. Yet, ironically, at the very time that his prestige was waxing strongest, Barkla was pursuing a line of research which was to lead him into isolation and neglect; he was soon to become in the eyes of his peers, a discarded relic, from an outdated scientific tradition.

Barkla had achieved scientific acclamation at a time when only multi-chromatic (multi-wavelength) beams of X rays were available for use in scattering and absorption experiments; and he had become perhaps *the* master of such techniques. In 1912 however, Barkla's rival, W. H. Bragg had with his son succeeded in separating the monochromatic (single-wavelength) components of X ray beams. Use of a monochromatic X ray beam rapidly became the norm in such scattering and absorption techniques because it was generally believed to allow greater energy-resolution; a vital point in attempts to discriminate via spectroscopy, the different energy states of electrons in the atom. For various reasons however, Barkla continued to employ the much more intense (ca. 1,000 fold stronger) but less energy-precise, multichromatic X ray beams. His prime reason was that he was searching for a J series of X ray emissions at frequencies above the L and K series, and since the J series was expected on theoretical grounds to be of extremely low intensity, Barkla decided that the newer monochromatic beams would not stimulate a detectable J emission even if it existed. Whereas orthodoxy consolidated around monochromatic beams, Barkla began to become isolated in his use of the (older) multichromatic techniques. Barkla's own multichromatic absorption results were ambiguous however, and in the light of criticisms of his J series idea, he was by 1921-22 exploring the rejection or radical revision of the theory. In an essentially turbulent theoretical situation with respect to the exact mechanism of X ray scattering and related atomic processes, Barkla became increasingly convinced from 1923 onwards, that some of the most fundamental tenets of physics required radical revision. Compton's widely and rapidly acclaimed quantum theory of the scattering process (1922) was unpalatable to Barkla, primarily for two closely related reasons:

a) its empirical foundations depended heavily upon the X ray spectrometer and monochromatic X ray beams.

b) it employed a quantised, atomistic model of electromagnetic radiation, whereas Barkla believed firmly in the ultimate *continuity* of radiation and matter in their shared ethereal essence.

Following a brief exchange of hostilities with Compton, in which Barkla appeared at first to reject Compton's interpretation entirely, the prevailing view in physics was that Barkla was pursuing an obscure and fantastic interpretation of scattering and absorption results from his complex multichromatic techniques, which could be explained away in the newly orthodox terms of Compton's quantum theory of X ray scattering. Whereas the orthodoxy consolidated around the confident acceptance of the separate action of monochromatic constituents of a multichromatic beam, Barkla argued that the supposedly separate and separable wavelengths acted in an organic, holistic fashion, transferring energy to matter by much more complex forms of organic, quasi-fluidic interaction. The whole was greater than the sum of the parts, so orthodoxy's separation of the parts was seriously misconceived. Barkla developed the view from 1924 onwards that in different experimental circumstances either Compton-type behaviour or his 'J phenomenon' behaviour could be systematically observed, and he called for recognition of this fundamentally novel idea about the structure of the ether, electromagnetic radiation, and its relation to matter. The J phenomenon and its wider theoretical metaphysical precepts was never seriously taken up and supported by any other research group outside Barkla's Edinburgh Department, and indeed perceptions of its content seem never to have gone beyond his 1924 position. The consolidated view in physics seemed to be that Barkla's J phenomenon was a tragic waste of time (though the *retrospective* account no doubt underplays the lesser confidence *at the time* that Barkla's 'will o' the wisp' was non-existent). Against such a solid mass of incredulity one would have expected a sharp decline in Barkla's ability to sustain his alternative research programme, and one would have expected Barkla himself either to have faded from the scene altogether, or to have accommodated his views to the predominant ones on this topic. (Barkla seems never to have even considered a third choice—to have taken up a new field of research. This would have been an acceptable way of maintaining 'insider' status). If he attempted actively to cultivate his alternative, we might have expected to see the full arsenal of overt and direct control employed against Barkla by the prevailing orthodoxy, and an ensuing battle of great ferocity.

What we find however, are five articles on the J. phenomenon between 1926 and 1932, all by relatively minor or obscure scientists. One of these was written in 1927 by R. T. Dunbar, who had actually obtained his Ph.D under Barkla in 1924, when he had concluded in favour of the J phenomenon. Dunbar at least accepted that there were systematic observations which required explanation but argued that the Compton theory embraced them. The others could not even find the systematic absorption—discontinuities which Barkla claimed as the basic empirical evidence for the J phenomenon. As I have demonstrated elsewhere however,[10] these 'refutations', for all the apparent confidence invested in them, were shrouded in uncertainty and confusion.

Barkla continued to publish extensively in the major journals on the J phenomenon—his only research topic and the only significant one in his Department—until 1933, with the help of several Ph.D. students, all of whom were successful in obtaining their doctorates. Even after 1933, when Barkla decided to abandon publication until he could find the final proof with which to disarm the sceptics, several Ph.D.s were obtained which concluded broadly in favour of the J phenomenon, right up to the time of Barkla's death in 1944. There is every reason to suppose that the J phenomenon research school would have continued indefinitely to reproduce itself at Edinburgh in this minimal but viable pattern had Barkla remained indefinitely. Given the recognised importance of recruits in the propagation or death of particular schools of thought, it is worthwhile to examine in more detail the role and destiny of Barkla's research recruits.

III Barkla's Research Students—Origins, Attitudes and Destinies

Between 1924 and 1944, Barkla supervised 14 Ph.D. students to successful completion of their doctorate.[11] Two of these (Watson and Khastgir) obtained D.Scs. Two further students, Paton and Carmichael, began on the J phenomenon in the 1930s, but Carmichael left to go to Cambridge after becoming sceptical, and Paton was the only student who—after also becoming sceptical and saying so to Barkla—was allowed to transfer to other work in Barkla's Department. Although the conclusions of most of the Ph.D. dissertations in the 1930s were less extreme than those in the 1920s, they all argued in the same deviant direction—that conventional quantum theoretical treatments of X ray scattering were inadequate and that urgent consideration of the 'other factors not yet considered in theoretical treatments of the subject'[12] was demanded by the empirical factors which Barkla's group were uncovering. Typical observations were that 'present theories . . . are not adequate to account for the behaviour of heterogeneous beams of radiation'[13] and that there was a whole range of significant effects which 'so far cannot be accounted for by quantum or classical theories of scattering'.[14] Unfortunately the examiners reports are confidential, but as far as can be told, none of the theses in question caused any demur on the part of its external examiner. The externals were G. P. Thomson (2), O. W. Richardson (2), H. S. Allen (2), C. T. R. Wilson (6), and Max Born (2). All of these were

74

eminent and respected physicists, though Wilson was by then retired
from Cambridge, and living near Edinburgh. It would be interesting
to know the criteria which the examiners felt it appropriate to employ
in acting as the gatekeeper to the qualified scientific community. The
only comments available—50 years or so afterwards—came from
G. P. Thomson, who noted that[15]

> 'it was a period when all sorts of fanciful ideas were around. Like Alice
> in Wonderland you were asked to swallow a thousand and one different
> ideas before breakfast. If a student had performed competent experi-
> ments and drawn balanced conclusions then there was no good reason
> not to pass him.'

Thomson acted as examiner in the 1920s; by the 1930s however,
much of this confusion he describes had receded, and even if not
resolved had at least been set aside. There were therefore more established norms by which to evaluate the standard of work offered, and
the accepted framework for scattering was quantum theory, which
Barkla and his Ph.D.s were explicitly repudiating. Passing the Ph.D.
even if not a positive vote in favour of the J phenomenon was
tantamount at least to an implicit vote in favour of those criticisms,
since they were based directly upon experimental evidence which, as
it was passed, was presumably 'competent'. Furthermore, the established *methodological* norms even by the early 1920s were based upon
monochromatic spectroscopic techniques. Whereas all Barkla students,
even in the 1940s employed the very outdated and discarded multichromatic absorption techniques and gold leaf electroscopes, so that
the question of 'competence' or otherwise of experiment seems,
curiously, not to have included the questions of which experimental
means to employ for given theoretical observational ends. The
conclusion which suggests itself is that the Ph.D.s were passed either
against the prevailing norms of judgement and scientific instincts of
the external examiners, or that Ph.D.s—the licence to enter the
legitimate research community, and of greater relative significance
in this respect than today[16]—were not in general quality-controlled
as rigorously as the important selection role of this function would
otherwise suggest. Usually of course supervisors only allow submission
of a thesis when in their judgement the thesis is acceptable, so that
refusal to grant the Ph.D. entails a direct conflict over scientific
standards and other substantive scientific questions, with the super-
visor. I shall suggest that there was a general desire to avoid such
official manifestation of conflict with Barkla, arising from the general

need for science to avoid overt conflict where it can. Unusually in this case, Barkla had the resources to create a substantial controversy had orthodoxy exercised its full powers of control upon him. Although in passing the Ph.D.s they risked loosing scientists of dubious loyalty to orthodox norms into science at large, there were other *informal* means of control at the disposal of orthodoxy, and these appear to have been successful.

Let us now look at the subsequent careers of Barkla's Ph.D. students. Of the 14, four were Indian, and returned to India to practice physics. Pal continued to work *inter alia* on the J phenomenon, from a purely theoretical-analytical perspective. Khastgir wanted to continue with the J phenomenon but was prohibited by his new superior, S. N. Bose. Neither of the other two Indians, Kubchandari and Sen Gupta, pursued the J phenomenon after leaving Barkla and never published the results of their Ph.D. Of the 3 women, McKenzie and Wilson married and abandoned a scientific career, but Ross pursued a successful career in physics at Edinburgh, though not on anything connected with the J phenomenon; nor did she publish the results of her initially controversial Ph.D. Four others, Honeyman, Kay, Winogradoff and Kellner, did not pursue research careers in physics after their Ph.D., even though the former two were widely regarded as top class. They both went into schoolteaching. The remaining three, Dunbar, Watson and Reekie, all obtained good academic posts after their Ph.D., Watson and Reekie going to Cambridge. However neither worked on the J phenomenon and Watson abandoned active physics for philosophy of science shortly after arriving at Cambridge. Dunbar obtained the Chair of Physics at Cardiff University in 1924, direct from his Ph.D. with Barkla. He continued for a few years to do research on the J phenomenon, but turned a complete volte-face as soon as he had left Edinburgh, to become the leading opponent of the J phenomenon.

In summary, it is immediately apparent that Barkla's research school never took off into a broadly based social community with supporting 'cells' in different places. If one discounts the Indians (who rightly or wrongly suffered a general lack of credibility) only 4 of 10 pursued subsequent academic careers, and either predisposition or pressure from new social reference groups or both, caused them to renounce the J phenomenon for something else, without any apparent stress of adjustment whatsoever.[17]

The scientific community at large seem to have accepted even very central and positive association with the J phenomenon (in the cases of Dunbar initially, and Watson more especially) as no stigma against competence and employability. There seems to have been a general recognition of the instrumental necessity for graduates in Barkla's Department, if they wanted an academic career at all, to sign up as a research assistant for Barkla; they had to do this work on the J phenomenon, or obtain no means of possible entry at all (short of getting a place elsewhere, which in the 1920s and 30s was extremely difficult). The research students' local situational adjustment to the Edinburgh Departmental framework of scientific judgement and practice was accepted by the orthodoxy as long as it did not take root, and to the extent that it could easily be discarded on leaving Barkla's sphere of control.

There are good reasons to conclude that all Barkla's research students adopted such an instrumental—even cynical attitude towards the paradigm they were supposed to be developing, and that as a result the morale of the group was virtually non-existent.[18] First of all, none of Barkla's graduates could come to his research school without running the gauntlet of a barrage of criticism of the J phenomenon in other undergraduate classes which they were obliged to attend as part of their degree.[19] These critics were the fierce E. T. Whittaker in Maths, and the less aggressive but no less destructive C. G. Darwin, in theoretical physics (Applied Mechanics). All physics graduates had to attend lectures and be examined in all three subjects, so that one entered Barkla's research school with few illusions about prevailing opinion on the J phenomenon in British physics at large. This undergraduate arena was probably the one in which most of the force of social control in physics actually took effect—in this case at least.[20] It so undercut the potential for Barkla to cultivate a 'sheltered' sympathetic cognitive climate, as to pre-empt the need for strong and *explicit* sanctions later in the careers of his 'followers', even if there intervened an intermediate process (the Ph.D.) which granted them 'official' licences to practise physics on supposedly the same terms and authority as orthodoxy. There seems in other words to have been a tacit agreement that the scientific beliefs and methods expressed by those under Barkla's patronage were a tiresome but necessary ritual process undergone to gain even a foothold on the academic career ladder. This throws an interesting light not only upon the attitudes of Barkla's students towards their research—something which can I suggest, be understood in terms of a situational adjustment model[21]—but also more importantly, upon the negotiability of scientific standards of acceptability.

IV Deviance Normalised

The very fact that Barkla's research students obtained their Ph.D.s; that two of them were awarded the further honour of the D.Sc.; that those of his students who *attempted* to do so, found academic posts; and that Barkla himself was in demand as an external examiner at King's College London, and at Liverpool, well into the 1930s, indicates that a significant amount of social exchange occurred between the deviant tradition and the orthodoxy during Barkla's supposed isolation. Although he was operating in a diminished world of status, nevertheless Barkla did receive some highly significant crumbs of scientific self-respect from orthodoxy, in spite of the general refusal to countenance his ideas and idiom of science. I suggest that Barkla and orthodoxy reached a steady state position in which he was defined as errant and pressured by criticism into silence and retreat into his own self-contained local scene; and at the same time in exchange for his non-aggression, Barkla himself was given a slimmer's diet of recognition which just allowed him to maintain sufficient self-respect not to be provoked into destabilising the situation by rendering what had been managed into a *muted* conflict, overt and 'officially' conflictual again. In other words, had Barkla been denied *any status at all* by orthodoxy, by e.g., refusing to pass his 'errant' Ph.D.s, refusing to consider them for posts, discontinuing his use as an external examiner, then he would have been forced by that complete starvation, into being more aggressively conflictual to orthodoxy, and to 'stir up' the difference of outlook into a highly visible controversy. He may even as a last resort have attempted to appeal over the heads of his scientific peers, to a different audience. With his recent great publicity, the formal trappings of prestige which few could match in British science, and the very considerable resources of power which he commanded in his institutional position at Edinburgh, he would presumably have found this a very tempting and (at least in the short term) fruitful course of action because of the public visibility which he would have had. The point is that it was in the interests of physics to avoid not only such direct public appeals and ensuing public conflict, but even 'official' internal conflict, which because Barkla was a very eminent figure, would have had external and internal repercussions whether or not Barkla or anyone else had cultivated an external audience.

Science like most social institutions seeks to supress overt conflict just because of the social uncertainty and threat to security which it entails. But science is even more unsettled by *overt* conflict than most institutions, because a vital part of the external ideology which it projects in the process of its authority maintenance to society at large, is the belief that science 'naturally' produces consensus by the collective pursuit of 'the scientific method' and of universal explicit standards of evaluation and commitment. When deviance goes 'official' therefore, this externally projected myth is threatened, along with the social authority which is based thereupon. Furthermore, not only is the ideology externally projected, but it is internally projected and assimilated too, so that scientists more so than social actors in most institutions, tend to react strongly against manifest internal conflict. The more it can be negotiated into tacit forms (e.g. via differentiation into two separate specialities, or normalisation of the kind described in this paper) the better.

Barkla's case is interesting because it falls outside the usually accepted categories of response to deviant ideas and methods. Because he was eminent and materially very powerful, able to exercise control over research assistants and grants, teaching, etc., he could not be entirely ignored or destroyed as a junior member (or aspirant member) of the scientific community could be without risking seriously unsettling retaliation. On the other hand, open conflict is bad for internal and external social relations, so that (after the brief period of overt conflict, mainly between Barkla and Compton) Barkla and the mainstream reached a stable situation in which each side tacitly yielded something to the other, and gained in exchange. Barkla's deviance became institutionalised as a normal—if localised and *contained*— subculture of X ray physics. In this way he was given just enough room to sustain a meaningful professional existence for himself, as long as he did not try to advance the J phenomenon into the wider scientific world. He was limited to arguing it as a *legitimate* position to hold, rather than the only, or the best one. Orthodoxy simply wrote off Edinburgh physics for the duration of Barkla's career at least; exercised some flexible criteria of acceptability in order to 'buy'

Barkla's peaceable, silent coexistence; and took the risk of allowing some potential scientific disciples of Barkla to enter the research community as fully licensed scientists. Given the availability of other, less formal and therefore less conflictual forms of social control, this was not a very serious risk.

V Discussion

It is important to emphasise that Barkla's relations with the mainstream of physics were not dictated solely by the naked institutional power which Barkla enjoyed. It was not a case of each antagonist pushing their power to the limits and reaching a stalemate as a result. As I have indicated, orthodoxy withheld one of its most important weapons of social control when it granted Ph.D.s to Barkla's research students, and even employed those who sought employment. Barkla also stopped short of exercising his full power, by suspending publications on the J phenomenon, (when at the very least he still—as a Nobel Laureate and Fellow of the Royal Society— had automatic access to *Philosophical Magazine*, the most important physics journal), and generally by not using his considerable power to proselytise aggressively in favour of the J phenomenon. (For example he could have used the public forum of the British Association for the Advancement of Science annual meeting to propagate his views and publicise the conflict, but he declined to do so after 1927). Thus a tacit 'agreement' seems to have been negotiated to stop short of full, open, and probably final conflict, and in the process to allow Barkla to survive in modest self-respect for the rest of his career. Obviously his material power and prestige was a central factor in pushing orthodoxy into 'normalising' his deviant subculture to the extent which it did so, because his autonomous power and his prestige beyond science represented a considerable threat of public scientific controversy with all its attendant embarrassments. The major point is that beneath the 'official' world of universal (at least throughout a single discipline or field) standards of evaluation and control, there is a flexible world of negotiated interpretations and real judgements which is influenced by concrete social factors of the kind I have outlined—material power, the professional ideology and authority of science (to society and to its new recruits), and the status—rewards received by different scientists from different (if overlapping) reference groups.[22] This is of course a world which cannot be acknowledged in the 'official' discourse of science. Because of its social importance, the official ideology (e.g. of uniformity of standards) is sacred, and to break the official seal, (e.g. in Barkla's case, had he actively advertised his deviant existence within the confines of scientific legitimacy), would be to invoke wrathful reaction because the collective myth is thereby threatened, even if one is actually behaving and believing in exactly the same way as before. Here is the analogy with Becker's example of public norms as a kind of social ritual. There seems to be some promise in treating the official norms of judgement of scientific disciplines in the same general way.

A final point which arises from this case concerns Barkla's own commitment to the J phenomenon and the negotiation of his normalisation. Another way of putting the foregoing analysis is to say that Barkla had essentially to be helped to adjust to failure. Given his own fundamental personal identification with the J phenomenon, this was equivalent to what Garfinkel has called 'moral degradation'.[23] Like the 'cooling out' of the con-man's 'mark',[24] the process is fraught with the danger that the subject—here Barkla—will rebel and opt out of the process of negotiation and adjustment, thereby recognising his own failure and (in the case of stronger commitments) self-destruction, but in the process publicising the hypocrisy or delusion entailed in the 'official' interpretation being negotiated, and thus seriously damaging the other side as a result, by blowing its cover. This seems an appropriate model to employ in looking at the tacit normalisation of deviance which occurred in Barkla's case. The intricate social delicacy of consensus in science, and the fearful proximity of cognitive and social anarchy, should be plain for all to see.

University of Lancaster.

[1] For example D. McKenzie and S. B. Barnes: 'Social Factors in Scientific Conflict: the Biometrician-Mendelian Controversy' in N. Stehr and R.Konig (eds.): *Wissenschaftssoziologie*, Westdeutscher Verlag, Opladen, 1975, pp. 165-196; J. Harwood: 'The Race-Intelligence Controversy: A Sociological Approach. I—Professional Factors', *Social Studies of Science*, Vol. 6, 1976, pp. 369-394; and, D. Robbins and R. Johnston: 'The Role of Cognitive and Occupational Differentiation in Scientific Controversies', *Social Studies of Science*, Vol. 6, 1976, pp. 349-368.

[2] For example Kammerer (see A. Koestler: *The Case of the Midwife Toad*, Hutchinson, London, 1971); Blondlot's N Rays (see M. Gardiner: *Fads and Fallacies in the Name of Science*, Dover, New York, 1957); Hagerstrand (see S. Duncan: 'The Isolation of Scientific Discovery: Indifference and Resistance to a New Idea', *Science Studies*, Vol, 4, 1974, pp. 109-134); Polanyi (see

M. Polanyi: 'The Potential Theory of Adsorption' in *Knowing and Being,* University of Chicago Press, Chicago, 1969); and perhaps Einstein's later career in pursuit of a general theory of relativity.

³ I am thinking particularly of the type of approach developed by Mary Douglas, analysing social structures according to 'grid' and 'group' dimensions. (See M. Douglas: *Natural Symbols,* Cresset, London, 1970; and M. Douglas: *Implicit Meanings,* Routledge & Kegan Paul, London, 1975.) For an application of this approach to modern science, see D. and C. Bloor: 'An Anthropological Approach to Industrial Scientists: An Empirical Test of Mary Douglas's Grid and Group Theory', University of Edinburgh, 1977, mimeo. One might predict that a scientific discipline with a strong grid social structure would tend to react very strongly to internal diversification, whereas a weak-grid structure would presumably entail a less rigidly structured cosmology, and thus a more benevolent attitude towards internal diversification. Strong group would tend to externalise any internal disorderings of the cosmology whereas weak group would tend to see little distinction between internally and externally generated diversification. The main problem in using these terms with reference to modern science seems to be in defining the scope of group. For example if one draws the boundary of group round particular *geographical*—social units (i.e. particular institutional research schools), then the discipline or speciality as a social-unit would be composed of several different (strong or weak group) sub-units. There may be some issues which engender uniform responses in terms of the larger group definition of group, and others which engender differentiated responses, in terms of the different constituent social sub-units.

⁴ The point is however, that Barkla supplemented his meagre diet of status from orthodox physics with a much richer diet from a social reference group of idealist philosophers and theologians at Edinburgh which was metaphysically compatible with the scientific outlook he had assimilated from his two mentors, Oliver Lodge and J. J. Thomson. Although a deviant in terms of orthodox science, Barkla was a conformist within the terms of this reference group. Given this alternative source of status, Barkla could afford to take his scientific isolation with equanimity. Without it, the course of the J phenomenon 'conflict' could have been much more vigorous because Barkla might have been forced to fight for more status and recognition within the terms of reference of orthodox physics. This is discussed in my M.Phil. thesis 'C. G. Barkla and the J Phenomenon: A Case Study in the Sociology of Physics', University of Edinburgh, 1977.

⁵ See B. E. Wynne: 'C. G. Barkla and the J Phenomenon—A Case Study in the Treatment of Deviance in Physics', *Social Studies of Science,* Vol. 6, 1976, pp. 307-347.
Even today, the J phenomenon has been actively suppressed as a live issue. Following a rather derogatory paper on Barkla by R. J. Stephenson: 'The Scientific Career of Charles Glover Barkla', *American Journal of Physics,* Vol. 35, 1967, pp. 140-152, two of Barkla's ex-students, H. K. Pal and S. R. Khastgir wrote an article which, they claimed, justified Barkla's approach to the problems of X-ray scattering, whilst not claiming (as Barkla originally did) that orthodox conceptions were wrong. The editor of *American Journal of Physics* refused to publish it, and the authors have not found another forum. In a letter to the author (18 December 1973) Khastgir complained that the article was not perfect but required scrutiny by competent peers, yet this was denied by the refusal to publish. Pal had in fact published several papers on the phenomenon in the *Indian Journal of Physics,* see H. K. Pal: 'The J Phenomenon: A Further Analysis', *Indian Journal of Physics,* Vol. 39, 1965, pp. 283-296.

[6] See, for example, J. Law and D. French: 'Normative and Interpretive Sociologies of Science', *Sociological Review*, Vol. 22, 1974, pp. 581-595; and, J. Law: 'Theories and Methods in the Sociology of Science', *Social Science Information*, Vol. 13, 1974, pp. 163-172.

[7] See S. B. Barnes and J. Law: 'Whatever Should be Done with Indexical Expressions?', *Theory and Society*, Vol. 3, 1976, pp. 104-118.

[8] See H. S. Becker: *Outsiders*, Free Press, New York, 1966, especially chapter 1.

[9] For further details, see my M. Phil. Thesis, op. cit. or Wynne: op. cit., 1976.

[10] Full references are contained in Wynne: op. cit., 1976.

[11] The full list of Ph.Ds after 1924 is as follows: R. T. Dunbar: 'Experiments on the Absorption of K Radiation of Short Wavelength, and on the Associated Scattered and Corpuscular Radiation', 1924; S. R. Khastgir: 'The Absorption and Scattering of X Rays: The J Phenomenon', 1924; W. H. Watson: 'Some Aspects of the J Phenomenon in X Rays', 1925; G. I. MacKenzie: 'Superposition of X Rays and the J Phenomenon', 1927; M. M. Sen Gupta: 'The Coherence of Superposed X Rays', 1929; J. S. Kay: 'Some Factors Influencing the Scattering of Heterogeneous X Radiation—the J Phenomenon', 1932; A. Honeyman: 'Investigations into Scattering of X Rays and the J Phenomenon', 1932; S. G. Kubchandari: 'Distribution of Scattered X Rays', 1935; H. K. Pal: 'A Study of the Energy Distribution of Heterogeneous X Rays', 1937; M. A. M. Wilson: 'Investigations on the Scattering of X Rays', 1939; M. A. S. Ross: 'The Scattering and Filtering of Heterogeneous X Rays by Matter of Small Atomic Weight', 1943; N. N. Winogradoff: 'Absorption and Scattering of Heterogeneous X Rays by Elements of Low Ab. Number', 1944; and, K. Kellner: 'Some Investigations of the Scattering and Absorption of Heterogeneous Beams of X Rays', 1944.

[12] Pal: op. cit., 1937. See especially C. S. Fisher: 'The Last Invariant Theorists', *European Journal of Sociology*, Vol. 8, 1967, pp. 216-244; T. S. Kuhn: *The Structure of Scientific Revolutions*, Chicago University Press, Chicago, 1970. Kuhn: op. cit., p. 158 notes that ' . . . if a paradigm is ever to triumph it must gain some first supporters, men who will develop it to the point where hard-headed arguments can be produced and multiplied'. At no stage in the history of the J phenomenon can it be said that Barkla generated supporters sufficiently committed to produce hard-headed arguments in the teeth of general antipathy.

[13] Reekie: op. cit.

[14] Wilson: op. cit.

[15] In an interview with the author, February 1973.

[16] In those days, many scientists went straight from a Ph.D. to senior posts, even Chairs on the strength of that Ph.D. This would be unheard of today.

[17] W. H. Stevens, Barkla's personal research assistant from 1919-1944 asserted in interview with the author (June 1973), that few if any of Barkla's research students believed in the J phenomenon, but merely followed in the wake of Barkla's determination to pursue it, because they had to.

[18] Watson is reputed in a visit to Edinburgh much later, to have dismissed the whole J phenomenon by observing that none of his research assistant colleagues had believed in it, implying that they simply told Barkla what he

wanted to hear. Kyles, Paton and Ross, three members of Barkla's staff in the 1930s issued the same general judgement upon the work of Barkla's research students. (In interviews, January 1973, March 1973, and May 1973.) Of course one must beware of post hoc rationalisation in attempting to assess the force of these judgements.

[19] Interestingly enough, the Indians were the only entry to Barkla's research school not to be exposed to this, and they were the most loyal to the J phenomenon.

[20] It appears to have been a common part of undergraduate culture to relate satires on the J phenomenon. Two examples are:
(a) 'J's a phenomenon known to the Prof.
   on Monday its working, and Tuesday it's off.'
   Tuesday it's off.'
(b) 'Prof's looking for kinks and ridges,
   caused by tramcars on the Bridges.'
(The J phenomenon was observed as discontinuous steps—'Kinks and ridges' —against the normal continuous curve in a plot of the intensity ratio of scattered and pre-scattered X ray beams. The Bridges is a busy street passing close to the Drummond Street Department of Natural Philosophy.)

[21] See, for example, H. S. Becker: 'Personal Change in Adult Life', *Sociometry*, Vol. 27, 1964, pp. 40-53; Becker: op. cit., 1966.

[22] See note 4 on this latter point.

[23] See H. Garfinkel: 'The Conditions of Successful Degradation Ceremonies' in J. G. Manis and B. N. Melzer (eds.): *Symbolic Interaction*, Allyn and Bacon, Boston, 1967, pp. 205-213.

[24] See E. Goffman: 'On Cooling the Mark Out: Some Aspects of Adaptation to Failure' in A. Rose (ed.): *Human Behaviour and Social Processes*, Routledge and Kegan Paul, London, 1962, pp. 482-505.

A STUDY IN THE LEGITIMISATION OF KNOWLEDGE: THE 'SUCCESS' OF MEDICINE AND THE 'FAILURE' OF ASTROLOGY

Peter W. G. Wright

THE sociology of science and knowledge are fields which have stimulated a considerable body of research over the last few decades both by sociologists and by historians. Surprisingly, however, until recently almost none of it has examined the processes by which the boundaries of particular areas of knowledge are established or created. This has meant that there has been an implicit tendency to regard forms of knowledge and the disciplines associated with them as demarcated from one another by divisions that are somehow natural and intrinsic to the structure of knowledge itself.

Recent work in different areas suggests, however, that there are very good reasons for doubting such an assumption. On a general level, Mary Douglas has shown that the social perception of borders and limits is one of the most fundamental social processes.[1] Pierre Bourdieu has further suggested that the erection of boundaries is an essential, and political, component of the creation of forms of knowledge both in the arts and in the sciences: it is, as he puts it, a characteristic feature of the market for symbolic goods.[2] Finally, sociologists of the professions such as Freidson have provided much evidence to show that the demarcation of the frontiers of competence is an important element in the construction of occupational control.[3]

Abundant evidence of the dangers of regarding the boundaries of knowledge as unproblematic can also be found in the writings of those authors who have made this assumption. This is particularly clear in the case of those using historical data: in their work a double distortion is all too frequently present. In medical history, for example, it has been common for researchers to begin by assuming that medicine is whatever the recognised modern professional bodies define it as being. As a result, medical sociology has concentrated on what doctors and other professionals do and especially on what they do in the most professionally dominated settings such as hospitals. This has resulted in a near total neglect of a whole range of factors such as working conditions, diet and transport policy which—despite their undoubted importance to health—are not usually regarded as medical issues by the dominant professional groups. What is more, in historical work an additional problem arises: here it is often further assumed that the current modern professional definition of the field is not merely an adequate one for today, but that it is also the same as that of the hegemonic profession in past periods too. As a consequence, it is now usual to find in histories of medicine chapters devoted to quackery, herbalism, astrological medicine, and so on; as if it were self-evident that these were not real or central elements in the medicine of other ages.

Such a tendency to read back modern professional ideologies into historical material has produced curious distortions: it has meant, for instance, that the existence and success of pre-scientific medicine has scarcely ever been perceived as something needing explanation. Because we today know that the medicine of Sydenham, or Boerhaave, or Bichat was a 'precursor' of our present enlightenment, its survival is usually seen as natural or to be attributed to its cognitive power. In contrast, the decline of astrology, phrenology, mesmerism or any of a number of historical 'failures' is commonly assumed to be the result of the inadequacy of their knowledge. It is the purpose of this paper to suggest that to adopt such conclusions uncritically is simply to accept the professional rationalisations of the groups that were victorious.

Let us take, for instance, the case of the fortunes of astrology and medicine in late seventeenth-century England. In the first years of that century astrology had held a position of great—but not unchallenged —dominance. By 1700, it had ceased to be accorded a serious status in educated circles.[4] The official medicine of the time, however, persisted and perhaps gained in influence. It will be argued that the changes in relative positions of these subjects are best understood as a reflection of the ideological and political power of the professions practising them, and not as a result of the truth or effectiveness of the knowledge which they utilised. In other words, medicine and astrology will not be seen as two naturally distinct fields based on different areas of knowledge (one 'true'; one 'false') but as two professional practices with different social positions and different success in delimiting and legitimating their activities.

Astrology and medicine do not usually appear from today's stand-point to have possessed many common features: in fact, however, they were alike in a number of respects. Both were generalising theoretical systems which claimed to give rise to a series of explanations that served as a basis for purposive, technical, action. Both presented themselves, to an extent, as 'scientific' and both were concerned with providing a framework of meaning for the misfortunes and anomalies of everyday life. In practice, there was also probably a considerable overlap between the concrete problems with which they dealt. The few surviving casebooks of seventeenth-century consultant astrologers show that a large proportion of their clientele came to them with straightforward health problems.[5] Similarly, astrological almanacs (which were published in vast numbers in this period) typically contained many references to illness and medical treatment. It was no chance, perhaps, that William Lilly (1602-81) the best-known astrologer of the period, despite his lack of formal medical training, obtained a licence to practice medicine in the last years of his life.[6]

It is sometimes assumed that the contrasting histories of these two subjects can be explained in terms of their respective effectiveness. The issue of effectiveness and its importance for the survival of a practice, is however, a complex one. On the simplest level there is, in my view, little evidence that official seventeenth-century medicine had any beneficial effect except as a placebo.[7] In fact, it is, if anything, quite likely—given that major therapies employed were bleeding and purging—that its results were generally harmful. Astrological practice is yet more difficult to assess. It is obviously likely that astrological consultants and almanacs from time to time provided their clients with information that was accurate or advice that was helpful. In general, their activities were unlikely to have been physically harmful because, even where dealing with matters of illness, the actions they prescribed were not usually drastic. As various writers have pointed out, astute practitioners of such 'bogus' subjects as astrology may well be capable of producing feelings of the recognition of truth, certainty and security in their clients very like placebo effects.

On a deeper level, issues of *real* effectiveness may be irrelevant to the understanding of the success of forms of practice. What is important is *perceived* effectiveness. Obviously, there is—at some point —a connection between the two: any form of treatment that is universally successful or harmful is likely sooner or later, to be perceived as such. These situations are rare, however, and slight differences in effectiveness may be of no importance in explaining success because they are imperceptible without sophisticated statistical techniques. What is likely to be far more important in deciding whether a form of treatment is felt to work or not is its compatibility with the dominant ideology of a period. This must mean that, whatever the real differences in effectiveness between seventeenth-century medicine and astrology may have been,they are not sufficient to explain the attitudes of contemporaries towards them. To discover what might have accounted for the decline in astrological belief we have to ask rather what was happening to the practices and forces which had previously sustained it. As to medicine, we have to ask what social factors were working to make its activities appear more plausible.

In principle at least, mid-seventeenth-century medicine was a highly regulated profession. This regulation took two forms: one applying to the city of London and a seven-mile radius around it; the other to the rest of England. In London, the only physicians who were permitted to practise were those who held a degree from Oxford or Cambridge and who had also been licensed by the Royal College of Physicians of London (afterwards to be referred to as RCP). In the provinces, the system was freer and practice was open to all with a degree or who had been licensed by a bishop. At times, the RCP had also tried to claim a monopoly of control outside the capital but, by the period we are discussing, had suffered serious reversals. Nevertheless, in the provinces too a minority of physicians also presented themselves to the College for examination and, if successful, were awarded extra-licenciates.

In addition to these arrangements which only concerned physicians, there were others regulating apothecaries and surgeons. In London, these were primarily forms of guild control supervised by the RCP; in the provinces, the system was more varied and also included the episcopal licensing of surgeons.

The distinctions between these various medical groups, however, was becoming increasingly blurred by the mid-seventeenth-century. Recent research has suggested that—in the provinces at least—there was a tendency for both surgeons and apothecaries to act as general practitioners.[8] Beneath and beyond those already mentioned were also multitudes of folk healers, 'wise women', herbalists, and others who had neither licence, formal training nor guild membership. Provided that they did not charge fees for their services, they were protected by a statute of 1542 (often referred to in established professional circles as the 'Quacks' Charter').

The essential point about the organization of health and healing in seventeenth-century England was its diversity: there was no single homogeneous group that could be referred to as a medical profession. Even regulated practitioners formed a hierarchy of several levels spanning wide differences in training, social origin, clienteles and treatment. The unregulated folk practitioners were almost certainly yet more heterogeneous. This variety, however, is frequently neglected because it is viewed with assumptions drawn from modern medical practice. In England today we experience a medical system that is the outcome of a further three centuries of dominance by the RCP and of other high status institutions modelled on it. To transpose it into the seventeenth century is to misinterpret the historical data and to obscure the various divergent forces at work in the healing arts of this time that conflicted with the (later triumphant) policy of the RCP.

Nonetheless, this is precisely what frequently occurs: until recently many writers seem to have assumed that the group of physicians involved with the RCP were the majority of those active. This is now known not to be the case. Beyond the 130 or so physicians licensed by that body were at least another 750 who practised by virtue of degrees or episcopal licences.[9] Beyond these again—to judge by recent research—were perhaps a thousand surgeons and apothecaries acting as general practitioners.[10] Apart from those too, there were countless numbers of unregulated healers. About the majority of practitioners, regulated and unregulated, little has been written. There is virtually no information available on the training they received, the knowledge they utilised, nor the therapies they provided. The bulk of writing on the medical knowledge and practice of the period relates only to those licensed by the RCP and, in particular to the activities of the forty or so fellows of that College. It is their knowledge and occupational definitions that have generally been taken as typical of medicine as a whole. This is a dangerous source of error since it has to be rememberd that their concepts were weapons forged in an ideological war, a war for professional dominance fought against surgeons, apothecaries, and quacks. It is as ideological weapons that they must be understood and not as dispassionate images of reality.

As soon as this is done it becomes clear that the boundaries between medicine and astrology, for instance, were by no means as clear and distinct as would appear from such a conventional study as Sir George Clark's *History of the Royal College of Physicians of London*. It also becomes evident both that the dominance of the RCP did not go unchallenged even by other physicians, and that there were divergent views on the role of the medical profession. These points will be discussed in detail later. Before doing so, however, it is necessary to give a brief account of the nature and organisations of astrology at the time.

Astrology, unlike medicine, did not benefit from protective legislation. Anyone was free to set himself up as a consultant astrologer; to cast nativities, answer horary questions, practise healing, and so on provided he did not infringe too openly the Church's prohibition of magic and witchcraft. The publication of almanacs was subject to regulation although this seems to have been somewhat relaxed during the Interregnum.

In at least one respect the structure of astrological practice resembled that of medicine: it too was both heterogeneous and hierarchical. Those practising the subject ranged from the eclectic folk healers of the countryside who frequently mixed the subject with elements of magic and divination, to the couple of hundred well-known London writers of almanacs who usually also gave consultations. The only vestige of professional organisations was a body named the Society of Astrologers which is known to have existed between 1649 and 1658 and to have been revived in 1682.[11] Unfortunately, little is known about it except that some dozen—at least —of the best-known London astrologers attended its annual Feasts where they were regaled with sermons from clergymen favourable to the subject. As far as can be gathered from the venues these events were fairly opulent and high-status occasions. Nonetheless, the organisation did not persist (the last surviving reference to it dates from 1683) and was certainly not able to preserve astrology as a respectable activity in the eyes of the educated.

To discover why this was so it may be useful to try to examine the respective practices of medicine and astrology in terms of Terence Johnson's concept of occupational control.[12] Johnson's view is that the relationship of professionals to their clients is merely one form of the producer-consumer relationship and, like all such, is characterised by a certain level of what he calls 'indeterminacy', a certain *'irreducible but variable* minimum of uncertainty'.[13] This uncertainty may be resolved in the interests of either the producer or the consumer and it will be their relative power which decides who shall dominate. A situation where the professionals define the needs of the consumers and how they should be catered for is termed collegiate control; one where the consumers define the needs and the means, one of patronage. Where a third party mediates the relationship between producer and consumer, the state of affairs is referred to as mediative.

The occupational situations of astrology and medicine in the mid-seventeenth century did differ in a number of respects. To begin with, they ministered to different groups of consumers. Those of astrology were almost certainly more numerous since they embraced virtually the entire adult nation; those of regulated medicine probably excluded at least the majority of the urban and rural poor. Given Johnson's scheme, the greater size and heterogeneity of the demand for astrology would have been likely to weaken the consumers' potential power and hence, make collegiate control more probable. On the other hand, the astrological consumers had far more occasion to define their own needs than those of medicine. People went to consultant astrologers with a vast and unpredictable range of questions: wives enquired whether their missing husbands were alive; men if they should enter a given trade. Astrologers were asked whether there was buried treasure on the questioner's property; the sick wanted to know of what they were ill and how they should be cured; young women might ask if they were pregnant. There was no way in which the astrologer could redefine these problems in terms of his own problematic. The best he could do was to prefer one technique for their solution to another: always he had to find an answer. As a result, astrology persistently tended to be very *ad hoc and* problem-centred: features which Johnson sees as typical of patronage.[14] Medicine was confronted with a rather different situation. Here it was far easier to redefine the client's symptoms and perceived needs in terms of an esoteric framework deriving from either the humoral theory or more modern empirical findings. It is perhaps this lack of problem-centredness which is reflected in the accusations of bookishness and lack of concern for patients which were sometimes directed against physicians.[15]

But what of the practitioners? How far did differences between astrologers and doctors make contrasting situations of occupational control seem likely? Medical practitioners taken as a whole were certainly heterogeneous but, within this heterogeneity existed particular groups of practitioners with rather similar origins. The most obvious example of such a cluster was the prestigious sub-group of university educated physicians composed of individuals who had not merely shared a certain classical education but had also been exposed, in most cases, to a fairly lengthy process of professional socialisation. There was no such group of individuals within astrology. Even the successful London almanac makers and consultants included men of the most diverse backgrounds and education.

Although on balance it may appear that, in Johnson's terms, an astrologer was in a somewhat weaker position *vis à vis* his clientele than was a doctor, the difference between their two practices cannot be represented as a simple contrast between patronage and collegiate control. On several occasions, Johnson makes clear that he considers pre-nineteenth century medicine to be an example of patronage;[16] using his criteria one can only conclude that astrology too falls in this category.

The difficulty with this early formulation of Johnson's theory is that it tells us nothing about the forces producing the needs for certain kinds of services.[17] If we are to understand the professional relationship as but one aspect of the general relationship between producer and consumer we need to extend the analogy further and examine the elasticity of demand for the activities of professionals. We need to enquire both why consumers felt themselves constrained to demand the services of doctors or of astrologers, and also ask to what degree the professionals were able to control and stimulate needs to which only they could minister. In view of what I have already said about the effectiveness of medical treatment it appears, in addition, that we need to examine the ideological significance of the two subjects and to investigate how this may have changed.

What I am going to suggest is that the seventeenth century was a period when medical practice and astrological practice came to be distinguished from one another not simply as a consequence of medicine eschewing astrological theory or incorporating the new science into its knowledge, but rather by establishing its elite as the possessors of a special professional domain bearing a distinctive ideological relationship to the developing capitalist mode of production. It is this process which now makes it appear in retrospect as if seventeenth-century astrology and medicine were far more clearly separated from each other than they actually were.

At the beginning of the century, it was not even easy to distinguish the two on the basis of the content of their knowledge. Late Elizabethan medicine was permeated with principles drawn implicitly or explicitly from astrological theory. Even leading members of the RCP were personally involved with it. The President elected in 1601, for instance, Dr. Richard Forster (1546?-1616) was the author of a book on astrological medicine. Even in the second half of the century such an intermingling of theories is still evident. As H. G. Dick has pointed out, there is even a sense in which Thomas Sydenham may be said to have held a number of astrological presuppositions.[18]

It also needs to be emphasised that the new knowledge of the period was by no means seen as inevitably undermining astrological theory. Indeed, the work of Paracelsus which contained an explicitly astrological element probably strengthened the subject as its influence spread in England. Perhaps the best way of illustrating the now largely forgotten interpenetration of the two fields is by looking at the connections and interests of a number of individuals.

Let us begin with Sir William Petty one of the founders of the Royal Society. Petty was a celebrated exponent both of the new science and of social reform, yet in his plan for a teaching hospital sent, in 1648, to Samuel Hartlib (d.1670?) he proposed that it should be administered by a mathematically trained 'steward' who should concern himself with judicial astrology, meteorology and medical statistics.[19] As we shall see, this association between astrology, social reform and the new science was by no means random. Astrology was frequently regarded, particularly during the Interregnum, as a practical technology both valuable to the masses and threatening to such learned monopolies as the RCP. It is perhaps significant that Petty himself only became eligible to practise medicine in the following year when he was given a Doctorate of Medicine by the University of Oxford after the intervention of Parliamentary Representatives and the Military Governor of the city. In 1652 he also became a Fellow of the RCP.[20]

Another representative of this tendency is the London astrologer and apothecary Nicholas Culpeper (1616-1654) who became famous for translating the RCP's Latin pharmacopoeia without their permission. Culpeper was a prolific systematiser and populariser of medical knowledge and translated numerous standard medical works from Latin into English. There can be no doubt that for him these activities were part of a campaign against the monopolisation of learning and for the widest possible diffusion of useful knowledge to the people. Their political nature was also obviously clear to his opponents who attacked him scurrilously. In 1649, the Royalist paper *Mercurius Pragmaticus* accused him of being:

> 'an absolute Atheist, . . . (who) by two yeares' drunken labour hath Gallimawfred the apothecaries' book into nonesense, mixing every recipe therein with some scruples, at least of rebellion or atheism, beside the poisoning of men's bodies. And (to supply his drunkeness and leachery with thirty shillings reward) endeavoured to bring into obloquy the famous societies of apothecaries and surgeons.[21]

Contact with the intellectual circles in which the leading astrologers moved was not limited, however, to physicians seeking to undermine professional monopoly, Dr. Jonathan Goddard (1617?-1675), for example, a Fellow of the RCP and author of a book which defended the College's regulation of the profession while criticising the apothecaries for undermining it, borrowed material from the astrologer and alchemist John Hunyades, an associate of many of the leading astrologers of his day.[22]

One further illustration will suffice to show the indeterminacy of the frontier between astrology and medicine. This is the case of William Salmon (1644-1713), a leading astrologer and almanac writer as well as an author of medical works. He is usually cited in medical histories as one of the most notorious quacks of the time. Whilst it is almost certainly true that he had neither university degree or licence, it is also true that he was a man of some considerable learning. Apart from translating the works of Dolaeus and Sydenham into English his own work, *Synopsis Medicinae* is commonly cited as a typical—if unoriginal—example of the medicine of the period.[23] Salmon's case epitomises the tendency of some historians to accept the ideology of the RCP at its face value: there can be no other reason why a recent writer should, without further justification, refer in passing to Salmon as, 'the most famous of the infamous'.[24]

As soon as one begins to examine in detail the practice of seventeenth-century astrology it becomes clear that no rigid barriers marked it off from that of medicine: indeed, the closer one looks, the more it becomes apparent that there was a significant intermixing of ideas, activities and personnel. What was distinctive about medicine—

or rather that sphere of medicine which has often been taken retrospectively to represent the whole—was that it was developing a form of professional regulation and control which astrology was not. It was the growth of this control and its associated ideology which was beginning to set medicine off from astrology and other, hitherto associated activities. It was for this reason that the unlicensed practice and advertising of Salmon was so derided and the democratising tactics of Culpeper were seen as such a threat.

The RCP and its dominance did not go unchallenged, however: at this period, at least two attempts were made to form competing organisations of physicians. In 1656, William Rand wrote to Samuel Hartlib suggesting the formation of a 'College of Graduate Physicians' to include all those who were either barred from the RCP for technical reasons (for example, holding a foreign not an English University degree) or who were unwilling to join it.[25] Again in 1665, there was a proposal to form a 'Society of Chymical Physicians' as a way of organising Helmontian and Paracelsian practitioners against the dominant Galenic orthodoxy. Neither plan reached fruition.[26]

Whilst there is no evidence of any direct association between astrology and these attempts to question and reform the prevailing definition of medicine, it is the case that such demands and the advocacy of astrology form part of a persistent sub-stratum of ideas in seventeenth-century radical thought. A good instance of this can be found in the work of John Webster (1610-1682), a sectarian preacher and advocate of the new learning, who published a biting (and perhaps unfair) attack on university education, *Academiarum Examen,* in 1654. Webster criticised the universities for their scholasticism and lack of interest in science and, with the support of numerous references to the most advanced seventeenth-century philosophical and scientific writing, called for a practical education to include—amongst other things—chemistry, astrology, and Helmontian medicine. The essence of his argument was that learning should be available to all, just as there ought to be a priesthood of all believers. Learning had become the private monopoly of the university elite and was maintained in this state by stress on the unpractical.

If astrology and medicine were not entirely separate and distinct fields, and if it is also the case that medical practitioners, taken as a whole, were not in a position especially favourable to exerting collegiate control, how then are the success of medicine and the

decline of astrology to be explained? I believe that this can be done
by trying to understand the social roles of the two practices; by
attempting to discover what needs they addressed and by what
criteria they were judged. To do this involves seeing both, to an
extent, as crafts. That is to say, in examining them as a set of techniques for the solution of socially given ends and considering their
position relative to other, more generally recognised, crafts of their
day.

The notion of a craft may be a useful concept for investigating such
practices provided one makes certain provisions about its use. To start
with, it is necessary to emphasise that the needs to which crafts
minister are not only physical needs, and that they are all socially
shaped. There is no sense in which there is an independent need even
for such essential crafts as baking, brewing or pottery-making. They
are all responses to material needs that have been generated in certain
—but not all—kinds of social formation. Obviously, these needs are
related to physical drives; nonetheless, they are always mediated by
the social form in which they occur. Similarly, just as there can be no
asocial, independent needs so there can be no neutral, purely instrumental crafts to provide for them. Crafts and technologies always
bear the stamp of the relations of production within which they have
been created.

What is necessary, I would argue, is to deny the implied distinction
between instrumental techniques and interpretative systems and to
envisage them as the two extremes of a continuum. If this is done,
technical needs can be understood as embodying, to various degrees,
both symbolic and material elements. To take but one example, the
notion of a good piece of furniture implies not merely 'material' but
also 'aesthetic' considerations. The craft of furniture design has therefore to be seen as responding to socially created needs which may
vary over time and from culture to culture. In the same way in
medicine, the development of therapies to treat forms of behaviour
which have only recently come to be labelled as pathological (e.g. the
'discovery' of hyperkinesis/Minimum Brain Dysfunction in the
USA)[27] must be understood not in terms of a technical response to
a pre-existing need, but as part of a social process whereby both need
and response are generated. Such a process can be analysed with
categories like power, ideology, deviance and control.

Seen from this viewpoint, the decline of astrology and the survival of medicine may be approached in a new way. It is no longer necessary either to search for differences in their cognitive power nor to see the two practices as operating in radically different situations of occupational control. Instead, one must ask what the connections of the two activities were with the material and ideological forces of their day. To do this is to begin to unravel how it was that both the needs and responses with which astrology was concerned came to lose their social legitimacy at a time when the reverse was happening to regulated medicine.

In order to begin this analysis I want to propose a tentative classification for both technical and interpretative systems which relates them to the relations of production. I shall argue that by placing seventeenth-century astrology and medicine in such a scheme it is possible to obtain new insight into their fates.

My main criterion for classifying different cognitive systems is that of their relationship to the needs of capitalist production (understood in what I take to be Marx's original sense and not in terms of a restrictively 'economic' view). In these terms, I would distinguish one group of symbolic and cognitive activities which, in general, would include most of what were considered as crafts in the 17th century. (Navigation, surveying, ship-building, metal-working, brewing, etc). The common element of such a group would be the directness of its contribution to capitalist production expressed by utility and profitability. This is not to ignore the possibility (as writers like Bravermann and Dickson have argued)[28] that many such techniques also possessed important ideological and social control features which may even have been the determining reason for their adoption by capitalists. I am merely suggesting that, analytically, the contribution of such subjects may be seen primarily as satisfying the socially-created economic needs of capitalist production.

A further group of symbolic activities might be identified whose relationship to capitalist production was primarily one of what one could call 'applied ideologies'. These I see as activities which, while principally concerned with generating a variety of ideological forms which legitimised capitalist domination, also pretend to manipulate nature in a utilitarian way. In retrospect, one may be inclined to view their manipulation of nature as ineffective even in terms of their own expressed intentions. To stress ineffectiveness, however, is in part to miss the point: the central issue from the perspective of this analysis is the contribution of such activities to the ideological structuring of a meaningful world. I would be inclined to see seventeenth-century licensed medical practice (as well, perhaps as political theorising and other activities) as suitable for inclusion in such a category. In my view, late seventeenth-century medicine, although of dubious utility as a *curing* activity may usefully be regarded as a *classifying* and *labelling* activity which appears to have been increasingly concerned with structuring everyday reality in terms akin to the new dominant ideological currents associated with the rise of capitalist production. I see these features as including the following.

Firstly, a Baconian emphasis on the domination of nature. In the medicine of the RCP this is expressed by therapeutics which stressed intervention at the expense of acquiescence to nature or notions of harmony. A trend at this time towards specifics (*i.e. ad hoc* remedies not deriving from the Galenic theory of humours) may also be seen as part of this tendency. Astrology and astrological medicine, in contrast, took universal harmony and its expression in the microcosm/macrocosm analogy as fundamental.

Secondly, the emphasis within regulated medicine on the lasting face-to-face relationship of learned doctor and patient for instrumental, curative, purposes is another aspect of practice congruent with ideologies of individualism. Again there is a contrast with astrology. There, individual consultation seems to have been fleeting and occasional: it seems that there was little tendency for the wealthy to have family astrologers in the way that they were beginning to have family physicians. What is more important, the tendency for astrology to be diffused by almanacs or popularised works like those of Culpeper and Salmon created a state of affairs where the relationship of professional and client were in large degree superfluous.

Thirdly, a further way in which regulated medicine was beginning to develop in accord with new ideologies was in its emphasis on an individualistic aetiology of disease. This parallel is apparent in many places, but most obvious, perhaps, in Sydenham's stress on the need for the close observation of the course of illness in a particular patient. This, like the supposed Puritan attitude to vocation, drew attention to immediate and individualised causes and drew away, precisely, from the cosmic factors that were the concern of the astrologers. The emphasis on mediate—as opposed to final—causes is again obvious in the attack on astrology by the licensed physician John Cotta (1575?—

1650) earlier in the century. Cotta's point was not that astrological forces did not exist, merely that they were mediated by other less remote factors which were more amenable to action by the doctor.[29]

The final, and perhaps most important, difference in the ideological roles of late seventeenth-century astrology and medicine concerns their different relationships to the newly institutionalised science of the Restoration period. Despite the establishment of the Royal Society and the self-evident enthusiasm of many of its early members for utilitarian applications of knowledge, the last quarter of the century, taken as a whole, was a period in which science became academic; was integrated into the restrictive educational monopolies of university learning; and was used as an advanced legitimisation for the dominant kinds of theology and political ideology. Licensed medicine, of course, was an integral part of this monopoly and benefitted accordingly. It is no chance that when Seth Ward (1617-89) wrote a strident defence of the universities against Webster's polemic he not only condemned astrology as a 'ridiculous cheat'[30] but cited medicine (licensed medicine) as an area which was benefiting from scientific advance. It is also interesting to note that he condemned Webster's advocacy of chemistry as too inappropriately utilitarian for the type of students that the universities then received.

The RCP may be seen as successful at this time because they were able to sustain and develop a definition of practice that was not merely in tune with the ideological needs of the social elite but which also suited the political conjunctures of the time. From this basis, they were able in later centuries to go on to impose their definition of practice on the whole of regulated medicine in England. The astrologers, in contrast, were carrying on activities that no longer harmonised—even positively clashed—with the role accorded to knowledge in Restoration England. Their professional organisation failed, one would imagine, as a result not of the ineffectiveness of their theory nor the intrinsic weakness of their professional position, but rather in consequence of the lack of fit between their doctrines and the newly dominant ideological concerns of the age.

The boundary which arose between astrology and medicine was, above all, one created and maintained by licensed medicine and other monopolies of learning as a means to mark out and appropriate fields of ideologically acceptable practice; only secondarily did it relate to the content and purpose of the two practices.

Peter W. G. Wright

All this is not to argue, however, that the decline of astrology among the educated at this time was historically inevitable. Had the Levellers triumphed in the late 1640s; had the education system been transformed along the lines suggested by Dell or John Webster; and had medical care evolved in ways advocated by Nedham and Culpeper, astrology might well have emerged strengthened and have persisted for a further period. My thesis is simply that the reasons for the success of licensed medicine and the failure of astrology as 'applied ideologies' lie not in their intrinsic qualities but in the particular outcome of the general social struggles of the time. It is in the interplay of these power and ideological relations that the boundary and fates of the two practices have to be understood.

Sheffield City Polytechnic.

[1] See for instance, M. Douglas: *Purity and Danger,* Routledge & Kegan Paul, London, 1966.

[2] P. Bourdieu: 'Le Marché des Biens Symboliques', *L'Année Sociologique,* Vol. 22, 1971, pp. 49-126.

[3] E. Freidson: *Profession of Medicine,* Dodd Mead, New York, 1970.

[4] For evidence of this decline see P. W. G. Wright: 'Astrology and Science in Seventeenth-Century England', *Social Studies of Science,* Vol. 5, 1975, pp. 399-422.

[5] For an account of these casebooks see K. Thomas: *Religion and the Decline of Magic,* Weidenfeld & Nicholson, London, 1971.

[6] See C. H. Josten (ed.): *Elias Ashmole (1617-1692),* Oxford University Press, London, 1966, p. 1197.

[7] Thomas McKeown, for example, has argued that the net effect of medicine before the nineteenth century was almost certainly harmful. T. McKeown: *Medicine in Modern Society,* Allen & Unwin, London, 1965.

[8] See R. S. Roberts: 'The Personnel and Practice of Medicine in Tudor and Stuart England: Part 1, The Provinces', *Medical History,* Vol. 6, 1962, pp. 363-382.

[9] This is the approximate number of practitioners listed in J. H. Raach: *A Directory of English County Physicians, 1603-43,* Dawsons, Folkstone, 1962.

[10] My estimate based on Roberts's findings, Roberts: op. cit.

[11] For evidence of these meetings see Josten: op.cit.

[12] Discussed in T. Johnson: *Professions and Power,* Macmillan, London, 1972.

[13] ibid., p. 41.

[14] ibid., pp. 72 ff.

[15] For example, in Culpeper's preface to his translation of the Royal College of Physicians' *Pharmacopoeia*, see N. Culpeper: *Pharmacopoeia Londoniensis or the London dispensatory further adorned*, 1653.

[16] Johnson: op. cit., 1972, p. 69.

[17] This is, however, an issue which he refers to by implication only in his 1975 paper. See T. Johnson: 'The Professions in the Class Structure' paper presented to the British Sociological Association Conference, 1975. Now published in R. Scase (ed.): *Industrial Society: Class, Cleavage and Control*, Allen and Unwin, London, 1977.

[18] See H. G. Dick: 'Students of Physic and Astrology. A survey of Astrological Medicine in the Age of Science', *Journal of History of Medicine*, Vol. 1 1946, pp. 300-315 and 413-432.

[19] Quoted in C. Webster: *The Great Instauration*, Duckworth, London, 1975, p. 294.

[20] For details see W. Munk: *The Roll of the Royal College of Physicians of London*, Vol. 1, Longman, London, 1861, pp. 252-253.

[21] Quoted in F. N. L. Poynter: 'Nicholas Culpeper and his Books', *Journal of the History of Medicine*, Vol. 17, 1962, pp. 152-167.

[22] See F. S. Taylor and C. H. Josten: 'Johannes Banfi Hunyades', *Ambix*, Vol. 5, 1953, pp. 44-52.

[23] For instance, A. W. Franklin: 'Clinical Medicine' in A. Debus (ed.): *Medicine in Seventeenth-Century England*, University of California Press, London, 1974, pp. 143-144.

[24] L.R.C. Agnew: 'Quackery' in Debus (ed.): op.cit., p. 321.

[25] See Webster: op. cit., 1975, pp. 300 ff.

[26] H. Thomas: 'The Society of Chymical Physicians' in E. A. Underwood (ed.): *Science, Medicine and History*, Oxford University Press, London, 1953.

[27] See P. Conrad: 'The Discovery of Hyperkinesis: Notes on the Medicalization of Deviant Behaviour', *Social Problems*, Vol. 23, no. 1, 1975, pp. 12-21.

[28] H. Bravermann: *Labour and Monopoly Capital*, Monthly Review Press, London, 1974; D. Dickson: *Alternative Technology*, Fontana, London, 1974.

[29] Cotta's views are described in Dick: op. cit., pp. 427-430.

[30] S. Ward: *Vindicae Academiarium, containing some briefe Animadversions, upon Mr. Webster's Book, stiled the Examination of Academies*, 1654, p. 30.

PROFESSIONAL DEVIANTS AND THE HISTORY OF MEDICINE: MEDICAL MESMERISTS IN VICTORIAN BRITAIN

Terry M. Parssinen

WHY has some knowledge been accepted by the medical community and other knowledge rejected? Most historians of medicine have assumed that knowledge-claims are eventually accepted if they correspond to scientific truth, and rejected if they do not. This 'correspondence' view of verification is implicit in the dominant tradition in the history of medicine which conceives of it, at least in modern times, as a march of progress toward truth, led by the discoveries of heroic physician-scientists. In this view, rational scepticism or misguided opposition sometimes prevails for a short period after the announcement of a discovery—the classic example being the resistance to Harvey's discovery of the circulation of the blood—but in time, truth prevails. In contrast to the heroes of science, purveyors of false knowledge are usually portrayed as unscrupulous charlatans or befuddled eccentrics, whose lives may have vexed their orthodox contemporaries, but which now provide us with amusing anecdotes.[1] If, however, one looks critically at why certain knowledge-claims were rejected by nineteenth-century medical men, one discovers that there are other factors than objective truth or falsity that determine whether knowledge is accepted or rejected by medical men.

In two recent papers, Dr. Jacques Quen has investigated unorthodox medical therapies which were anathema to the great majority of medical men in nineteenth-century Europe and America. Dr. Quen concludes each paper with suggestive questions. In 'Case Studies in Nineteenth Century Scientific Rejection: Mesmerism, Perkinism, and Acupuncture,' Dr. Quen notes:

> 'It was a confirmed observation, in the history of each method, that patients, who had not been relieved by conventional medical treatments, were relieved by these therapies. What factors in the medical and scientific communities determined the responses?'[2]

In 'Mesmerism, Medicine, and Professional Prejudice,' Dr. Quen asks:

Terry M. Parssinen

'What determines which therapeutic modes a medical community (or a society) will accept and which it will reject? What factors other than objective performance criteria enter into the evaluation of a proposed treatment method?'[3]

This latter formulation, in particular, recognises the significance of a broad range of factors to explain why particular therapies were unacceptable to medical men. Yet Dr. Quen offers no definite answers to the questions which he has posed. In spite of a qualified nod to Thomas Kuhn in both papers, and a suggestion in the former that 'political, economic, and social' factors might have played a role in the process of medical rejection, each article leaves the reader with his curiosity whetted, but unsatisfied.

It is my purpose to address the questions which Dr. Quen has raised: first, by constructing a theoretical perspective on professsional deviancy in medicine which I believe will bring the problem into sharper focus; second, by using this theoretical perspective to answer the specific question of why mesmerism was anathema to medical men in Britain in the 1840s; and third, by suggesting how this perspective might be applicable to the history of medicine beyond the narrow boundaries of early Victorian Britain.

Professional Deviants

In a now-classic article, William J. Goode argued that a profession is a community, in all the most meaningful senses of that word, a fact which we acknowledge informally by making reference to 'the legal community', 'the medical community', or 'the academic community.'[4] Communities, whether they are geographically situated, like neighbour-hoods, or less visible but no less real, like professions, spawn deviants. That is, there are those individuals, and even groups who operate in and around communities, but whose ideas and behaviour are un-acceptable by community standards. Some sociologists, like Kai T. Erikson, push the argument even further by claiming that com-munities *need* deviants.[5] A community ascribes deviant status to individuals who violate its norms, thereby strengthening the com-munity by differentiating sharply between insiders and outsiders. Presumably professions, like other communities, create deviants whose existence is functional in that they mark out the ideas or behaviour that the professional community considers unacceptable.

The utility of Goode's insight to historians of medicine is limited, however, by the fact that his model is static. It is meant to describe professionalism, not professionalisation. For historians, concerned with change over time, the medical profession is not a community with well-defined boundaries. Rather it is a community whose values and norms are constantly in flux; indeed, at any given time, the profession may encompass several distinct and possibly competing groups who are trying to define community standards quite differently. Thus certain ideas or behaviour that might be judged deviant by the medical community in, say, the mid-nineteenth century may be considered quite orthodox by the beginning of the twentieth. In asking why certain ideas or behaviour were considered unacceptable or deviant to the profession at any particular period, a historian must carefully elucidate their relationship to contemporary medical standards. Thus the study of professional deviants can be an important heuristic device; they are, ironically, mirrors to the very profession which spurned them. From this perspective of professional deviancy, then, I would rephrase Dr. Quen's question about medical mesmerism by asking, 'In what ways did mesmerists violate the boundaries of professional respectability in early Victorian Britain?'

Medical Mesmerists in Victorian Britain

It is not my intention to write a narrative history of the controversy between mesmerists and the British medical profession. Dr. Quen and Jon Palfreman have done that admirably.[6] Instead I intend to explain the controversy by illuminating the issues that underlay it.

Animal magnetism, or mesmerism, as it was called after its founder, first flourished in France in the 1770s and 1780s. Anton Mesmer believed that he had discovered the existence of an invisible, rarefied liquid that permeated all bodies in the universe, animate and inanimate. He claimed that a person's state of health depended upon a proper ebb and flow of the liquid throughout his body. Certain individuals have the power to alter a person's bodily fluids by moving their hands in patterns around the person's body —rather like a magnet that can change the configuration of iron filings—and thus restore him to health.[7]

Mesmer's theories proved to be extremely popular, at least in part because he combined in a single system particular elements that resonated with older traditions. His idea of an invisible but powerful liquid was not unlike the theory of aether, which had long been a staple of Western natural philosophy; his theory of disease, based on the idea of bodily fluids, resembled humoural pathology; and his therapies were reminiscent of 'touch-healing,' which still enjoyed a strong popular following. Thus Mesmer drew on existing intellectual and social traditions, and welded them into a unified system that had great appeal.

After a long and controversial life as a medical and scientific doctrine on the Continent, mesmerism was finally introduced into England in 1837 by one of the most formidable medical men of the age, Dr. John Elliotson (1791-1868).[8] He was Professor of Medicine at the young but prestigious University of London, one of the founders of University College Hospital, and the translator of Blumenbach. In addition to his academic qualifications, he was known as an innovator who had been one of the earliest English proponents of the stethoscope, and had experimented boldly and successfully by using large doses of drugs on his patients. Elliotson became the leader of a small group of medical mesmerists, only some of whom had received medical training. Under Elliotson's leadership, they flourished through the 1840s, and early 1850s.

Elliotson did not claim that mesmerism was a medical panacea that would invalidate all existing therapies. However, he did claim that the discovery of the power of mesmerism was akin to Harvey's discovery of the circulation of the blood, both in terms of the irrational resistance which it encountered among medical men, and in terms of its potential for furthering medical knowledge. In addition, mesmerism had two immediate applications: as a therapy for patients suffering from neurological disorders, and as an anaesthetic for surgical patients.

In his own journal, *Zoist*, begun in 1843, Elliotson cited scores of cases of patients suffering from hysteria, epilepsy, tic doloreaux, and other nervous disorders, who had been treated unsuccessfully by traditional therapies, but who had recovered when they were treated mesmerically. A typical example was the case of a woman, aged thirty, who had been deeply affected by the business reverses suffered by her father eleven years before. She was subject to fits of jumping up and down and clapping her hands together until they bled. For the past five years, she had been in and out of various London hospitals, and had been treated by forty practitioners.

'Dr. Watson shaved her head and electrified her. Under the others she was bled in the arm TWENTY-FIVE times; *cupped* SEVEN-TEEN *times;* had TWO setons, THREE issues, leeches and blisters WITHOUT NUMBER, and was in bed for SEVENTEEN days in a state of salivation. One practitioner attended her for a year and gave her carbonate of iron largely, and made her wear bags of steel filings on her back and feet, silk stockings and gloves: but the filings increased her sufferings when she jumped. She was mesmerised daily for periods of two weeks or a month when she felt the fits coming on. After a year of such treatment, the fits ceased entirely, and have not returned in the three years since she was treated.'[9]

If the use of mesmerism as a therapy was promising, its use as an anaesthetic was startling. Before the introduction of ether into Britain in 1847, British surgeons either drugged their patients with alcohol or opium, or gave them nothing at all. Especially after 1842, mesmerists began to report large numbers of cases in which their patients underwent major surgery—for example, the removal of a tumour or a limb—completely insensible to pain while in a mesmeric trance.[10]

One might expect that the new science, which enjoyed the support of one of the leading medical men of the day, and which seemed to counter important weaknesses in contemporary medicine, would have aroused considerable interest and even support among Victorian medical men. Quite the contrary. Elliotson was forced to resign from his position at the University of London, his experiments were denounced or ignored, his followers were ridiculed, and medical men went to great lengths to castigate mesmerically-induced insensibility to pain as either a fraud, or a perversion of God's will. Why did mesmerism evoke such impassioned negative response?

From early Victorian medical journals and pamphlets, one can cull hundreds of denunciations of mesmerism as quackery, fraud, and chicanery usually punctuated by the choicest expletives of the day: 'Humbug!' 'Errant Nonsense!' and so on. But these are mere shell explosions. What one would like to have is a detailed plan of battle, or even better, a Thucydidean explanation of why the war was being fought. But these do not exist; they can only be inferred from the odd outbursts.

We can understand the motivation behind this reaction if we go beyond the stated denunciations to an appreciation of the mentality of medical men, and of the social standing of their profession. I wish to argue that mesmerism was considered pro-

Terry M. Parssinen

fessionally illegitimate in mid-Victorian Britain because on one
level, it contradicted so completely the contemporary theory and
practice of medicine, and because on a second, and more significant level, it threatened the social and professional aspirations of
medical men during a critical period in their history.

In what way did mesmerism challenge contemporary medical
theory? Elliotson and his followers endorsed the classic 'fluidist'
interpretation of mesmeric phenomena. Mesmerism was, according
to Elliotson, a scientific discovery of great human power, whose
medical potential was undeniable, but as yet only partially understood.
Nineteenth-century medical men denounced most of the quacks of
their day as 'empirics;' that is, as mere opportunists who claimed that
a specific remedy 'worked' without understanding why.[11] The
dangers of this kind of medicine were clear. An empiric lacked the
comprehensive knowledge to deal effectively with the whole health
needs of the patient. Seen from another perspective, however, the
denunciation of empirics underscored an important and timeless
claim by medical men that they, and they alone, have access to an
esoteric body of knowledge which is essential to professional
practice. While empirics annoyed orthodox medical men—and often
drained away a part of their livelihood—they did not challenge them
theoretically. But mesmerists did, by claiming that the orthodox theory
of the origin of disease was incorrect, or at best woefully incomplete.
Mesmerism thus threatened the legitimacy of medicine by disputing
its claim to possess exclusive, esoteric knowledge about the nature of
disease and health.

Occasionally, a medical man would admit that the success of mesmerism, and other medical heresies of the 1840s, was a commentary on
the lack of public confidence in heroic medical practice and the
prevailing localised theory of disease. J. Evans Riadore noted that the
popularity of 'new fangled systems' could be attributed to

> 'the want of success attending the old practice, arising from the too
> generally contracted opinion, that diseases originate either in the
> stomach, liver, or the brain, and that the remedial means consist in
> administering mercury, purgatives, starving diet, and employing bleeding
> and cupping, and afterwards some preparation of iron, with or without
> bitters, and walking exercise; without sufficiently regarding other sources
> of disease, particularly the constitutional predisposition to certain
> diseases.'[12]

But most medical men regarded mesmerism, along with homeopathy
and hydropathy, as fraudulent systems, reminiscent of eighteenth-

108

century medical panaceas. Samuel Flood, a surgeon of Leeds, called them 'little truths run mad,' and compared them to astrology and alchemy. For Flood, as well as other medical men, it was sufficient to be convinced that mesmeric phenomena could be explained by 'the force of imagination, and the influence exerted by the mind upon the body' to label mesmerism 'a delusion.'[13] It is a measure of the commitment of orthodox medical men to a purely somatic explanation of disease that they could consider mesmerism a hoax if they were convinced that it worked through the imagination, regardless of its efficacy.

But mesmerism's challenge to medical theory was indirect, and only dimly perceived; its threat to contemporary medical practice was much more obvious. Except for Elliotson and a few others, most mesmerists who practised as healers were not professionally-trained seekers after truth. It required no special training or formal education to acquire, and it could be practised by anyone who believed that he was in possession of that knowledge. In 1844, the *London Medical Gazette* sputtered that mesmerism

> 'admits the humblest and most insignificant, unrestrictedly for a time, into the society of the proud and lofty; it enables the veriest dunderheads to go hand in hand, as "philosophical inquirers" (forsooth!) with men of the highest scientific repute!'[14]

In addition, mesmerism was an economic challenge to orthodox medical practice. Unlike many of the more traditional medical quackeries, the medical heresies of the 1840s—mesmerism, homeopathy, and hydropathy—were patronised by an affluent, urban clientele. Even the *Dublin Medical Press,* in an antagonistic editorial on the subject, admitted that mesmerism's patrons included 'successful lawyers, good generals, wealthy merchants, and great politicians.'[15] Since medical fees were generally high, and those who could afford them relatively scarce, this competition was a source of considerable discomfort to medical men. They were particularly vexed by licensed practitioners who began to practice one of the 'new systems' of medicine. Medical men castigated such renegades as unprincipled mercenaries and saw the process as being the result of 'the difficulty in the present overcrowded state of [medical] society of gaining an honest livelihood.'[16]

Another aspect of mesmeric healers which particularly rankled medical men was their resemblance to magico-religious healers of the recent past who cured their patients by touching them. Valentine Greatrakes, a seventeenth-century Irishman, who was widely known for his healing power throughout the British Isles, was the best-known practitioner in this tradition. And, as recently as the early eighteenth century, English monarchs had treated scrofula by the 'royal touch.' Naturally physicians had striven to differentiate their form of scientific medicine from what they characterised as superstitious magic. They greeted mesmerism with a flurry of articles claiming that it was only the most recent example of this spurious form of healing.[17] Mesmerists, meanwhile, welcomed the comparisons, claiming on their part that touch healing was simply an unselfconscious form of mesmerism.[18]

Yet it was only in part because of its challenges to contemporary medical theory and practice that medical men considered mesmerism illegitimate. Of greater importance was the fact that mesmerism threatened to taint it at the very time when the leaders of the profession felt it extremely important to maintain a spotless reputation.

In the 1840s, the institutions and legal boundaries of the medical profession were changing. The tripartite division of the British medical profession into physicians, surgeons, and apothecaries, derived from a late medieval distinction among functions which no longer corresponded to medical practice. Physicians were limited to practice among the very wealthy in large cities, and the number of 'pure' surgeons was very small indeed. The overwhelming majority of medical men were general practitioners (the term became widely used in the early nineteenth century) who had qualified as surgeon-apothecaries, but who usually practised all forms of medicine. Yet politically the general practitioners were virtually powerless, as the profession was dominated by the fellows of the elitist Royal Colleges of Physicians and Surgeons in London, Edinburgh, and Dublin. There were no common standards in medical education, the quality of which varied widely, and there were nineteen different bodies which had the power to license medical practitioners according to their respective regulations. While the Royal Colleges and the Society of Apothecaries had the power to sue unlicensed practitioners who operated within their jurisdictions, they were usually unwilling to do so because of the expense involved, and the reluctance of the juries to find for the plaintiffs in such cases.[19]

Moreover, medical men had a poor reputation with the general public, for a variety of reasons. Medicine was often characterised as a profession filled with marginal men: drunken, randy medical students; half-caste army and navy surgeons; impecunious Scots with dubious medical degrees in their kits; and irreligious professors of anatomy who furtively purchased exhumed corpses from graverobbers. But if some medical men were marginal because they lacked respectability, most were marginal simply because they seemed to be tradesmen rather than gentlemen. Particularly in small towns and rural areas, where medical men dispensed drugs as well as medical advice, and were paid for the former but not the latter, the line between the 'doctor' and the shopkeeper, at least in the eyes of the lay public, was very thin indeed.[20]

These unsettled conditions spawned a reform movement which had grown to considerable strength by the late 1830s. The movement had three principal foci: the firebrand Thomas Wakley, surgeon, radical MP from Finsbury, and editor of the popular medical weekly, *Lancet;* the Provincial Medical and Surgical Association (later the British Medical Association), an organisation whose strength lay in its broad base among provincial general practitioners; and John Forbes, publisher and editor of *British and Foreign Medical Review,* a scholarly and respected spokesman for reform.

From the late 1830s through the early 1850s, reformers petitioned Parliament in support of a succession of bills to reform the profession. Although the specific provisions varied from one bill to another, the reform program consisted of the following essential demands: 1) the supersession of existing bodies by a single medical organisation which would register all medical practitioners, and administer a qualifying examination to all candidates; 2) the standardisation of medical education; and 3) criminal sanctions against unlicensed practitioners.[21]

This program stressed what Eliot Freidson has identified as the core of 'the profession of medicine;' namely, an autonomous body which sets standards for education and licensing, and which may enlist the police power of the state to suppress unlicensed practitioners.[22] These demands, however, were not easily won. It was first necessary to convince the lay public, and their representatives in Parliament, that medical men were sufficiently knowledgable and selfless to deserve the power of autonomous decision-making.[23]

To the dismay of the reformers, their lay opponents continued to insist on the right of every Englishman to select his own brand of medical treatment, without the interference of laws and licensing bodies. Thus Wakley, Forbes, and the Provincial Association saw the necessity of changing public opinion by trying to enhance the public image of medical men. For example, one of the reformers' burning causes of the late 1830s and 1840s was their campaign to force repeal of a provision of the New Poor Law of 1834 which established a competitive bidding system for the appointment of medical officers of Poor Law Unions. Although this system harmed medical men economically, its most deleterious effect was on the image of the profession. The public was treated to the squalid sight of impoverished country surgeons, scrambling to underbid one another for a contract from a union, often at £11 or £12 per year, like purveyors of potatoes or bread. By reinforcing the unprofessional image of medical men as tradesmen, this practice sharply undercut the reformers' attempts to raise the social status of the profession.[24]

Still another aspect of the reformers' campaign to enhance the public image of the profession was their attempt to expose, to discredit, and if possible, to prosecute quacks. According to contemporary medical literature, the kingdom abounded with quacks in the early nineteenth century as never before.[25] Thomas Wakley felt especially impelled to protect the public's health and the reputation of the profession by exposing some of the more blatant of these practitioners in London. In the 1830s he attacked them recklessly, risking libel suits in order to expose them. The public, he reasoned, could not be expected to empower the profession to regulate itself if it allowed medical quacks to practise unchecked. His campaign against them was a demonstration of his power, and his good faith with the public, which was intimately tied up with his overriding campaign for professionalisation. In one of his many editorial denunciations of quackery, Wakley specifically linked it to the issue of the profession's image:

> 'We propose to extirpate unsparingly everything that openly or secretly lowers the dignity or rank of medical science and its professors. The IDEA of a Profession, of a Faculty, in the maintenance of which all, the highest and lowest, are alike interested, and which the elder medical men held in such reverence, has well nigh disappeared from us. This must be restored. Every offence, every injury done to the profession thus embodied, whether by members of the profession or by interlopers, is *quackery* to our code.'[26]

Wakley's attack on mesmerism was of a piece with his ongoing struggle against medical quackery. In the summer of 1838, John

Elliotson began to give public demonstrations of his mesmeric manipulations of two teen-aged sisters, Elizabeth and Jane O'Key. Elliotson did not limit his demonstration to the so-called 'lower' phenomena: somnambulism, cataleptic rigidity, and insensibility to pain. Instead he seemed to endorse the much more controversial belief that mesmeric entrancement raises certain individuals to a higher plane of knowledge. For example, after becoming convinced that the O'Key sisters had the power of medical diagnosis while entranced, he took them to the men's ward of the Hospital late one night, where they caused complete disruption by not only 'diagnosing' certain cases, but by loudly prophesying the imminent deaths of several patients. As a result of his experiments with the O'Key sisters, Elliotson was savagely attacked by his former friend Wakley, and forced to resign his professorship at the University of London.[27] Wakley's attack on Elliotson was the first and most important, although not the only medical denunciation of mesmerism. The attacks came continuously from all quarters of the reforming party in the 1840s.[28] Why did they feel so compelled to denounce the mesmerists?

In the 1830s and 1840s, mesmerism became a popular culture phenomenon. Self-proclaimed 'professors' of the subject swarmed throughout the kingdom, demonstrating their subjects' clairvoyant powers through 'experiments' in which the entranced subjects would read from a book or paper while blindfolded and the like.[29] Often these itinerant performers also claimed to practise medical mesmerism in private consultations. In the eyes of orthodox medical men, this was a reincarnation of the seventeenth- and eighteenth-century tradition of medical mountebanks, who performed a short entertainment before hawking their patent medicines at fairs and carnivals.[30] It was bad enough that the public equated medical men with tradesmen; would they now equate them with showmen as well?

Moreover, mesmerism was not taken seriously by the great Victorian quarterly reviews, the pace-setters of upper-middle-class opinion. Indeed, the quarterlies treated mesmerism as an object of ridicule. Those who dabbled in it were either tricksters or fools. J. F. Ferrier, writing in *Blackwood's* echoed the majority opinion when he explained the apparent success of mesmerism:

> 'Imbecility of the nervous system, a ready abandonment of the will, a facility in relinquishing every endowment which makes man *human—*

these intelligible causes, eked out by a vanity and cunning which are always inherent in natures of an inferior type, are quite sufficient to account for the effects of the mesmeric manipulations on subjects of peculiar softness and pliancy.'[31]

Finally, mesmerism was suspect because it seemed to place one person so totally in the power of another. While that idea in the abstract was unsettling enough for ordinary Victorians, it assumed an even more sinister meaning when the operator was an older man, and the subject, as was usually the case, a young girl. While this sexual tension in mesmeric performances made for good entertainment, it did nothing to enhance the public image of the science. Furthermore, the power of mesmerism was transportable. What a gentleman had seen performed on the stage one night he might try in his own home the next. As mesmerism spread across the breadth of the Kingdom, outraged Victorians railed against it, as though an army of seducers had been set loose to prey on the unsuspecting virgins of the land. Wakley's editorial in the *Lancet* of 15 December 1838 reflected this fear:

'Mesmerism, according to its advocates, acts most intensely on nervous and impressionable females. What father of a family, then, would admit even the shadow of a mesmeriser within his threshold? Who would expose his wife, or his sister, his daughter, or his orphan ward, to contact of an animal magnetiser? If the *volition* of an ill-intentioned person be sufficient to prostrate his victim at his feet, should we not shun such pretenders more than lepers, or the uncleanest of the unclean? Assuredly the powers claimed by MESMER will eventually prove their own ruin. In endeavouring to raise themselves above ordinary mortals, they lay claim to attributes and powers which must place them, forever, beyond the pale of civilized society.'[32]

Mesmerism was regarded as disreputable, for all of these reasons, by important segments of middle-class opinion. To alienate that opinion would be damaging to the goals of Wakley and the reform party. Their struggle to upgrade the status of the medical profession would be badly, perhaps irretrievably damaged, if Elliotson and his followers were allowed to continue their experiments without reproach by the profession. Mesmerism was moral leprosy which contaminated the persons and institutions it touched.

Nowhere was this attitude better shown than in the debate amongst the medical students of University College on 4 January 1839, over whether or not to support Elliotson in his dispute with the Council. The discussion centred on a single issue: Irrespective of the truth or falsity of mesmerism, how badly had the reputation of the institution been damaged by Elliotson's experiments? A speaker named Mr. George summed up the case against Elliotson:

> 'Carried on as mesmerism had been, in defiance of the whole profession, it must be injurious to the institution. Mesmerism was so disgraceful to the character of a public institution—so derogatory to the dignity of a physician—so opposite to everything that should have been expected from Dr. Elliotson—that he blamed the Council for not having stopped it before.'[33]

Confronted with the potential damage to their College, and possibly to their careers, a number of Elliotson's devoted students apparently had second thoughts about his work. While the pro-Elliotson organisers of the meeting had expected the students to vote three- or four-to-one for his retention, in fact they split just about evenly.

Both because of their challenge to medical theory and practice, and also because of their threat to the social and political goals of the reformers, medical mesmerists were regarded by orthodox practitioners as deviants, who were outside the boundaries of professional respectability in the 1840s. However, the story of mesmerism in Victorian Britain does not end quite so abruptly. It has a curious addendum.

Braid and Hypnotism

In 1843 the Manchester surgeon, James Braid, published a book on mesmeric phenomena, which he called 'hypnotism.'[34] He argued that the lower phenomena are induced by the suggestion of the operator, acting on the imagination of the subject. (He did not believe that the 'higher' phenomena existed.) In spite of the good sense of Braid's book, and his later articles, he was denounced by Elliotson's party, and largely ignored by orthodox medical men.[35] The reasons for his rejection tell us something further about the limits of medical thought in the 1840s. Elliotson and his followers held tenaciously to a physical model of explanation because non-somatic explanations of disease, even of nervous disorders, were not considered to be professionally respectable. To embrace Braid's explanation, they would not only have had to renounce their earlier commitment to a fluidist theory, but also to surrender one of their last ties to the mainstream of medical thought. Such an imaginative leap was too much, even for Elliotson. As for orthodox medical men, their unwillingness to take Braid seriously is further evidence that what troubled them about mesmerism went far beyond the particular theory which explained its phenomena. By 1843 they were unwilling to be associated with mesmerism regardless of how it might be re-christened or re-interpreted.

After Braid's death in 1860, hypnotism and animal magnetism disappeared as topics of debate amongst medical men. In the 1870s and 1880s, however, the work of several French physicians on hypnotism attracted the interest and eventually the respect of their colleagues. At Salpêtière Hospital in Paris, Jean-Martin Charcot, the prestigious medical director, began hypnotic experiments on hysterical women in 1878. The culmination of his work was a paper presented to the Académie des Sciences in 1882, which was very well received. Charcot argued, as had Elliotson, that mesmeric phenomena were produced by physical means. In Nancy, meanwhile, Hippolyte Bernheim, Professor of Medicine at the University, and Auguste Liébeault, a private practitioner, also carried on experiments with hypnotism. In contradistinction to Charcot, Bernheim argued, as had Braid, that hypnosis was the product of suggestion. Although the substance of the debate was a recapitulation of positions that had been defined by previous debators, both in France and in England, the setting was rather different. It took place entirely within the professional community. The disputants were all medical men; they wrote in medical journals and spoke before reputable professional organisations; and they managed to avoid association with hucksters.[36]

Renewed interest in the topic, as a result of the reports on the French work, and the appearance of several books in English[37] induced the British Medical Association, in 1891, to establish a committee of prominent medical men to investigate hypnotism. Their report was cautiously favourable. In several key paragraphs, the investigators revealed the extent to which their guarded interest was tempered by memories of the mesmeric controversies a half century earlier:

'The Committee have satisfied themselves of the genuineness of the hypnotic state. No phenomena which have come under their observation, however, lend support to the theory of "animal magnetism."

'The Committee are of opinion that as a therapeutic agent hypnotism is frequently effective in relieving pain, procuring sleep, and alleviating many functional ailments.

'The Committee are of opinion that when used for therapeutic purposes its employment should be confined to qualified medical men, and that under no circumstances should female patients be hypnotised, except in the presence of a relative or a person of their own sex.

'In conclusion, the Committee desire to express their strong disap-
probation of public exhibitions of hypnotic phenomena, and hope that
some legal restriction will be placed on them.'[38]

As long as hypnotism's ties with animal magnetism were severed,
its therapeutic scope was limited, and its practice was confined to
medical professionals, British medical men were willing to consider it.
In 1893, the entire BMA, in a decision that reflected its tentative view
of the subject, agreed to 'receive' the report but not to endorse it.
Nevertheless, this was the beginning of hypnotism's emergence as a
legitimate medical procedure. What had changed was not so much the
theory or even the practice of hypnotism, but rather the professional
community that received it. By the 1890s, the British medical profession was established legally rather than struggling for acceptance, and
hypnotism was not associated with a dangerous popular culture
phenomenon as mesmerism had been. Moreover, etiology and therapeutics were not areas of contention as they had been, and the
profession was not beset by such fundamental challenges as it had been
in the 1840s. In short, the acceptance of hypnotism as medically
respectable in the 1890s and after is a measure of change, less of the
theoretical differences between mesmerism and hypnotism than of the
boundaries of the profession from the 1840s to the 1890s.

Professional Deviants and the History of Medicine

Finally, I wish to suggest how this perspective on professional
deviants might have meaning for the history of medicine generally.
Historians of medicine have so deeply internalised a correspondence
theory of verification and the 'march of progress' historiography that
proceeds from it that they are largely unaware of how this has restricted their vision of the past. They often refuse to acknowledge—
or even consider—that medical knowledge is not received in pristine
form by disembodied intellects. Rather it originates and is judged
by men who, both singly and in groups, have traditions, prejudices,
and ambitions that influence their judgement. Usually, these norms
are powerful but unexpressed. Because they are not articulated,
they are rarely visible to historians. But when they are challenged,
medical men, like all men, articulate these norms. They are like
fortifications that suddenly appear when the citadel is under attack.
Thus conflicts over knowledge-claims can reveal to historians, as
archaeologists of the mind, a part of the hidden mentality of the past;

Terry M. Parssinen

and professional deviants can show him where to start digging.
The research for this paper was supported by grants from the
American Philosophical Society and the Temple University Faculty
Senate.

Temple University, Pennsylvania.

[1] E. Maple: *Magic, Medicine, and Quackery*, London, 1969; E. Jameson:
The Natural History of Quackery, C. C. Thomas, Springfield, Illinois, 1961;
W. G. Rothstein: *American Physicians in the Nineteenth Century: From
Sects to Science*, Johns Hopkins University Press, Baltimore, 1972.

[2] Jacques Quen: 'Case Studies in Nineteenth Century Scientific Rejection:
Mesmerism, Perkinism and Acupuncture', *Journal of the History of the
Behavioural Sciences*, 1975, p. 154.

[3] Jacques Quen: 'Mesmerism, Medicine, and Professional Prejudice',
New York State Journal of Medicine, Vol. 76, 1976, p. 2222.

[4] William J. Goode: 'Community Within a Community: The Professions',
American Sociological Review, Vol. 22, 1957, pp. 194-200.

[5] Kai T. Erikson: *Wayward Puritans: A Study in the Sociology of Deviance*, Wiley, New York, 1966.

[6] J. Quen: op. cit., 1976; Jon Palfreman: 'Mesmerism and the English
Medical Profession: A Study of Conflict', *Ethics in Science and Medicine*,
Vol. 3, 1977.

[7] Robert Darnton: *Mesmer and the End of the Enlightenment in France*,
Harvard University Press, Cambridge, Massachusetts, 1968.

[8] Fred Kaplan: ' "The Mesmeric Mania": The Early Victorians and
Animal Magnetism', *Journal of the History of Ideas*, Vol. 35, No. 4, 1974, pp.
691-702; George Rosen: 'John Elliotson, Physician and Hypnotist', *Bulletin
of the Institute of the History of Medicine*, Vol. 4, 1936, pp. 600-603; John H.
Harley: *Doctors Differ*, London, 1946.

[9] *Zoist*: 'Cures of Epileptic and Other Fits with Mesmerism', Vol. 1, No.
4, 1844, pp. 407-469.

[10] John Elliotson: *Numerous Cases of Surgical Operations without Pain in
the Mesmeric State*, London, 1843; James Esdaile: *The Introduction of Mesmerism as an Anaesthetic and Curative Agent, into the Hospitals of India*,
Perth, 1852.

[11] Erwin H. Ackerknecht: *Therapeutics from the Primitives to the Twentieth Century*, New York, 1973; Alex Berman: 'The Heroic Approach in 19th
Century Therapeutics', *Bulletin of the American Society of Hospital Pharm-
acists*, Vol. 11, No. 5, 1954, pp. 321-327.

[12] J. Evans Riadore: *On the Remedial Influence of Oxygen or Vital
Air . . .*, Churchill, London, 1845.

[13] Samuel Flood: 'On the Power, Nature, and Evil, of Popular Medical
Superstition', *Lancet*, Aug. 16, 1845, pp. 179-181; Aug. 23, 1845, pp. 201-204.

14 *London Medical Gazette*: 'On the Absurdities of Mesmerism', Aug. 23, 1844, pp. 704-706.

15 *Lancet*: 'Who are the Quack Fanciers', Sept. 20, 1845, p. 328.

16 *London Medical Gazette*: 'Mesmerism Exposed', July 26, 1844, p. 575.

17 *Lancet*: 'Mesmerism', Sept. 8, 1838, pp. 834-836; *Provincial Medical and Surgical Journal*: 'Letter to the Editor', Aug. 12, 1843, p. 417.

18 John Elliotson: 'On Valentine Greatrakes and Local Mesmerisation', *Zoist*, Vol. 3, 1845, pp. 98-102.

19 W. J. Bishop: 'The Evolution of the General Practitioner in England', in E. A. Underwood (ed.): *Science, Medicine and History*, Oxford University Press, London, Vol. 2, 1953, pp. 351-357; Charles Newman: *The Evolution of Medical Education in the Nineteenth Century*, Oxford University Press, London, 1957; Paul Vaughan: *Doctors' Commons: A Short History of the British Medical Association*, London, 1959.

20 *Lancet*: 'Remuneration of General Practitioners', June 1, 1839, pp. 382-383; *Lancet*: 'On the Present Mode of Remuneration in the Medical Profession', May 13, 1843, p. 235.

21 *Lancet*: 'State of the Medical Profession', Feb. 5, 1841, pp. 655-656.

22 Eliot Freidson: *The Profession of Medicine*, Dodd Mead, New York, 1970.

23 *Lancet*: 'Progress of Medical Reform', Jan. 4, 1840, p. 539.

24 *Lancet*: 'Medical Officers Under the Poor Law', July 9, 1842, pp. 524-525.

25 *Institute*: 'Mesmerism', Dec. 7, 1850, pp. 228-229; *Provincial Medical and Surgical Journal*: 'Quackery and its Pretension', Sept. 9, 1843, pp. 490-492.

26 *Lancet*: 'The Lancet in 1846', July 4, 1846, p. 16.

27 *Lancet*: 'Animal Magnetism; or Mesmerism', Sept. 1, 1838, pp. 805-814; *Lancet*: op. cit., 1838, 'Mesmerism'; J. F .Clarke: *Autobiographical Recollections of the Medical Profession*, London, 1874, pp. 155-194.

28 George Sandby: *Mesmerism and its Opponents*, London, 1848.

29 Terry M. Parssinen: 'Mesmeric Performers', *Victorian Studies*, Vol. 21, No. 1, 1977, pp. 87-104.

30 *Medico-Chirurgical Review*: 'Animal Magnetism', 1839, pp. 630-631; *Medical Times*: 'On Mesmerism', July 13, 1844, p. 311; *Dublin Journal of Medical Science*: 'The Early Irish Mesmerists', 1847, pp. 254-271.

31 J. F. Ferrier: 'Postcript to Eagles's Article, "What is Mesmerism?"', *Blackwood's*, Vol. 70, 1851, p. 84.

32 *Lancet*: 'Animal Magnetism', Dec. 15, 1838, p. 450.

33 *Lancet*: University College and Hospital', Jan. 12, 1839, p. 594.

34 James Braid: *Neurypnology: or the Rationale of Nervous Sleep, Considered in Relation with Animal Magnetism*, Churchill, London, 1843.

35 John Elliotson: 'Case of a Contracted Foot with Severe Pain, Cured with Mesmerism', *Zoist*, Vol. 3, 1845, pp. 339-379.

[36] Maurice M. Tinterow: _Foundations of Hypnosis, from Mesmer to Freud_, C. C. Thomas, Springfield, Illinois, 1970; Peter W. Sheehan and W. P. Campbell: _Methodologies of Hypnosis; a Critical Appraisal of Contemporary Paradigms of Hypnosis_, Lawrence Erlbaum, New York, 1976; H. F. Ellenberger: _The Discovery of the Unconscious: The History and Evolution of Dynamic Psychiatry_, Basic Books, New York, 1970.

[37] Charles L. Tuckey: _Psycho-Therapeutics: or Treatment by Sleep and Suggestion_, Bailliere, London, 1889; George C. Kingsbury: _Practice of Hypnotic suggestion: Being an Elementary Handbook for the use of the Medical Profession_, Wright, Bristol, 1891.

[38] J. Milne Bramwell: _Hypnotism: Its History, Practice and Theory_, Rider, London, 1921, pp. 36-37.

SCIENTIFIC CONTROVERSY AND SOCIO-COGNITIVE METONYMY: THE CASE OF ACUPUNCTURE

A. J. Webster

'Groups of roving troubadours of acupuncture are giving acupuncture lectures and sideshows.' H. A. Ross, 1973.

CONTEMPORARY research in the sociology of science expresses a strong though theoretically diverse commitment to an explanation of the social and conceptual factors effective within the evolution of scientific disciplines and specialisms.[1] Recent work has been especially interested in such issues as: how is the conceptual marginality of fields defined according to the jurisdictional boundaries between scientific professions?;[2] under what conditions is conceptual migration stimulated and when does it generate new areas of research?;[3] to what extent does the speed and direction of research within and between disciplines depend on the cognitive structure of those disciplines?;[4] and so on. Such questions have promoted an increasing interest in scientific controversies wherein the complex relationship between social and conceptual factors is perhaps more visibly displayed, expressed in terms of explicit (at times, hostile), negotiation over particular orthodox and heterodox knowledge-claims advanced by identifiable groups.[5] The specific processes associated with scientific conflict and controversy reveal general socio-cognitive patterns describing the promotion and degeneration of scientific specialisms. With this in mind, this paper reports on the current controversy within Western allopathic medicine over the status of Chinese acupuncture.

This paper introduces the notion of 'socio-cognitive metonymy'. As a figure of speech a metonymic expression occurs when a part stands for the whole, and where that which signifies the whole is intrinsically correspondent with or contiguous to the signified: for example, within a monarchy a crown is a sign for sovereignty. Though contiguous the elements of the expression are not necessarily reducible to one another. Accordingly, the phrase 'socio-cognitive metonymy' posits a contiguous but non-reducible relationship between cognitive and social processes whereby the constitutive features of scientific cognition are effectively signified by and in part genetically linked to the social processes of the scientific institution. The heuristic value of the concept is that it indicates the socio-cognitive production and legitimation of knowledge-claims in science without requiring that the rather problematic distinction be made between 'purely' cognitive practices and 'purely' social practices. The paper suggests the conditions under which socio-cognitive metonymy occurs by reference to the professionalist strategies through which orthodox allopathy establishes its jurisdictional boundaries relative to acupuncture.

The paper proposes that there is a metonymic or contiguous relationship between those social and conceptual processes that delimit the medical status of acupuncture. This metonymic dynamic is especially apparent in professionalisation and specialism strategies that allopathic and non-allopathic groups adopt. It is argued that such strategies reveal the competition between and within medical groups for the ownership and control of a particular form of social capital, i.e. scientific knowledge. I shall describe how orthodox allopathic groups—in particular neurophysiologists, anaesthesiologists, and dentists—can move into a new area of research conventionally perceived as being nonscientific without devalorising, and indeed actually revalorising, their ownership of scientific capital.[6] Tactics designed to maximise this form of capital are discussed and shown to be conditioned by specific factors. In general, these factors indicate that the present state of acupuncture in Western medicine is neither purely the result of scientific inquiry nor wholly determined by the ideological interests of the medical professions: these scientific and social processes are mediated through each other. The first task is to describe the development of the controversy over acupuncture and the latter's contemporary status.

Before 1972, acupuncture analgesia had relatively little exposure in the major Western medical journals. Within the West, research was confined to three mid-European private medical centres, (France Sweden, and Germany), and the lack of English language reports restricted the flow of information about ongoing experiments at such centres. Reports from China, often only available as highly condensed English abstracts in the *Chinese Medical Journal*, prompted little response from Western allopathy, despite the not insignificant claim that from 1958-1970 over 400,000 operations had been successfully performed in China using acupunctural analgesia. Most of the papers and correspondence published in Western European, American, and Australian medical journals by members of allopathic specialisms questioned the significance of the Chinese reports. Substantively, the papers argued, first, that acupuncture 'meridians' and 'needle-points' had no objective basis,[7] and second, that consequently acupuncture's pain killing power if it did exist at all, must be based on some form of hypnosis and/or placebo mechanism, not the putative meridians.[8] The first argument involved an explicit ontological investment in Western neurophysiology and anatomy. The meridian theory of classical acupuncture proposes that there are twenty-six energy ('Ch'i') circuits in the body all of which need to be in balance if the body is to be healthy. The analgesic capacity of the acupuncture needle derives from its ability to block the flow of energy along the meridian circuits. The links between different parts of the body described by the meridians do not conform to any Western neurological models. The latter typically favour a mechanistic energy theory that specifies measurable physical and chemical reactions between proximate segmental neurological structures of the body.[9] Thus the explanatory models provided by neurophysiology and acupuncture have generally been regarded as incompatible. The belief that acupuncture was based on hypnosis involved a psychogenic interpretation of the Chinese claims of analgesia that effectively relegated acupuncture to the para-medical domain of psychosomatics. Prior to 1972, therefore, acupuncture was placed at the margins of medical practice, and, more importantly, medical research; neurophysiological models remained intact.

Events occuring during 1972, however, quickly altered the situation. James Reston, columnist and vice-president of the *New York Times,* developed acute appendicitis while on a visit to China. He received acupuncture therapy for post-operative complications and his report of its success was syndicated in most of the national American press. After Reston's report, a group of prominent neurophysiologists and anaesthetists visited China as guests of the Chinese Medical Society. Here they witnesed and were later to report the use of acupuncture as an analgesic in major surgery. Media coverage of Nixon's call on acupuncture clinics during his own trip to China was particularly important in generating widespread public interest in the technique, especially from those suffering with chronic disorders who requested that it be made generally available. The official response by the

American medical elite came in terms of an announcement from the National Institutes of Health of a '. . .commitment to study the use of acupuncture in surgical anaesthesia and in the treatment of pain resulting from chronic disorders.' This led to an injection of State funds, the very availability of which in part legitimated experimentation in acupuncture. The new and extensive interest was not restricted to the United States. Scientific gate-keepers in Western Europe, Canada, and Australia called for research in the area in line with the American national policy statement.[10] From 1971-6 there was an exponential growth in research, a four-fold increase in publications over the period. By 1975 there had accumulated approximately 1200 contributions almost 50% of which were published in English.

Since 1972 papers have attended not so much to the ontological status of traditional or classical acupuncture accounts but to the experimentally specific issue of producing statistically significant tests of acupuncture analgesia.[11] This does not necessarily mean that an ontological commitment to Western neurophysiology had been abandoned through research, merely that this was given virtually no formal expression in the literature; there were some notable exceptions.[12] The new tests focused on pain, its mechanism, measurement, and control. There had already been a long history of research into this area by orthodox neurophysiology, so there was readily available a large body of literature the findings of which could be, and were, brought to bear on the acupuncture problem. Investigation in this area gave rise to a number of neurogenic, e.g. 'neurohumoural', as opposed to the earlier psychogenic theories of analgesia, explanations originally developed to cope with problems generated by previous neurophysiological research. Requiring little adaptation these theories were generally considered to handle most of the anomalies of acupunctural analgesia. Thus, for example, the 'Gate-control theory' of 'presynaptic inhibition', first devised in 1965[13] was, and still is, regarded as being one of the most likely explanations of the analgesia.[14] Areas of research now include measuring the electrical sensitivity of acupuncture points and the general electromagnetic field of the body (particularly through the use of Kirlian photography), tests of alternative types of acupuncture, such as sonopuncture, and the production of double-blind control studies of the nature of placebo mechanisms and the bodily sensation as opposed to electronic registering of pain. In short, from 1972 to 1976 research on acupunctural analgesia expanded rapidly as a variety of allopathic specialists moved into the area, defined the problems, and established both formal and informal channels of communication such as the British Medical Acupuncture Society, and the *American Journal of Chinese Medicine*.

Though the cognitive disjunction between Western neurology and traditional acupuncture was gradually set aside as allopathic investigators developed an interest in experiment-design problems associated with the measurement of pain and its alleviation, the general research status of acupuncture remained problematic. As a modality with a long and rather hybrid heritage[15] acupuncture was already constituted as a medical practice for a number of 'marginal' groups, including homeopaths, naturopaths, osteopaths, and chiropractors. Typically, members of such groups had used acupuncture along with other modalities as a therapy for the relief of chronic pain, such as migraine, and were not primarily concerned with investigating the analgesic properties of the needles. They nevertheless constituted a significant Western population who had a strong interest in any attempts to define the socio-cognitive status of the modality. Hence, given these existent, albeit 'marginal', groups, the post-1972 allopathic intervention does not exemplify what has been called a 'movement into a new area of ignorance'.[16] The allopathic investigation made research problematic from the beginning: the inquiry must not be seen as an association with and tacit support of marginal groups. The problem, then, for orthodox specialists, particularly neurophysiologists and anaesthesiologists, was to generate knowledge claims about acupuncture without risk to their ownership of social capital, expressed in the forms of institutionalised professional reputation: one of the first knowledge-claims made was that acupuncture be considered a 'medical practice' and thus for the sole use of licensed, i.e. allopathic, practitioners,[17] the irony of which was not lost on at least one traditional acupuncturist.[18] The socio-cognitive strategies whereby the allopathic intervention was legitimated remain concealed within the rather eliptical commentary offered by an eminent British neurophysiologist who, in private correspondence, declared that 'Since we are in a position of power, I would have thought that we could magnanimously adopt certain aspects of folk medicine without feeling threatened.' Though it is true that the effective challenge of traditional acupuncture would always be circumscribed by the existent professional structures of institution-alised medicine, the widespread and prolonged use of professionalist strategies by allopathic groups ensuring non-identification with 'marginalism' indicates that more than magnanimity was required to exercise a legitimated patronage over acupuncture research.

The primary interests of traditional acupuncturists within medical groups were similarly mediated through proto-professionalist strategies designed to increase their ownership of scientific capital expressed in terms of (non-marginal) medical 'competence'. The following remarks to be found in the British Acupuncture Association's 1976 *Year Book*, typify proto-professionalism: the Association informs its inquirers that '(It) is concerned to have official registration for all qualified acupuncturists and is actively pursuing this policy. If an acupuncturist does not appear in this register, please check his qualifications. If in doubt please contact us and we will obtain information for you. Do not go to a quack. You may be harmed by people with inadequate training.'

In short, it is suggested that the various professionalist strategies adopted by both orthodox and marginal groups to specify what can be called the 'research-programmatic' of acupuncture express historically the development of the controversy and signify analytically the process of socio-cognitive metonymy in science.

The stance of medical orthodoxy to marginal groups will vary according to a number of considerations, including: a) the range of alternative marginal groups in existence at any one time; b) the relative size, popular support, and political influence of each group; c) the extent to which the competitor group is unified on all fronts; d) whether the group's leadership is effective; and e) whether the marginal group strives to maintain independence from orthodoxy or seeks some sort of alignment with, or perhaps complete incorporation within the dominant medical profession.[19]

The decision for independence or incorporation does not involve unproblematic alternatives. Coe[20] has described the predicament faced by marginal groups:

> To obtain public acceptance, (. . . a group must . . .), among other things, be able to legitimise its own existence through performing certain functions which characterise its uniqueness. In some cases, however, this very uniqueness or individuality may prevent the acceptance by the public, which has been conditioned to some other professional groups

> which perform similar functions. Thus to obtain public recognition, (the group) must give up some of its uniqueness . . . In doing so, (it) risks becoming merged with allopathic medicine, but in a minority status.[21]

The significance of those features listed above (a-e) is that they relate directly to the process of professional monopolisation through which occupational groups maintain and protect the exchange-value of their (mental) labour over and against that of other groups providing the 'consumption-market' of medical knowledge. A number of tactics have been employed by groups seeking acceptance, though of course, allopathy has been the most successful in this regard.[22]

First, in terms of the restriction of group membership within the medical occupation there is the tendency towards the creation of scarcity through the institutionalisation of licensing procedures which control the number of agents allowed to practise medicine. Secondly, educational institutions are established to monopolise the control of the production of medical knowledge as a saleable commodity.[23] Thirdly, the elimination of external competition is sought through a) denouncing as false the knowledge-claims that marginal groups advance—i.e. as 'quackery'; b) legal moves to force the political machine, (governmental agencies, State licensing Boards in the U.S.A.), to act against competitors; and c) insisting on a higher ethical pedigree such that ethical claims improve the marginal utility of (usually allopathic) knowledge-claims for the consumer of medicine. Fourthly, strategies are also encouraged that regularise the potential for, or better, minimise the possibility of fractioning within the group through intra-group competition for scientific capital: one such strategy involves a normative ideology that demands members' elective obedience to a putative set of professional ethics. Finally, the status of medical knowledge as a saleable commodity—the condition of its level of consumption on the public market—depends on the degree to which its producers justify the separation of the practice of their medical skill from the satisfaction of their clients' health interests. The socialised acceptance of this separation has in practice legitimated the notion that the provision of allopathic medical care does not guarantee a cure for ill-health. This means that the supply of allopathic medicine can be sustained even though it does not reflect the demands of its consumer market. The point about these monopolisation tactics is that they are not confined to the consumption market of medical science: they express processess directly associated with knowledge production and certification within medical science itself, which are then continued into the professional-lay situation. These internal processes are connected with specialisation.

Freidson[24] has argued that the specialism boundaries within medical science are not derived from differences in conceptual inquiry or the control of technical resources alone, but rather, are more a reflection of 'conventional institutional distinctions that have grown up out of the way in which specialisation happened to have developed in a particular market place, organised in a historically specific way.'[25] These distinctions are patterned upon 'jurisdictional boundaries' which define the parameters, and to some extent the hierarchy, of the various medical sciences. I suggest that such boundaries reflect the fragmentation of scientific labour—i.e. the specialisation of production. As such, specialisation represents an institutionalised factor of control in the competition for scientific capital: it not only allows for the privatised group ownership of scientific capital, but also protects a group's possession of such capital.

There are different risks attached to the movement into an area of research: those richest in scientific capital (the elite, the scientific 'gate-keepers') who sponsor, both through their call on material resources and through the association of their professional reputation, a new field of inquiry, are at greatest risk for they face the possibility of an almost complete devalorisation of their scientific capital, particularly when the new area threatens to subvert the reigning conceptual paradigm, i.e. threatens the existing distribution and control of scientific capital.[26]

Different specialist groups can move into an area of research through different forms of capital investment. The three most important groups of allopathy involved in acupuncture research are neurophysiologists, anaesthesiologists, and dentists.[27] These specialisms represent highly developed fields of medical inquiry, both in terms of their professional academic research traditions and technical resources. Dividing the research on acupuncture analgesia into two areas, the technical or *practical efficacy of* acupunctural analgesia and its *conceptual significance,* then I suggest that the intervention of these groups in acupuncture research has involved a process of selecting between the two areas of inquiry in such a way as to maintain and revalorise each group's ownership of scientific capital.

Here, I shall indicate briefly how this process informed the participation of dental specialists in acupuncture research.

Thus, dentists have been especially concerned with the *technical* potential of acupuncture. Papers by dentists have been particularly concerned with the practical demonstration of acupuncture as a therapeutic aid in the control of pain. The papers are typically reports on the use of 'double-blind control studies' of acupunctural analgesia, and acupuncture is indicated, or acceptable in practice so long as the tests demonstrate the 'statistical significance' of the technique's efficacy relative to other forms of induced analgesia.

I suggest that we can explain the dentists' concern with such technicist matters through reference to the jurisdictional boundary of dentistry relative to neurophysiology. In an important sense, dentistry involves the practical implementation of the conceptual models provided by theoretical neurophysiological research: it is, in a sense, parasitical on this research. In concentrating on the practical utility of acupuncture as a technique, dentistry maintains its boundary of competence relative to neurophysiology, thereby posing no threat to the status of theoretical neurological models, while simultaneously appropriating the scientific value of acupuncture according to its own form of scientific capital production.

Dentists have been able to maximise the potential gain in scientific capital that is available to their own specialism through engaging in strategies of socio-conceptual conservation and subversion. First, on the conservation side, the researchers have minimised the challenge acupuncture might pose to conventional techniques used by practitioner dentists by advising that it requires little training to master. And yet secondly, on the subversive side, the researchers have been the first to invest their scientific reputations in a new area of research within allopathy and will therefore be those members of the specialism who will be recognised as the experts in the area, enjoying the material and conceptual capital such recognised expertise brings.

Furthermore dental specialists have successfully defined acupuncture as being peripheral to the specialism ostensibly because of its restricted technical practicability with regard to analgesia induction: anaesthesiologists, as will be seen, considered this to be a crucial issue in the debate. Finally, within the field of dentistry itself, the competition between groups to produce 'statistically significant' results depends on those groups' respective access to a particularly important form of scientific capital: the research laboratory in a dental school or hospital.

The general proposition can be made that the theoretical and practical scope of acupuncture did not depend primarily upon the theoretical and technical propositions or observations investigators produced: its 'research-programmatic' was more the product of specialist and professionalist strategies adopted by allopathic groups. At first glance, the notion that the scientific status of acupuncture depends solely on the quality of the research seems reasonable; but this belief must be challenged, since, from 1972, propositions have been developed in the course of allopathic investigation that could have generated a number of radically different research programmes. Though research conducted by prestigious and core members of specialisms led, for example, to a recognition of the potential disciplinary status of acupuncture—the more radical of these investigations even suggested the complete overthrow of conventional neurophysiological models[28]—despite this, it has generally been allocated the rather minimal programmatic status of a para-medical therapy with restricted analgesic usage.

I suggest that the gradual definition of acupuncture as a limited analgesic and therapeutic technique represents the process of reducing the cost of entry into the area for allopathic groups, where 'cost' is measured in terms of the scientific capital required for entry. The non-field status of acupuncture meant that traditional acupuncturists' knowledge-claims had little effect on the scientific capital reproduced within the disciplinary structures of professionalised allopathy. Within the conceptual arena of scientific practice, this social reduction in cost was effected by a distantiation from the potentially revolutionary theoretical significance of acupuncture through a concentration on its technical utility and efficacy as an analgesic.[29] Papers appearing during the period 1972-5 were much more concerned with claims and counter-claims about secondary, environmental implications of acupuncture than with claims over its primary theoretical implications for neurophysiology.[30]

In the United States, the reduction in the cost of entry for orthodox allopaths simultaneously increased the entry cost for traditional acupuncturists: because acupuncture was defined as a 'medical practice' by official Federal and State Medical Boards, it could only be practised by licensed physicians or by the traditional acupuncturist working under the supervision of a physician. Thus acupuncturists had to qualify as physicians or assume the inferior status of para-medical technical assistants to licensed doctors. Furthermore, Federal licensing and training requirements introduced in 1973 in effect cost the acupuncturists their traditional theory since the authorities considered that 3-6 weeks training was sufficient for a doctor to be licensed to practise the technique: most acupuncturists consider that full knowledge can come only after three to six *years* of intensive instruction in not only the technique of acupuncture but also the 'ancient' Taoist philosophy of life.

A similar situation has developed in the U.K., the British Acupuncture Association, with the majority of its practitioners working in England, has only three fully registered members who are orthodox licensed doctors in a total population of 186.[31] None of the higher officers of the Association are orthodox doctors. In this situation the insistence of neurophysiologists that acupuncturists must first be registered doctors poses a threat to the legitimacy and cohesion of the Association. Most of its members have practised various modes of marginal medicine—chiropratic, naturopathy, homeopathy, herb-alism—for many years. Though it is true that all members of the Association work independently, controlled only in a limited way by the Association,[32] they nevertheless regard it as the main public platform through which their various medical practices, including acupuncture, may be legitimated. Members of the Association have privately told of their strong resentment against the Medical Acu-puncture Society, whose membership consists entirely of licensed allopaths. The ostensible reason for their hostility is based on the allegation that the Society does not give its members sufficient training in traditional Chinese philosophy and its relationship to diagnostic techniques used in acupuncture. Like their American counterparts, the British Association claims that in China it takes 3 years to be a Western trained doctor in comparison with 5 years to be an acupuncturist, though Riddle[33] would dispute this assertion.

A significant feature of the debate is that interested parties profess certain norms such as universalism and disinterestedness in an attempt to establish the ethical pedigree of their research procedures. Such norms were originally identified by Merton[34] as crucial components of an institutionalised 'scientific ethos.' Merton emphasised the importance of norms and values as institutional mechanisms of social

A. J. Webster

control guaranteeing scientific progress, and, more importantly, the maintenance of a meritocratic, democratic, and informally organised social system of science. Merton claimed that the norms are derived from and encouraged the development of scientifically efficacious 'technical' or methodological norms. Mulkay[35] has argued, however, that the Mertonian portrayal of the function of norms is based on an unjustified assumption, i.e. that *verbally* professed values have an *institutionally* warranted significance for rewards. In support of Mulkay's position that norms be regarded merely as standardised verbal formulations, during the progression of the acupuncture debate, both allopathic and marginal groups deploy a variety of normative principles that champion both universalism, impartiality, and disinterestedness, and at the same time opposing norms such as particularism and the necessity of subjective and emotional involvement in research. What is significant here is that both sets of norms have been used by one or another of the groups involved as justifications before specific audiences—both professional and lay—for their involvement in the constitution of acupuncture's research-programmatic. The analytical problem is that of specifying the conditions under which medical scientists tend to adopt certain norms in preference to alternative counter-norms. Norms can be seen to be primarily associated with specialist and professionalist interests, and, insofar as they successfully promote a group's interests then they function as an ideological resource in the competition for scientific capital. Within the medical profession it is likely that some groups deploy a rhetoric of norms more effectively than other groups. In short, normative claims can be envisaged as a strategic ideology in support of a professional status. In the interchange with lay society, orthodox medical scientists, as all other scientists, advocate the neutrality, practical 'pay-off', and independence of their science, all prominent values of the 'ethos.' The declaration is delivered in such a way, however, as both to challenge the relevance and experience of public regulation and yet to ensure their continued financial sponsorship from public funds. Medical allopathy has carved out for itself a special political status that minimises the liability and necessity for accountability to the public. This status was won in particular through the ideological deployment of the norm of 'service', closely associated with those monopolisation tactics discussed earlier.

As suggested, within medical science itself certain groups have more successfully employed the rhetorical use of norms for the protection of their socio-cognitive status. This has occurred in the course of the investigation into acupuncture. For example, traditional acupuncturists agree with the position generally adopted by Western allopathy that acupuncture research should go hand in hand with conventional neurophysiological investigation. This prescription is typically legitimated through the profession of the norms of universalism and impartiality,[36] the argument being that a scientific acupuncture can only be established in accordance with universal and impersonal criteria. But, from their institutionally stronger position, allopathic specialists measured normative conformity not so much in terms of the respect that any given researcher has for the technical and moral norms of science, but rather in terms of an investigator's willingness to accept the allopathic control of research.[37] This professionalist strategy clearly involves a socially divisive use of the norms of universalism and impartiality. From the late 1960s to around 1972 orthodox Western specialists complained that traditional acupuncturists did not abide by the norms of openness and impartiality, relying instead on popularisation and sensationalism to attract support for their technique.[38] This complaint featured predominantly in the editorial columns of the medical journals. Gradually, however, after 1972, the normative rhetoric rapidly disappears from the literature. Tentatively, it is suggested that its relative absence was due to acupuncture being restricted in the West to the rather poorly defined status of a para-medical therapy, under the control of licensed allopathic practitioners. Through establishing both informal[39] and formal[40] control the scientific capital of orthodox neurophysiology and anaesthesiology not only remained intact but was actually revalorised both materially, in terms of increased public funding and renewed and expanded control of the consumption market, and cognitively, in terms of the development of new neurological models of the mechanics of pain and its control.

By way of summary, the paper has suggested that competition for what has been called 'scientific capital' occurs, first, within the productive sector of the scientific enterprise promoting the fragmentation of labour expressed in terms of specialisation strategies. Secondly, this competition is augmented to include the consumption market and is displayed through professionalisation tactics. Within the productive sector the power of any one allopathic specialism is significant not only inasmuch as it indicates a crystallisation of recognition at group level, but also insofar as it can be used to gain new facilities and resources and thereby extend its own hegemony. This suggests that rank-ordering within medical science tends towards an oligopolistic structure. Within this structure particular specialisms enjoy a structurally favorable position with regard to the receipt of recognition which *as such* is *independent* of the quality or significance of work produced. Weingart[41] touches on this when he notes:

> The fact that evaluation processes are consolidated in the institutional structure indicates the tendency towards the independence of reputation. It, in turn, retroacts, mediated by institutional factors, on the evaluation process.

This situation clearly exhibits socio-cognitive metonymy, since the scientific and social practices exist in an inter-mediate relationship wherein the signifiers of the one practice are continually transformed into the signifiers of the other practice, and vice versa. Weingart's argument is supported by the discussion of the acupuncture controversy, for, as was argued, the process through which knowledge claims were evaluated was only a partial reflection of decisions based on criteria of scientific adequacy: a primary determinant of the research-programmatic of acupuncture were the specialist and professionalist strategies deployed by the dominant allopathic groups, both internally among their number, and externally, against the marginal traditional acupuncturists. It was further noted that the influence of a rhetorical appropriation of norms depended on the relative strength of the groups competing for scientific capital: hence the norms of universalism and impartiality, professed by *both* marginal and allopathic groups, were more effective as legitimators of the professionalist claims of the latter group.

The prospects for traditional acupuncture are somewhat restricted. The current neurophysiological position is that it could possibly be accepted as a therapeutic modality or 'reflexotherapy.' This would give it the same sort of paramedical status as basic physiotherapy. Its practical anaesthetic capabilities are considered so inferior to conventional anaesthesia that there is little possibility of its being used extensively for surgery in America or Britain.

In conclusion, it is suggested that the mediated relationship between social and cognitive processes is exhibited most clearly in situations of controversy, particularly when orthodox and marginal groups are involved, for then the influence of professionalist strategies on the acceptance and rejection of knowledge claims can be identified with greater facility.

University of York.

1 For a recent overview see G. Lemaine *et al.* (*eds.*): *New Perspectives on the Emergence of Scientific Disciplines*, Mouton, Paris, 1976.

2 D. Robbins and R. Johnston: 'The Role of Cognitive and Occupational Differentiation in Scientific Controversies', *Social Studies of Science*, Vol. 6, 1976, pp. 349-368.

3 N. C. Mullins: 'The Development of a scientific Specialty', *Minerva*, Vol. 10, 1972, pp. 51-82; M. J. Mulkay: 'Conceptual Displacement and Migration in Science', *Science Studies*, Vol. 4, 1974, pp. 205-234.

4 T. E. Huff: 'Theoretical Innovation in Science', *American Journal of Sociology*, Vol. 79, 1973, pp. 261-277.

5 S. S. Duncan: 'The Isolation of Scientific Discovery: Indifference and Resistance to a New Idea', *Science Studies*, Vol. 4, 1974, pp. 109-134.

6 For a full discussion of the notion of the production of knowledge-claims as the competition for scientific capital, see P. Bourdieu: 'The Specificity of the Scientific Field and the Social Conditions of the Progress of Reason', *Social Science Information*, Vol. 14, 1975, pp. 19-47.

7 M. Kelly: 'Some Medical Myths', *World Medical Journal*, Vol. 11, 1964, pp. 205-207.

8 I. Veith: 'Acupuncture Therapy: Past and Present', *Journal of the American Medical Association*, Vol. 180, 1962, pp. 478-484.

9 M. Porkert: *The Theoretical Foundations of Chinese Medicine*, M. I. T. Press, Cambridge, Massachusetts 1974.

10 *Lancet*: 'Editorial: 20th-Century Acupuncture', June 17, 1972, p. 1321.

11 B. Lynn and E. Perl: 'Tests of Acupuncture', *Proceedings of the Physiological Society*, 1974, pp. 83-84; L. C. Mark: 'Double-Blind Studies of Acupuncture', *Journal of the American Medical Association*, Vol. 225, 1973, p. 1532.

12 A. Taub: 'Acupuncture', *Science*, Vol. 178, 1972, p. 9.

13 R. Melzack and P. Wall: 'Pain Mechanisms: a New Theory', *Science*, Vol. 150, 1965, pp. 971-979.

14 S. A. Andersson: 'On Acupuncture Analgesia and the Mechanism of Pain', *American Journal of Chinese Medicine*, Vol. 3, 1975, pp. 311-334.

15 J. M. Quen: 'Acupuncture and Western Medicine', *Bulletin of the History of Medicine*, Vol, 49, 1973, pp. 196-205.

16 M. J. Mulkay: 'Three Models of Scientific Development', *The Sociological Review*, Vol. 23, 1975, pp. 509-523.

17 J. W. Riddle: 'Report of the New York State Commission on Acupuncture', *American Journal of Chinese Medicine*, Vol. 2, 1974, p. 293.

[18] C. P. Li: 'A Policy Towards Chinese Medicine', *American Journal of Chinese Medicine*, Vol. I, 1973, p. 689.

[19] W. Wardwell: 'Orthodox and Unorthodox Practitioners: Changing Relationships and the Future Status of Chiropractors', in R. Wallis and P. Morley (eds.): *Marginal Medicine*, London, 1976.

[20] R. M. Coe: *The Sociology of Medicine*, McGraw-Hill, New York, 1970, p. 219.

[21] The distinctive feature of acupuncture is the philosophy behind the 'meridian' theory. At the British Acupuncture Association's annual conference (1975), York, a traditional acupuncturist declared: 'We welcome research so long as it maintains the notion of meridians', and when asked about the possible incorporation of acupuncture into the National Health Service an informant replied, 'If acupuncture was used throughout the N.H.S. imagine the difficulty this would bring about. Overnight we would have a great deal of acupuncture without its philosophical basis.'

[22] For a detailed historical account of the strategies of professionalist monopoly in medicine see, J. Berlant: *Profession and Monopoly*, California University Press, London, 1975.

[23] The establishment of medical schools has been a crucial factor in the search for acceptance pursued by marginal groups, as is well demonstrated by the 'Report of the Committee for the Study of the Relations between Osteopathy and Medicine', *Journal of the American Medical Association*, Vol. 152, 1953, pp. 734-739.

[24] E. Freidson: *Doctoring Together*, Elsevier, New York, 1975.

[25] ibid., p. 71.

[26] See A. De Grazia (ed.): *The Velikovsky Affair*, University Books, New York, 1966 and the account of the dismissal of Gordon Atwater from his positions as Curator of Hayden Planetarium and Chairman of the Department of Astronomy at the American Museum of Natural History for recommending that Velikovsky's book *Worlds in Collision* be published.

[27] Taken together, these groups account for approximately 70% of all published results and correspondence. See B. and M. Tam: *Acupuncture: An International Bibliography*, Scarecrow Press, New Jersey, 1974, and; D. L. Davis: 'The History and Sociology of the Scientific Study of Acupuncture', *American Journal of Chinese Medicine*, Vol. 3, 1975, pp. 5-26.

[28] G. Looney: 'Autonomic Theory of Acupuncture', *American Journal of Chinese Medicine*, Vol. 2 1974, pp. 332-333.

[29] From 1972-75, the literature is dominated by communications about the statistical significance of acupuncture as a successful analgesic compared to placebos, hypnosis, and the use of chemical drugs.

[30] Thus, anaesthesiologists criticised the environmental implications of acupuncture inasmuch as they claimed it works only on patients who have been 'preconditioned' to the analgesic powers of the needle, thus that it cannot be used in an emergency when the patient is unconscious, causes unnecessary pain with manipulation of internal organs during surgery, may transmit disease because of insufficiently sterilised needles, and finally needle insertions may damage vital organs.

[31] Figures correct at October 1975.

[32] The Association claims that it 'guarantees the training and ethics of a practitioner'.

[33] Riddle: op. cit., p. 303.

[34] R. K. Merton: 'Science and the Social Order', *Social Theory and Social Structure*, Free Press, New York, 1968.

[35] M. J. Mulkay: 'Norms and Ideology in Science', *Social Science Information*, Vol. 15, 1976, pp. 637-56.

[36] A. Feibel: 'Acupuncture: Dilemmas, Problems, Perspectives', *Archives of Physical Medicine and Rehabilitation*, Vol. 55, 1974, pp. 524-525; W. B. Shute: 'East meets West', *Canadian Medical Association Journal*, Vol. 107, 1972, pp. 1002-1003.

[37] L. R. Rice: 'Letter: Acupuncture', *New Scientist*, 1972, p. 262.

[38] D. N. Goldstein: 'The Cult of Acupuncture', *Wisconsin Medical Journal*, Vol. 71, 1972, pp. 14-15.

[39] The President of the British Acupuncture Association has stated that the *British Medical Journal* will not publish research reports submitted by traditional acupuncturists. Obviously the Editor could assert that such reports were not worthy of publication according to certain criteria of scientific adequacy.

[40] On February 21, 1973, the U. S. Federal Food and Drug Administration required that acupuncture needles and electronic equipment be labelled 'For investigational use by licensed medical or dental practitioners only'.

[41] P. Weingart: 'On a Sociological Theory of Scientific Change', in R. Whitley (ed.): *Social Processes of Scientific Development*, Routledge and Kegan Paul, London, 1974, p. 59.

THE POLITICS OF OBSERVATION: CEREBRAL ANATOMY AND SOCIAL INTERESTS IN THE EDINBURGH PHRENOLOGY DISPUTES

Steven Shapin

Hamlet: Do you see yonder cloud that's almost in shape of a camel?
Polonius: By the mass, and 'tis like a camel, indeed.
Hamlet: Me thinks it is like a weasel.
Polonius: It is backed like a weasel.
Hamlet: Or like a whale?
Polonius: Very like a whale.

A widely distributed conception of scientific knowledge is that it is generated, and acquires its objective character, by processes of disinterested contemplation. The effect of social interests on knowledge would be to distort reality, hence such interests are not expected to attend the production of knowledge which we regard as reliably scientific.

In the past, historians of science wrote as if they universally subscribed to such conceptions. More recently, however, some historians of science have been able to exhibit in detail the political and social interests that have informed the general styles, orientations, metaphors and *Weltanschauungen* of certain pieces of scientific knowledge.[1] With few exceptions,[2] the newer social history of science leaves itself open to the sometimes legitimate (often pedantic) charge that it has not shown the presence of social interests in the esoteric and technically most detailed content of that knowledge.

Thus, the concrete practice of even the more sociologically-minded historians of science might serve to reinforce the following conclusion: social factors can inform only certain layers of scientific work—the 'theoretical scaffolding' of scientific work, but not the esoteric, and really detailed, scientific content. This wuold be to subscribe to a version of empiricism, with its well-known fact-theory dichotomy. The short-comings of such a dichotomy have been widely publicised by detailed demonstrations of the ways in which theory and fact, or style and content, are intimately connected in one interacting network of meanings Likewise the conclusion that a social analysis must stop at the point at which knowledge begins to reflect or correspond to directly observed fact is not binding on historians. The present paper aims to display the influence of social interests on an esoteric body of scientific knowledge. Specifically, it treats the rapid growth of the knowledge of cerebral anatomy in the context of the disputes over the validity of 'phrenology' in the Edinburgh of c. 1800-c. 1830.

This paper also aims to bring out a further point. It is indeed difficult for historians of science to detect the operation of social interests in the detailed knowledge generated by their subjects. There may be a reason for this; one which relates the historian's predicament to the actual role of social interests in the generation of knowledge. In many cases the reason may be that for the actors, just as for most historians, the identification of such interests would have left that knowledge open to the charge of bias—of not being knowledge at all. In the Edinburgh disputes over phrenology, as in most other scientific contexts, a participant could hope to discredit the knowledge of his opponent by detecting the presence of social interests in it. Where the effect of social interests on knowledge is held to be corrupting, the display of the presence of such interests in knowledge seems a sound strategic move. Of course, a controversy between interested parties, both of whom subscribe to this conception of knowledge and who deploy this strategy, will be one where interests are either obscured or minimised.[3] That is, each party may actually encounter or prefigure an 'exposure of interest' by its opponents. Each party's reaction may then well be to produce accounts in which it becomes more and more difficult for its opponents to expose interests. There is a risk of apparent sophistry in making this point: one does not propose immediately to infer from the absence of apparent interests to their real presence, but, rather, to introduce a further tactic into the search for such interests, viz. the realisation that it may be the operation of such interests which has been responsible for their very invisibility. Of course, this process must itself be historically identifiable, and it will be one of the aims of the present paper to show it at work.

What follows is divided into eight parts. In the first I briefly introduce the nature and historical origins of phrenology. In the next two I situate certain controversies over the status of phrenology in a defined local social and ideological context—the Edinburgh of the first three decades of the nineteenth century. I then examine a series of four increasingly esoteric issues in cerebral anatomy which were objects of dispute in the Edinburgh context, and I conclude by offering some speculations of general relevance to our conceptions of the relationship between social interests and esoteric bodies of knowledge.

Phrenology: *Its Doctrines and Origins*

The roots of phrenology may almost certainly be traced to Lavater's eighteenth-century physiognomical system of judging character from facial appearance, and probably penetrate even deeper, into folkloric techniques of psychological imputation. But the formal, codified corpus with which we are concerned here owed its origins to the work of two German-born, Vienna-trained physicians—Franz Joseph Gall (1758-1828), and his associate Johann Gaspar Spurzheim (1776-1832).[4] Working first in Vienna as a physician to a lunatic asylum, Gall developed a 'cranioscopic' system upon which he lectured to fashionable audiences, before the lectures were banned in 1802 by an Austrian government concerned about their tendency to the subversion of religion. From 1804 he was assisted in anatomical researches by Spurzheim, shortly undertaking a joint lecture tour through Germany, before settling in Napoleonic Paris, where Gall remained for the rest of his life. Spurzheim, who popularised the name 'phrenology' and who had major conceptual disagreements with Gall, was the main agent of the system's dissemination abroad, especially to Great Britain and the United States, where it developed in different directions from the Continental formulation and obtained massive popularity.[5]

The major tracts on the new system began to appear in Paris from 1810, but even as early as 1803 the *Edinburgh Review* could rhetorically ask its readers: 'Of Dr Gall, and his skulls, who has not heard?'[6] British medical men and scientists began to be apprised of the debate then raging in France over Gall and Spurzheim's claims in 1806,[7] and, in 1809, general publicity was given to the findings of an inquiry conducted into Gall and Spurzheim's neuro-anatomical work by a committee of the French National Institute, under the auspices of the eminent comparative anatomist Cuvier.[8] The massive *Anatomie et physiologie du systême nerveux en général et du cerveau en particulier* was published from 1810 to 1819, and from 1822 to 1825 Gall brought out his *Sur les fonctions du cerveau*.[9] In 1815 Spurzheim rendered the elements of the system accessible to English-speaking readers with his *Physiognomical System of Drs. Gall and Spurzheim*,[10] and, when, in 1816, he arrived in Britain for the first time, the controversy with which we are concerned here was set alight, raging through the 1810s and 1820s until phrenology was effectively rejected as a scientific system in the 1830s.

As phrenology's intellectual structure and historiography have been fully detailed elsewhere,[11] I shall confine myself here to a brief synopsis of its three fundamental tenets. First was the contention that the brain was the organ of the mind. In itself an unexceptional proposition at the beginning of the nineteenth century, it might be seen (in Gall's case, quite rightly) as the foundation of a materialist programme, intended to assert the non-existence of an immaterial soul. Certainly, both Continental authorities and the Presbyterian Kirk in Scotland were put on their guard by this primary phrenological claim. Second, the phrenologists argued that the mind was not a single psychological entity, nor was the brain a single unified organ. Rather, the brain was a congeries of organs, topographically distinct, each of which subserved a distinct mental function. Thus, there was an organ of 'adhesiveness', the role of which was to manifest individuals' tendency to cling to surrounding objects, such as one's house. Another organ subserved 'hope'; yet another expressed 'philoprogenitiveness' (the tendency to procreate and nurture children). In various phrenologists' systems the number, naming and location of organs varied, but in the period we are discussing there were generally agreed to be from 27 to 33 such organs, displayed on phrenological busts and skulls like that shown in figure 1. The third basic dictum of phrenology was that, all things being equal, the size of the cerebral organ was a measure of the power of its functioning. In other words, if one had a large organ of 'amativeness', one might tend towards 'la disposition fortes à l'amour physique'. Similarly, an unusually small organ of 'tune' tended to render its possessor insensible to melody or even make him tone-deaf. An important corollary of this doctrine was that the contours of the skull were shaped by, and followed, the variations in the sizes of the underlying cerebral organs, so that one could diagnose innate mental make-up from the 'bumps' and depressions apparent on the exterior surface of the skull.[12]

Again, it is impossible here to go into great detail about how Gall and Spurzheim derived their 'organology', but it is important in this connection to stress that it was *not* by means of cerebral anatomy—the investigation of actual structures in the brain and on its surface. Three sources for the organology were repeatedly mentioned by Gall and Spurzheim. Gall himself liked to emphasise how he observed clear correlations between the behaviour of his school-mates and their external cranial contours. Later on, he and Spurzheim displayed busts and portraits of individuals celebrated for certain traits and abilities, pointing out their possession of the appropriate 'bumps'. Thus, engravings of Chaucer ('ideality' large) and Locke ('ideality' small) were crucial visual confirmation of the organology. The second alleged line of research derived from cranial comparative anatomy. The skull shapes of various animals were displayed as evidence of their accurate reflection of the beasts' 'known' psychic and behavioural attributes. Thus, the 'bump' for amativeness is appropriately large in rabbits; that for 'cautiousness' is well-reflected in the crania of birds. And, finally, 'knowledge' of racial and sexual traits was also brought to bear in the construction of an organology. 'Veneration' was found to be large amongst the superstitious and credulous Negroid races; 'amativeness' was well-known to be small in women.[13] This sort of evidence, which correlated structure and function and made each illuminate the other, the phrenologists liked to term 'physiological', and it was by physiological, and not by anatomical, investigations that the enumeration and mapping of organs was achieved. The skull did *not* require to be opened up and the brain displayed in order for the system to be established. Gall, as Temkin reveals, made his conjecture about the multiplicity of cerebral organs years before he undertook anatomical research on the brain.[14]

Phrenology and Social Interests in Edinburgh

Phrenology was in one sense a system of psychological diagnosis, a technique for discerning mental characteristics from external appearances. But if it had been merely a diagnostic tool, phrenology would never have aroused the intensely polemical opposition, and gained the wide public acceptance, which we know it did. Nowhere was critical reaction to the phrenological system more virulent than in the Scottish capital of Edinburgh, which was likewise the capital for the dissemination of the British form of phrenology to a popular audience.

As we know, phrenology was not merely a diagnostic tool. It was very rapidly developed by Spurzheim and his Scottish disciples into the foundations of a far-reaching programme of social and cultural reform. This explicit development took time, although George Combe's characteristic interest in educational reform and the de-mystification of academic mental philosophy began to appear very shortly after Spurzheim's 1816-17 visit to Edinburgh.[15] Gall and Spurzheim's Continental system was, as we have seen, well known in Edinburgh from at least 1803. At the time of Spurzheim's first English publication in 1815 phrenology already appeared as an anti-establishment 'breaker' of systems; as an anti-academic, scientistic de-mystifier of idealist philosophies; as a materialistic *bête noire* of spiritual religions; and as a deviant new body of neuro-anatomy. Although Scottish phrenology clearly developed in response to local social and cultural conditions, its initial image in the Edinburgh of 1815 situated it quite clearly in a system of conflicting social interests. It was this system which provided the context for the development of phrenology into an explicit social programme, and which was the background against which the Edinburgh disputes over technical anatomical issues occurred.[16]

The introduction and early career of phrenology in Edinburgh has been well detailed by Cantor.[17] The 1815 publication of Spurzheim's *Physiognomical System,* and his subsequent visit to Edinburgh to publicise the doctrine, triggered the initial outburst of local criticism and resulted in the recruitment of his major British convert, the lawyer George Combe (1788-1858). From 1815 until the end of the 1820s phrenology was under almost continuous siege from Edinburgh intellectuals. The city was very well equipped to combat a deviant new system of mental science. It was the home of a great scientific and philosophical University, with a world-renowned clinical medical school; it had Royal Colleges of Physicians and Surgeons, as well as numbers of highly qualified 'extra-mural' lecturers in anatomy and surgery. Edinburgh's politically and culturally dominant legal corporations were practically concerned with the springs of human behaviour, and their favoured schema was the Scottish Common-Sense philosophy taught in the University by Dugald Stewart, and defended in the *Edinburgh Review* by his Whig disciples.

In an earlier paper I offered an interpretation of the Edinburgh phrenology debate which linked conflicting social interests in the city to the career of the new system.[18] As I wish to use that analysis as background to the technical anatomical issues with which this paper is mainly concerned, I shall offer here only the most sketchy synopsis and refer the reader to that paper itself for substantiating evidence.

There were four main ways in which adherence to phrenology, and critical reactions towards it, were related to social interests in early nineteenth-century Edinburgh.

(1) Phrenology can be fairly precisely located on a social map of the city from the 1810s to the 1830s. Phrenological doctrine (and practice) proved markedly more attractive to 'outsider' intellectuals, and to their audience of superior working-class and petty-bourgeois groups, than it did to establish elites. The University professoriate universally condemned it; as did the Established Kirk, the *Edinburgh Review*ers, and the upper echelons (but by no means all) of the legal and medical professions. The ability to map phrenology in this way follows from its development into an instrument serving certain social interests.

(2) The phrenological system of Gall and Spurzheim was initially attractive to these 'outsider' intellectuals as a symbolic system which could be used as a juxtaposition to the institutionalised mental philosophy of local elites. Precisely because phrenology proceeded from the identification of what was innate in the human constitution, and because it identified the limits of human plasticity, it could be used to criticise the Enlightenment environmentalism of the Scottish Common-Sense philosophical tradition whose ideology reigned supreme among Edinburgh elites in the 1810s and 1820s.[19] Thus, phrenology furthered the symbolic expression of disaffected groups in Edinburgh, insofar as it could be seen as the 'not—x' to the 'x' of elites.

(3) Phrenology in Edinburgh was developed as the naturalistic basis for a programme of social change and institutional reform which served the interests of those groups which espoused it. The programme, broadly speaking, was to the right of the Owenites and to the left of the Whigs. The development proceeded in this manner: only when the actual innate constitution of an individual mind was scientifically diagnosed could rational and effective social policies be designed to improve individual behaviour, and, by extension, to ameliorate the social condition. Only when one knew the 'limits' could one move within what 'nature' allowed. George Combe and his Edinburgh colleagues thus elaborated a vast programme for the re-distribution of rights, privileges and priorities within British society, which followed from the premise that one could assess innate character scientifically, and then act to shift it in the desired directions. Edinburgh phrenologists

developed and lobbied for changes in the provision of education, for penal reform, the more effective treatment of the insane, 'enlightened' colonial policies, and a more humane system of factory production (identifying the disastrous consequences of capitalist exploitation of labour for the workers' psychic well-being).[20]

(4)   Finally, the phrenological system of naturalistic psychology and sociology amounted in Edinburgh to an important social statement about the boundaries of participation in literate culture and commented upon the access of social groups to certifiable natural knowledge. One could, the phrenologists claimed, be fitted to employ the system in a day. The reason one could was that phrenology, like the other recognised natural sciences, was based upon observation, and, therefore, upon capacities common to *all* competent members of society. It was not, like the mental philosophy of the universities, based upon the mystifying and biassed 'method' of introspection. Hence, the ability of any competent member to 'read-off' innate character from the exterior of the skull was central to the phrenologists' social programme, and was in itself a proposition of great social significance. It re-defined the boundaries which had separated disaffected social groups from a source of crucial legitimation. An observation-based psychology opened up the social system, by opening up access to resources for its criticism and change.

These are the lines along which one can say that the debate that took place in Edinburgh during the 1810s and 1820s was basically structured by conflicts between social interests—even, to some extent, by 'class' interests. It was, in this interpretation, fundamentally a dispute over the distribution of rights and privileges in society, and it was as a symbolic and technical *instrument* in that dispute that the validity of phrenology as natural knowledge was assessed.

The Role of Anatomy in the Edinburgh Disputes

However much one feels it correct to stress the primacy of social interests in structuring the career of the Edinburgh disputes over the status of phrenological knowledge-claims, there is no reason to deny that many aspects of the controversy centred upon highly technical and esoteric cerebral anatomical matters. In certain of these issues it is extremely difficult for historians to discern the action of wider social interests. Hence, there is the temptation to divide the Edinburgh disputes into those aspects influenced by social interests and those informed solely by idle curiosity. Before proceeding to discuss four increasingly esoteric issues in cerebral anatomy, it is necessary to make some general introductory remarks on the status of the phrenologists' anatomical work and the circumstances under which cerebral anatomy entered into the Edinburgh controversy.

Almost needless to say, no one currently believes that one can read-off character traits from the exterior of the skull, in the manner the phrenologists claimed. Phrenology is an approved object of laughter for psychologists and intellectual historians. But the cerebral and neuro-anatomy the phrenologists generated and defended is not, and was not then, entirely an object of derision. 'Truth', as historians of medicine and science are prone to use the notion, does not lie wholly on one side in the phrenology disputes. Especially as regards the fine structure of brain tissues, the phrenologists are frequently admitted to have 'got it right'. Some historians have argued that Gall and Spurzheim contributed to the progress of cerebral anatomy by focussing attention on the problem of cerebral localisation of function, which was then subjected to 'disinterested' inquiry later in the nineteenth century.[21]

Yet contemporaries and historians, while often disposed to 'give credit' to the phrenologists for acute observations, are prone to prise apart what they regard as true and worthwhile in the phrenologists' anatomy from the 'illegitimate' interests with which the observations were associated. Thus, Clarke and Dewhurst, amidst jocular references to cranioscopic claims, allow that Gall was 'an outstanding anatomist'[22] and the great medical historian Erwin Ackerknecht has gone so far as to say of Gall that 'his anatomy still stands, while his physiology has fallen long ago'.[23] The partisan biographer of one of the most bitter Edinburgh opponents of phrenology's anatomical basis admitted that, before Gall and Spurzheim, there was general 'ignorance of [the] minute structure of the brain.'[24]

Cuvier, one of the arbiters appointed by the National Institute of France to adjudicate Gall and Spurzheim's claims, credited the two with some original observations which were correct and further instances in which they provided confirmation of existing ideas of cerebral and neural structure. But Cuvier, like Ackerknecht and Clarke, was at pains to point out that 'the anatomical questions with which we have been engaged in this report, have no immediate and necessary connection with the physiological doctrine taught by Dr. Gall . . .'.[25] What was true, in other words, had no apparent relationship to the 'illegitimate' interests of the observers.

The second prefatory point I wish to make is that the role of the phrenologists' cerebral anatomical work in the Edinburgh context was secondary and derivative. We have already seen that Gall himself developed the organology from other resources. Andrew Combe, the Edinburgh phrenologist-physician, after vigorous defence of the anatomical findings in phrenology's favour, asserted that the system 'rests almost entirely upon physiological evidence'.[26] In addition, no phrenologist (arguably including Gall himself) was primarily concerned to further disinterested advance in the knowledge of cerebral anatomy.[27] While knowledge of brain anatomy advanced during the Edinburgh controversies, no British phrenologist sought to do more than to master and defend the anatomical foundations laid down by Gall and Spurzheim. Spurzheim, who carried the system to Britain, made his interest in cultural warfare and institutional change apparent from the outset.[28] George Combe records how, in his first encounter with phrenology, at Spurzheim's 1816-17 Edinburgh demonstrations, 'he saw, from the first, that the new doctrines if true, were eminently practical; and he earnestly and deliberately, and through many difficulties, set about the task of ascertaining whether nature supported them or not.'[29] No Edinburgh phrenologist—not George Combe, his brother Andrew, Sir George Stewart Mackenzie, nor the numerous local contributors to the *Phrenological Journal*—undertook research in cerebral anatomy, except to *defend* specific components of the system. On the other hand, the Edinburgh phrenologists were assiduous in using the anatomical 'evidence' as a naturalistic resource in an increasingly elaborate and confident programme of social policy. Indeed, they constantly expressed their Baconian belief that the utility of knowledge was the only true test of its validity.[30] The success of the social programmes would prove the correctness of phrenology's anatomical basis. Thus, in terms of the founders' accounts of how phrenology was established, in terms of the motives of those who did anatomy in the phrenological context, and in terms of the hierarchy of interests in the phrenological movement, cerebral anatomical research was derivative and secondary.

What I shall do now is to present a series of four cerebral anatomical issues discussed during the Edinburgh disputes. The issues are ordered so that each appears more esoteric and arcane than the one preceding; each takes us literally 'deeper' into the structure of the brain; and each seems more difficult to connect with wider social interests. So we can, if we like, conceive of the following as a trip into the interior of the brain, and a trip away from the apparent action of social interests on technical bodies of knowledge.

The Frontal Sinuses

The frontal sinuses are cavities between the two tables of the cranial bones, situated above and to the sides of the nose. Although their filling up with fluid is now known to contribute to the symptoms of many a 'common cold', the sinuses were not, at the beginning of the nineteenth century, subjects of medical interest nor of any significant anatomical curiosity. Alexander Monro, then professor of anatomy at Edinburgh University, depicted the frontal sinuses in 1783 as 'stylised', almost perfectly circular structures, no attention being paid to them in the accompanying text.[31] Gall and Spurzheim also paid little attention to the frontal sinuses prior to the Edinburgh controversies. Figure 2, taken from their 1810 *Atlas,* illustrates the *sphenoidal* and *ethmoidal* sinuses (situated below no.38), but the frontal sinuses are not indicated at all. Although Edinburgh phrenologists showed themselves to be generally aware of the frontal sinuses from very early on,[32] their local critics were far more intrigued by this feature of cranial anatomy. Figure 3 shows how anti-phrenologists in Edinburgh 'saw' the frontal sinuses. The relevant point to note here is that the sinuses, wherever they extend, create non-parallelism between the two tables of the cranial bones. It is also evident from figure 3 that care has been taken to depict them in a naturalistic, as opposed to a stylised, manner.

Notice the implications of structures which cause non-parallelism. Wherever there is cranial non-parallelism, at that point there is no reason to expect that the exterior contours of the skull reflect the contours of the underlying brain surface. And, if the exterior of the skull gives an imperfect account of what lies underneath, then phrenological diagnosis is impossible.[33] One might, for example, find an individual with a big 'bump' over 'individuality' which was caused not by a big cerebral organ of 'individuality', but by the appropriately shaped sinus. More generally, any instance of imperfect parallelism between the two surfaces of the skull might be instanced as evidence of the futility of the phrenologists' diagnostic ambitions.

The Edinburgh anatomist John Gordon (1786-1818), in a scathing assault on phrenology in the 1815 *Edinburgh Review*,[34] maintained it to be common knowledge that 'the two surfaces of the bones which form the cerebral cavity of the cranium are not everywhere parallel to each other.' And, while Gordon, curiously, did not draw special attention to the frontal sinuses, he did generally contend that:

> . . . There are often considerable depressions within, where the corresponding surface without, does not exhibit the slightest appearance of projection, but is quite flat or even hollow; and that there are often large prominences without, where there are no corresponding concavities within . . .[35]

Gordon also faulted Gall and Spurzheim for failing to assign 'organs' to the inner surfaces of the temporal and occipital lobes, or to other surfaces of the cerebrum not facing the overlying cranial bone,[36] thus identifying other anatomical features which seemed to present problems for phrenological character diagnosis.

In 1824 the physician P. M. Roget critically reviewed 'Cranioscopy' in the *Supplement* to the Edinburgh-edited and published *Encyclopedia Britannica*,[37] pointing out difficulties in Gall and Spurzheim's claim that the 'bony processes' of the skull adapt 'themselves exactly to the form and size of the cerebral parts they are destined to inclose and protect'. Roget observed that there are several 'natural protuberances' on the skull which interfere with diagnosis—the mastoid processes (behind the ears), the zygomatic processes (just in front of the ears), the 'crucial spine of the occiput' (above the foramen magnum), and, most importantly, the frontal sinuses.[37a]

When, from 1826 to 1829, a sustained final assault on the anatomical basis of phrenology was mounted in Edinburgh, its leaders were the metaphysician Sir William Hamilton, Bart., (then professor of civil history and later professor of logic) and Thomas Stone (then a medical student). Both Hamilton and Stone focussed upon the issue of the frontal sinuses, their size, shape and distribution in the population.[38]

In a lecture at the University in 1827, Hamilton, who described himself as a 'mere interloper in anatomy', opened and displayed crania collected both by phrenologists and non-phrenologists. Hamilton contended (1) that no skull, including those collected by phrenologists, was totally devoid of the frontal sinuses; (2) that large sinuses were a normal structural feature, not a feature associated solely with old age and disease; (3) that one could not tell from external signs (such as a bony ridge) whether or not the individual in question had large sinuses; (4) that the frontal sinuses were of great extent, covering as many as one-third of the phrenological organs and that they 'interpose an insuperable obstacle to observation'.[39] Hamilton, well satisfied with his anatomical findings, was

> . . . not afraid, if Phrenology is found a *phantom* as to one-third of its organs, that it will prove a *reality* in respect to the other two.[40]

Hamilton and Stone's findings did not go unchallenged in Edinburgh. George and Andrew Combe replied to their critics and enlisted the help of Spurzheim, who undertook a second visit to the city. Their responses took several tacks. Edinburgh phrenologists first of all alleged that anti-phrenologists were incompetent to judge of the anatomical issues 'through deficiency of elementary information' and through 'partiality'.[41] They maintained that the sample of skulls selected by Hamilton, even those derived from their own collections, was unsuitable for the purposes at hand, and that Hamilton had not prepared the skulls in such a way as to exhibit the true structure of the sinuses.[42]

Before his chosen audience (a public assembly for 'the relief of the distressed operatives'), George Combe displayed a collection of skulls belonging to the Edinburgh Phrenological Society and to Syme, a prominent anti-phrenological anatomist.[43] Here he showed, to the evident satisfaction of members of the audience, (1) that departures from parallelism in the two tables of the skull were negligible; (2) that the frontal sinuses did not exist in young children; (3) that they did exist after puberty, but even then to a very limited extent (such as to present some difficulty in determining perhaps two organs (fig. 1, nos. 23-24); (4) that the sinuses were occasionally found to be very large, but only in the elderly and the diseased (these categories being routinely excluded from the ambit of phrenological diagnosis anyway).

'Appeals to nature', to the 'evidence of one's senses', were made by both sides, in a vain attempt to secure public consensus and the conversion of the heathen. Skulls were sawn open, along one axis and then along another, as well as being probed by needles. They were displayed to the interested of all classes and standing. Accounts of what was seen were published in the popular press, in medical journals, in the organ of the Phrenological Society, and in books and pamphlets for professional anatomists and the generally curious. Umpires to decide the issue by expert opinion were proposed by Hamilton and company, and an appeal to the general public was suggested by the phrenologists. A panel of umpires was duly appointed, but failed to come to a definitive finding.[44] A challenge to a *mano-à-mano* public dissection between Hamilton and Spurzheim was proposed by the latter, and declined. Exchanges grew increasingly acrimonious and undignified. Accusations of bad-faith and fraud mounted, as reality refused to be successfully negotiated, and the discussions finally collapsed in invective. Thomas Stone continued the assault into the 1830s, and George Combe intermittently responded, but it had by then long been clear that the phrenology controversy was not to be decided by appeals to anything so apparently problematic as 'nature' or the 'evidence of one's senses'.

The historian who wants to take advantage of modern knowledge in order to make his best *guess* as to how 'nature' figured in the accounts is in something of a quandary here. It is not easy to find modern medical texts which offer the sort of detailed information about the exact shape, size and demographic distribution of the frontal sinuses which (various) actors in the 1820s believed they possessed. One can argue that knowledge of these structures in fact reached its high point (although not consensus) in the context of these exchanges, and has since declined. No modern technical concern seems to require the sort of knowledge in which protagonists in the phrenology disputes evinced their interest. (In general terms, however, the standard modern teaching text *Gray's Anatomy* tends to support the phrenologists' account more than it does their opponents).[45]

That this knowledge was not generated by idle curiosity, and that this debate was not a manifestation of the intrinsic fascination frontal sinuses have for people, is readily apparent. If the sinuses were large and were universally distributed, then one could not *do* phrenological character diagnosis. And, if one could not do phrenological diagnosis, then one could not *use* it as a naturalistic resource for constructing a scientifically-legitimated social programme. This was a dispute in which anti-phrenologists attempted to demonstrate, through anatomical research, the impossibility of diagnosing structures (the cerebral organs) which, in any case, they did not believe *existed*. Hence, there is little problem in seeing what this anatomical dispute, in the course of which esoteric knowledge advanced so markedly, was, so to speak,

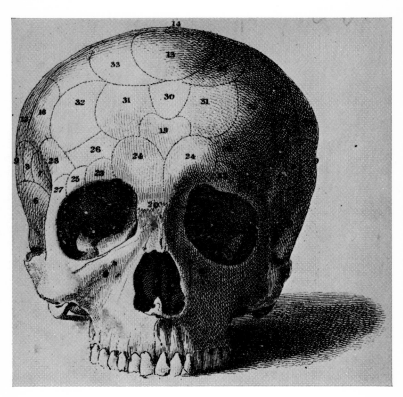

Figure 1

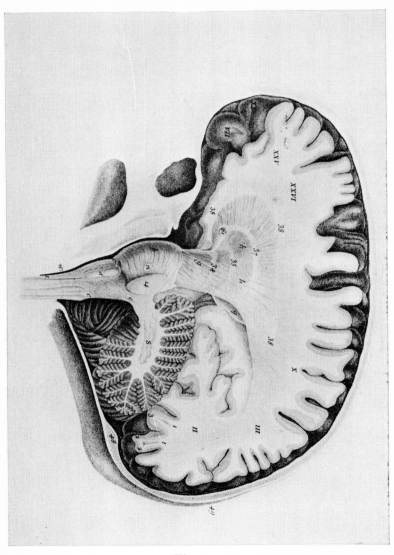

Figure 2

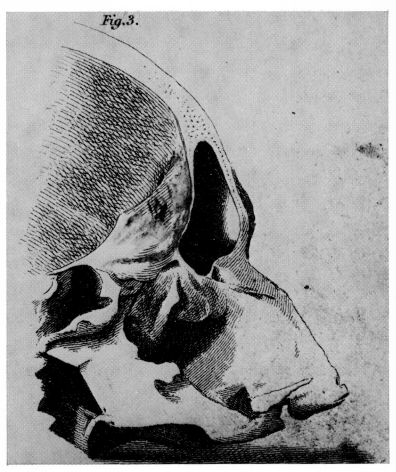

Figure 3

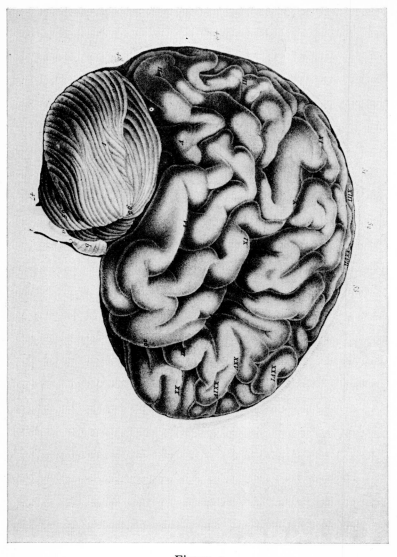

Figure 4

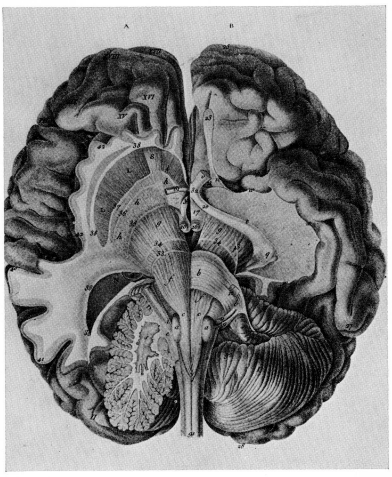

Figure 5

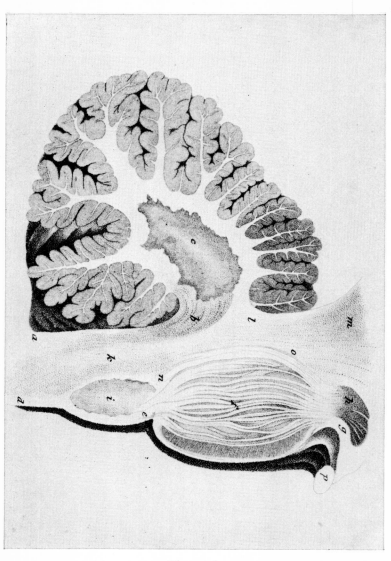

Figure 6

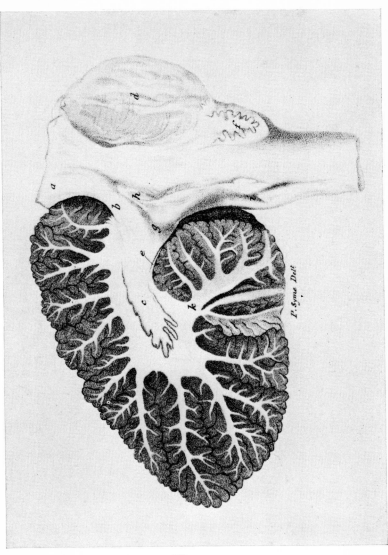

Figure 7

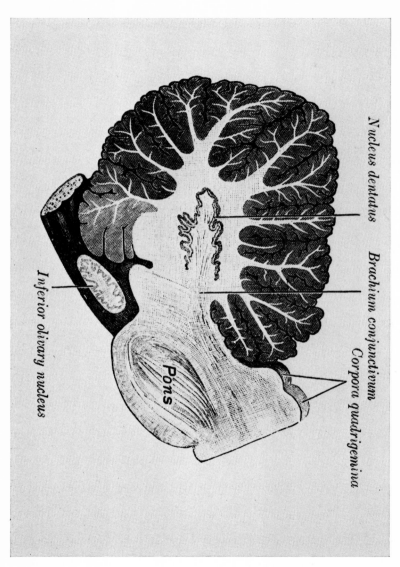

Figure 8

'all about'. The action of wider social interests in the controversy, and in the positions taken up by each side, are apparent. We see anatomical research as a clear deviation from normal practice for Hamilton, and to a lesser extent, for the Combes and Stone. Natural reality, as displayed by a properly sawn-open skull, would oblige one's opponents to accept as fact anatomical features uncongenial to their own interests. But as we have seen, perceptual accounts were quite open to question and the interests of the 'other group' were quite capable of being discerned in the accounts offered. Our 'anatomists' may have been common-sense realists, but perceptual accounts of reality were incapable of doing the job of social suasion the 'anatomists' required of them. This is a feature of all of the following anatomical issues to be discussed.

The Convolutions of the Cerebral Cortex

The convolutions of the cerebral cortex are the wavy surface features seen in figure 4. In previous centuries anatomists thought that the cerebral convolutions looked like intestines, and they used that 'syntax' to make pictorial statements about them.[46] The actual tissues of the convolutions are referred to as 'gyri' and the 'valleys' between them are called 'sulci or, if major, 'fissures'. At the beginning of the nineteenth century a few of the fissures had been recognised as constant from one individual to another, and symmetrical between right and left hemispheres, e.g. the fissures of Rolando and Sylvius.[47] But no functional significance was attached to the pattern of gyri and sulci, nor was it thought that there was a standard pattern of convolutions.

In his 1815 anatomy teaching text, written before Spurzheim came to Edinburgh, John Gordon expressed what seems to have been the general view:

> These Convolutions are seldom precisely alike, either in shape or size, in any two corresponding points of the opposite Hemispheres. In different Brains, I do not know that any two corresponding points, in either Hemisphere, have ever been observed exactly alike.[48]

This was all Gordon had to say on the subject; he did not offer a pictorial statement of how the convolutions appeared; there were no illustrations of any sort in the text. Despite the fact that Gall and Spurzheim's 1810 *Atlas* contained many engravings of the cerebral convolutions, Gordon had nothing to say on the subject in his

Edinburgh Review critique;[49] neither did he refer to the subject in his
1817 *Observations on the Structure of the Brain*,[50] which was a
concerted attempt to discredit the phrenologists' cerebral anatomy.

However, in 1822 John Barclay, the distinguished Edinburgh
anatomist who had taught both Gordon (now deceased) and George
Combe, treated the convolutions in his *Life and Organization*,[51] a
section of which sought to undermine the anatomical foundations of
phrenology. The phrenologists, said Barclay, have claimed real
existence for 'no fewer than thirty-three species of organs', yet

> If you ask for any ocular demonstration respecting the existence of these
> organs, you are told they are indicated by thirty-three modifications
> that have been observed in the form of the skull, and these occasioned
> by thirty-three modifications in the form of the brain . . .[52]

But, if one opened up the skull and inspected the cortical surface on
which these organs were said to be situated,

> it seems to require no small share of creative fancy to see any thing more
> than a number of almost similar convolutions, all composed of cineritious
> ['grey'] and medullary ['white'] substance, and all exhibiting as little
> difference in their form and structure as the convolutions of the
> intestine . . .

How could distinct cerebral organs be said to exist if there were no
cortical areas which were distinct in their appearance?

And what of the neat lines which bounded off one organ from
another on the busts manufactured by the phrenologists (e.g. fig. 1)?
'No phrenologist,' Barclay ventured, 'has ever yet observed the
supposed lines of distinction between them.' Where were these lines on
the gyri of fig. 4? Why had no phrenologist, during public dissection,
endeavoured to map the organology shown on busts on to the actual
cerebral cortex? The reason, Barclay was confident, was that it could
not be done.[53]

Moreover, Barclay argued that these supposed distinct organs could
not be morphologically distinguished. If one dissected a brain, and
separated out all the putative 'organs', then mixed them up and
presented them to a phrenologist, could he tell the dissociated organ of
'sentiment' from that of 'reflection'? Again, Barclay wagered that it
could not be done. Here, as in the instance of Hamilton and Stone on
the frontal sinuses, we have an attack upon the possibility of discerning
organs which were not even believed to exist.

The actual stand of the phrenologists on the connection between
their organology and the convolutions is not readily evident. None

of the engravings in Gall and Spurzheim's *Atlas* manifests an attempt
to display bi-laterally symmetrical standard pattern (e.g., Plate IX),
nor was there much of an attempt to display even the 'known' fissures.
Figure 4 clearly shows the fissure of Sylvius (running from roman
numeral IX to the lower right), but the fissure of Rolando is not
clearly indicated. Moreover, there are signs of an unwillingness to
associate specific organs with specific gyri. Note, for example, in fig. 4
that several roman numerals, indicating the area of an organ, straddle
gyri, e.g. VI, VIII, X and XI. Gall himself, long after the 1810
engravings were made, confirmed this:

> We acknowledge ourselves not yet in a condition to specify the precise
> limits of all the cerebral organs . . .[54]

This all appears to suggest that the phrenologists, initially at least,
were not ready to make a wager as to how the convolutions related to
their organs.[55]

Whatever Gall and Spurzheim's initial position had been, it was the
responsibility of their Edinburgh disciples to deal with Barclay's objections. Andrew Combe, not unnaturally, turned to Spurzheim for assistance. Quoting a personal letter from Spurzheim, Combe sought to
refute Barclay's suggestion that the brain appeared to be composed of
nothing more 'than a number of almost similar convolutions'.[56] How
should Barclay decide that distinguishing gyri was 'impossible, merely
because he has not examined it with due attention in nature'. Surely,
there was no difficulty in distinguishing the *lobes* of the brain from
each other? And could not all agree that the organ of amativeness,
which was the cerebellum (fig. 4, roman numeral I), was distinct from
the cerebrum proper? Perhaps, *close* observation would similarly
reveal morphological differences between gyri which had hitherto
been ignored. 'Dr. Barclay may be sure,' Spurzheim continued, 'that,
if he makes it a study to compare the configurations of the cerebral
convolutions, and of the different organs, he will find great differences,
which he has hitherto overlooked.' 'It will not be denied', Spurzheim
was quoted, 'that frequently some convolutions of the brain are much
more developed than others . . .'

Andrew Combe went on to describe a number of instances in which
phrenologists correctly diagnosed an individual's character, not from
his living skull, but from the appearance of his *brain* after death. He
himself was inclined to Barclay's view of the convolutions as 'nonsense' until his 'attention was directed particularly to this subject',

and he had 'seen many brains'. He had *learnt* to see 'the characteristic differences' to which he 'had not previously attended'.[57]

But what of the thought-experiment of identifying dissociated cerebral 'organs'? Here Spurzheim was bold in reply:

> . . . I maintain that he who has studied the forms of the peripheral expansions of the cerebral organs, will always be able to distinguish, in man, the organ of acquisitiveness from that of destructiveness . . . as easily as an ordinary observer will the olfactory from the optic nerve. I am ready at any time, personally, to verify the above statement.[58]

But there is no record that he did, or that anyone required him to do so.

On the question of a standard pattern of convolutions, the 'joke', as it were, was on both sides. What the phrenologists, under attack, weakly asserted, but always declined to display, was, within forty years, firmly established by Turner in Edinburgh and Ecker in Germany. To be sure, the patterns they mapped corresponded in no way to the phrenological bust, but then, perhaps the bust would have looked differently had the phrenologists endeavoured to map the convolutions. Later in the century, histological studies (by Betz, Lewis and Ramón y Cajal) established differences in the cellular constitution of different cortical areas.[59] Historians of medicine are almost right when they claim that phrenology focussed attention on the problem of the convolutions.[60] However it was not the phrenologists, but their opponents, in an attempt to discredit the system, who focussed their attention on the convolutions, and *they* made a 'wrong' guess about the possibility of discerning an 'image in the clouds'. The phrenologists, under duress, ultimately made the 'right' guess, but either were not confident enough to pursue it, or felt its pursuit might jeopardise their investment in the existing organology. In the end, their strongest statement was this:

> The general form and direction of the convolutions, even of the human brain, in its complications, are, in fact, remarkably regular.[61]

The connection here between social interests and the anatomical matters discussed should be evident, although perhaps it is less clear than in the preceding case. If the phrenological organs existed, and existed in the mapping offered, then there ought to be morphological support for them. If they didn't, then there should not be. Hence, opponents of phrenology could point to the convolutions as nonsense, to the lack of differentiation between gyri and to the absence of dividing lines between organs situated on a single gyrus, as evidence for the non-existence of any such things as the 'organs'. The phrenologists made the best 'bet' they felt they could in linking convolutions and organs, but, as we have seen, that 'bet' was never very confident. The question at issue was not the convolutions as objects of disinterested inquiry, but the brain as a legitimating resource for the policies the phrenologists espoused, and the responses their usage elicited.

The Cerebral Fibres

Until the advent, in the 1870s, of microscopic instruments and staining techniques adequate to the task, cerebral anatomists had to content themselves with making mainly macroscopic observations of the constitution of the two main tissue types of the brain—the 'grey' (cortical, or 'cineritious', matter) and the 'white' (medullary) matter. Hence, the debate with which we are now concerned occurred on what anatomists recognised to be the margin of their perceptual resources.

The general contention that the medullary substance of the brain (the main mass of the hemispheres) was fibrous in appearance was by no means novel or contentious at the beginning of the nineteenth century. The conception goes back at least to the seventeenth-century anatomist Malpighi, and may be found, in one or another form, in Willis and de Vieussens, and in Vicq-d'Azyr and Reil, who were roughly contemporary with Gall.[62] It should, however, be pointed out that when anatomists in the early nineteenth century referred to 'fibres', they might have had various structural notions in mind, but they were certainly not aware of the more modern concept of the 'neuron' and its functions.

Thus, the basic assertion that the white matter was fibrous in appearance and was in fact composed of fibres was unoriginal when, in the first decade of the nineteenth century, Gall and Spurzheim articulated and refined the notion in their phrenological context.[63] What precise relationship existed between their view of the fibres and their phrenological system is not only problematic for historians, but was equally puzzling to contemporary anatomists. The committee of the French National Institute requested to judge their anatomical claims credited Gall and Spurzheim as being the 'first to have distinguished the two orders of fibres, of which the medullary matter of the hemisphere appears to be composed', but added the caveat that 'the anatomical questions with which we have been engaged . . . have no immediate and necessary connection with the physiological doctrine taught by Dr. Gall . . . All that we have examined with respect to the encephalon might be equally true or false, without any conclusion being drawn for or against this doctrine'.[64] And the medical historian Erwin Ackerknecht, while palpably overstating Gall's claim to originality, praises him for recognising 'the fibrous nature of the white matter, hitherto regarded as a kind of gruel, and its conductor function', but does not say what relation the phrenologists' 'contribution' bore to their system.[65]

Let us now briefly outline the phrenologists' view of the fibres of the medullary matter. Gall and Spurzheim discerned two distinct types of fibre in the white matter of the brain. The one they called the 'diverging system' (what is now termed 'projection' fibres) and the other the 'converging system' (now called 'association' fibres).[66] The diverging fibres may be clearly seen in figs. 2 and 5. Gall and Spurzheim contended that the diverging fibres took their origin from 'grey' ganglia in the medulla oblongata (or brain stem) (fig. 2, no. 1; fig. 5, no. 91). One set going out of the cerebrum proper emerged from grey ganglia in the pyramidal bodies (figs. 2 and 5, 'e'), then continued upwards through the pons Varioli (or annular protuberance) (figs. 2 and 5, 'b') and crura cerebri (figs. 2 and 5, 'g'), to the inner surfaces of the convolutions on the frontal and parietal lobes (follow nos. 34-38 in both figures). Another set of diverging fibres emerged, they claimed, from grey ganglia in the olivary bodies (figs. 2 and 5, 'a'), passing upwards behind the pons and through the crura, the optic thalami and corpora striata, to the convolutions of the 'posterior' (temporal) lobe (fig. 2, 'II'). The two diverging systems of Gall and Spurzheim therefore go from brain stem to convolutions, functionally connecting the surfaces of the 'organs' to the motor apparatus of the spinal cord.

The 'converging' system of medullary fibres was held to originate from the convolutions of one hemisphere, proceeding medially, where they unite and connect opposite hemispheres in the great 'commissures' of the brain, such as the corpus callosum (not shown in our figures, but see Gall and Spurzheim's *Atlas*, Plates VI and XI '$\lambda - \mu - \lambda$'). The converging system thus served the function of bringing organs on opposed areas of the bi-laterally symmetrical brain into systemic connection. At the bottom of each convolution, the two systems cross each other and form a tissue. Distal to this tissue the convolutions may be separated along their median line (fig. 2, '1—2', '1—3'). Hence, the phrenologists' system of medullary fibres was involved in long debates over the tissue composition of the convolutions and the processes involved in the disease of hydrocephalus.

The phrenologists' anatomical findings about the cerebral fibres encountered, as we have seen, relatively little disapproval from the French Institute, but John Gordon, in Edinburgh, reacted hostilely to their claims. Gordon's position on these matters was both idiosyncratic and ambiguous, but a quotation from his 1815 anatomy text provides a succinct expression of his views:

> It is difficult to convey any accurate idea of the consistence of the White Nervous Matter. It varies a little in different parts. In general it is less elastic than Jelly, but somewhat more glutinous or viscid.
> When we make a section of it in any direction, with a sharp scalpel, the surface of the section is perfectly smooth, and of a uniform colour. There is no appearance of any cells, or globules, or fibres whatever.[67]

Gordon recognised, however, that when the white matter was subjected to various preparatory treatments, e.g., maceration in acid or alcohol, or when it was 'scraped' rather than sliced, it might be 'made to exhibit a fibrous appearance'.[68] Here, in a context in which he was not concerned to discredit the phrenologists, but to provide learning materials for his extra-mural classes, Gordon strongly suggested that the fibrous 'appearance' thus induced is an indication of the white matter's actual fibrous nature.[69]

However, in his *Edinburgh Review* assault on phrenology, as well as in his critical pamphlet occasioned by Spurzheim's Edinburgh demonstrations, Gordon now adopted a more suspicious posture on the question of the cerebral fibres. 'We are by no means satisfied,' he cautioned,

> . . . how much of the White Matter throughout the brain is capable of exhibiting this fibrous appearance when coagulated. This point, as well as the cause of the fibrous appearance in general, requires to be further investigated . . .[70]

Where Gall and Spurzheim 'scraped' and 'tore' the white matter to display its 'real' fibrous nature, Gordon now asserted that their techniques resulted only in the display of artifacts, and that his (the traditional 'slicing') technique showed the matter as it naturally was. Thus, even the phrenologists' display of a fibrous appearance was insufficient evidence of a real fibrous nature: 'a fibrous appearance, and a fibrous structure, are two different things . . . the former is not always caused by the latter'.[71] And even if Gall and Spurzheim happened to have hit upon the truth, Gordon was keen to ensure that the credit was not to be theirs. These fibrous 'appearances', whose correspondence to structural reality was queried, had in fact been observed and recorded by previous anatomists, most particularly by Gordon's favourite authority the German *Naturphilosophe* J. C. Reil.[72]

To all this, Spurzheim, then in Edinburgh, responded that the procedures by which the fibrous 'appearances' were produced were those which displayed the structures in their most natural state:

> We seldom cut, but mostly scrape; because the substance, on account of its delicacy, when cut, does not show its Structure.[73]

Fresh brains as well as coagulated ones might be used, if that was insisted upon, but here one ran the risk of meeting up with a bad brain, so soft and pulpy that it was 'entirely unfit for demonstration'.[74] In any case, what could one do with a man like Gordon who, when asked at a public dissection to 'give a name to what he saw, called it a "fibrous appearance"?'[75] It was an idiot's ontology. Yet phenomenological gymnastics of that sort were in part responsible for the considerable refinement and clarification of the phrenologists' accounts which occurred during the Edinburgh disputes.

While anti-phrenologists showed themselves quite capable of discerning the 'interests' which lay behind the phrenologists' views of the frontal sinuses and the convolutions, neither Gordon (who contended that Gall and Spurzheim 'got it wrong' on the fibres), nor the French Institute (which generally agreed they 'got it right'), provide evidence that they saw any connection between the phrenological system and particular accounts Gall and Spurzheim offered of the cerebral fibres. Yet it is possible for a historian to suggest such a connection.

It must be emphasised here, as the phrenologists themselves frequently did, that the 'organs' were not merely composed of the surface layer of grey matter but were, rather, the whole mass of the brain. They were to be viewed as 'wedges', of which only the distal surface faced the skull, and which 'extended from the pyramidal bodies of the medulla oblongata, to the external surface of the convolutions'.[76] They ran, as it were, from the 'bumps' down to the spinal cord, connecting the visually apprehensible contours of the head to the motor apparatus for translating 'faculties' into behaviour.[77]

It is arguable that the major concern connecting the phrenologists' cranioscopic system to their work on the anatomy of the brain was to find and display any anatomical bases for a conception of the brain as a congeries of distinct organs. While they were evidently unwilling to make such a display of the cerebral convolutions, they were more certain that visible nature was on their side in the matter of the medullary fibres, and they pursued this line of research with great vigour. To those philosophers and psychologists who contended that the mind was a unity, and that the brain itself appeared as an undifferentiated mess of porridge where 'all the parts are blended together in common union', Gall replied:

> The whole substance of the brain, moreover, is far from exhibiting such a commingling of its parts as is affirmed; no such blending exists: on the contrary, fibres and fibrous fasces are in every part very distinctly visible . . ., they form their own expansions and convolutions . . . It is true, that all these parts are connected; but this connection does not prove the impossibility of each being an independent organ.[78]

Gall claimed that 'there is no common centre for all the cerebral fibres' and that the 'fibrous fasces are really distinct'.[79] Indeed, they do appear as 'really distinct' in the engravings—far more distinct than fibres do in the pictures of non-phrenological contemporaries or of more modern neuro-anatomy texts. It is quite possible, then, that the phrenologists' work on, and accounts of, the cerebral fibres was linked to their interests in displaying a pluralistic brain, as naturalistic basis for their pluralistic psychology, the diagnostic system erected thereon, and the programmes advocated on the possibility of such a diagnosis. Hence, at a highly mediated level, the phrenologists' view of the cerebral fibres was generated and developed in a context of conflicting wider interests, for the purpose of making the system more plausible by securing for it a naturalistic base consistent with their other anatomical contentions. And, although we have no evidence that John Gordon discerned the posited connection between interests and fibres, his developing notions of the medullary substance were hardly impelled by disinterested contemplation or the inherent interest of these 'appearances'.

The Corpus Dentatum of the Cerebellum and Related Matters

The cerebellum (the 'hind brain', or what the Germans call the 'kleines Gehirn') is a bi-lobed structure, situated below the posterior portions of the two cerebral hemispheres and lying on the dorsal surface of the medulla oblongata. It is easily distinguished from the hemispheres proper by its closely ridged laminar surface (see fig. 4, 'I', and also the cross-sections in figs. 2 and 5), which contrasts markedly with the convolutions of the rest of the brain. Like the cerebrum, the cerebellum is composed of an exterior capsule of grey matter, enclosing a central core of white, medullary matter. Within its white core, the cerebellum contains a number of ganglia or nuclei whose existence was not disputed in the early nineteenth century but whose tissue composition was a matter of divided opinion. The fibrous connections extending from the medulla oblongata to the cerebrum (views of which were described in the last section) have their counterparts in the cerebellum. Again ,it was not doubted that there were such connections between cerebellum and brain stem, but, in the setting we are dealing with, the precise nature of these fibre bundles and their pathways were disputed.

Phrenologists devoted much of their anatomical work to the cerebellum, its internal structure and fibrous connections. Seven plates in the 1810 Gall and Spurzheim *Atlas* were specifically concerned to display these aspects of the cerebellum. In 1838 George Combe translated from the French a series of essays by phrenologist-anatomists on the structure and functions of the cerebellum, this amounting to the single most sustained and focussed effort by phrenologists to study a part of the brain.[80] Not surprisingly, the accounts the pherenologists offered of cerebellar structure were severely criticised in Edinburgh, most particularly by John Gordon.

One of the most noteworthy features of the Edinburgh debate on cerebellar structure was that, for the first and only time during the Edinburgh phrenology controversies, we have the purposeful juxtaposition of published *pictorial* statments of what the disputed struc· tures 'really' looked like; in this case, of two almost exactly comparable copper-plate engravings prepared under the respective supervisions of Gordon and Gall and Spurzheim.[81]

Fig. 6 is a reduced copy (commissioned by Gordon) of Plate XII from Gall and Spurzheim's 1810 *Atlas*, showing a section taken through the cerebellum and medulla oblongata. Fig. 7 was specifically done for Gordon to display the 'actual' appearance of these parts. The two were published on the same page in Gordon's 1817 examination of Gall and Spurzheim's anatomical claims.[82] It was the first and only time that John Gordon published a *picture* of any brain structure.

Let us first summarise some of the features of the cerebellum and its connections as seen by Gall and Spurzheim:

(1)   They noted a fibre bundle ('e-e' in figs. 2 and 5; 'a-b' in fig. 6), running from a grey ganglion (not shown) in the medulla oblongata (called the corpus restiforme) to the entrance to the cerebellum, thickening as it ascends. These are Gall and Spurzheim's 'diverging fibres of the cerebellum', analogous to their diverging system of cerebral fibres.

(2)   As this fibre bundle enters the cerebellum it meets with and enters a mass of grey matter (fig. 6, 'c'; figs. 2 and 5, 's') called the corpus dentatum (or dentate nucleus) of the cerebellum. The function of this grey nucleus, like that of grey ganglia generally in Gall and Spurzheim's schema is to increase, 'nourish' and thicken the (white) fibres along their course.

(3)   From the serrated edges (the 'teeth') of the corpus dentatum issue forth augmented white fibre bundles (not shown), proceeding in several directions. One set proceeds medially to form the central vermiform process of the bi-lobed cerebellum; another proceeds outwards to form the laminae (the convolutions) of the cerebellum.[83]

(4)   Other features of fig. 6 of relevance to the Edinburgh debate included the appearance of the fibre bundles passing through the pons ('f') and the appearance of the grey mass ('i') which is the dentate nucleus of the corpus olivare.

Having reproduced this portion of a Gall and Spurzheim account as an exemplar of error (bearing 'no resemblance to nature'), Gordon commissioned the artist-anatomist P. Syme to produce fig. 7 as a representation of the 'real appearance' of these structures.[84] *This,* according to Gordon, was how the cerebellar and brain-stem structures actually appeared:

(1)   The corpus dentatum of the cerebellum 'has no connexion whatever with the corpus restiforme'. Except at one point, 'it is impossible to demonstrate a single filament either entering or leaving it'.[85] In fig. 7 Gordon showed only one type of connection between the corpus dentatum and the brain-stem, what he called a pillar of the 'Vieussenian valve' (now termed the anterior

medullary velum) (fig. 7, 'a-b'). So the only fibrous link between cerebellum and brain stem was upwards rather than downwards.

(2)   The corpus dentatum of the cerebellum was not in fact a mass of grey matter as Gall and Spurzheim claimed. In his 1815 text Gordon had described it as 'a nucleus of Orange-White Matter, contained in a capsule of Wood-Brown Matter, not more than a fiftieth part of an inch in thickness', although he acknowledged that the presence within the nucleus of venous structures 'has led some Anatomists, to describe the nucleus as being intermixed with Brown Matter'.[86] In fig. 7 the corpus dentatum ('c') is shown as white matter, encapsulated by a very thin 'grey' shell.

(3)   The corpus dentatum is shown, as in the phrenologists' account, to be serrated, but these serrations are insisted to be composed of white matter and not of 'grey'. No fibres are shown leaving the serrations, and in the accompanying gloss, it is asserted that no fibres can be observed to leave them.

(4)   In fig. 7 the corpus olivare is sliced open to show the 'real' structure of its dentate nucleus ('f'). It may be seen that it is displayed in the same 'syntax' as that used to show the cerebellar dentate nucleus, just as Gall and Spurzheim's representation uses the same 'syntax' to display the dentate nuclei of cerebellum and corpus olivare (fig. 6, 'c' and 'i'). Although, curiously, Gordon did not elect in his picture to show the interior structure of the pons (fig. 7, 'd'), he asserted that Gall and Spurzheim's representation was seriously in error. And, further, he showed a structure (the posterior medullary velum) (fig. 7, 'e') which Gordon claimed existed, but which Gall and Spurzheim's representation omitted altogether.

Not having provided a single illustration in his 1815 text, Gordon clearly expected that his juxtaposition of cerebellar 'reality' with the obvious 'distortions,' 'omissions' and 'misrepresentations' of the phrenologists' picture would have the effect of rendering them speechless and destroying their credibility. But Spurzheim, then in Edinburgh, preferred his own representation and argued that Gordon's was the one which was in error. In his lengthy reply to Gordon's attack, Spurzheim developed his case:

(1)   The passage of fibres from the corpus restiforme to the corpus dentatum is 'easily shown'; one merely has to scrape away some obscuring nerves in order to observe it. Spurzheim, having

already shown this feature in Barclay's dissecting room, offered to display it again 'to every one who produces a fresh brain'.[87]

(2)   The corpus dentatum of the cerebellum (as that of the corpus olivare) was indeed 'greyish matter', as previously stated. However, Spurzheim complained, with good reason, that the portion of the original engraving which Gordon had copied (Plate XII of the 1810 *Atlas*) showed a corpus dentatum containing 'more white matter than he has represented in the copy which he has taken from our plate'. (Compare the corpora dentata shown in accompanying figs. 2 and 5, 's'.) 'Is this whole proceeding', Spurzheim asked, 'consistent with candour?'[88]

(3)   On the form of the corpora dentata of cerebellum and corpus olivare, Spurzheim declined to defend his representation as the only accurate one, nor did he contend that Gordon's was necessarily faulty. These structures appear in different lights depending upon how one views them, and from what perspective the view is taken. So the two engravings, which Gordon claimed to be comparable in these respects, are not necessarily so. 'How then could he', Spurzheim inquired,

compare his figure of the corpus dentatum with one of ours, while both cerebella were different in size and form, and the corpora dentata are not cut in the same direction? . . . We have cut more towards the medial line; he more externally.[89]

Similarly, the representations of the dentate nucleus of the corpus olivare are not fit to be juxtaposed:

[Gordon] has not yet learned that it varies, like the corpus dentatum [of the cerebellum], in size and form, in different individuals, and that the form appears different according to the section. His is horizontal, and ours vertical; hence the appearance must be different.[90]

Knowledge of the structures in their totality was thus said to be generated from a number of partial views. Arguably, knowledge of these esoteric structures *was* so generated during the course of the Edinburgh disputes.

As a matter of interest (but not central to the argument of this paper) we can turn to the modern anatomy text as a highly developed, stable account of the structures disputed in early nineteenth-century Edinburgh. Fig. 8, and the accompanying text, indicates that 'honours' must be considered shared. The dentate nuclei of cerebellum and corpus olivare both appear much as Gordon contended— white with a thin grey capsule—although the text confirms that the nuclei appear more as a greyish mass when sections are taken towards the lateral edges.[91] The interior of the pons is shown much as Gall and Spurzheim represented it. When Gordon and Spurzheim discussed fibres entering the cerebellum, modern knowledge would lead us to suspect that they were 'actually' dealing with what are now referred to as the three cerebellar peduncles. The superior cerebellar peduncle, shown as the 'brachium conjunctivum' of fig. 8 is very probably what Gordon showed in fig. 7, 'a-b', connecting, as he argued, the corpus dentatum upwards to the hemispheres by way of the brain-stem. On the other hand, the inferior cerebellar peduncle (not shown in fig. 8) is in fact part of the corpus restiforme, and, thus, may correspond to 'a-b' in fig. 6. It does, as Spurzheim averred and as Gordon denied, enter the cerebellum and constitutes a group of fibres radiating out to various parts of its surface, but only a few of its fibres enter the corpus dentatum. The middle cerebellar peduncle connects pons to cerebellar convolutions, but does not enter the corpus dentatum. The implication, although nothing in this paper hinges thereon, is that no party to this dispute 'conjured up' any structure in his representations; there is an agreed-upon modern basis for all that was seen, although much was left 'unseen' and the connections between 'real' structures were made differently from the way they would be today.

Surely, representations of structures as esoteric as these could not have been influenced by considerations of social interest. Certainly, neither Gordon nor Spurzheim provide us with evidence that they detected the workings of social interests in the other's representations of the internal structure of the cerebellum and its fibrous connections. Indeed, partly because we cannot employ actors' own detections of the link between social interests and these representations, such a link is exceedingly difficult to discern and to make historically plausible. Yet, the following is a hypothesis about such a connection:

(1)   In the phrenological system the cerebellum, in its entirety, is a single 'organ', that of 'amativeness'.

(2)   The cerebellum is the only 'organ' which was undeniably morphologically distinct from all other areas of the brain. Were it excised from the rest, there would have been no problem for phrenologists in identifying it as the organ of amativeness. The cerebellum was therefore generally appealing to phrenologist-anatomists as a subject relating function to structure.

(3)   The material basis for a functional 'organ' would therefore be worked out in detail in the particular case of the cerebellum.

(4)   The interest phrenologists had in the display of the cerebral fibres would be reflected in the cerebellum. If the fibres entering the cerebellum from the brain-stem entered it from *above* (as Gordon asserted), the cerebellum would be an anomaly in the general anatomical scheme. If, as Gall and Spurzheim claimed, the fibrous connection was from *below* (linking the organ to motor mechanisms), then desired consistency in this most visible of organs would be preserved, and the plan as a whole would be supported.

Social Interests and Esoteric Knowledge: Some Speculations

In the series of increasingly esoteric anatomical issues discussed above, the influence of social interests becomes more and more difficult for both actors and historians to discern. One possible conclusion from this impression would be that social interests affected representations of some anatomical structures and not others; for example, those structures on or near the cranial surface were liable to be infected by social interests, while representations of those more interior, more esoteric structures were manifestations of pure contemplation. The sociology of scientific knowledge, in this case at least, would have a limited role to play, literally and figuratively a superficial one.

However, such a conclusion would neither be a necessary nor an accurate inference from the episodes discussed. Indeed, these materials provide support for a rather different conception of the relationship between social interests and the development of esoteric bodies of knowledge.

Let us first examine the predicament of the phrenologists. Various phrenologists were committed to different moral and social policies, but all were committed to securing credibility for some such policy. In Gall's work one finds an apparent interest in the debunking of idealism, *Naturphilosophie,* Enlightenment optimism, and, presumably, Catholic theology. His expressions of these interests pre-date his anatomical work (see note 27). Spurzheim broke with Gall to develop phrenology into the legitimation of meliorist social policies, and the Edinburgh phrenologists were almost uniform in their adherence to the Whig-to-Owenite social programme previously outlined. All had social commitments to further and all were deviant iconoclasts in their contexts.

While it is one thing to argue social policies on the basis of their inherent justness or 'rationality', it has often seemed a more persuasive strategy to argue them upon the basis of 'nature' and 'how things really are' in the natural order. Philosophical flaws in the 'naturalistic fallacy' do not diminish its obvious appeal as a social strategy.

The argument is that phrenologists did anatomy, defended and developed the anatomy of their canon, in an attempt to secure social credibility and to conceal the role of their social interests. The phrenologists' social interests may therefore be conceived as a sort of motor, driving them to produce and develop knowledge in which ideally it would become impossible for their opponents to discern the action of these interests. Such a motor might operate on a diachronic sequence, as the result of criticism from opponents, or it might equally operate by the imaginative rehearsal of *possible* criticisms prior to the enunciation of 'findings'. In our material, we see both modes of operation.

Credibility may be secured by the production of apparently naturalistic knowledge, in which it is impossible for opponents (or historians) to discern social interest, but not *any* naturalistic account will best further a particular social interest. Certain natural realities are better for some purposes than for others. Your enemies will, for example, be delighted to believe you if you prove them right, but that does you little good.

Hence, the naturalistic anatomical knowledge the phrenologists produced may be seen as the resultant of the forces of these two social motors. The first is the felt necessity to secure a naturalistic basis for one's policies, and, thereby, credibility in society. This encourages one to make a 'bet' about reality as it may be and as others, in a concrete social context, may perceive it to be. The 'bettor' may then produce a perceptual account which, considering all the contingencies of the setting, will maximise the probability that specified others will 'match' the account and the object portrayed; in other words, that some other person or persons will see (or be encouraged to see) the account as a reliable rendering of perceived reality. The push this social motor exerts towards naturalism, as actors in the setting recognise it, is obvious.

The second social motor reflects the *particular* legitimating require-ment actors feel they have, as contrasted to the general desire to secure credibility for their perceptual accounts. This social motor pushes the perceptual accounts in the direction where they are best suited to the legitimating tasks at hand. Hence, Gall was concerned to display a brain with no common origin of the nerves and fibres, in order to argue against the idea of a 'common seat' of an immaterial soul. The skull with frontal sinuses 'little' was better for the phrenologists' social purposes than the skull with frontal sinuses 'large'. Each account offered reflects both these social motors.

What of the phrenologists' Edinburgh opponents? They too had their interests to defend. As custodians and practitioners of an institutionalised body of anatomical knowledge, they were concerned to defend the existing model of the brain as a reliable account of reality, and at the same time to expose the new, deviant account as deficient. Inasmuch as their enemies' brain-model stressed its dif-ferentiation, they had an interest in displaying lack of differentiation. In defending the existing model of the brain, they were defending their social situation as expert anatomists in that setting.

And what of the intellectual strategies professional anatomists employed to defend and further their interests? Are they symmetrical with the strategies employed by phrenologists? Arguably, they are. Barclay and Gordon responded to the phrenologists' threat by articulating more naturalistic-appearing, more esoteric bodies of knowledge. Greater refinement of focus was developed and more rigorous perceptual accounts were offered of structures hitherto of little interest to them. John Gordon produced a *picture* of the internal structure of the cerebellum, where before he devoted few *words* to its elucidation. These accounts were, like those of the phrenologists, manifestations of a 'bet' that they would be accredited as reliable accounts by specified others in a particular social setting, and they therefore reflect a push towards that setting's sense of naturalism. But, again, not any naturalistic account will serve the particular interest. Cerebral reality ideally had to be such as would preserve the greatest stock of institutionalised knowledge while discrediting as much as possible of the phrenologists' central claims to naturalism. Gordon and Barclay's behaviour manifests both these social interests.

But here many historians will object that, while the point relating social interests to knowledge may be granted for the phrenologists, the evidence for a symmetrical treatment of their opponents seems weak. Perhaps one can make such a case for Sir William Hamilton, but surely not for Barclay and Gordon. Hamilton, who deviated from his normal ambit by learning cerebral anatomy precisely for the purpose of discrediting phrenology and upholding the validity of the Scottish Common-Sense philosophy of which he was such a leading exponent, provides historians with 'good' evidence of his social interests; he had little to gain by tolerating a psycho-philosophical system whose local leaders advocated the overthrow of the existing educational order, at both university and popular levels.

What historians take to be 'good' evidence for sustaining such an imputation is usually evidence of an individual's *motives* or *intentions,* in any case, evidence of that person's subjective state of mind. The phrenologists supply us with such information, relating the knowledge they produced to their intentions; Hamilton perhaps does as well; but Barclay and Gordon surely do not. There is not a shred of evidence which would support an interpretation which claimed to discern in their writings a special desire, for example, to thwart the social ambitions of the rising petty-bourgeoisie. The interpretation developed in this paper does not depend on a diagnosis of any given individual's subjective motives; it does, however, depend upon a notion of what his social interests may be.

The historiographic problems of distinguishing between motives and interests seem especially important when one is dealing with a comparative analysis of institutionalised and 'new' or deviant bodies of knowledge. In a new or deviant body of knowledge, we will typically see the social interests of those who produced it being closely 'coupled' to the actual form of their production. Typically also, we will have rather 'good' evidence as to their motives, and these will be uniformly expressed in the producing group. When, however, we come to look at 'old' or institutionalised bodies of knowledge, a different situation seems to obtain. Apart from their interest in defending the institutionalised body of knowledge and attacking its enemies, the social interests of its practitioners *may be* effectively 'de-coupled' from the actual content of the knowledge, and their motives in practising that body of knowledge may be very various.

Perhaps a concrete example will help to get this notion across: When the Romans occupied Britain, they built a road from what is now Cambridge to what is is now Godmanchester, passing on the way the site of what is now Girton College. They built this road, like most of their British highways, with the intention of ferrying armies and military supplies as rapidly as possible between two, rather distant, points, and, because of their intention, the road, straight as a die, directly reflects their interest in making the Imperial occupation as effective as possible. That Roman road is now the A604, and it is used by many individuals, for very various purposes. Anyone who, observing a King's man cycling at evening towards Girton, decided that the scholar was intending to further Roman imperialism, might be guilty of an error of imputation. It would, of course, be equally incorrect, although less bizarre, to claim that the scholar's behaviour that evening, whatever his state of mind, owed nothing to Roman Imperial social interests.

There may be an interesting consequence of historians' preference for evidence linking actors' intentions to their knowledge when making social imputations. Such information, we have suggested, will tend preferentially to be available for new and, especially, for deviant bodies of knowledge, and will tend, correspondingly, to be unavailable for institutionalised or old bodies of knowledge. The consequence may therefore be that the usual canons of historical procedure will sustain a sociological approach to deviant bodies of knowledge, but not to institutionalised ones. Indeed, there is some evidence that this is what is developing in the social history of science: a sociology of error, of deviance and of rejected knowledge but not, as yet, much in the way of a sociology of 'truth'. Social interests may be *discerned* in the former, but not in the latter.

Yet the major concern of this paper has been to prise apart the notion of social interest in knowledge from the notion of error and distortion. Science does not guarantee its growth towards esoteric naturalism by systematically immunising itself from the action of social interests. Rather, it may be the action of conflicting social interests, and actors' ability to assign ideological concerns to knowledge claims, which provide a significant push towards the development of increasingly naturalistic forms. It is when the 'pressure is on' that knowledge develops most intensely in these directions. Hence, social conflict and ideological considerations may be seen as an important element in the development of bodies of knowledge valued as 'interest-free', rather than as a feature of the environment which retards such development.

We should, however, make it very clear that this thesis is not the same as the proposition that no interests other than social bear upon the development of naturalistic bodies of knowledge. This would be obviously incorrect. Practical interests of all kinds, the use of knowledge as an instrument for prediction and control of natural and technical processes, clearly act upon and influence the development of knowledge. The general argument has not been that such interests are unimportant; far from it. But I have not been able to see how such manipulative interests may have borne upon the material just discussed. No surgical procedures, for example, in the early nineteenth century, depended upon the elaboration of knowledge about the convolutions, the cerebral fibres, the sinuses or the corpus dentatum and its peduncles. Likewise, I have found it very difficult to see how these episodes may be dealt with by an analysis which stresses contemplation and the disinterested desire to know as the motors of knowledge. The fundamental argument has been that social interests act upon knowledge in ways rather different from those usually assumed; that it is the effect of such interests to conceal their action; and that, because of this, it may well be that social interests influence knowledge more pervasively than the usual canons of historical procedure can persuasively demonstrate.

Acknowledgements

I wish to thank my colleagues at the Science Studies Unit, David Bloor and Barry Barnes, for their critical comments on an earlier version of this paper. I owe a particular debt to Dr. Christopher Lawrence of the Wellcome Institute for the History of Medicine, who gave generously of his time and expertise and who helped me to make my own observations of the brain.

---

[1] For example, Ruth S. Cowan: 'Francis Galton's Statistical Ideas: The Influence of Eugenics', *Isis*, Vol. 63, 1972, pp. 509-528; P. Forman: 'Weimar Culture, Causality and Quantum Theory, 1918-1927: Adaptation by German Physicists and Mathematicians to a Hostile Intellectual Environment', *Historical Studies in the Physical Sciences*, Vol. 3, 1971, pp. 1-115; R. M. Young: 'Malthus and the Evolutionists', *Past and Present*, no. 43, 1969, pp. 109-145 and, 'Darwin's Metaphor: Does Nature Select?', *The Monist*, Vol. 55, 1971, pp. 442-503.

[2] For example, Donald Mackenzie: 'Statistical Theory and Social Interests: A Case Study', *Social Studies of Science*. Vol. 8, 1978, pp. 35-83.

The Politics of Observation

3 Karl Popper espouses the view that error will be systematically eliminated by the operation of critical debate in science, and that, provided a liberal and competitive 'open-market' obtains, those interests which produce error will be vanquished by those which produce truth or the progress of knowledge. In certain respects the present model is similar to Popper's, but there is no concern here with epistemological evaluation. What is at issue (to use the jargon of the ethnomethodologists) is the process whereby disinterested *appearances* are 'practically accomplished' in particular settings and contexts and against a particular background, not whether that 'accomplishment' is correct or not.

The present conception of the role of social interests in the production of knowledge owes much to the work of my colleague Barry Barnes (e.g. B. Barnes: *Interests and the Growth of Knowledge*, Routledge & Kegan Paul, London, 1977, expecially his discussion of Habermas (J. Habermas: *Knowledge and Human Interests*, Beacon, Boston, 1971) in chapter i of Barnes: op. cit. The idea of 'experiments in social control' invoking a nature which, over time, becomes increasingly naturalistic, is introduced in S. Shapin and B. Barnes: 'Science, Nature and Control: Interpreting Mechanics' Institutes', *Social Studies of Science*, Vol. 7, 1977, pp. 31-74.

4 Owsei Temkin: 'Gall and the Phrenological Movement', *Bulletin of the History of Medicine*, Vol. 21, 1947, pp. 275-321.

5 John D. Davies: *Phrenology, Fad and Science*: *A Nineteenth Century American Crusade*, Yale University Press, New Haven, Conn. 1955; David A. De Giustino: *Conquest of Mind*: *Phrenology and Victorian Social Thought*, Croom Helm, London, 1975.

6 [Thomas Brown]: 'Villers *Sur une Nouvelle Theorie du Cerveau*', *Edinburgh Review*, Vol. 2, 1803, p. 147.

7 'Review of "Account of Dr. Gall's Discoveries regarding the Structure of the Brain." By T. C. Rosenmuller . . .', *Edinburgh Medical and Surgical Journal*, Vol. 2, 1806, pp. 320-324.

8 'Report on a Memoir of Drs. Gall and Spurzheim, relative to the Anatomy of the Brain . . .', *Edinburgh Medical and Surgical Journal*, Vol. 5, 1809, pp. 36-66.

9 F. J. Gall: *On the Functions of the Brain and of Each of Its Parts*, Boston, 1835, 6 vols. (translation of *Sur les Fonctions du Cerveau*, Paris 1822-25).

10 J. G. Spurzheim: *The Physiognomical System of Drs. Gall and Spurzheim*, London, 1815.

11 Temkin: op. cit., 1947; E. Ackerknecht and H. V. Vallois: *Franz Joseph Gall, Inventor of Phrenology and His Collection* (Wisconsin Studies in Medical History, No.1), University of Wisconsin Medical School, Madison, 1956; Robert M. Young: *Mind, Brain and Adaptation in the Nineteenth Century*, Clarendon Press, Oxford, 1970; Roger Cooter: 'Phrenology: The Provocation of Progress', *History of Science*, Vol. 15, 1976, pp. 211-234.

12 For example, see the engraving of such 'bumps' and depressions on the skull in F. J. Gall and J. G. Spurzheim: *Anatomie et Physiologie au Systéme Nerveux en General et du Cerveau en Particulier, Atlas*, Paris, 1810, Plate XCIX, reproduced in E. Clarke and K. Dewhurst: *An Illustrated History of Brain Function*, Sandford, Oxford, 1972, p. 92.

13 Occasionally, phrenologists used evidence derived from instances of the destruction of parts of the brain, although they expressed reservations about the value of this sort of data; see Spurzheim: op. cit., 1815, pp. 239-241.

Steven Shapin

[14] Temkin: op. cit., 1947, pp. 278-279.

[15] [G. Combe]: 'Explanation of the Physiognomical System of Drs. Gall and Spurzheim', *Scots Magazine*, Vol. 79, 1817, pp. 243-250 and his *Essays on Phrenology*, Edinburgh, 1819; J. G. Spurzheim: *A View of the Elementary Principles of Education* . . ., Edinburgh, 1821.

[16] A quite useful, although biassed, contemporary account of most of the Edinburgh controversies is R. Chenevix: *Phrenology. Article of the 'Foreign Quarterly Review', with notes from G. Spurzheim*, London, 1830. (Original publication in *Foreign Quarterly Review*, Vol. 2, 1828, pp. 1-59.)

[17] G. N. Cantor: 'The Edinburgh Phrenology Debate: 1803-1828', *Annals of Science*, Vol. 32, 1975, pp. 195-218.

[18] S. Shapin: 'Phrenological Knowledge and the Social Structure of Early Nineteenth-Century Edinburgh', *Annals of Science*, Vol. 32, 1975, pp. 219-243. Also see S. Shapin: 'Homo Phrenologicus: Anthropological Perspectives on an Historical Problem', in B. Barnes and S. Shapin (eds.): *Natural Order: Historical Studies of Scientific Culture*, Sage, London, 1979.

[19] G. E. Davie: *The Social Significance of the Scottish Philosophy of Common Sense*, Dundee, 1972.

[20] De Giustino: op. cit.; Roger Cooter: 'Phrenology and British Alienists, c. 1825-1845', *Medical History*, Vol. 20, 1976b, pp. 1-21, 135-151.

[21] Young: op. cit., 1970; Clarke and Dewhurst: op. cit., pp.91, 101-102.

[22] Clarke and Dewhurst: op. cit., p. 91.

[23] E. Ackerknecht: 'Contributions of Gall and the Phrenologists to Knowledge of Brain Function' in F. N. L. Poynter (ed.): *The History and Philosophy of Knowledge of the Brain and Its Functions*, Blackwell, Oxford, 1958; cf. Owsei Temkin: 'Remarks on the Neurology of Gall and Spurzheim', in E. A. Underwood (ed.): *Science, Medicine and History*, Oxford University Press, London 1953, Vol. 2, pp. 282-289; McD. Critchley: 'Neurology's Debt to F. J. Gall (1758-1828)', *British Medical Journal*, Vol. 2, 1965, pp. 775-781; Erna Lesky: 'Structure and Function in Gall', *Bulletin of the History of Medicine*, Vol. 44, 1970, pp. 297-314.

[24] D. Ellis: *Memoir of the Life and Writings of John Gordon, M.D., F.R.S.E.*, Edinburgh, 1823, pp. 41-42.

[25] 'Report on a Memoir': op. cit., p. 65.

[26] Andrew Combe: 'Dr. Prichard and Phrenology', *Phrenological Journal*, Vol. 8, 1834, p. 650.

[27] Biographical information on Gall and his motives is scarce and mostly unreliable. The crucial evidence is his 1791 *Philosophisch—medicinische Untersuchungen* . . . which, prior to his anatomical investigations, set out his views on the relationship of body and soul; see Temkin: op. cit., 1947, pp. 276-278, 313-314. Gall's intention to debunk idealist philosophies is evident in this text.

[28] Spurzheim: op. cit., 1815, pp. 2, 543-551.

[29] George Combe: *The Life and Correspondence of Andrew Combe, M.D.*, Edinburgh, 1850, p. 44; cf. G. Combe: op. cit., 1819, pp. 304-342.

[30] Shapin: op. cit., 1975, pp. 234-235.

The Politics of Observation

[31] Alexander Monro: *Observations on the Structure and Functions of the Nervous System*, Edinburgh, 1783, Table II, p. 106.

[32] For example, Sir George S. Mackenzie: *Illustrations of Phrenology*, Edinburgh, 1820, pp. 227-230.

[33] Shapin: op. cit., 1975, pp. 239-240.

[34] [John Gordon]: 'The Doctrines of Gall and Spurzheim', *Edinburgh Review*, Vol. 25, 1815a, pp. 227-268.

[35] ibid., p. 252.

[36] ibid., p. 249; cf. John Barclay: *An Inquiry into the Opinions, Ancient and Modern, Concerning Life and Organization*, Edinburgh, 1822, pp. 375-379; A. Combe: 'Observations on Dr. Barclay's Objections to Phrenology', *Transactions of the Edinburgh Phrenological* Society, Vol. 1, 1824, pp. 406-407.

[37] P. M. Roget: 'Cranioscopy', *Encyclopedia Britanica Supplement to 4th, 5th and 6th edns.*, *Edinburgh*, Vol. 3, 1824, pp. 419-437.

[37a] ibid., p. 428.

[38] 'Controversy with Sir William Hamilton', *Phrenological Journal*, Vol. 4, 1827, pp. 377-407; 'Sir William Hamilton, Bart., and Phrenology', *Phrenological Journal*, Vol. 4, 1829, pp. 1-69; Thomas Stone: *Evidence against the system of phrenology . . .*, Edinburgh; 1828, *Observations on the phrenological development of Burke, Hare . . .*, Edinburgh, 1829, and 'On the Frontal Sinus', *Edinburgh New Philosophical Journal*, Vol. 14, 1833, pp. 82-89; Alexander Monro: *The Anatomy of the Brain* (with an account of experiments conducted by Sir William Hamilton), Edinburgh, 1831.

[39] 'Controversy with Hamilton': op. cit. pp. 390-391; Stone: op. cit., 1828, p. 54.

[40] 'Controversy with Hamilton': op. cit., p. 395.

[41] ibid., pp. 392, 401.

[42] ibid., pp. 386-387; 'Sir William Hamilton . . .': op. cit., p. 9.

[43] 'Controversy with Hamilton': op. cit., pp. 388-389n.

[44] 'Sir William Hamilton . . .': op. cit., pp. 11-12.

[45] Henry Gray: *Gray's Anatomy*, London, 1913, 18th edn, pp. 190, 221.

[46] Francis Schiller: 'The Rise of the "Enteroid Processes" in the 19th Century: Some Landmarks in Cerebral Nomenclature', *Bulletin of the History of Medicine*, Vol. 37, 1965, pp. 326-338; Clarke and Dewhurst: op. cit., pp. 60-67.

[47] It is important here to stress the ambiguity inherent in the notion of what structures were 'known' at any given time. The fissure of Rolando, for example, was 'shown' in various anatomists' representations prior to 1810 (or at least it has been 'shown' by historians to have been 'shown'). But it was not 'named' and assimilated to modern conceptions of pattern until much later. On this particular subject, and for an emphasis on the importance of 'naming', see Schiller: op. cit.

[48] John Gordon: *A System of Anatomy*, Vol. 1, Edinburgh, 1815b, p. 81.

[49] Gordon: op. cit., 1815a.

Steven Shapin

50 John Gordon: *Observations on the Structure of the Brain, comprising an estimate of the claims of Drs. Gall and Spurzheim to discovery in the the anatomy of that organ*, Edinburgh, 1817.

51 Barclay: op. cit.

52 ibid., pp. 375-377.

53 cf. Stone: op. cit., 1828, pp. 15-17.

54 Gall: op. cit., ii, p. 249.

55 Clarke and Dewhurst: op. cit., pp. 94, 101-102; E. Clarke and C. D. O'Malley: *The Human Brain and Spinal Cord: A Historical Study Illustrated by Writings from Antiquity to the Twentieth Century*, University of California, London, 1968, pp. 391-395; J. G. Spurzheim: *Examinations of the Objections made in Britain against the Doctrines of Gall and Spurzheim*, Edinburgh, 1817, p. 43.

56 A. Combe: op. cit., 1824, p. 399; J. G. Spurzheim: *The Anatomy of the Brain, with a General View of the Nervous System*, London, 1826, pp. 110-111.

57 A. Combe: op. cit., 1824, p. 403.

58 Spurzheim: op. cit., 1826, p. 112; Stone: op. cit., 1828, p. 17.

59 Clarke and O'Malley: op. cit., pp. 415-457.

60 Clarke and Dewhurst: op. cit., p. 91.

61 Spurzheim: op. cit., 1826, p. 111.

62 Clarke and O'Malley: op. cit., pp. 566-567.

63 ibid., pp. 598-599.

64 'Report on a Memoir': op. cit., pp. 64-66.

65 Ackerknecht: op. cit., p. 151.

66 Spurzheim: op. cit., 1815, pp. 36-43 and 1817, pp. 32-42.

67 Gordon: op. cit., 1815b, p. 121.

68 ibid., p. 123.

69 ibid., pp. 123-124.

70 Gordon: op. cit., 1815a, pp. 255-256.

71 ibid., p. 256. It is interesting to note that Gordon expressed two, rather different, views of the value of direct sensory evidence. In this context he asserted that 'mere' appearances may be bad indicators of structural reality; elsewhere, as we have seen, he chided his opponents for doing other than describing 'mere' appearances.

72 Gordon: op. cit., 1817, pp. 11-16.

73 Spurzheim: op. cit., 1817, p. 20; cf., Spurzheim: op. cit., 1815, pp. 13-14.

74 Spurzheim: op. cit., 1817, p. 21.

75 ibid., p. 25.

76 A. Combe: op. cit., 1824, p. 408.

The Politics of Observation

[77] This is not to say that the fibres had a common origin or that the nerves were 'prolongations' of the brain. Phrenologists, especially Gall, were keen to deny these notions; for example, Spurzheim: op. cit., 1815, pp. 15-18.

[78] Gall: op. cit., ii, pp. 248-249.

[79] ibid., ii, pp. 247, 250.

[80] George Combe: *On the Functions of the Cerebellum*, Edinburgh, 1838.

[81] The subject matter of this section might easily have been addressed from a rather different perspective, that of the cognitive aspects of visual communication. Indeed, my attention was originally drawn to these issues by a reading of William Ivins: *Prints and Visual Communication*, M.I.T. Press, Cambridge Mass., 1953; and H. E. Gombrich: *Art and Illusion*, Phaidon, London, 1959. Ivins stresses the difficulty of relating a published engraving to what the anatomist may actually have 'seen', whereas Gombrich emphasises the relationship between 'schema' of artistic production and 'schema' for seeing. In any case, it is important to know that a number of people were involved in the production of these representations. The Gall and Spurzhiem plates were drawn by the artist Prêtre and engraved by Bouquet; the 'Gordon' cerebellum was in fact drawn by Syme and engraved by one W. Miller. Both artist and engraver impose their 'syntax' on the representation, which may result in the loss or distortion of those features of reality which most closely relate to the anatomists' concerns. However, the end-products become representations of 'reality' to which anatomists, and those they are able to persuade, give their assent as reliable accounts.

[82] Gordon: op. cit., 1817, figs. 1 and 2, pp. 209-215.

[83] Spurzheim: op. cit., 1815, pp. 34-35 and 1826, pp. 121-125; Gordon: op. cit., 1817, pp. 191-193, 198-199.

[84] Gordon: op. cit., 1817, pp. 39, 209-210.

[85] ibid., p. 38.

[86] Gordon: op. cit., 1815b, pp. 144-145.

[87] Spurzheim: op. cit., 1817, p. 15.

[88] ibid., p. 29.

[89] ibid., pp. 28-29.

[90] ibid., p. 39.

[91] Personal experience with dissection of these structures (aided by Dr. C. J. Lawrence) indicates that if one cuts the corpus dentatum towards its lateral edges it does appear to be a greyish mass, wheras slicing it medially produces a section which appears much as Gordon represented it. I should like to thank the Anatomy Department of the University of Edinburgh Medical School for providing us with the necessary material.

NOTES ON FIGURES

Figure 1: Sir George Stewart Mackenzie: *Illustrations of Phrenology*, Edinburgh, 1820, Plate IV, figure 1.

Figure 2: F. J. Gall and J. G. Spurzheim: *Anatomie et Physiologie du Système Nerveux . . . Atlas*, Paris, 1810, Plate X.

Figure 3: Mackenzie: op. cit., Plate I, figure 3.

Steven Shapin

Figure 4: Gall and Spurzheim: op. cit., Plate VIII.

Figure 5: Gall and Spurzheim: op. cit., Plate V.

Figure 6: John Gordon: *Observations on the Structure of the Brain . . .,* Edinburgh, 1817, figure 1 (This is a reduced copy of Plate XII of Gall and Spurzheim: op. cit.)

Figure 7: John Gordon: op. cit., figure 2.

Figure 8: *Gray's Anatomy,* 18th edn., London, 1913, p. 771; cf. J. C. Brash (ed.): *Cunningham's Text-Book of Anatomy,* Oxford University Press, London, 1953, 9th edn., p. 910, fig. 797.

I should like to thank the Royal Society of Medicine (London) for their permission to use the Gall and Spurzheim *Atlas* and to publish photographs taken from it. I should also like to express my appreciation of work done by the Photographic Unit of the University of Edinburgh Library, only a small part of which could be printed with the present paper.

IN THE BEGINNING: THE BATTLE OF CREATIONIST SCIENCE AGAINST EVOLUTIONISM*

Eileen Barker

WHETHER or not one agrees with the general theoretical position of Thomas Kuhn in *The Structure of Scientific Revolutions*[1] there can be little doubt that the theory of evolution does constitute an overwhelmingly pervasive paradigm not just for modern science but for almost the whole of modern thought. There are, however, those who operate outside the paradigm, rejecting evolution and all the assumptions and implications of that perspective, adhering instead to a fundamentalist view of the Bible and accepting as literal the account of Creation as it is presented in Genesis and elsewhere in the Scriptures.

The particular conflict between science and religion which was engendered by the publication of Darwin's *The Origin of Species*[2] has been faced in a variety of ways which basically involve either accommodation or rejection.[3] The accommodators believe that evolutionary theory and Christianity can be seen as compatible. The Bible is interpreted as partially allegorical or perhaps as only relating to things spiritual, and some kind of theistic evolution is adopted. In other words evolution is accepted as the Creator's way of doing things. The rejectors continue to argue that Christianity and Evolution are incompatible and as a consequence deny the truth either of religion or of evolutionary theory.

Those who reject evolution may do so unobtrusively, withdrawing from situations in which their beliefs will be questioned or threatened by the 'domain assumptions'[4] of the community at large. The division of labour, the general compartmentalisation and the heterogeneity of contemporary industrial society allow an individual Creationist to lead

* This study of Creationist Science forms part of a larger study on the ideologies of scientists which has been funded by the Nuffield Foundation to whom I wish to extend my thanks. I would also like to thank the Creationists who have given up valuable time to talk to me, often in the hospitality of their own homes.

a comparatively unremarkable life, whispering his beliefs to God when no one else is listening or, while secure in the fellowship of like-minded believers, openly declaring a faith which is reinforced by corporate affirmation and time-honoured ritual.

But what if he is a scientist? If he is a student or even a researcher or teacher of science, how can he work within the evolutionary paradigm? If he wants to get or keep jobs he may feel it necessary to keep his beliefs to himself. This he can do by choosing areas where affirmation of evolution is comparatively irrelevant. Or he may, by carefully compartmentalising his psyche, convince himself in a somewhat schizoid fashion that while the Genesis story is the truth, the whole truth, and nothing but the truth, this is a metaphysical belief while evolutionary theory is an occupational or methodological heuristic. Evolution thus becomes tolerable as a working hypothesis, but it is awarded no existential status and it is abandoned as soon as the scientist steps out of his world of work.[5]

There are, however, others who feel the evolutionary paradigm has gone too far—that it is *not* useful but is in fact positively harmful both to the furtherance of true science in particular and to the state of the world in general. Creationist scientists must stand up and be counted not just as fundamentalists who happen to be scientists, but as Creationist scientists who happen to believe in the Bible. This in its present form is a recent and rapidly growing phenomenon.

Entrenchment of the Evolutionary Paradigm

The idea of evolution is an old one but the growth of acceptance of modern evolutionary theory can easily be dated from the publication of Darwin's *The Origin of Species* in 1859. In this natural selection was put forward as the mechanism whereby more complicated species, including man himself, had evolved from the 'lower' animals. The most spectacular dramatisation marking the 'paradigm shift' from Genesis to Darwinism took place at the British Association confrontation between T. H. Huxley and Bishop Wilberforce in 1860. In 1900 Mendel's earlier work on genetics was discovered and although Creationists would claim this supported Genesis rather than evolution[6] it was in fact followed by the development of Neo-Darwinianism.

Fundamentalist churches continued to exist of course, but their beliefs were based on faith rather than on scientific support. A few scientists vociferously insisted on the Genesis account of creation but theirs tended to be voices crying in the wilderness. As the twentieth century progressed the evolutionary paradigm became more and more established in scientific circles and there was little institutional support for those who rejected it—little, but some. The Victoria Institute (V.I.), or Philosophical Society of Great Britain as it was originally called, had been founded in 1865 'To promote investigation into the relation between science and Christian faith at a time when many people believed science to be an enemy of revealed religion and irreconcilable with it'. But while the V.I. certainly provided a forum for those wishing to promote the Creationist perspective, the organisation as a whole increasingly tended to embrace theistic evolutionism. In 1932 the Evolution Protest Movement (E.P.M.) was founded with the stated aims of publishing scientific information supporting the Bible and demonstrating that the theory of organic evolution is not in accordance with scientific fact. But although the E.P.M. numbered some eminent scientists among its members (Sir Ambrose Fleming was its first president) most of its literature was written by non-scientists and the criterion for assessing truth tended to be the Book of Scripture rather than the Book of Nature, or when the Book of Nature was invoked it was to lend support for the Argument from Design—'consider the wondrous works of God'.

On the whole those who, by the end of the first half of the twentieth century, turned to science for reassurance that the evolutionary paradigm was not omnipotent might find a few scien*tists* publicly affirming their belief in Genesis as literal[7] truth, but these scientists rarely *used* their science to support their belief.

In order to try to understand why there should at the present time be a growth in Creation science—something which would still nevertheless undoubtedly fall into the category of rejected knowledge for the overwhelming majority of modern scientists—the phenomenon will be looked at from two distinct but interrelated perspectives. First it will be suggested that one can at a macro level locate certain features which might promote a need for, or, to be more cautious, a receptiveness towards such a growth; secondly one can look at the growth itself and see the generation of a healthy spiral of reinforcement of the rejected knowledge, providing support for a deviant 'plausibility structure'.[8] The first approach assumes the operation of negative feedback or reactions, while the second assumes a positive feedback or reinforcement mechanism.

Cultural Climate of Receptiveness

To make generalisations at the macro level is to invite instant repudiation as myriad qualifications are ignored by the bold or fool-hardy strokes of the generaliser's brush. Nevertheless it is sometimes possible to recognise drifts or changes which are of sufficient substance to facilitate the understanding of certain phenomena. The argument, which I have elaborated elsewhere,[9] is that the growth of certain kinds of rejected knowledge can be more comprehensible if they are seen in a context in which the paradigm of normal science is itself *both* rejected *and* accepted in a somewhat paradoxical fashion.

For well over a century and until the end of the Second World War, or even possibly as late as the 1960s, science was increasingly turned to in order to provide many of the answers to men's predicaments. It was science that embodied the respected values, attitudes and standards of excellence. According to most commentators there was a generally accepted and generally acceptable trend towards a decline in religion, or at least in the scope and range of religious beliefs and institutions, while science, almost, it seemed, on a zero-sum principle, surged ahead, penetrating into ever more aspects of our lives with ever increasing efficiency and commanding ever more the awe and wonder demanded of an esoteric religion. There are indeed still scientists who believe an enlightened interpretation of modern science provides the only source of moral or ethical knowledge.[10] However, during the sixties it started to become clear that there was a discernible disillusionment with science. Bombs and pollution, uncertainty, relativity, rationality, empiricism, deterministic materialism and the dehumanising loss of individuality through generalisation—all these and other aspects and attitudes of modern science contributed towards a new questioning of the sort of society associated (especially among sections of the affluent youth) with a focus on scientific enquiry. There must, the argument went, be a greater, warmer Quality which transcends the quantifying rationality and cold, impersonal objectivity of mechanistic science.

It was almost as if Sorokin's pendulum had swung to its sensate maximum and was on the return journey to the ideational. The Puritan Ethic, when fully explored as the Ethic of Science, was found to have exhausted its own enthusiasm of hope and was recognised as devoid of the basic religious answers and reassurances that had been carefully cast off by the Puritanism of science.

But history shows us that pendulums do not swing backwards and forwards along the same path. Those rejecting the values and consequences of a scientific world-view are nonetheless children of the age of science. They have been imbued with the spirit of the era of the scientific expert and it is from him that they will seek a justification of their rejection. The community of scientists has taken over the role of the priest as the guardian of truth. While there is a realisation that science cannot provide all the answers and that 'real truth' goes beyond science, there is also the belief that it is necessary to take up the gauntlet that science has thrown at Biblical revelation and thus to use the methods and reliability of true science to overcome false scientism.

The initial swing was largely a radical one. Large areas of conventional wisdom were rejected in favour of spontaneity, exploration, freedom from constraint, communing and the commune. Consciousness was sought at the Aquarian Frontier, and the Invisible Religion blossomed into Flower Power, The Jesus Movement, the Gay Church and all manner of effervescent and esoteric Eastern type religions. But this very swing has itself produced a further reaction, this time against the antinomian heresy of anything-goes-Hippydom.

Among some of those more firmly attached to the traditional institutions and values of Western society, the reaction against the uncertainty, materialism and secularism of science took a different form. Their commitment to cosmic rules and order would certainly allow them to accept the new *means* of science to reveal truth, but the meanings to be found in such revelations could only reflect those eternal truths which had been embodied in the threatened traditions and beliefs of the past.

Thus, the argument at the macro level has been: first, that the second half of the twentieth century has seen a reaction against science as the provider of the highest form of truth and an increasingly articulated belief that something exists beyond science which in some ways corresponds to and would meet the problems met by traditional religion. Secondly, science as a form of knowledge had nevertheless been impressive and successful enough to be able to lay claim to a superior epistemology so that if one were looking for an expert in knowledge to justify one's claims about reality it would be to the new priesthood of science that one would turn. Thirdly, the initial direction in which the rejection of science (and not only science, of course) took place was anti-traditional in its search for spontaneity and freedom, but fourthly, a further response, in part a reaction to this youthful antinomianism, sought to preserve traditional values and moral standards. For some of those concerned, the paradigm of evolution with its denial of the fundamental importance and implications of a Creator, its apparent insistence on moral relativism rather than absolutism, and its assertion that man was merely a complicated beast, epitomised and was responsible for the undermining of all that was sacred, good and true.

In other words, searching among the many options offered in the contemporary supermarket of truths there will be those who are receptive to a traditional religion packaged by science and for whom evolution can be identified as one of the primary causes of present-day ills.

The Growth of Creation Science

Having suggested a social context in which a certain phenomenon *might* occur, we still have to see whether or not it *does* in fact occur, and if so how. The sociologies of knowledge and of religion are sadly silent on detailed explanations as to why different truths should be *differentially* accepted within a particular class or group. It does, however, seem fairly clear that once a movement *starts* to grow it provides its own impetus for *further* growth so long as there remains a general climate of receptiveness. In other words, acceptance, *ceteris paribus,* encourages further acceptance. The laws of supply and demand of knowledge, like other commodities, enjoy their own multiplier effect. Availability and visibility of what is supplied is necessary to initiate, keep up and bolster demand. A process of positive feedback or reinforcement can be seen to operate as knowledge becomes more widely disseminated and as it proclaims legitimation from respectable backers.

First a fairly obvious but nonetheless important point to note is that the recent growth in Creation science has by no means been a phenomenon *ex nihilo,* nor has it been associated with a charismatic figure. Where there is no demand for his knowledge, it is a rare man who upholds his beliefs in complete isolation from his fellows. Society tends to allow individuals who persevere with non-popular beliefs only limited hearing outside mental institutions and the supply of such knowledge soon peters out. But while those upon whom society had conferred the status of purveyors of scientific truth had rejected the Genesis account of Creation, and the paradigm of evolution had become firmly entrenched, the Bible could still be cited as a respectable source of religious or spiritual knowledge and fundamentalist beliefs continued to survive, if not exactly to prosper, throughout the twentieth century. Churches and small groups provided sufficient fellowship to protect small pockets of believers, and into these preserves children were born and carefully socialised in the belief of the literal truth of Genesis. This was, however, at the cost of isolation and a retreat from a direct confrontation with science. The religious organisations tended to be sectarian in character or, among those like Baptists who could be classified as denominational, congregations could be found putting considerable pressure on their members not to take up the study of biology. This is understandable as it would be a not infrequent occurence for those who *did* take up science to renounce their faith completely—particularly on being taught evolutionary theory.

Today, however, there are those with undoubted membership of the new priesthood of science who are prepared to declare that Genesis has nothing to fear from science—*true* science that is. In the light of such declarations, the Genesis believer becomes less isolated from the dominant paradigm which is no longer seen as something to fear but rather as something to ridicule and show to be mistaken; more established scientists are prepared to come into the open; more young people are prepared to go into science and stay within the faith; and a few—as yet only a few, but an increasing number—are turning *from* an atheistic belief in science *to* belief in the Bible.

Creation Science in America

The impetus for the growth in Creation science can be traced to North America—particularly the West Coast of the United States.

The debate between Evolutionists and Creationists in the United States came to a head considerably later than it had in Britain. By the early 1920s several organisations had tried to pass anti-evolution laws. When a high school teacher, John Scopes, was convicted of teaching evolution, his lawyer, Clarence Darrow, provided a public dramatisation of the evolutionary arguments with an effect not dissimilar to that which had occurred in The British Association meeting half a century earlier. The evolutionary paradigm became more and more firmly entrenched and fundamentalist churches, as in Britain, relied on faith and fellowship rather than on science for support of beliefs. In 1949 the American Scientific Affiliation was formed. Initially it supported the Genesis account of Creation but gradually it moved towards an acceptance of theistic evolution. In 1963 this became so marked that a group of ten members broke away and formed the Creation Research Society.[11] This grew rapidly and within ten years was claiming a membership of 450 voting members (with post-graduate degrees in science) and over 1600 non-voting members. All members have to subscribe to the official Statement of Belief which summarises the fundamental tenets of the movement as a whole:

1. The Bible is the written Word of God, and because it is inspired throughout, all its assertions are historically and scientifically true in all the original autographs. To the student of nature this means that the account of origins in Genesis is a factual presentation of simple historical truths.

2. All basic types of living things, including man, were made by direct creative acts of God during the Creation Week described in Genesis. Whatever biological changes have occurred since Creation Week have accomplished only changes within the original created kinds.

3. The great Flood described in Genesis, commonly referred to as the Noachian Flood, was an historic event worldwide in its extent and effect.

4. We are an organisation of Christian men of science who accept Jesus Christ as our Lord and Saviour. The account of the special creation of Adam and Eve as one man and woman and their subsequent fall into sin is the basis for our belief in the necessity of a Saviour for all mankind. Therefore, salvation can come only through accepting Jesus Christ as our Saviour.

The Society publishes a quarterly journal of research articles with the goal of realigning science within the framework of Biblical creationism.

In 1970 Christian Heritage College and its research division, now known as the Institute for Creation Research (I.C.R.), were established in San Diego, California. The Institute declares that it 'recognises the Bible as the source of all truth and meaning of life and God as the Creator and Sustainer of all things. Its goals are to re-establish these principles in the educational and scientific worlds'. It is, it claims, the first known time in history that an educational and research centre has been founded strictly on Creationist principles and purposes. Current projects include a search for Noah's Ark on Mount Ararat; research for fossil anomalies; field studies on inverted geo-

logical sequences as well as library research in current scientific publications dealing with origins. A monthly newsletter 'Acts and Facts'
is available free. This describes the successes of I.C.R. scientists as
they travel all over North American churches (usually Baptist) and
campuses, giving lectures, holding seminars, and engaging in debates
with Evolutionists who are always reported to have come off the
worse for wear. 'Acts and Facts' also gives advance details of the
scientists' itineraries and of their nationwide weekly broadcasts.
Among other I.C.R. publications there is a considerable number of
books which range from High School texts to 'technical monographs
on specific evidences for recent creation'.

The existence of the C.R.S. provided an undoubted boost to the
creation science movement in Britain. Membership of the E.P.M.
was 200 in 1966. In 1970 it had 850 fully paid up members but in
1972 the secretary reported that, unlike their American friends, they
were making little numerical progress. The E.P.M., possibly because
of its Biblical rather than scientific focus, did not seem to provide an
adequate forum for Creationist scientists and in 1972 the Newton
Scientific Association (N.S.A.) was started by the Pastor of the
Metropolitan Tabernacle and a few young scientists. The group
advertised in religious magazines such as the *Evangelical Times,* and
sent invitations to colleges giving information about their meetings.
This, together with personal contacts and a long letter on the origin
of life in the *School Science Review* of September 1975, resulted in
a total membership of 160 by the beginning of 1977.

Membership of the N.S.A. falls into two categories:

(1) *Subscribers* who primarily enrol to express their support but
also receive a periodic newsletter and are invited to occasional meetings.

(2) *Participants* who must be graduates and able to affirm the 1846
Evangelical Alliance Statement of Faith. Over half have in fact joined
as Graduate Participants. Of the scientists (chemists, engineers and
biologists being most prominent), over 40 per cent make their living
by teaching, nearly half of these being in higher education. While
all the Participants hold at least one degree, 22 per cent of them have
also been awarded doctorates. A quarter (perhaps more) of the Subscribers hold at least one degree. While all the Participants are Pro-
testants, the vast majority of them are Non-conformists. Only 12 per
cent of the membership is female.[12]

Attendance at the twice yearly N.S.A. meetings has been steadily increasing to about 150 over the last 4 years. Roughly three-quarters are male and most of them under 35. The audience is dressed in respectable, casual clothes; slacks and jackets for the men and skirts and blouses or jumpers for the women. Hair is clean and controlled. Nearly all are English, all are pleasant and courteous in manner and speech. At the earlier meetings there was little 'group feeling' but at later ones considerably more fellowship developed as people began to recognise each other and chat over the sit down high tea which breaks up the proceedings. Books can be bought and participants are invited to stay and talk after the last lecture. The lectures delivered at these meetings are impressive. Visual aids are well used and the speakers are genuine experts in their subject, most of them being university teachers, some of professorial status. As yet, however, few but the converted attend and there is no public debate with evolutionists. The continually reiterated expression of emotion at the gatherings is one of relief, especially from school teachers; relief that at last they can mix with fellow teachers and discuss shared problems; and relief that at last they can hear and buy the works of scientists who support their anti-evolutionary beliefs. The dangers of the evolutionary paradigm are discussed and agreement is reached that something must be done, especially in the important field of education.

Attitudes to Science and Scripture

The Creationists with whom we are concerned accept the validity of *both* science *and* a literal interpretation of the Bible. God is seen to reveal himself both in the scriptures *and* through nature. As God does not contradict himself there must be a basic compatibility between the two sources of revelation, so if scientific research is carried out honestly and carefully it will become obvious that it fits the Genesis explanation far more neatly than the evolutionary one.[13]

The exact emphasis in the degree and kind of possible support for creation varies between individuals and the organisations.

While the Evolution Protest Movement describes itself as a 'scientific, educational and religious organisation' its focus has been on the last two functions rather than the first, the literature being more of an exegesis of the Bible than a scientific contribution. 'If the science of biology is at any point at variance in what it teaches with what we find written in God's word, then let us cleave to the latter and not to the former. We ought to obey God rather than men.'[14]

The I.C.R. claims that it 'seeks to educate scientists, teachers, students and the general public on the *scientific evidence supporting* Biblical creationism', (my italics) and that it 'conducts and sponsors research on projects which bear promise of significant impact in the scientific realm supporting creationism'. Even more boldly one can find such statements as 'The Bible *is* a textbook of Science'.[15]

The Newton Scientific Association is particularly concerned not to resort to Biblical reference at all in its work but to stick solely to secular references. The members are well aware that they could easily be accused of being 'religious' and they are insistent that it is not a religious crusade that they are conducting. Their interest is in good *science* and this they believe is non-evolutionary. To claim they could prove a Biblical revelation, which is by its very nature a supernatural revelation, would be self-defeating. They would only be making the mistake that they accuse the evolutionists of making—that is of accepting as fact what can only be an unprovable, metaphysical theory. Science has to be reproducible, the origins of the world not being reproducible must remain speculative. It is necessary for the Creationist scientists to try to claim superior knowledge but they too must beware of becoming too dogmatic. The important thing is to understand the difference between scientific *facts* which the Creationist will not only not be afraid of, but will delight in accepting, and scientific *theory* which is man-made and subject to the vagaries of man's limited understanding.[16]

The Creationist scientist must then try to produce all the facts that he can for which evolutionary theory cannot account and he must try to show that Creation theory provides a more plausible interpretation of *all* the facts.[17]

Creation science arguments[18]

The attack on evolution takes place on various fronts, some of which will be accepted by most Creationist scientists but some of which (such as the Gosse argument[19] that God created the world *as though* it had evolved over millions of years) will be rejected by others as not being legitimate in a rational or scientific debate. What follows is a brief, non-technical summary of some of the main arguments, but in the actual literature elaborate technical detail is often presented.[20]

It is important to emphasise that none of the 'facts' of nature is denied, only an evolutionary interpretation of them.

First of all, it is pointed out that classification is nothing more than a taxonomic device. If one arranges the species in order of increasing complexity it does not follow that we must therefore have evolved from the amoeba to man.[21] To the believer in the Bible similarity of structure among living organisms just establishes the fact of the One Great Architect who had in mind one great pattern which He used while making His natural species with such modifications as were necessary for their different conditions in life. Anyway, it has been claimed, the similarity of structure is only superficial. One of the youngest of sciences called cyto-chemistry can actually show that formulae for specimens of treated cytoplasm of the cells of different animals are different for each species. All mankind belongs to one species or has one formula—birds, apes and so on each have their own formulae.[22]

According to the evolutionists it is possible to see vestigial organs and limbs as morphological lags, or 'left overs' from earlier states which have lost their function. The Creationist denies such vestiges exist. Because an organ's function is not known it does not mean it has not got one.[23]

Palaeontology (the study of extinct, organised beings) provides a crucial battle ground. The Creationists have various arguments here.[24] Those concerning dating question the evolutionists' assumption of 'Uniformitarianism'—that processes occurring *now* can explain what happened in the past.[25] Also when 'earlier' fossils are found above 'later' ones, evolutionary geologists say on *this* evidence that the earth must have had an upthrust fold and *therefore* show the fossils in the wrong order but this, of course, is purely circular.[26] The fossil evidence instead suggests the truth of the Noachian flood.[27]

Another line of argument rests on the paucity of evidence of links connecting the different species—or 'kinds' as the Creationists prefer to call them (not wishing to assume that modern taxonomy necessarily coincides with the Biblical 'kinds'). The problem of 'the missing link' is of course of particular importance and the story of the Piltdown forgery is often raised as an example of the evolutionary scientist's gullibility if not downright incompetence.[28]

Creationists do not deny that *variations* can occur *within* the different kinds of animals. The well known example of the development of black moths in the north of England during industrialisation is accepted. But to prove evolution one would have to show that each kind evolved *from* another kind. The Bible does not speak of any fixity of a species. It only speaks of kinds reproducing 'after their kind' because 'the seed is in itself'.[29] Similarly natural selection is recognised as an integral part of the current creation model but only acting *within the gene pool* of a particular population.[30]

Another popular argument concerns the second law of thermodynamics. If entropy is increasing, and the world is continually undergoing increasing disorganisation, how can it be argued that evolution, which concerns increasing organisation, could occur?[31]

Many more arguments are advanced on such subjects as mimicry,[32] embryology, probability[33] and the age of the world,[34] our galaxy and the universe;[35] and, of course, the Argument from Design is continually reiterated. The details need not concern us here. What is of relevance is that the Creationists believe that if the facts are examined closely enough then they all point to creation rather than evolution. It is by doing science properly, not just accepting a theoretical position blindly, that the Bible is vindicated. 'As more and more scientists adopt the creation model, there ought to be an increasing emphasis on examining data from a Creationist viewpoint and a decreasing emphasis on searching out failures of the evolution model to make true or testable predictions. More than enough of the latter has been done than is needed to convince anyone not hindered by non-scientific considerations such as ignorance, prejudice or philosophy'.[36]

The Demand for Creation Science

Demand for creation science comes from a wide range of religious organisations. Baptists, Christadelphians, Seventh Day Adventists and many other fundamentalist sects are eager to promote the new justifications. Various publications such as *Plain Truth* proclaim the scientific basis of creation[37] and even the Hare Krishna magazine *Back to the Godhead*[38] scientifically shows how Darwin was wrong, although here, for an alternative explanation, one turns to Vedic literature rather than to Genesis. Jehovah's Witnesses who have published their own book on the subject are gratefully reproducing the scientific evidence which now supports their beliefs. Christian bookshops now stock whole shelves with Creationist literature whereas four or five years ago it was difficult to find any books on the subject by scientists. There are also cassettes on sale giving series of lectures on 'the Bible and Science' which confirm the Genesis account of origins. Although Pius XII allowed that 'the doctrine of Evolution is an open question' so long as it confines its speculations to the development of the *body* as opposed to the *soul,* the teaching of the Catholic Church is emphatic that the first eleven chapters of Genesis come under the heading of history and Catholic teachers of science are warned against disseminating false conjectures rather than true science.[39] Occasionally students from Catholic backgrounds receive something of a shock when they go up to read biology at university and hear for the first time about evolution.

It is impossible to estimate the extent to which news of creation science has spread but there can be no doubt that one can find oneself constantly being told by fundamentalists that proper science is now producing evidence to show that evolution is wrong. This knowledge may have been gained from the literature, either in books or magazines, from the pulpit or from special lectures at meetings organised by the various bodies. It is not unusual to talk to people who have travelled over 50 miles to attend such special meetings. At a recent EPM meeting in Manchester the room that had been booked provided insufficient accomodation for the audience which had to move into the adjoining Methodist Church for the lectures.

As well as meeting the demand from lay Creationists, Creationist science has started to reach those who had reluctantly or unthinkingly accepted evolution as a scientific fact. Most of those who are now told it is no such thing and turn to Creationism tend to be from evangelical Christian backgrounds, but there are those who have turned *to* Christianity *because* for them scientific knowledge points more directly to the Genesis account than to evolution. Such cases are admittedly rare but they certainly do exist.

Attitudes to others

Attitudes towards Creationists of scientists who accept the evolutionary paradigm tend to vary according to the type of belief held by the evolutionist. Although the growth of Creation science is widely recognised in America, few non-Christian scientists in Britain have heard about it and most tend to disbelieve that Creationists still exist. The general opinion seems to be that they can not be *proper* scientists, and/or they must be crazy—Flat Earthers. There is a marked unwillingness to consider any of the Creationist arguments and if pressed, amusement soon gives way to irritation rather than to debate.

Christian scientists tend to be more concerned. Liberals or modernists will, like the atheist or agnostic, tend to be slightly incredulous but not perhaps to doubt the Creationist's sanity so emphatically. They will insist he is wrong rather than mad. Evangelical scientists who accept theistic evolution are the most concerned for they will see and fear the reaction of others and believe that the Creationists are giving Biblical Christianity a bad name by clinging to 're-jected knowledge' and thus exposing the Scriptures to ridicule and opting for an easy way out of the laborious but necessary task of interpretation.

When considering the attitudes of Creationists towards others it is not perhaps altogether surprising that the more Popperian of them show greater respect for certain evolutionists than they do for some of their fellow Creationists. Members of the NSA are likely to be embarrassed by what they consider the Bible-thumping approach of the EPM which is seen as doing more harm than good to the cause. EPM members on the other hand are dubious about the apparently secular attitudes of the NSA, and the way members of the latter appear to leave the Scriptures out of their calculations as, for them, the whole point of the exercise is to show that God's word is true, and that therefore we should believe and live by the Bible. While there is certainly some overlap in the membership, one rarely sees the same faces at the meetings of the two organisations. There may, however, be some change in the future as the EPM has begun involving younger, scientifically trained speakers and officers.

Creationists' attitudes to evolutionists do vary of course but when asked why the theory of evolution has had such a success they will usually blame man's fallen nature, present day attitudes to science, and the mass media. The BBC is particularly subject to a conspiracy theory interpretation as one of the greatest institutions devoted to spreading the evolutionary ideas and refusing to give a hearing to the other point of view. Like the rest of society, the mass media are extremely reverential of science which is seen as a 'sacred cow' by non-scientists.[40] The Creationists believe that evolutionary scientists are reluctant to meet them on a public platform because they realise they would be forced to concede too much. Often teachers and text books and indeed public figures are regarded by Creationists as performing confidence tricks in the name of science, glossing over the shaky aspects of evolutionary theory, telling children a smooth, convincing story in place of the uncomfortable and difficult truth. In the end, Creationists feel, it comes down to the fact that evolution represents a Theophobia. People will believe anything rather than facing up to the implications of accepting creation, that there is a Creator, a personal God who created man with a purpose and destiny and to Whom they will one day be held personally responsible. Evolution removes such spiritual constraint and responsibility and presents man with a justification for submitting to his fallen nature.

Christian scientists who accept theistic evolution are seen as having compromised their position by trying to keep their beliefs in water-tight compartments and not wishing to expose them to the attack of rationalists. Such a strategic withdrawal is thought to lead non-Christians into saying that if evolution *is* the case then theism is nothing but the icing on the cake. Theistic evolutionists are there-fore seen as suffering from guilty consciences. It is admitted by Creationists that theistic evolution is still the most *comfortable* position for a Christian to take. They recognise full well the problem that testifying to other beliefs could risk isolating them from the rest of the scientific community. Also specialists in one area are frequently afraid to speak out against specialists in another area.

In fact the setting up of the N.S.A. has brought several scientists to declare openly their commitment to Creationism. They have been asked to speak on their own particular subjects and have been en-couraged by the public testimony of some of the more eminent of their colleagues. So far I have come across no instance of discrimin-ation when scientists in universities or research institutions have spoken out. On the whole, Creationists report that while some of their colleagues might be mildly amused and question them, most tend to avoid the subject, possibly, it is thought, through embarrass-ment. Occasionally public affirmation leads to a surprised discovery of fellow travellers, for example, in one London teaching hospital there were at least four Creationists on the staff (and several students) who were unknown to each other until one senior physician made his beliefs public.

But while British Creation scientists at the level of research and further education are tolerated within the scientific community—

possibly because they are not taken all that seriously—the situation might be different in the schools.

Creationism and Education

Given that the Creationists believe that the evolutionary paradigm is responsible for many of the ills in contemporary society and that it is bad science, it is to be expected they will be anxious that good and true science should be taught in the schools.

In America there has recently been a remarkably successful lobby by Creationists for alternatives to evolution being presented to school children and a few states have now had legislation passed to this effect. According to Dorothy Nelkin there have been three themes pervading 'The Science Text-Book Controversies'.

> 'First, the protests reflected the fact that a non-negligible fraction of the population is disillusioned with science and is concerned that it threatens traditional religious and moral values. Second the protests reflect the fact that many people clearly resent the authority represented by scientific dogmatism, particularly when the authority is expressed in an increased professionalism of the school curriculum. Third the protests reflect the fact that many people are afraid that the structured, meritocratic processes operating within science threaten more egalitarian, pluralistic values.'[41]

There has as yet been no comparable movement in Britain—nor indeed is it likely to occur in a similar form since there is no equivalent system of text book control in this country. The British science teacher who does not accept evolution has an uphill job if he tries to do something about it in his classes. The children are likely to regard him with a certain amount of patronising sympathy if he voices objections to evolution. As one Creationist told me with a wry smile, he was informed 'But, Sir, I saw a programme about it on the telly. It really is true you know'. Some teachers use such ploys as 'not quite managing to get to the bit in the syllabus where evolution is covered' but then there is the problem that the examination system is not only evolution-orientated in G.C.E. papers but Creationists are afraid their pupils might suffer a disadvantage if they do not give orthodox answers. The most they can really hope to do is to make the children aware that there are questions that *could* be asked and that evolution is not a hard fact but a theory which makes certain assumptions. But here again too nice an argument on the philosophy of science can lead to confusion at O level or even A level and as yet there is little overt debate in this country during science lessons.

When confrontation does occur it is more likely to be in the field of religious education. It is in fact interesting that early in 1977 when the local authority in Dallas was *insisting* that the historical story of Adam and Eve must be taught to students, an English local authority was upholding the *dismissal* of a religious education teacher for doing that very thing.[42] At the time of writing the case has yet to appear before an industrial tribunal,[43] but it already promises to be something of a *cause célèbre* in Creationist circles. The teacher concerned has received considerable support from fellow Creationists such as the ten scientists (comprising 10 per cent of the staff and research workers in the Faculty of Enginering of one of the better British universities) who wrote a letter to the local authority stating that there is 'a significant number (of scientists) who, having undergone a conventional scientific training are able to affirm their belief in the Genesis account of the origin of all things'. The dismissed teacher has also received support from many who, while believing in the theory of evolution, nevertheless believe he should have been allowed freedom to express his views. It could in fact be argued that this case and the situation in America as described by Professor Nelkin highlight a curious phenomenon prevalent in sections of modern society which is that while there is a growing clamour *against ethical relativism* in favour of absolute values, at the same time there is a growing demand *for epistemological relativism* where all knowledge should, in the name of some sort of absolute egalitarianism, be regarded as having validity. It may well be that such disinterested (or uninterested) tolerance will yet allow considerable further development of the movement from those who are themselves operating within the evolutionary paradigm. It is also, however, likely that such relativistic tolerance is confined to the middle class intelligentsia and should the creation science movement develop beyond a certain limit there may well be a reaction from those who, like the fundamentalists themselves, tend to seek an absolute truth and the reassurance that their children will be taught proper science as it has been defined for them—that is within the evolutionary model—without the confusion of liberal choice.

Conclusion

Today an individual scientist working by himself or with *only* the fellowship of a religious community behind him, is unlikely to get much of a hearing if he proclaims knowledge rejected by the scientific community at large. For organisations of like-minded scientists, however, there is more chance of making some kind of impact. The organisation can perform the functions of providing a haven of protection and reinforcement for those who feel isolated in the world of conventional science. Also, through the pooling of resources such as energy, knowledge and money, the organisation can act as a base for concerted proselytisation. Once such organisations get under way they can themselves provide the impetus for further growth so long as there is sufficient demand for their services. Theologically conservative science, whether concerned with creation or the Biblical record in general, eliminates an area of ambiguity and uncertainty between the demands and criteria of the present and the inheritance of the past. Perhaps it is not crucial for the majority of lay Creationists whether or not the intricacies of the arguments put forward by the scientists are grasped. What does matter is that there are those who undoubtedly possess membership of the new priesthood who claim that the heritage of the ages is validated by the criteria of the present.

It might however be a mistake to assume that the Creationist scientists *only* have a role to play in providing a justification for fundamentalist beliefs. They could well be seen as being capable of performing a much wider function. Detailed arguments over substantive issues cannot be entered into here but even a cursory examination of the literature suggests that there is enough sloppy thinking by Evolutionists to allow the Creationists to point legitimately to difficulties which the former all too often smugly ignore. Many Creationist scientists have a sophisticated grasp of the philosophy of science and they are by no means all living in a world of their own so far as scientific discoveries are concerned. It could indeed be argued that *because* they work within a 'rejected paradigm' they are sometimes more open to new facts than are those working within 'normal science'. Where the battle of Creationist science involves a challenge within the battlefield of science (as defined by the prevailing paradigm) it is Evolutionism which risks the consequences of complacency when it does not pick up the gauntlet.

Just as Durkheim suggested the pathological or the deviant can serve a positive function by defining what is 'right' and what 'wrong', so, it could be argued, those whose work outside an accepted paradigm can clarify boundaries of knowledge, highlighting the distinctions

Eileen Barker

between fact and interpretation of fact, between beliefs, metaphors, heuristic organising principles, theories, laws and all the other paraphernalia of categories that man employs in his search for truth. What is unknown and what unknowable can be made clearer and the bases of what knowledge we have can be more scrupulously examined.

Creationists may not win the battle within the scientific community but they can certainly provide proof for those who need and desire such proof that the battle is not lost. Old faith can appeal to the new knowledge, ancient certitude to modern proof.

London School of Economics and Political Science.

[1] Thomas Kuhn: *The Structure of Scientific Revolutions*, University of Chicago Press, Chicago, 1970, 2nd edn.

[2] Charles Darwin: *On the Origin of Species by Means of Natural Selection* or *The Preservation of Favoured Races in the Struggle for Life*, Watts, London, 1921 (reprint of 1st edn., 1859),

[3] E. Minter (ed.): *Evolution and Christian Thought Today*, Paternoster Press, London, 1961, 2nd edn.

[4] Alvin Gouldner: *The Coming Crisis of Western Sociology*, Heinemann, London, 1970.

[5] Eileen Barker: 'Apes and Angels: Reductionism, Selection and Emergence in the Study of Man', *Inquiry*, Vol. 19, 1976, pp. 367-399.

[6] Sylvia Baker: *Bone of Contention*, Evangelical Press, Welwyn, 1976, p. 15.

[7] It should perhaps be noted that some Creationists are worried about the use of the word 'literal' in describing their interpretation of scripture. The Creationist, it is pointed out, does not rule out poetical or even allegorical interpretations of scripture where these appear to be the writer's intention. For example, Psalm 8:3—'When I consider thy heavens, the work of thy fingers . . .' does not imply that God has fingers. Nor is Psalm 98:8 'Yet the floods clap their hands: let the hills be joyful together' to be taken literally.

[8] Peter Berger: *The Social Reality of Religion*, Faber, London, 1969, p. 126.

[9] Eileen Barker: 'Biologists on Religion: Contributions offered by contemporary biology to religious knowlege in the face of the changing image of science' in *Religion and Social Change*, Acts of the 13th International Conference on Sociology of Religion (C.I.S.R., Lille), 1975, pp. 253-284.

[10] Eileen Barker: 'Value Systems Generated by Biologists', *Contact*, Vol. 55, No. 4, 1976b, pp. 2-13.

[11] Vernon Bates: 'Defenders of the Faith', unpublished draft paper made available privately, 1973, pp. 13 ff.

[12] These figures are from an analysis I carried out on the membership list which the secretary of the NSA went through with me. A comparison with analyses of membership lists of other organisations of religious groups of scientists shows that all are strongly male dominated. Class membership of Evangelical groups which espouse theistic evolution is slightly higher than for the Creationists and much higher for 'Liberals' and 'Modernists' (see Barker: op. cit., 1975 for a typology and description of the various categories).

[13] P. Zimmerman (ed.): *Darwin, Evolution and Creation*, Concordia, St. Louis, 1959, p. x.

[14] Evolution Protest Movement: pamphlet No. 209.

[15] Henry Morris: *Studies in the Bible and Science*, Baker Book House, Grand Rapids, Michigan, 1966, p. 108.

[16] Edgar H. Andrews: *Is Evolution Scientific?*, Evangelical Press, Welwyn, 1977.

[17] P. Masters: *A Scientfic Approach to Origins*, Newton Scientific Association, London, 1975, pp. 7-8.

[18] The references given in this section are somewhat arbitrary as it in fact summarises arguments which appear over and over again in slightly varying forms throughout the literature.

[19] Edmund Gosse: *Father and Son*, Heinemann, London, 1907 (also Penguin, Harmondsworth, 1949, p. 76).

[20] For example, Walter Lammerts (ed.): *Scientific Studies in Special Creation*, Presbyterian and Reformed Publishing Company, Nutley, New Jersey, 1971.

[21] H. Douglas Dean et al.: *The Living World*, Creation-Science Research Center, San Diego, California, 1971, p. 22.

[22] H. Enoch: *Evolution or Creation*, Evangelical Press, London, 1967, p. 7.

[23] Henry Morris, William Boardman and Robert Koontz: *Science and Creation—A Handbook for Teachers*, Creation-Science Research Centre, San Diego, California, 1971, pp. 42-43.

[24] Lammerts: op. cit., 1971, pp. 72 ff.; William W. Boardman et al: *Science and Creation*, Creation-Science Research Center, San Diego, California, 1973, pp. 141 ff.

[25] Baker: op. cit., p. 3.

[26] ibid., pp. 14, 24.

[27] John C. Whitcomb and Henry M. Morris: *The Genesis Flood*, Presbyterian and Reformed Publishing Company, Nutley, New Jersey, 1961.

[28] Francis Vere: *Lessons of Piltdown*, Evolution Protest Movement, Stoke, Hampshire, 1959, p. 51.

[29] Enoch: op. cit., p. 107.

[30] Minter: op. cit., p. 129.

[31] Bolton Davidheiser et al.: *The Beginning of the World*, Creation-Science Research Center, San Diego, California, 1971, p. 6.

[32] Lane Lester: 'Mimicry', *Impact Series*, No 18, Institute for Creation Research, San Diego, California.

[33] S. Ellacott: *Mathematical Problems in the Evolutionary Model,* Newton Scientific Association Report, London, 1977, pp. 1-5.

[34] William W. Boardman *et al*: *Worlds Without End,* Creation-Science Research Center, San Diego, California, 1971, p. 20.

[35] Minter: op. cit., p. 41.

[36] Lester: op. cit.

[31] *Plain Truth,* Sept./Oct., 1976.

[38] *Back to the Godhead,* Vol. 10 No. 10.

[39] Pius XII: 'False Trends in Modern Teaching', *Evangelical Letter 'Humani Genesis',* Catholic Truth Society, London, 1950, pp. 21-23.

[40] David Watson: *The Great Brain Robbery,* Henry Walter, Worthing, 1975, p. 86.

[41] Dorothy Nelkin: 'The Science Text Book Controversies', *Scientific American,* Vol. 234, No. 4, 1976, p. 35.

[42] *Sunday Telegraph,* 6th February 1977.

[43] In the event, the industrial tribunal upheld the dismissal.

BETWEEN SCEPTICISM AND CREDULITY: A STUDY OF VICTORIAN SCIENTIFIC ATTITUDES TO MODERN SPIRITUALISM

Jon Palfreman

'Nothing is so difficult to decide as where to draw a just line between scepticism and credulity'

So wrote Charles Darwin[1] confused and disturbed by what he had heard of William Crookes's investigations with the American medium Daniel Dunglas Home. Darwin had always felt a certain antagonism to the alleged phenomena of such practices as mesmerism and clairvoyance. But in the 1870s he was to see Crookes, A. R. Wallace,[2] his cousin Francis Galton and other scientists attend seances and come away impressed and convinced. When in January 1874 Darwin attended his first seance with the medium Charles Williams—in the illustrious company of G. H. Lewes, George Eliot, Hensleigh Wedgwood and Francis Galton—he became tired and left before effects began happening. Galton's account of how things subsequently 'moved about the room' was very disturbing to Darwin until the following week T. H. Huxley attended a seance in disguise and satisfied himself that Williams was a fraud.[3] Darwin gladly accepted Huxley's version and regained some peace of mind.

Darwin's confusion was indicative of the mood of a decade in which no scientist could be indifferent to the alleged phenomena of spiritualism. While spiritualism had been a controversial issue in the 1850s and 1860s which had attracted the attention of scientists, it was really with William Crookes's investigations in 1870 that the whole area became of major concern to the scientific community. The next ten years saw a hardening of attitudes and the abuse and counter-abuse which appeared in Victorian periodicals, newspapers and public meetings allied individuals in various camps. To some extent this polarisation has obscured the full complexity of the situation. The changing attitude of Victorian science to modern spiritualism reflected the preoccupations and conflicts of the period, which included such things as: the issue of the endowment of Victorian science; the disenchantment with scientific naturalism; the particular financial interests of certain groups (e.g. conjurors); personal ambitions and desires, etc. As will be shown, different individuals were motivated to investigate spiritualism for differing reasons and the public discussion of the alleged phenomena often concealed conflicts of interest quite unrelated to the subject itself.

If examples can be found of the extremes in the controversy—examples of marked scepticism and credulity—they are respectively the distinguished physiologist and essayist W. B. Carpenter and the co-discoverer of the theory of evolution by natural selection, Alfred Russell Wallace. W. B. Carpenter, over a period of forty years, continually attacked the phenomena and exponents of the 'occult' studies of mesmerism, clairvoyance and spiritualism. His view was that such 'phenomena' resulted either from fraud or the deficient scientific training of the investigators, or both. In a celebrated exchange of articles in 1877-8 involving five journals[4] Carpenter and Wallace both argued the other's prejudice. Carpenter developed his theme of the 'psychological curiosities of credulity'. How was it, he asked himself, that men like Crookes and Wallace—who had apparently done exemplary work in orthodox science—could be so willing to accept the phenomena of spiritualism? Wallace's reply was an attempt to turn Carpenter's thesis on its head. 'The Psychological Curiosities of Scepticism'[5] discusses how Carpenter, apparently a sane and reasonable man when working on orthodox scientific subjects, had resorted to perpetrating damaging falsehoods about his opponents when dealing with spiritualism. The scepticism which Carpenter displayed in this sort of behaviour was not, in Wallace's view, the noble scepticism of the scientist but rather

'. . . a blind, unreasoning, arrogant disbelief that marches on from youth to age with its eyes shut to all that opposes its own pet theories; that believes its own judgement to be infallible; that never acknowledges its errors. It is a scepticism that clings to its refuted theories, and refuses to accept new truths'.[6]

But to Carpenter, Wallace was so credulous in regard of spiritualism that his testimony was almost worthless. In a discussion of the mediumship of Mrs. Eva Fay, who—despite William Crookes's endorsement—was widely held to be fraudulent, Carpenter says

'The fundamental difference between Mr. Wallace and myself as to the validity of testimony in regard to the "occult" sciences comes out so strongly in this case that I really have no common ground for a discussion which I cannot consider it profitable to continue'.[7]

Both men had a more realistic picture of the other's faults than of his own. As will be shown, Carpenter's behaviour displayed considerable prejudice and malice. On the other hand, Wallace came to be regarded as credulous by a great many of his fellow scientists. He played a minor role in the Society for Psychical Research (SPR) after its foundation in 1882, finding the atmosphere far too sceptical.

Most other scientists, or 'scientifically minded individuals' held positions in between that of Wallace and Carpenter. In the many clashes in the newspapers, periodicals, Court Trials and public meetings which took place in this decade a number of the fundamental issues and difficulties connected with the 'scientific' investigation of a heterodox area like spiritualism emerged. By the time the SPR was founded its leading representatives had a remarkable grasp of the problems. The purpose of this paper is to outline the history of the interaction between science and spiritualism (in the context of Victorian society) which led up to that understanding.

1. The Introduction of Modern Spiritualism to England

Modern Spiritualism arrived in successive waves from America where it had from its outbreak in 1848 attracted enormous interest and comment.[8] It was formally introduced to England when Mr. Stone brought the first professional medium, Mrs. Hayden, from the United States in October, 1852. The country was recovering from a heated controversy over the use and doctrine of animal magnetism or mesmerism in medical practice, and the new heresy soon inflamed the same organs of prejudice which had been very active in attacking animal magnetisers.[9]

Mrs. Hayden was a professional medium who only performed for the well-to-do, but the particular phenomenon of 'table rapping' which she (and several continental mediums) exhibited was to spread to all sectors of English society. Seances were held in which spirits would communicate with the sitters by rapping, turning or tilting the table when the correct letter of a printed alphabet was touched by the questioner. The early comments of those who had investigated Mrs. Hayden were largely unfavourable.[10] It included an article by G. H. Lewes 'The Rappites Exposed'[11] ridiculing the whole affair and explaining how the trick was done. But Robert Chambers wrote favourably of his experiences[12] and the famous mathematician Augustus de Morgan was clearly markedly impressed by what he saw.[13]

In 1853 table-turning spread to all classes of Victorian society and fast became a national pastime.[14] As in the case of the popular spread of animal magnetism in the 1840s the orthodox practitioners of science and medicine felt the time had come to 'restore sanity'. James Braid the Manchester surgeon who had attempted to explain animal magnetism in terms of involuntary muscular action and unconscious expectation on the part of the subjects[15] attended a conversation on table turning in Manchester and wrote up his deliberations.[16] *The Medical Times and Gazette* largely agreed with Braid.[17] But the most famous and convincing 'exposure' of table turning was due to Michael Faraday. Faraday, who never regarded the phenomena of spiritualism as anything but rooted in fraud or ignorance,[18] performed an ingenious experiment whereby he placed a movable table-top upon an ordinary table. In the seance Faraday observed that the table-top always started moving before the lower one under the influence of the hands of the sitters. Table moving was simply the result of involuntary muscular movement and unconscious expectations. Faraday completed his account with the words 'I must bring this long description to a close. I am a little ashamed of it, for I think, in the present age, and in this part of the world, it ought not to have been required'.[19]

A similar view was expressed by W. B. Carpenter both in a lecture at the Royal Institution on March 12, 1852,[20] and in an important article.[21] This article was the basis for his later writings. Apart from these responses from orthodox scientists a sizable literature[22] emerged on the subject including some trying to reconcile table-rapping with mesmerism.[23] But in 1853 interest began to decline rapidly and Mrs. Hayden returned to America.[24]

Apart from the interest caused by the brief visit of the American medium, D. D. Home,[25] little serious attention was paid to the phenomena of spiritualism until after 1860. Home's return to England in 1859 was undoubtedly partly responsible for this revival. His itinerary was markedly more spectacular than had been the case in 1855. He was followed by a series of American mediums including Squire, Foster, Redman, Colchester, Conklin and the Davenport brothers, giving rise to what Podmore has aptly termed 'the American Invasion'.

2. *The Second Phase*: *Mediums and Magicians*

Spiritualism had taken the United States by storm[26] but by this stage (1860) Britain could only boast one indigenous medium, Mrs.

Marshall. And this state of affairs was to continue until the closing years of the decade. It was the American mediums who received the comments in the periodical literature[27] inlcuding the newly founded *Spiritualist Magazine*.

Of the early American invasion the Davenport Brothers caused considerable interest. The brothers would typically be bound hand and foot and placed in a cabinet with certain musical instruments out of reach. When the cabinet doors were shut or the hall put in darkness,[28] music (of the spirits) would resound. Comments on the Davenports came thick and fast. *The Lancet*[29] described their performance and concluded that there was nothing in it which could not be achieved by trickery. They continued 'that the Davenports are quick and adroit we freely admit; that they possess any extraordinary power beyond that of highly exercised dexterity we altogether deny.'[30]

Was the *Lancet* being fair? Some evidence in support of their claim began to emerge from the people whose full time business was trickery —the conjurors and magicians. The financial success of professional mediums both in America and England had undoubtedly taken away some of the trade which magicians enjoyed, it was therefore very much in their interests to show that the activities performed by mental and physical mediums were just conjuring tricks. And indeed it was not long before conjurors were freely imitating many, if not most, of the phenomena produced in seances.

The most famous and colourful of the British conjurors was John Nevil Maskelyne. Maskelyne was responsible for a number of 'exposures' of fraudulent mediums and was called on to give testimony at legal trials.[31] When the Davenport[32] brothers performed at Cheltenham Town Hall, Maskelyne was on the investigating committee. Detecting the method used by the brothers he offered to repeat everything they had done. The Davenports challenged him and, together with his colleague from the Egyptian Hall, Mr. Cooke, he was able to repeat all the effects within six weeks. While Maskelyne admitted that they were fairly slow at the beginning, they became very much quicker with practice and performed the experiments with great success.

> 'So successful were we, that I finally determined to throw up the horological in favour of the mystical business—a much better paying concern as you might imagine'[33]

Maskelyne was to deride the performances of most of the American invasion and their British counterparts in his little book, *Modern Spiritualism* which came out in 1876. Throughout he takes a very strong line against the phenomena of spiritualism and its exponents. Home, the Davenports, Miss Nichols (Mrs. Guppy), Mr. and Mrs. Holmes, Miss Eva Fay, all came under his attention. In several cases he showed that the phenomena could be produced by trickery.[34]

In others he questioned the competence of the testimony,[35] having no doubt about the problems of accepting the positive testimony of scientific men. Of William Crookes he was particularly critical:

'Mr. Crookes puts forward "proofs" so ingeniously, with such an air of good faith, that one might be startled if we did not know how easily the gentleman can be hoodwinked . . . As a believer Mr. Crookes is all very well; as an investigator he is a failure'.[36]

Maskelyne's lack of confidence in Crookes was based on his perceived loopholes in the latter's investigations of D. D. Home and Mrs. Eva Fay (discussed below). Whilst not all of Maskelyne's explanations have stood the test of time, he was undoubtedly very important in demonstrating just how easy it was to fool sensible quick-witted people including scientists. Magicians were to be involved[37] in the arguments surrounding mediumship, particularly the physical mediumship which became widespread in the 1870s. Their function as psychic investigators was recognised then perhaps more widely than today. Houdini also made a career of exposing fraudulent mediums, doing so with consummate skill.[38] For this he earned the wrath of the spiritualist community.

3. *Wallace and the Sceptics*

Towards the end of the 1860s a number of significant things happened: a trial involving D. D. Home sparked off a controversy in the *Pall Mall Gazette;* Alfred Russell Wallace converted to spiritualism and began proselytising fellow scientists; and the London Dialectical Society set up a Committee to investigate spiritualism.

D. D. Home was in many ways *the* outstanding Victorian medium.[39] Virtually alone he survived with his reputation intact. He was well liked by most people and was prepared in general to operate in good light under comparatively good test conditions. F. W. Myers and W. F. Barrett who undertook a thorough study of Home's mediumship as one of the first tasks of the SPR concluded

'We have found no allegations of *fraud* on which we should be justified in laying much stress . . . there has been nothing we can style conviction of fraud . . . and so far as regards conjuring, we may say with confidence that there has been neither actual exposure nor even inferential ground for explaining his phenomena in this way'.[40]

At the height of his fame, Home became embroiled in a celebrated Court case involving a wealthy widow, Mrs. Lyon.[41] Central to the case was the allegation that Home's mediumship was fraudulent and —as was to become customary in such cases—scientific testimony was sought. In this trial Cromwell Varley,[42] Robert Chambers, Dr. Gully and others furnished evidence in support of Home. The favourable publicity which Home was receiving induced Professor J. Tyndall —Faraday's successor at the Royal Institution—to write to the *Pall Mall Gazette* on May 5th 1868. Tyndall's letter related a situation which had occurred some years earlier. Faraday—who had been besieged by requests to investigate mediums ever since his 1853 paper on table-turning—was asked via Sir Emerson Tennant to investigate D. D. Home. According to Tyndall, Faraday had reluctantly consented, provided he could apply his own conditions and tests in the investigation, but Home was not willing to submit to these tests and they never took place. Home's reply (5, 8 and 9 May 1868) denied this story claiming that he had not seen Faraday's conditions and that Robert Bell (who had arranged the affair) had called the examination off. In the resulting correspondence, Home's account was endorsed by various people (8 May 1868), and Tyndall published Faraday's set of conditions as contained in his letter to Sir Emerson Tennant.

Faraday's letter demonstrates a high degree of prejudice in an elderly paragon of science

'I cannot help feeling that you are indiscrete in your desire to bring me into contact with the occult phenomena which it is said are made manifest in Mr. Home's presence. I have investigated such in former times . . . it would be a condescension on my part to pay any more attention to them now'.[43]

He continues delineating a set of questions to which Mr. Home is to agree before the investigation. Question number seven is quite remarkable:

'If the effects are miracles, or the work of spirits, does he (Home) admit the utterly contemptible character both of them and their results, up to the present time, in respect either of yielding information or instruction, or supplying any force or action of the least value to mankind?'

When the full facts began to emerge[44] and Home's name was cleared at Faraday's expense, Tyndall tried to defend Faraday's repu-

tation as an impartial man (18 May 1868) 'Faraday regarded the
necessity even of discussing such phenomena as are ascribed to Mr.
Home as a discredit, to use no stronger term, to the education of this
age'. Yet even given that the 'repeated spiritualistic phenomena were
only worthy of the scorn or pity of all intelligent persons' he was still
willing to examine them. Tyndall then offered to investigate in Faraday's place provided that Home would submit to certain tests. Home
declined on the ground that Tyndall was not impartial. G. H. Lewes
also joined in the debate (12, 16 and 19 May 1868) and reiterated his
earlier charge (1853) that all the effects were accomplished by trickery,
evasion or natural effects.

These events were remarkable because the implication of Tyndall
and Lewes is one of evasion on the part of the spiritualists. But in
fact it is well documented that Wallace had tried and failed to induce
Tyndall and Lewes (not to mention Huxley and Carpenter) to come
to seances with Miss Nichols (see below). Wallace had been introduced
to the ideas of mesmerism and phrenology when, as a schoolteacher,
he had attended some of Spencer Hall's lectures. Wallace continued
working on mesmerism and phrenology during his long absences from
England (e.g. his trip to the Malay Archipelago 1854-1859). On his
return to England he began working on the problem of the origin
of man[45] and his conviction that natural selection alone was insufficient
to explain the development of man set him on the path to spiritualism.

Wallace attended his first seance in July 1865[46] and this led to
many investigations with professional mediums. In 1866 he produced
a pamphlet based upon his documentary research into the area 'The
Scientific aspect of the Supernatural' and discovered a new medium,
Miss Nichols (who was to become the powerful Mrs. Guppy). By
1867 Wallace, having been convinced of the truth of spiritualism,
began his attempts to convert other scientists. By sending his pamphlet
with an appeal to come and attend seances with him, he hoped to
convince Huxley, Tyndall, Lewes and Carpenter. The record of his
failures is highly interesting[47] especially in view of the attitude of
Lewes and Tyndall in the *Pall Mall Gazette* correspondence later
in 1868.

Huxley's[48] response is famous for its indifference

> 'I never cared for gossip in my life and disembodied gossip, such as these
> worthy ghosts supply their friends with, is not more interesting to me
> than any other. As for investigating the matter, I have half a dozen
> investigations of infinitely greater interest to me to which any spare time
> I may have will be devoted'.[49]

His appeal to Tyndall,[50] Carpenter and Lewes was no more successful. Wallace's request that they come to a *series* of seances with Miss Nichols, being prepared for initial failure, was not heeded. Both Tyndall and Carpenter came once but when nothing significant happened they never returned. G. H. Lewes never came at all.

The debate in the *Pall Mall Gazette* is all the more remarkable against this background. Wallace was at this stage seeking to establish an understanding of the phenomena via the notion of a possible new force and this view is characteristic of William Crookes's early work. His actions merited a more positive response than he received. Early in 1869, however, Wallace was asked by the London Dialectical Society, a debating club (founded in 1867) to join a Committee to investigate the alleged phenomena of spiritualism. Wallace accepted but a number of scientists rejected their offer including again Huxley, Tyndall, Carpenter and Lewes.

The Committee of the London Dialectical Society[51] had some thirty members but numbered very few recognised scientific men among its ranks—A. R. Wallace being the only distinguished scientist to take part. The Committee received both written and verbal reports from leading Spiritualists and mediums and undertook some first hand investigations in special committees. Most of the six sub-committees observed very little of significance but committees one and two did observe 'positive results'.

The Committee attracted the attention of *Punch* in December 1869 which jibed:

'Wanted a ghost of whatever variety,
Fitted to mingle in learned society,
Able to work on the feelings electric
Of *savans* devoted to themes dialectic'

And indeed when the Committee's deliberations were published in its *Report* in 1871 they were not taken very seriously. The standard of investigation, reporting, and analysis was sadly inadequate. Podmore observed that there were discrepancies between the *Report* and the written minutes of the sittings. 'These discrepancies are not, perhaps, in themselves serious; their real importance lies in their revealing such slovenliness in the recording as justifies us in attaching little value to the record'.[52] And the *Saturday Review*, 21 October 1871, questioned the conclusion of the *Report* saying: 'Half the sub-committees saw nothing whatever, and of the remaining three, one only held the so-called communication by means of signals; and yet the committee calmly states that the reports substantially corroborate each other'.

With the publication of the Report of the Committee of the London Dialectical Society the interaction of science and spiritualism entered a new phase. The *Report* came on the heels of the early investigations of William Crookes and became involved in the intense debates that were to follow.

4. *From Crookes to the SPR—Resumé*

Up until this date, spiritualism had been 'contained' by the scientific community with very little effort. Whenever public interest had become too great, as in the table-turning epidemic or in the publicity surrounding the Davenport brothers, 'men of science' had stepped in to criticise and ridicule the situation. It was classed with a whole range of similar fads including mesmerism, electro-biology, etc. and generally explained in terms of fraud, scientific incompetence, or the unconscious expectation and involuntary muscular activity of the subjects.

But this state of affairs was to change radically. After 1870, the number of indigenous private and professional mediums increased greatly. Moreover, physical effects (levitation, the remote moving of bodies, etc.) became both more common and more extreme— including spirit materialisations. But if the range and tenor of the phenomena increased, the methods of investigation changed also. Following the example of William Crookes to whom we now turn, a number of scientists or scientifically minded individuals became involved in the investigations. In an effort to rule out fraud new tests were introduced and methodological questions were discussed. With Maskelyne and other magicians continuing to deride all positive results, considerable progress was made.

Crookes

In 1870 William Crookes, the eminent physical chemist, announced his intention to investigate the phenomena of spiritualism. Over the next five years he was to investigate most of the leading mediums of the day and testify repeatedly to the genuineness of their mediumship. Crookes's approbation of mediums such as D. D. Home, Kate Fox, Charles Williams, Florence Cook and Mrs. Eva Fay caused a sensation. For convinced spiritualists he was a heaven-sent gift whom they could cite in support of their case, but for many scientists he was an embarrassment and disturbance. Crookes's experimental skills and breadth of scientific knowledge were well attested and he had been elected a Fellow of the Royal Society at the age of 31 in recognition of this. His endorsement of the phenomena of spiritualism therefore could not easily be dismissed.

Crookes became the centre of a major conflict the effects of which were felt to some extent by most (if not all) leading scientists of the day. He was undoubtedly responsible for involving (or at least fostering the interest of) many scientists like Rayleigh, Barrett, Galton, etc. At the same time he received the brunt of the reaction of the scientific establishment against this unorthodox development. In his attempts to present the results of his investigations with D. D. Home before the Royal Society and British Association for the Advancement of Science (BAAS), Crookes was thwarted as will be shown. Moreover in a series of articles and public lectures his character and competence were severely attacked by W. B. Carpenter.

Crookes, however, gave as good as he got and the Victorian periodicals resounded with the controversy. Crookes gave a comprehensive and devastating account of his 'noble quest' and his partisan opponents, in his *Researches into the Phenomena of Spiritualism.*[53] But after his investigation of the American medium Mrs. Eva Fay, in the following year, he completely withdrew from publicly stating his views on spiritualism. He returned to his orthodox scientific studies which were to make him famous. He went on to receive virtually all the scientific distinctions that were available[54] and received the Order of Merit and a Knighthood before he died.

While Crookes participated in the Committee of the SPR on physical effects (1888-90) and accepted the Presidency of that body in 1896-9, his involvement in psychical research was now low key. As far as most of his scientific colleagues were concerned he had 'reformed'. When he was elected President of the British Association in 1898, some who remembered his 'renegade period' 1870-75, wondered whether he would refer to this episode and use this opportunity to express bitterness about his earlier treatment by the scientific community. Crookes addressed himself to this question

'Some may feel curious as to whether I shall speak out or be silent. I elect to speak, although briefly . . . I have nothing to retract. I adhere to my already published statements. Indeed I might add much thereto. I regret only a certain crudity of those early expositions which, no doubt justly, militated against their acceptance by the scientific world'.[55]

This 'episode' in William Crookes's life is especially important; apart from Wallace's belief which failed to convince his colleagues, this is the first example of a reputable scientist endorsing the phenomena of spiritualism after apparently serious investigation. Crookes was not a 'crank' and could not therefore be cursorily dismissed. Also he had not simply invited his colleagues to seances as Wallace had done, but had allegedly performed controlled experiments recorded by reputable witnesses. It was therefore incumbent on the orthodox practitioners of science, who felt antagonistic towards Crookes's conclusions, to explain them away.

Crookes's remarkable behaviour (1870-75) has attracted a lot of attention[56] and various theories have been put forward. Historians have pointed to an apparent discrepancy between his early, methodically sound investigations of D. D. Home (c.1870-72) and his later inquiries into the mediumship of such individuals as Florence Cook and Charles Williams (1872-75).

These latter investigations, where very radical effects such as full form spirit materialisation[57] occurred, were very much more suspect and were published in the spiritualist press (*The Spiritualist; The Medium and Daybreak;* etc.)

It has also been pointed out that—with the exception of Home—all the mediums Crookes worked with were exposed as frauds, sometimes on very strong evidence.[58] In order to fathom this complex behaviour it is necessary to examine those investigations in which he interacted most strongly with his fellow scientists—the D. D. Home sittings (1870-72) and the investigations of Mrs Eva Fay (1874-75).

D. D. Home

Crookes's opening article[59] in *The Researches* 'Spiritualism viewed in the light of Modern Science' reviews previous attempts to investigate spiritualism and criticises the techniques employed. It is on the face of it an indictment of earlier attempts to investigate the phenomena. He draws a distinction between the spiritualist and the man of science delineating the kind of evidence the latter would require before being convinced of the genuineness of the phenomena. His first thoughts were positive but non-committal

'That certain physical phenomena such as the movement of material substances, and the production of sounds resembling electric discharges, occur under circumstances in which they cannot be explained by any physical law at present known, is a fact of which I am as certain, as I am of the most elementary laws of chemistry. My whole scientific education has been one long lesson in exactness of observation, and I wish it to be distinctly understood that this firm conviction is the result of most careful investigation'.[60]

One year later he was ready to go further. The experiments appeared 'to conclusively establish the existence of a new force, in some unknown manner connected with the human organisation, which for convenience be called [sic] the psychic force'.[61]

This psychic force theory was along the same philosophical lines that Wallace had suggested some years before. In defence of it Crookes reported how D. D. Home was able to perform certain effects like altering the weights of bodies and playing musical instruments remotely. These effects were corroborated by Dr. William Huggins[62] and Serjeant Cox.

The records of the D. D. Home seances are[63]—while incomplete— the best records we have of Crookes's work and they show a reasonably critical standard of investigation. Crookes was sufficiently satisfied to submit the results of these investigations formally to the two secretaries of the Royal Society. He received a polite refusal from Dr. Sharpley and a longer one from Professor Stokes, a longstanding friend and colleague, in which he discussed a possible fallacy in the apparatus.

A technical correspondence followed between Crookes and Stokes which revealed that the latter was clearly not eager to publish the papers. But shortly afterwards on 22 July an editorial note in the *Spectator* blew the whole affair open. The note claimed bluntly that Crookes's paper had been rejected 'as one not deserving the attention of the Royal Society'.

Crookes was astounded. As far as he had known[64] the Royal Society Committee which considered papers was not quorate and discussion of the Crookes submissions had been deferred to their next meeting in November.

The *Spectator,* however, was quick to clear its name

'Our note was not founded on any mere rumour. The words used contained an exact copy of the words conveyed to us as used, not as we inadvertently stated, by the Committee, but by one of the secretaries, Professor Stokes, who in the absence of a quorum exercised, *pro tempore,* the usual discretionary authority in regard to the papers offered'.[65]

Stokes, in Crookes's view had acted in an unprofessional manner by conveying the decision resulting from a Royal Society Committee to a popular weekly newspaper and the latter was understandably annoyed. Crookes's papers in the *Quarterly Journal of Science* had attracted some negative comment in the scientific press,[66] but again at the British Association for the Advancement of Science meeting in Edinburgh, he tried to present his work formally to the world of science. The officer who considered his paper for discussion at Section A (Mathematics and Physics) was Stokes. His report was guarded and said that while he did not see much use discussing it in the section he did not see any objection to setting up a committee to investigate it. He added however that he would not participate personally. 'I have heard too much of the tricks of Spiritualists to make me willing to give any time to such a committee myself'.[67]

The meeting itself contained some controversial references to spiritualism, mostly hostile, from eminent scientists such as Professor Tait and Professor Alan Thomson[68] and the spiritualist press acted as a forum for the ensuing argument.

Crookes published another paper on Home: 'Some Further Experiments on Psychic Force'[69] in which the experimental conditions were tightened up—in response to comments he had received. In these experiments Home was prevented from having any direct physical contact with suspended objects being weighed, and the room was well-lighted. Crookes reported

'These experiments *confirm beyond* doubt the conclusions at which I arrived in my former paper, namely the existence of a force associated in some manner not yet explained, with the human organisation, by which force, increased weight is capable of being imparted to solid bodies without physical contact. In the case of Mr. Home, the development of this force varies enormously, not only from week to week, but from hour to hour . . . It is capable of acting at a distance from Mr. Home (not infrequently as far as two or three feet), but is always strongest close to him'[70]

Crookes then had made his position clear but had failed to get his papers read before the Royal Society or British Association. Yet he had begun to attract attention from his fellow scientists. Crookes for example corresponded with the physicist W. F. Barrett who later (in 1876) was to alarm the world of science with an address to the Anthropological Section of the BAAS on Thought Transference. Crookes asked Barrett to come and see Home,[71] an offer which Barrett was not able to take up. It is clear however that on 15 May

1871, Crookes was clearly seeking an explanation in terms of a new force.

> 'I must have some conversation with you respecting these obscure phenomena. If you could help me form anything like a physical theory I should be delighted. At present all I am quite certain about is that they are objectively true. I have had all my wits about me when at a seance, and the only person who appeared to be in a state of semi-consciousness is the medium himself. The other evening I saw Home handling red hot coals as if they had been oranges. Will you favour me with a visit one evening when you are disengaged?'[72]

Crookes also attracted the attention of William Huggins the astronomer; Lord Rayleigh[73] who soon began to investigate mediums; Cromwell Varley; and the Cambridge Group of Sidgwick, Myers and Gurney (see below). Francis Galton also appears to have been fascinated by his experiences in seances. While originally sceptical, his letters to Charles Darwin indicate that he was eager to participate and was waiting for the approval of Crookes or Home.[74] On 19 April 1872, Galton wrote to Darwin describing a seance in full gas light in which Home played an accordian with one hand under the table.

> 'Crookes, I am sure, so far as it is just for me to give an opinion, is thoroughly scientific in his procedure. I am convinced, the affair is no matter of vulgar legerdermain and I believe it well worth going into, on the understanding that a *first rate medium* (and I hear there are only three such) puts himself at your disposal'.[75]

He went on to propose that Darwin join him in a seance—a seance which never happened.

But this informal interest in Crookes's work was formally contradicted by the official criticism of the scientific establishment. In October 1871, an anonymous review appeared in the *Quarterly Review*[76] entitled 'Spiritualism and its Recent Converts'. The article savagely and comprehensively attacked the exponents and defenders of 'occult phenomena' including Crookes and his co-workers. Everybody knew from the outset that the author was W. B. Carpenter. Carpenter's earlier ideas on unconscious expectation and involuntary muscular action are referred to but his main criticism of Crookes and his collaborators concerns the 'adequacy' of their scientific training.

Underlying Carpenter's Review article one can observe one of the major preoccupations of Victorian Science—the Endowment of Science Movement.[77] At the beginning of the 19th century very little 'science' was taught at the English Universities or public schools. Throughout the century a reform movement characterised initially by such figures as Brewster, Babbage and Playfair gathered momentum. Concern about the degeneration of the Royal Society,[78] the low state of physics and mathematics,[79] the lack of scientific and technical training and its effect on industrial performance etc. were felt strongly and widely discussed. Included among the many issues which were involved was the desire (held by many) that science should be a profession. A man, properly trained and examined, should, they argued, be able to earn his living by doing scientific research and/or teaching.

Throughout the century a new breed of professional scientist, Carpenter, Huxley, Tyndall, Crookes, Lodge, etc.—who had at times great difficulty in supporting themselves—co-existed with amateurs such as Darwin, Galton, Huggins and Rayleigh. This latter group did not really need to work for a living and studied science—often very brilliantly—as a leisure activity.[80] In the Endowment of Science movement, this heterogeneous set were by no means unanimous—many felt that government support would lead to government interference and control. The complex pattern of resentments and conflicts which existed between certain career scientists and their amateur counterparts can be seen as one element in the controversy over spiritualism. Many of the individuals who were to become involved in spiritualism in the 1870s—partly as a result of Crookes's work—were wealthy amateur scientists or 'philosophers'—Rayleigh, Huggins, Myers, Sidgwick, Gurney. They often spent considerable amounts hiring professional mediums for their investigations[81] and later the Sidgwick group was to subsidise the SPR[82] by several hundred pounds per annum.[83] It was no accident in Carpenter's view that the leisured amateur inquirer should 'fall for' spiritualism rather than the professional scientist. In his Review of 'Recent Converts' to spiritualism he picks on William Huggins the noted amateur astronomer, one of the key witnesses to Crookes's investigations of D. D. Home.

'Dr. Huggins is one of a class of scientific amateurs who hold a most important position in our community, as helping to maintain for British Science that place which would be imperilled by the paucity of its professional defenders: men who, either born to independence, or honourably acquiring it by their own exertions, apply themselves to scientific pursuits with as much earnest devotion as if their livelihood depended on their success. When such amateurs have shown the capacity, as well as the will to labour for the advancement of Science in any department they may select, they are invariably welcomed by its professors as most valued allies. . . There can be no question however, that such scientific amateurs labour, as a rule, under a grave disadvantage, in the want of a broad basis of *general* scientific culture, which alone can keep them from the narrowing and perverting influence of a limited *specialism*. And we have no reason to believe that to this rule Dr. Huggins constitutes an exception. Of his acquaintance with any other department of science than the small subdivision of a branch to which he has so meritoriously devoted himself, we are not aware that he has given any evidence whatever'.[84]

In short he concludes that Dr. Huggins is skilled at *observation* (which is essential to astronomy) rather than *experimental inquiry* which is essential to spiritualist investigations. It follows that his word cannot really be relied upon. The other main witnesses, Serjeant Cox and Cromwell Varley, are sharply dismissed. Mr. Cox is described as 'the most gullible of the gullible as to whatever appeals to his organ of wonder'.[85] Cromwell Varley is summed up as a man '. . . possessing considerable technical knowledge . . . but his scientific attainments are so cheaply estimated . . . that he has never been admitted to the Society'.[86] Varley had in fact been elected a Fellow of the Royal Society in June of that year.

Carpenter subjects Crookes to the same scrutiny but also makes baseless accusations to which Crookes is well able to reply. Why, asks Carpenter, has Crookes not read the works of other scientists like himself who have studied the question before, and seen that there was 'nothing left to investigate except the knavery of one set of performers and the self-delusion of others?'.[87] The reason can only be in Crookes's defective scientific training. Carpenter's diatribe, questions Crookes's election to the Royal Society and demeans him as a narrow specialist not competent to see through the subtle devices of tricksters. In fact as Crookes argued in his *Researches* (see note[59]) both criticisms were totally incorrect.[88]

Carpenter's attack on Crookes continued the following year with a series of public lectures specifically aimed at Crookes and his fellow-travellers. In one (at Vestry Hall) Carpenter again raised the issue of Crookes's 1871 papers claiming that they had been rejected by the Royal Society because they were 'good for nothing'. In the outcry that followed, Carpenter was forced to reveal his sources as Professor Stokes and Sir Charles Wheatstone.

This fiasco had gone too far and Crookes wrote to the Royal Society demanding an explanation on two points. Firstly, Carpenter's allegations concerning Crookes's election to the Society, and secondly his Vestry Hall statement that 'in the opinion of the Royal Society it (Crookes's paper) was good for nothing'. In both cases, Carpenter—

not a member of the Royal Society Council—was expressing a personal opinion based on hearsay, in the name of that body.

The Royal Society replied on 18 April 1872, resolving:

1. 'That the President and Council of the Society regret that the statements in question should have been published, both because they are incorrect in point of fact, and because the unauthorised publication of the deliberations of the Council is contrary to the usage of the Society.
2. That the above resolution be communicated to Mr. Crookes'.[89]

Carpenter's 'outburst' on the subject of spiritualism now temporarily subsided. He had every opportunity to speak out against Crookes and others who were investigating spiritualism in his capacity as President of the BAAS which met at Brighton that year. But his Presidential Address avoided the subject completely. Carpenter wasn't to indulge in a public debate on the subject again until 1876.

The informal interest which Crookes had generated incited several parties to investigation. Rayleigh was to investigate Kate Fox and Mrs. Fay. Huggins and Galton were interested for a while and attended seances, but their involvement was temporary. W. F. Barrett began a series of experiments into Thought-Transference. But the greatest interest came from Trinity College, Cambridge in what Gauld has called the Sidgwick group—Henry Sidgwick, F. W. H. Myers and Edmund Gurney.

This group, all sons of clergymen,[90] became actively involved in the phenomena of spiritualism in the early 1870s. Crookes in sparking this group into action helped liberate a deep-rooted feeling of unrest widely characteristic of the time. In the 1870s the temple of science was under attack. While by no means all scientists accepted the extreme representations of Darwinism or for that matter Tyndall's scientific materialism, science was fast losing popular sympathy and support. As MacLeod remarks

'For wide sections of the public, the concepts of unity and uniformity of nature, established first by geology, then by biology and physics, brought what seemed like a threatening prospect of an encompassing atheistic materialism'.[91]

Myers, Sidgwick and Gurney had undergone grave personal doubts about their religious beliefs under the impact of contemporary science and philosophy. But, as Turner[92] has argued they did not find an adequate replacement in the prevailing dogmatic scientific naturalism of Huxley, Tyndall, and Spencer.

The doubt felt by many of the pioneers of psychical research and their desire to demonstrate the existence of a spiritual dimension to human life, was clearly a key motivating force. Indeed the fanatical zest with which they undertook their research in the early years of the SPR is otherwise difficult to comprehend. As Myers later put it:

> 'To be able to say to the theologian or philosopher: Thus can we demonstrate that a spiritual world exists—a world of independent and abiding realities . . . This would indeed, in my view, be the weightiest service that any research could render to the deep disquiet of our time'.[93]

While Crookes was to continue (for two years) his investigations into spiritualism in isolation from the scientific community,[94] the Sidgwick group began conducting experiments.[95] The three of them met with the medium and investigator the Reverend Stainton Moses in May 1874,[96] and began to devise a programme of research. The enthusiasm spread to an informal group connected with Trinity College (including Rayleigh). Investigations were made of Charles Williams, and others were planned for the investigation of the American medium Mrs. Eva Fay. It was with this latter medium that a joint series of seances with Crookes and Rayleigh was proposed.

Mrs. Eva Fay

Mrs. Eva Fay arrived in England with her husband in 1874, and immediately began giving seances and stage performances. She demonstrated a variety of telekinetic effects, remotely moving objects while apparently being securely bound in a cabinet. Despite arousing the interest of Myers, Sidgwick, Crookes, Rayleigh and others, her performances were likened by many to conjuring exhibitions and even some of the most convinced spiritualists considered her a fraud.[97]

Yet despite some of the unflattering things which were said about Mrs. Fay before and after her visit to England (1874-5), a joint investigation of her mediumship was proposed, to include Myers, Sidgwick, Crookes, Rayleigh (and perhaps Gurney). The initiative for these seances (which were never in fact held as intended) came from Myers and Sidgwick and it is from their letters and notebooks (preserved at Trinity College, Cambridge) that most of our information comes. It is quite clear that the efforts to set up a joint inquiry were plagued by personal difficulties and distrust. The correspondence between Rayleigh, Myers and Sidgwick show concern with the test conditions under which Mrs. Fay should operate and also refer to the strange behaviour of William Crookes. Already by this time he was regarded suspiciously by his fellow psychic inquirers, because of his continual 'success' as an investigator. 'The never failing Crookes' as Sidgwick called him, always seemed to get positive results. But there was an additional 'complaint' in this case which concerned Crookes's desire to get *control* of the investigation.

Myers records seances with Mrs. Fay in his diary for June, November, December, 1874 and January 1875. Sidgwick left the joint sittings in November 1874, after accusations by Mrs. Fay that he was a 'bad sitter'[98] and wrote to Myers suggesting that Rayleigh should become involved. He clearly thought Rayleigh's word would carry weight.[99] Rayleigh was definitely interested in spiritualism, but in a letter on 23 November 1874, he indicates his mixed feelings about whether it is worthwhile paying Mrs. Fay a sum of £400 for a long series of sittings.

> 'I do not know what evidence you or Crookes may have for Mrs. Fay's genuineness, and so I am writing rather in the dark . . . I should attach great importance to the terms of the arrangement that it will be possible to make e.g. whether Mrs. Fay is to be eliminated and the general control is to be in our hands . . . I ought perhaps to say that I am not as yet satisfied that there is any such thing as so called spiritualism'.

Crookes was certainly present at many of the seances after November and his monopolistic behaviour was noted with concern by his colleagues. In a letter to Myers, Sidgwick records 'The (more the?) man Crookes gives himself the air of tyranny, the more needful it is that (you) . . . should have the power of the purse.' And Rayleigh wrote an indignant letter to Myers on 15 January 1875—disturbed by his experiences of investigating Mrs. Fay.

> 'I scarcely see my way to asking Mrs. Fay here again without a better explanation of her extraordinary conduct, but I have written to Gurney, and perhaps something may still be arranged. I received a strange letter from Crookes saying that an explanation was certainly due to me from Mrs. Fay but not giving it, as he said he did not wish to put anything upon paper upon this subject. If I could give him an interview he had no doubt he could satisfy me that no other course was open to Mrs. Fay. I do not feel much disposed to recognise him in the matter at all . . . I must confess all these difficulties share the limited belief that I had arrived at—probably more than is reasonable. Crookes' behaviour seems so odd that I cannot help attaching less value to his testimony on which I had mainly relied. What was it to him whether I was a believer or not?'

All the parties became aware that Crookes was trying to monopolise the investigation and might well succeed, and it appears from other documents that by January 1875, Crookes had effective control over the investigation of Mrs. Fay. Crookes conducted a series of seances with the American medium in February of that year, employing the same electrical test which had been designed by Cromwell Varley and used on Florence Cook in 1874. One was attended by Lord Rayleigh (probably February 6) and long accounts survive of two of the sittings.[100] At the seance which Crookes records, we know the sitters to be Crookes, Galton, Huggins, Ionides, Cox and Harrison (editor of the *Spiritualist*). At the seances Mrs. Fay was connected to an electric circuit by holding two conducting handles while sitting in a cabinet. It was thus intended that her absence from the cabinet (to impersonate a spirit) would break the circuit and be seen on a galvanometer. The account records that the seance was successful and a spirit materialisation was effected, *but* the meter readings did not vary from those expected of a human sleeping in a cabinet.

Crookes had yet again obtained positive results with a medium and soon suggestions of trickery were made.[101] Podmore[102] suggested that Mrs. Fay had inserted a resistance coil into the circuit thus leaving herself free to impersonate the spirit. A recent investigation of this theory by Broad[103] shows it to be incorrect. Probably incorrect also is Maskelyne and Houdini's explanation that she placed one handle under her knee leaving one hand free (the handles were nailed down in the February 19 seance).[104]

Mrs. Fay returned to America soon afterwards and continued her performances. She was to make good currency of the endorsement she had received from Crookes for her mediumship in the advertisement which preceded her stage acts—this was to be the centre of another bitter attack on Crookes by Dr. Carpenter.

But what relation did this work have to Crookes's orthodox scientific investigations? The evidence is highly suggestive of some link between the two and it may be the case that his decision to eschew the public defence of spiritualism in 1875 was related to his changed views in physical chemistry.

Crookes's Physics—the Radiometer.

In an attempt to weigh accurately his newly discovered element Thallium, Crookes refined the technique of determining weights in a high vacuum.[105] In his 'scientific' work in the early 1870s he observed the mechanical effect of radiation and became convinced that it (radiation) could exert a pressure directly; this action was only detectable, however, in a high vacuum. Crookes thought he had discovered a new 'force' and he was optimistic about the range of its explanations.

'Although the force of which I have spoken is clearly not gravity solely
as we know it, it is attraction developed from chemical activity, and
connecting that greatest and most mysterious of all force, action at a
distance, with the more intelligible acts of matter. In the radiant
molecular energy of solar masses may at least be found that "agent
acting constantly according to certain laws" which Newton held to be
the cause of gravity'.[106]

In April 1875 he made the first radiometer which he described to
the Royal Society.[107] It is clear from a letter of Galton to Darwin that
Crookes may have thought this 'radiation force' was connected with
the psychic force as demonstrated by (say) D. D. Home

'What will interest you very much, is that Crookes had needles (of some
material not yet divulged) which he hangs *in vacuo* in little bulbs of glass.
When the finger is *approached* the needle moves, sometimes (?) by
attraction, sometimes by repulsion. It is not affected at all when the
operator is jaded but it moves most rapidly when he is bright and warm
and comfortable after dinner. Now different people have power over the
needle and Miss F (medium) has extraordinary power. I moved it
myself and saw Crookes move it, but I did not see Miss F (*even* the
warmth of the hand cannot radiate the glass). Crookes believes he has
hold of quite a grand discovery . . .'[108]

But early in 1876 two papers,[109] by Osborne Reynolds and Arthur
Shuster, criticised Crookes's interpretation. In the ensuing discussion
Crookes was forced to retreat on the notion of a 'new force' but soon
began to see the effect as the product of a new 4th state of matter.
This was to be the basis of all his later work on radiation.[110]

The Scientific Community was by no means unanimous and a long
correspondence entitled 'The Radiometer and its Lessons' ensued in
Nature. Carpenter who joined in to make a general point attacked
Crookes's articles in both *Nature* and *Fraser's Magazine* in November
1877. In these, Carpenter accused Crookes of having lowered the
reputation of English science through the Eva Fay business; claiming
that he had given her a letter of endorsement which she had displayed
all over America.

This baseless charge, which Wallace defended in his long periodical
debate with Carpenter, was the last straw for Crookes. After replying
in detail to the charge and reaffirming his belief in Mrs. Fay he writes
deploring the time he has spent over the years in contact with
Carpenter:

'So great a tax for so trivial a purpose is monstrous in its disproportion,
and I can waste on this fruitless discussion no more precious time—time
stolen from my physical work in the laboratory, already too much
curtailed by the pressure of outward business'.[111]

It may in fact be the case that the notion of a new force in physics, which he was forced to amend, altered Crookes's attitude to the phenomena of spiritualism.[112] The combined effects of this and the continued attacks of Carpenter caused him to leave the subject alone forthwith. Crookes's complex behaviour is extremely puzzling. His strange relationship with his mediums (particularly Florence Cook), his monopolistic behaviour,[113] his belief in the genuineness of mediums who later were proved fraudulent are well known. As I have argued elsewhere,[114] the evidence surviving is insufficient to explain the behaviour of this man but Medhurst and Goldey[115] are probably close to the truth.

> 'If he (Crookes) was in fact systematically deceiving the public and his colleagues during all those years, the motive is surely to be sought not in an isolated sexual adventure, as Mr. Trevor Hall suggests, but rather in some form of megalomania in perhaps a vision of himself as the Newton of a vast new realm of psychic science.'

But if Crookes now withdrew, sufficient interest had already been generated for a concerted study of the multifarious phenomena of spiritualism. In 1876 the extent of this interest among scientific men was recognised and this led ultimately to the foundation of the SPR.

The Slade Affair

1876 was an important year for spiritualism. Many of the scientists who had been most involved in the debates were brought together at the BAAS meeting in Glasgow when a storm broke. At this meeting two separate issues were discussed which became fused—the case of Henry Slade and W. F. Barrett's address on Thought Transference.

'Dr.' Henry Slade arrived from America in July 1876. He was immediately investigated with enthusiasm by men like Cox, W. H. Harrison, Lord Rayleigh and also Myers and Sidgwick.[116] Slade's forte was slate writing. He would place a piece of chalk in between two slates and bolt the slates together. After a time a scribbling noise would be heard and later, on opening the slates, a message (from the spirits) would be seen to have been written. Many of the first investigators who saw Slade were favourably impressed or at least undecided. Lord Rayleigh, took a conjuror with him to see Slade, but neither he nor the conjuror could see how the writing could be achieved by trickery.

In September of that year however Professor E. R. Lankester of Exeter College, Oxford attended two sessions with Slade. At the second, which was also attended by his colleague Dr. H. B. Donkin (of

Queens College, Oxford), Lankester pretended for a time to be completely 'taken in' by Slade's mediumship. But at a critical stage he seized the slate from Slade before the scratching (writing) had begun and discovered that the 'spirit message' had already been written. Lankester wrote up his exposure in the *Times* 16 September and Dr. Donkin confirmed his account.

A few days prior to this 'exposure', William Fletcher Barrett presented his paper on Thought-Transference to the Anthropological Section British Association meeting in Glasgow. The decision to allow this paper had been taken on the Chairman Wallace's casting vote. As well as Wallace, Carpenter, Crookes, and Rayleigh were all at the meeting and discussion was active.[117] After describing his experiments, Barrett had speculated that the extreme cases might be explained by hypnosis or hallucinatory factors. Crookes spoke out against this saying that if this argument was accepted it would 'entirely stop the whole progress of research in any branch of science'.

It was not long before members of the audience began discussing Henry Slade. Several, including Rayleigh and Barrett, spoke of their positive impressions. Even Carpenter admitted to having seen some effects which were difficult to explain, but he claimed that he would want to investigate Slade carefully in his own (Carpenter's) house in order to be satisfied. Several members of the group strongly objected to Barrett's remarks, but Wallace (as Chairman) exerted a firm and far from impartial control. He interrupted the Reverend R. Thomson's objection, telling him to produce 'facts not opinions' and eventually silenced him. Another individual, the Reverend McIlwane, claimed that some of Barrett's witnesses were known to him personally and were unreliable. Again Wallace silenced him. After a lengthy discussion people called for a special committee to be set up to investigate spiritualism.

Lankester found this type of discussion among men of science deplorable. In his letter to the *Times* (16 September) exposing Slade he attacked the decision (and particularly Wallace's role in it) to allow Barrett's paper to be read at all. His exposure of Slade now showed how unreliable the word of these scientists was.

'the public has learned . . . that "men of science" are not exempt as a body from the astounding credulity which prevails in this country and in America. It is, therefore, incumbent upon those who consider such credulity deplorable to do all in their power to arrest its development'.

A heated correspondence in the *Times* followed[118] in which Wallace defended the decision to allow Barrett's paper to be read and argued that his experiences with Slade were quite different from those of Lankester.[119] Slade tried to defend his mediumship (21 September) by arguing that the spirits had begun writing at the instant that the slate was seized. Slade also dismissed the claim that he himself did the writing by concealing a crayon under his fingernails, saying that his nails were cut short. Lankester and Donkin totally rejected this account (23 September).

But if these discussions helped set the direction for the SPR, the fate of Henry Slade was still in the balance. Lankester brought a lawsuit against Slade which reached the court room on 3 October of that year.[120] The case was somewhat of a 'cause célèbre' for spiritualists and for its duration the courtroom was packed. The prosecution presented the testimony of Lankester and Donkin and also brought Maskelyne into the witness box.[121] Maskelyne gave testimony that slate writing was a very old trick—he had in fact done it many years ago. He was about to demonstrate how, when objections were made about the relevance of his testimony which were sustained by the judge.

The defence used the testimony of persons who believed Slade to be genuine. These included Wallace and Serjeant Cox (a written statement). The judge found it a difficult case to adjudicate on but eventually sentenced Slade to three months imprisonment with hard labour. Slade left the country for America before his Appeal, but he only faced more exposures and his career as a medium was over.[122]

It had been Barrett who had urged most strongly for a committee of scientific men to be set up at the Glasgow BAAS meeting, and it was Barrett who did more than anyone to bring this about. The discussion following Barrett's paper on Thought-Transference brought forward many alleged instances of this phenomenon from the public. These Barrett personally investigated communicating his results to Sidgwick, Myers, Gurney, Wallace, *et al.*

The common interest of these and other people in the phenomena of spiritualism led Barrett to convene a conference at 38, Great Russell Street (the location of the British National Association of Spiritualists) on 5 and 6 January 1882 and it was proposed that a society be set up for the scientific examination of psychic phenomena. A working party examined the question and reported to the reconvened conference on

20 February 1882 causing the SPR to be formally constituted with
Henry Sidgwick as its first President. Their stated aim was as follows:

> 'to investigate that large body of debatable phenomena designated by such
> terms as mesmeric, psychical and spiritualistic . . . without prejudice or
> prepossession of any kind, and in the same spirit of exact and un-
> impassioned enquiry which has enabled science to solve so many
> problems, once not less hotly debated'.[123]

The Society which issued a *Proceedings* from July 1882 and a
Journal from February 1884, was run by a President and a Council.
Its membership and that of the Council was initially formed from
two main camps—a group of neutral as yet unconvinced investigators (Rayleigh, Myers, Gurney, etc.) and a group of 'spiritualists' like Stainton Moses and C. C. Massey who were strongly
disposed towards acceptance of the phenomena. From the outset
however the first group were in control and this led to a confrontation.
In 1886 a row sparked off by Mrs. Sidgwick's critical comments on
the medium W. Englinton, led to a 'walk-out' by many of the
spiritualist faction.[124]

The SPR set up five working parties to look into thought-reading,
mesmerism, Reichenbach's phenomena,[125] apparitions and haunted
houses, physical phenomena, and one to perform a literary or
documentary survey. The Committees reported regularly and the work
done by certain members like Myers, Sidgwick, Gurney, Podmore,
Barrett, etc. was phenomenal. The reports were of a high calibre
certainly by contemporary standards. But the control of the Society
rested firmly in the hands of the Sidgwick group and the tenor of
investigations became too sceptical for some members. Wallace played
a very small role from the start and refused Barrett's request that he
stand for President of the Society 'I am so widely known as a "crank"
and a "faddist" that my being President would injure the Society as
much as Lord Rayleigh would benefit it'.[126] For Barrett also, the
Society was rather too sceptical. While he had been instrumental in
founding both the English SPR and its American counterpart in 1884
he soon came into conflict with the Cambridge trio.[127] He wrote to
his good friend Wallace on 3 November 1905[128] again begging him to
accept the nomination of President. 'Podmore, who is proposed as
President, represents the attitude of resolute incredulity, and I
consider this line of action has to some extent been injurious to the
SPR'.

The extensive studies of the SPR in the 1880s seemed to show that a distinction could be drawn between two kinds of mediums—physical and mental. It also became clear that the power of both mental mediumship (i.e. trance-writing, visions, clairvoyance, etc.) and the physical mediumship (which we have discussed), almost never occur in one individual at the same time. Of the two categories virtually none of the physical mediums investigated by the SPR survived with their reputation intact. The area of physical mediumship was permeated by fraud and sophistry,[129] and after 1890, very little work was done by the Committee on physical effects. It was really the mental mediumship which interested the Sidgwick group and in particular the issue of survival of the soul after death. This was where most research was concentrated. There is evidence that Myers, Sidgwick, not to mention Podmore, Lodge and others all came to a conviction, albeit a tentative one, in some kind of existence after death and it was this that they had sought. On his deathbed, when suffering from a fatal illness, Sidgwick wrote to Myers 'This *may* be farewell, but I hope not.'

As the SPR became interested primarily in mental phenomena—clairvoyance, thought-transference, etc.—spiritualism ceased to be such a contentious issue within the scientific community. Victorian scientists did of course have many other important interests and it seemed to many that the SPR was proceeding in a systematic and uncontroversial way. Great attempts were made by the SPR to establish links with other more orthodox branches of psychological science, but these were not very successful. Psychology was itself at a very uncertain stage and sought its own scientific respectability. It selected to develop in an experimental and physiological way and so had little to do with psychical research.

Carpenter had argued in his *Mesmerism, Spiritualism, etc.*[130] that there was a variety of reasons for rejecting the alleged phenomena of spiritualism. When a piece of evidence was produced which seemed to contradict the vast weight of orthodox science it was absurd to accept it. An explanation should rather be sought in terms of an experimental oversight, observational errors, incompetence, bias, irrational credulity, etc. This line of argument was not altogether unreasonable. In the case of Home's famous levitation—where he passed out of one window and in another—a reconciliation with orthodox concepts of gravity, mechanics, etc. is clearly very difficult. Hence Carpenter feels justified in explaining the testimony of the sitters away in terms of their desire to believe.

> 'A whole party of believers will affirm that they saw Mr. Home float out
> of one window and in another, whilst a single honest sceptic *declares*
> that Mr. Home was sitting in his chair *all the time.*'[131]

Carpenter's scepticism shows clearly that ultimately the truth of many of the alleged phenomena depended upon one's opinion of the character and competence of the investigators. This caused individual scientists great difficulty; for, given that the field was largely inhabited by charlatans, what response was possible when an eminent FRS testified that some mediums were genuine?

This paper has argued that this difficulty was greatly augmented by various distorting factors rendering any uniform scientific response an impossibility.

Firstly it has been demonstrated that the special interests of conjurors and magicians exercised a significant influence on the fortunes of spiritualists in the 1860s and 1870s. Their public exhibitions and court evidence were taken very seriously by scientists who became involved in the area. Secondly, the issues of the support and professionalisation of Victorian science have been shown to be an important underlying factor in the disputes over spiritualism. In particular, it has been suggested that the concern of university scientists to professionalise their occupation produced in many of them a hostile reaction against 'pseudo-science' and 'quackery'. This hostility sometimes extended to the amateur scientists who expressed an interest in spiritualist investigation. Thirdly, it has been argued that the intellectual crisis caused by Darwinism and the scientific naturalism of the 19th century, led a number of scientists and philosophers to investigate spiritualism in the hope that it would eventually provide evidence of the existence of a spiritual aspect to the universe and the survival of the human soul after death. This hope was particularly characteristic of the Sidgwick group, who dominated the SPR for the first 30 years of its existence. And fourthly, the personal ambitions and idiosyncracies of individual scientists has been shown to be of great importance to the development of spiritualist investigation in this period. It has been argued that Crookes, more than any other factor, caused the scientific community to take some account of the phenomena of spiritualism. His role as investigator, proselytiser, advocate and tyrant has been discussed and analysed.

The interaction between science and spiritualism was therefore highly complex. It was not just a question of methodology, as many issues were involved. It is not therefore surprising that most scientists took up a position on the spectrum between the scepticism of Carpenter and the credulity of Wallace. No uniform scientific response was possible.

Hatfield Polytechnic.

[1] F. Darwin (ed.): *The Life and Letters of Charles Darwin*, Murray, London, 1887, Vol. I, pp. 373-374; K. Pearson (ed.): *The Life, Letters and Labours of Francis Galton*, Cambridge University Press, Cambridge, 1924, p. 167.

[2] A. R. Wallace had been attending seances and writing on spiritualism since 1865 and was a convinced spiritualist by this time (see below). For Wallace his ideas on spiritualism were closely related to his quest to explain satisfactorily the origin of man. He felt that the theory of evolution by natural selection which he and Darwin had independently created was quite insufficient for this. See M. J. Kottler: 'Alfred Russell Wallace, the origin of man and spiritualism', *Isis*, Vol. 65, 1974, pp. 145-192.

[3] Darwin: op. cit., Vol. III, pp. 186-188.

[4] The controversy began when Carpenter gave a series of lectures on Spiritualism to the London Institution in 1876, and spread to the *Quarterly Journal of Science, Frasers Magazine, Nature, the Atheneum* and the *Contemporary Review*.

[5] A. R. Wallace: 'The Psychological Curiosities of Scepticism'. *Frasers Magazine*, Vol. 16, 1887, pp. 694-706.

[6] ibid., p. 694.

[7] W. B. Carpenter: *Nature*, 1887, pp. 122-123.

[8] A. Gauld: *The Founders of Psychical Research*, Routledge & Kegan Paul, London, 1968, pp. 3-31; F. Podmore: *Modern Spiritualism*, Methuen, London, 1902, Vol. I; A. Conan Doyle: *History of Spiritualism*, London, 1926.

[9] I have written elsewhere of this remarkable episode in the history of the medical profession. See J. Palfreman: 'Mesmerism and the English Medical Profession: A Study of a Conflict', *Ethics in Science and Medicine*, Vol. 4, Nos. 1-2, 1977, 51-66; also, Parsinnen, present volume.

[10] See *Blackwoods Magazine*, May, 1853 and *National Miscellany*, 5 May, 1853.

[11] G. H. Lewes: 'The Rappites Exposed', *The Leader*, Vol. 4, 1853, pp. 261-63.

[12] *Chambers Journal*, 21 May, 1853.

[13] S. E. de Morgan: *Memoirs of Augustus de Morgan*, Longman, London, 1882, pp. 221, 222. Augustus de Morgan later wrote a preface to his wife's book *From Matter to Spirit* in which he confessed his belief in spiritualism (pp. v, vi).

[14] Gauld: op. cit., p. 66 and seq.; Podmore: op. cit., Vol. 11, pp. 5 and seq.

[15] See James Braid: *Neurypnology,* John Churchill, London, 1843; *The Power of the Mind over the Body,* John Churchill, London, 1846; and *Magic, Witchcraft, Animal Magnetism etc.,* John Churchill, London, 1852. Braid coined the term hypnotism in his studies in trying to explain the phenomenon of mesmerism (see Palfreman: op. cit., 1977).

[16] See *The Times,* 13 June 1853 and the appendix to James Braid: *Hypnotic Therapeutics,* Murray and Gibbs, Edinburgh, 1853. At this converzatione Braid suggested his own conditions and theories. Braid remarked that the direction of rotation was always announced in advance and that this effected the outcome.

[17] *The Medical Times and Gazette,* 11 June, 1853.

[18] His account was written up in *The Times:* 30 June, 1853 and *The Atheneum:* 1853, pp. 801-803. His position was clear:
'The object which I had in view in this inquiry was not to satisfy myself, for my conclusion had been formed already on the evidence of those who turned tables—but that I might be enabled to give a strong opinion, founded on facts, to the many who applied to me for it. Yet, the proof which I sought for, and the method followed in the inquiry, were precisely the same as those which I should adopt in any other scientific investigation'. (p. 801.)

[19] *The Atheneum:* 1853, p. 883.

[20] W. B. Carpenter: 'On the Influence of Suggestion in Modifying and Directing Muscular Movement Independently of Volition', *Proceedings of the Royal Institution,* Vol. 1, 1852, pp. 147-53.

[21] W. B. Carpenter: *Quarterly Review,* October 1853.

[22] A number of treatises associating table-rapping with Satanic influence came out. For example, E. Gillson: *Table-talking: Disclosures of Satanic Wonders,* Bath, 1853; N. S. Godfrey: *Table-moving Tested and Proved to be the Result of Satanic Agency,* London, 1853. The Socialist reformer Robert Owen attended a seance of Mrs. Hayden and was very impressed. He wrote it up in *The New Existence of Man upon the Earth,* London, 1854.

[23] Podmore: op. cit., Vol. II, p. 10 records that an anonymous pamphlet *Table-turning by Animal Magnetism Demonstrated,* London, 1853, went through 110 editions in one year. The possible relationship of table-turning with animal magnetism was taken up by the mesmerists' journal *The Zoist.*

[24] It is generally thought that the work of Faraday, Braid, G. H. Lewes and Carpenter was partly responsible for this decline.

[25] The events concerning the investigation of D. D. Home by the eminent scientists David Brewster and Lord Brougham are brought together in the *Spiritualist Magazine,* 1861, pp. 540 and seq. See also M. M. Gordon: *The Home Life of Sir D. Brewster,* Edinburgh, 1869, pp. 257-8.

[26] Podmore: op. cit., Vol. I, pp. 202-220.

[27] For example see *Cornhill Magazine,* August 1860 where Robert Bell the dramatist describes seances with Mrs. Marshall and D. D. Home.

[28] See *The Times:* 30 September, 1864.

[29] *The Lancet:* 8 October, 1864, pp. 418-420.

[30] *The Lancet*: 29 October, 1864, pp. 500-1.

[31] See his role in the Slade case discused below—and details in J. N. Maskelyne: *Modern Spiritualism*, London, 1876.

[32] See T. L. Nichols: *A Biography of the Brothers Davenport*, London, 1864; J. W. Truesdell: *The Bottom Facts Concerning the Phenomena of Spiritualism*, London, 1884, pp. 228 and seq.

[33] J. N. Maskelyne: *Pall Mall Gazette*, 18 April, 1885.

[34] Details on these and other prominent mediums can be found in a series of articles by R. G. Medhurst: 'Stainton Moses and Contemporary Mediums', *Light*, 1963-66.

[35] See for example Maskelyne: op. cit., 1876, pp. 35-6, 50-7, which relates the celebrated seance where Home was alleged to have levitated himself and passed out of an upstairs window—returning through another window to the room.

[36] ibid., p. 173.

[37] See *The Times*: 27 April, 30 April and 1 May, 1907, and a discussion 'Archdeacon *versus* Conjuror—a Challenge and a Lawsuit', *Annals of Psychical Science*, Vol. 4, 1906, pp. 333-335 and Vol. 5, 1907, pp. 397-398.

[38] See Houdini: *A Magician among the Spirits*, Harper, New York, 1924; W. B. Gibson and M. N. Young: *Houdini on Magic*, Dover, New York, 1953.

[39] See Jean Burton: *Hey-day of a Wizard*, George C. Harrap, London, 1948; and, Count Perovsky-Petrovo-Solovo: 'Some Thoughts on D. D. Home', *Proceedings of the Society for Psychical Research*, Vol. 39, March 1930.

[40] F. W. Myers and W. F. Barrett: *Journal of the Society of Psychical Research*, Vol. 4, 1889, p. 249.

[41] See *Journal of the Society for Psychical Research*, July 1889. Miss Lyon had befriended Home giving him several large gifts of money, in return he changed his name to Lyon-Home. Some of the gifts were the result of seances which Home had given for her. In the Court case she alleged that he had 'contacted' her dead husband who had put pressure on her to marry Home and give him money.

[42] Cromwell Varley was a well known electrician who became a Fellow of the Royal Society. Varley designed an electrical test in 1874 which was used by William Crookes on the mediums Florence Cook and Eva Fay.

[43] Faraday: *Pall Mall Gazette*, 8 May, 1868.

[44] See for example Mr. Wilkinson and Mr. F. T. Palgrave: *Pall Mall Gazette*, 16 May, 1868.

[45] Kottler: op. cit.

[46] I am inevitably following the same path of evidence here as Kottler: op. cit., and should like to express my debt to him.

[47] A. R. Wallace: *On Miracles and Modern Spiritualism*, London, 1875, pp. 214-17, 225; A. R. Wallace: *My Life: A Record of Events and Opinions*, Chapman and Hall, London, 1905, Vol. II, pp. 278-281; J. Marchant: *Alfred Russell Wallace: Letters and Reminiscences*, Vol. 11, Cassell, London, 1916, pp. 187-188.

[48] Huxley had attended a seance earlier with Mrs. Hayden but had been unconvinced.

[49] Marchant: op. cit., pp. 187-188.

[50] Tyndall had attended a seance in 1864 and later wrote his experiences up in 'Science and the Spirits', *Fragments of Science for Unscientific People*, Appleton, New York, 1871. His attitude was similar to Faraday's.

[51] See Podmore: op cit., p. 147 and seq.; B. and P. Russel (eds.): *The Amberley Papers*, London, 1937, Vol. II, pp. 115-118, 167-173.

[52] Podmore: op cit., p. 150.

[53] W. Crookes: *Researches in the Phenomena of Spiritualism*, 1874a, reprinted in R. G. Medhurst (ed.): *Crookes and the Spirit World*, Souvenir, London, 1972.

[54] He was variously President of: the Chemical Society; the Institute of Electrical Engineers; the British Association for the Advancement of Science; the Society for Psychical Research; and the Royal Society. Additionally, he acted as Foreign Secretary to the Royal Society and received its Davy, Royal and Copley medals and was Honorary Secretary to the Royal Institution.

[55] W. Crookes: *Proceedings of the Society for Psychical Research*, 1898-9, p. 2.

[56] J. Palfreman: 'William Crookes: Spiritualism and Science', *Ethics in Science and Medicine*, Vol. 3, No. 4, 1976, pp. 211-227; R. G. Medhurst & K. M. Goldney: 'William Crookes and the Physical Phenomena of Mediumship', *Proceedings of the Society for Psychical Research*, Vol. 54, 1964, pp. 24-157; T. M. Hall: *The Spiritualists: The Story of Florence Cook and William Crookes*, Duckworth, London, 1962.

[57] Between 1872-80 a large number of mediums allegedly exhibited powers of materialisation. The typical procedure—of which Florence Cook was a master—was to use a cabinet. The medium was bound to a chair in the cabinet and the lights were dimmed. After a time a 'spirit' would emerge from the cabinet and walk around. At the end of the seance the medium would be found still in her chair in a deep trance. Often the medium was found to be impersonating the spirit materialisation, indeed this was the allegation made against Florence Cook.
See S. Cox: *The Spiritualist*, 5 June 1874; *Proceedings of the Society for Psychical Research*, Vol. 48, p. 45 and Vol. 49, p. 58; and *Journal of the Society for Psychical Research*, Vol. 39, p. 189, Vol. 41, p. 205, Vol. 42, p. 47, Vol. 43, p. 19, Vol. 44, pp. 98 and 203.

[58] For the evidence see Palfreman: op. cit., 1976.

[59] This was the first of a series of papers describing his experiments with D. D. Home. *The Researches* was the name familiarly given to a collection of Crookes's Essays, entitled *The Researches in the Phenomena of Spiritualism*, 1874a, and originally published in the *Quarterly Journal of Science*, between 1870 and 1874.

[60] ibid., p. 15.

[61] ibid., p. 22.

[62] William Huggins: *The Spiritualist*, 15 July 1871, He was a gifted amateur scientist, a pioneer of astrophysics, who later became President of the Royal Society. He was interested in spiritualism only for a few years becoming convinced that the subject was too closely tied to trickery.

[63] See Palfreman: op. cit., 1976.

[64] See *The Spiritualist*, 15 August 1871.

[65] The *Spectator*, 29 June 1871.

[66] Balfour Stewart reviewed Crookes's June article for *Nature*, 27 July 1871, suggesting that observers may have been hallucinating under a 'hypnotic influence'. Mr. Coleman Sellers, writing in *Journal of the Franklin Institute*, October 1871, claimed that a mahogany board of the dimensions stated by Crookes did not weigh the amount presented in the article. This latter objection was cursorily dismissed.

[67] The report is reproduced in *The Spiritualist*, 15 August 1871.

[68] Thomson after being attacked in the August 15 edition of *The Spiritualist* apologised promising to amend his speech for the written transactions of the British Association. See BAAS 1871, Presidential Address by Professor Alan Thomson to Biology Section pp. 114-122 and Presidential Address by Professor P. G. Tait to Mathematics and Physics Section, p. 75.

[69] W. Crookes: 'Some Further Experiments on Psychic Force', *Quarterly Journal of Science*, 1 October, 1871; Crookes: op. cit., 1874a, p. 34.

[70] Crookes: op. cit., 1874a, p. 57.

[71] W. F. Barrett: 'Some Reminiscences of Fifty Years of Psychical Research', *Proceedings of the Society for Psychical Research*, Vol. 34, 1924, pp. 275-310.

[72] ibid., p. 283.

[73] The Third Lord Rayleigh (1842-1919) was a mathematician and physicist of the first order. He was to investigate spiritualism from the early 1870s including Kate Fox and Eva Fay and retained an active interest throughout his life. He was appointed President of the SPR in 1919.

[74] Pearson: op. cit., p. 65.

[75] ibid., p. 64.

[76] So intense was the outcry that the *Quarterly Review* was compelled to go to press with a second issue containing a supplement. In this the author (Carpenter) admits his mistakes with respect to Huggins and Varley (see below).

[77] There is a large literature on this subject. See, for example, Roy MacLeod: 'The Support of Victorian Science: The Endowment of Research Movement in Great Britain, 1868-1900', *Minerva*, Vol. 2, 1971, p. 197; D. S. L. Cardwell: *The Organisation of Science in England*, Heinemann, London, 1972, revised.

[78] See, For example, Brewster: *Reflections on the Decline of Science in England*, 1830.

[79] See, for example, P. G. Tait: *Lectures on Some Recent Advances in Physical Science*, Macmillan, London, 1876, p. 13.

[80] Darwin when on his voyage on the Beagle wrote home ecstatically about his naturalist studies:
'There is nothing like geology; the pleasure of the first day's partridge shooting or first day's hunting cannot be compared to finding, a group of fossil bones, which tell their story of former times with almost a living tongue'.

Sir Roderick Murchison a Scottish gentleman took up geology as an alternative hobby to shooting, at his wife's suggestion, and went on to become one of the most important geologists of the 19th century.

81 In an undated letter of Sidgwick to Myers they are discussing finance for an investigation of a professional medium.
'As to the guarantee I will take my share: and could probably persuade Arthur Balfour if not Rayleigh—Crookes and Wallace I should think too poor'.

82 The early membership of the SPR included some famous and wealthy people—Gladstone, Arthur Balfour, eight Fellows of the Royal Society, two Bishops, Ruskin, Tennyson, Lewis Carroll, J. A. Symonds and William Bateson.

83 Gauld: op cit., p. 145.

84 [Carpenter]: 'Spiritualism and its Recent Converts', *Quarterly Review*, October 1871.

85 ibid., p. 343.

86 ibid., p. 348.

87 ibid., p. 328.

88 The controversy between Crookes and Carpenter is dealt with fully in Palfreman: op. cit., 1976.

89 *Daily Telegraph*, 2 May 1872.

90 Sidgwick originally went to Cambridge intending to be ordained.

91 MacLeod: op. cit., p. 221.

92 F. M. Turner: *Between Science and Religion: The Reaction to Scientific Naturalism in Late Victorian England*, Yale University Press, London, 1974.

93 F. W. H. Myers: *Human Personality and its Survival of Bodily Death*, Vol. 2, London, 1903, p. 292.

94 Crookes's investigations in 1873-75 with mediums like Williams, Cook, Showers were written up in the mainstream spiritualist press. See Medhurst and Goldney: op. cit., and Palfreman: op. cit., 1976.

95 See Gauld: op. cit., pp. 88-114.

96 Moses was an Oxford graduate, who had been ordained in 1863. Through reading Robert Dale Owen's *Debateable Land* he became interested in spiritualism and went on to investigate and practise it.

97 On Mrs. Fay see Truesdell: op. cit., pp. 240-275; *Proceedings of the Society for Psychical Research*, Vol. 4, 1886, pp. 45-79; and more recently E. J. Dingwall: *The Critics Dilemma*, Crowhurst, Sussex, 1966, pp. 40-45.

98 Mrs. Fay thought that he was too fidgity and too sceptical. Many of Sidgwick's colleagues thought him to be decidedly unpsychic—nothing ever seemed to happen in his presence.

99 'He (Rayleigh) is more useful for my special purpose of convincing . . . the world: being Senior Wrangler, physicist, and understood to be mainly an inquirer . . .'

[100] W. Crookes: 'A Scientific Examination of Mrs. Fay's Mediumship' *The Spiritualist*, 12 March, 1875, pp. 126 and seq; S. Cox: *Mechanism of Man*, London, 1876.

[101] Mrs. Fay wrote denying that she had tricked Crookes. See *The Spiritualist*, 4 January 1878.

[102] Podmore: op. cit., p. 158.

[103] C. Broad: 'Cromwell Varley's Electrical Tests', *Proceedings of the Society for Psychical Research*, Vol. 54, 1964, pp. 158-172.

[104] Maskelyne: op. cit., 1885; Houdini: op. cit., 1924, p. 204.

[105] W. Crookes: 'On the Existence of a New Element. Probably of the Sulphur Group', *Chemical News*, Vol. 3, 1861, pp. 193-195; and, 'Researches on the Atomic Weight of Thallium', *Philosophical Transactions of the Royal Society*, Vol. 163, 1873, p. 279.

[106] W. Crookes: 'On Attraction and Repulsion Resulting from Radiation', *Philosophical Transactions of the Royal Society*, Vol. 164, 1874b, p. 527.

[107] W. Crookes: 'On Repulsion Resulting from Radiation—Part III', *Philosophical Transactions of the Royal Society*, Vol. 166, 1876, pp. 328-329. Crookes's physical investigations are treated at length in Rober K. De Kosky: 'William Crookes and the Fourth State of Matter', *Isis*, Vol. 67, 1976, pp. 36-60.

[108] Pearson: op. cit., 63-65.

[109] Osborne Reynolds: 'On the Forces Caused by the Communication of Heat between a Surface and a Gas; and on a New Photometer', *Philosophical Transactions of the Royal Society*, Vol. 166, 1876, pp. 725-735; Arthur Schuster: 'On the Nature of the Force Producing the Motion of a Body Exposed to Rays of Heat and Light', *Philosophical Transactions of the Royal Society*, Vol. 166, 1876, pp. 715-724.

[110] De Kosky: op. cit.

[111] W. Crookes: 'Letter', *Nature*, Vol. 17, 13 November 1877, pp. 44-45.

[112] This is not to say that Crookes stopped believing in spiritualistic phenomena, but only that the psychic force theory had ceased to be quite so attractive. Crookes was in fact led in later life to a belief in spiritualism and in survival after death.

[113] We see evidence of Crookes's monopolistic behaviour earlier in a letter to William Huggins on 6 June 1871 (see E. D. Fournier D'Albe: *The Life of Sir William Crookes*, Fisher Unwin, London, 1923, p. 210). Huggins had apparently suggested that a committee of scientists be set up to investigate Home to verify Crookes's work.
'It would be a confession of weakness and doubt on my part for me to take the initiative in calling together a scientific committee to help me. You do not ask for a committee to examine spectra. I did not ask for one to convince me that Thallium was true.'

[114] Palfreman: op. cit., 1976.

[115] Medhurst and Goldey: op. cit., p. 150.

[116] Myers and Sidgwick suspected fraud.

[117] See *Glasgow Herald*, 13 September 1876.

118 *The Times,* 18 September 1876, where Lankester is criticised for his so-called exposure and J. A. Clarke, a colleague of Maskelyne, claims that it could all be accomplished by trickery.

119 *The Times,* 19 September 1876. On 20 September 1876 a letter was received which revealed that it was Wallace's casting vote which allowed Barrett's paper to be read. Also a letter from Donkin, arguing that Lankester's work was the only serious scientific work on the subject.

120 Reports can be found in *The Times,* 3, 11, 21, 23, 28 and 30 October and 1 November, 1876.

121 *The Times,* 11 October, 1876. Maskelyne argued that slate writing could be done by trickery by wiping down a marked slate with a wet rag. When the slate dried the writing would appear.

122 Podmore: op. cit., pp. 89-91; Truesdell: op. cit., pp. 143-159.

123 *Proceedings of the Society of Psychical Research,* Vol. 1, 1882, p. 3.

124 Podmore: op. cit .,p. 177, wrote
'It is enough to say here that the avowed spiritualists who joined its Council in the first instance have all since dropped off'.

125 The Baron Reichenbach undertook a series of experiments in 1884 on animal magnetism. His results were quite spectacular and caused a resurgence of interest in England. See Palfreman: op. cit., 1977; Podmore: op. cit., pp. 117-120 and 132.

125 The Baron Reichenbach undertook a series of experiments in 1844 on *Scientifically Considered,* Appleton, New York, 1877.

127 A letter from Sidgwick to Myers, 12 February 1884, perhaps refers to that conflict.
'Barrett's letter is a bore! I can hardly think it much worthwhile to write at length about it; he seems so determined. Can a confirmation be found? We cannot of course give way . . .'

128 Marchant: op. cit., pp. 210-211.

129 Many mediums argued that the power they possessed varied greatly and sometimes disappeared for a time. In order to maintain their following they were forced to resort to a little conjuring. Such an explanation if widely used would clearly render psychic investigation of little purpose.

130 W. B. Carpenter: *Mesmerism, Spiritualism, etc. Historically and Scientifically Considered,* Appleton, New York, 1877.

131 W. B. Carpenter: 'Fallacies of Testimony', *Contemporary Review,* 1876, p. 268.

All uncited letters are from the Library, Trinity College, Cambridge.

THE CONSTRUCTION OF THE PARANORMAL: NOTHING UNSCIENTIFIC IS HAPPENING*

H. M. Collins and T. J. Pinch

Introduction

RECENT studies have exposed the social components involved in the assessment of the validity of scientific findings, a process normally thought of as being in some way immune to social forces. This programme has developed from the work of Wittgenstein[1] through the 'Copernican Revolution' in the history and philosophy of science, associated with the writing of Kuhn, Lakatos, Feyerabend, and Lakatos and Musgrave,[2] to an explicitly relativistic sociology of science, as argued, for instance, by Barnes, and Collins and Cox.[3] Detailed case-studies of the social processes involved in knowledge production have been carried out by the present authors. Collins[4] has attempted to show the social component involved in the process of 'testing' findings by the replication of experiments in the case of the physical phenomena of gravity waves, and extended this analysis to the case of replication in parapsychology.[5] Pinch,[6] by considering the part played by a particular proof, has attempted to show the social components associated with the rejection of the work of the physicist, David Bohm, on the foundations of quantum theory.

In this paper we will be concerned with examining the processes involved in the attempt to establish the existence of a certain class of phenomena referred to as paranormal phenomena. In particular we intend to analyse the tactics used by parapsychologists in their efforts to gain scientific recognition for their discipline and its findings, and the tactics used by orthodox scientists to deny them this stamp of legitimacy. In analysing these tactics it is hoped that something will

---

* Our subtitle refers to the paper 'Nothing Unusual is Happening' in which Emerson discusses the interests and techniques of actors trying to establish that nothing, or something, unusual is happening in situations such as hold-ups and gynaecological examinations. The parapsychologists' tactic of meta-morphosis, and their critics' attempts to prevent its success, can be seen in these terms.[1a]

We are grateful to David Travis for his helpful discussion of the paper, and to the Social Science Research Council for supporting our fieldwork.

be learned about the social processes involved in introducing radically new or strange elements into an established culture, and indirectly about the social processes which maintain science as a part of an established culture.

Paranormal phenomena are defined by Beloff (a leading parapsychologist) as:

'. . . phenomena which in one or more respects conflict with accepted scientific opinion as to what is physically possible . . .'[7]

The element of conflict within the parapsychologist's programme is rewarding in the context of a sociological study, for controversy highlights social processes with particular clarity. But it must be borne in mind that parapsychological and scientific man is not a 'cultural dope'. Unfortunately, for the possibility of ever doing really neat quantitative fieldwork in this area, there are an embarrassing number of orthodox scientists actively experimenting with psi (see note 7); an embarrassing number who, if not actually engaged in such research, are at least prepared to entertain it; and an embarrassing number of critics of psi experimentation among the ranks of the experimenters themselves. What is more, a recent survey of *New Scientist* readers has shown that attitudes are becoming more open, for 70 per cent of the respondents claimed to be believers in the phenomena or the possibility of the phenomena.[8] Furthermore, in our own discussions with physicists investigating Uri Geller-type metal bending, little open hostility from the physics community has been mentioned.[9]

But survey results do not make an area scientific, and even a cursory look at parapsychology produces concrete evidence of the conflict with orthodox science. For instance, articles have been rejected by orthodox journals, often with no reasons given, and sometimes referees' reports recommending publication have been overruled by journal editors.[10] In fact there is evidence that the refereeing system has broken down for parapsychology papers. The editor of a well known science journal told us that there is little point in sending out parapsychology papers for refereeing because opinions are so polarised as to render the content of referees' reports entirely predictable. (This particular editor overcame the problem by evaluating nearly all parapsychology papers himself.) Again, our respondents often reported adverse effects on their careers due to their involvement with parapsychology, and any university academic is likely to suffer amused patronisation from his colleagues

238

should they discover his involvement with psi—it is best kept secret as long as possible in most departments. The authors have both done experiments in areas of parapsychology and we have quickly discovered the importance of telling our sociologist colleagues that our interest was strictly that of the participant observer building up the background for good sociological fieldwork. Another survey compared the reported results of experiments published in psychology journals with those published in parapsychology journals.[11] The findings were that psychology journals preferred to publish negative results, when they published at all. Unfortunately this study lacked conviction, for only six parapsychological articles could be found in the psychological literature, though this is indicative in itself. Finally, parapsychology (at least in the U.K.) does not attract any government funding. Not surprisingly some parapsychologists were bemused by our sociological project, which is, ironically, probably the only government-funded research connected with parapsychology in the U.K.

1. *Modes and Forums of Conflict Within Science*

Sociologists have learned about conflict within science through one or two celebrated case studies, but this may have obscured the variability of the phenomenon. To put our discussion of parapsychology into perspective, it may be useful to point to the distinction between explicit and implicit conflict, and, to help with the analysis, a distinction between 'constitutive' and 'contingent' forums of debate will be drawn.

Implicit rejection operates when rival knowledge claims are ignored by orthodoxy, whilst explicit rejection is characterised by controversy where the objects of dispute are articulated by individual scientists or opposed groups of scientists. Implicit rejection has received very little discussion in the sociological literature, which is somewhat surprising, considering that it appears to occur rather often in modern science. For example, many new and challenging physical theories, even when they are published, disappear into the literature ignored rather than contested. In accord with this, there appear to have been comparatively few cases of explicit rejection with its associated controversy, in modern physics.

Both implicit and explicit rejection operate within two forums. On the one hand there is what we will call the 'constitutive' forum, which comprises scientific theorising and experiment and corresponding publication and criticism in the learned journals and, perhaps, in the formal conference setting. On the other hand, there is the forum in which are set those actions which—according to old-fashioned philosophic orthodoxy—are not supposed to affect the constitution of 'objective' knowledge. We will call this the 'contingent' forum, and would expect to find there the content of popular and semi-popular journals, discussion and gossip, fund raising and publicity seeking, the setting up and joining of professional organisations, the corralling of student followers, and everything that scientists do in connection with their work, but which is not found in the constitutive forum. Within this classification, early work in the sociology of science can be seen as first discussing the explicit values of the constitutive forum,[12] and then showing the influence of the contingent forum upon it.[13] Later work can be seen as showing that even actions properly within the constitutive forum do not have any specially privileged epistemological status, so that, within certain sociological perspectives, the separation of the two forums relates to no underlying distinction in the construction of 'scientific' knowledge *per se*.[14]

Nevertheless, despite this sociological subtlety it is possible to generalise about the type of arguments and actions which may be legitimately expressed, in the normal way, within these forums. In the constitutive forum, actions should be *seen to be* based on universalisable non-contingent premises, whereas, in the contingent forum, actions may be of any kind, but normally they will not *look as though* they are constitutive of scientific knowledge.[15]

Returning now to the question of the mechanisms of rejection of knowledge claims, we can construct a fourfold classification and give some examples of knowledge claims where the mode of rejection has been largely of one type.

		Forum	
		CONSTITUTIVE	CONTINGENT
Mode of	IMPLICIT	1	4
Rejection	EXPLICIT	2	3

Into category 1 for example, would fit the rejection of many rival interpretations of the quantum theory. These are (were) certainly presented in the professional journals, but have been allowed to fade quietly from the scene without any explicit rejection.[16] Examples of category 2 include the rejection of the knowledge claims of Bohm[17] and

Barkla[18] and of the phenomenon of high fluxes of gravity waves.[19] Such knowledge claims all produced controversy but this was seen to be confined in the main to the constitutive forum—the professional journals and the conference presentation. The Velikovsky affair seems to fit into category 3, with his knowledge claim promoting a controversy, but a controversy which did not impinge much on the professional journals and which was conducted more over a popular front.[20] Finally, in category 4 are all the knowledge claims which are so radical as to produce no controversy within science, but are rejected out of hand, and without explicit mention. For example, the knowledge claims of scientologists or followers of the Reichian "orgone energy" concept would fall into this box.[21]

Our discussion here is of explicit mechanisms only, and we will consider both forums in turn, pointing out especially those illuminating cases where anomalous activity is found within a forum, that is when the normal boundaries are seen to be crossed, and are allowed to be crossed. However, it is important to bear in mind that the paper as a whole is informed by 'recent work in the sociology of science' which accepts no epistemological distinction between the two forums. That is, for the authors, contingent actions do constitute scientific knowledge, and the constitutive actions are as much a social construct as anything else. Only in this light can one of the parapsychologists' main strategies for gaining scientific legitimacy be understood, this strategy being one of physical metamorphosis—of changing themselves into scientists. In getting chairs, students, university posts, funding from legitimate sources and publication in recognised journals, and in looking like ordinary quiet members of the scientific community, parapyschologists may construct scientifically acceptable telepathy, clairvoyance, and psychokinesis.[22] If this were not the case, then the appropriate strategy would surely, be simply to perform and report the 'definitive' experiment!

2. *Tactics of Legitimation and Rejection in the Constitutive Forum*

In nearly every classificatory scheme such as this, certain items will be found which do not fit unambiguously into either category. Our policy is as follows. Correspondence to constitutive journals such as *Nature* or *Science* has been treated as belonging to the constitutive forum, as have books which have been reviewed in constitutive journals. Arguments which have been used in both forums are fully discussed when they appear under the constitutive heading so that they do not need to be redescribed under the other heading.[23] A list of sources of constitutive-and contingent-forum material is given in the appendix.

Before looking at the detailed tactics of the parapsychologists and their critics we must explain that our notion of tactics is a way of 'making sense' of individual actions, though not all individual actors (not cultural dopes) need be consciously committed to what we see as an overall strategy. Other parapsychologists (not discussed here) are consciously committed to a quite different strategy. They prefer to work within the institutions of parapsychology external to the main body of science and are happy, for example, to publish only in parapsychology journals. The basis of another route to legitimacy can be seen in this attitude. The internal institutions of parapsychology themselves provide a cognitive and social framework within which credibility can be sought. Such a path will not directly concern us here.[24]

The tactics of the parapsychologists

(i) *Using Symbolic and Technical Hardware of Science*

Parapsychology presented its first important knowledge claim to science in the 1930s with the work of J. B. Rhine. His experiments had many of the characteristics of legitimate scientific experiments; they involved meticulous observations done over a period of years within a university laboratory, and presented in a similar way to the reports of orthodox psychology experiments (Rhine was trained as a botanist.)

A typical experiment within the field might consist of a subject making guesses at the order of a randomly ordered pack of cards while the subject was isolated from any possible sensory channel of communication with the cards, or anyone knowing the order of the cards. The subject's guesses would be compared with the actual order of the cards, at the termination of the experiment, and usually these guesses would deviate only slightly from chance expectation. But if the subject's guesses were consistently better than chance over a long period, the total effect might be highly statistically significant, and in these cases, the subject's success could be attributed to some sort of E.S.P.

Rhine's early experiments of this type were open to a number of criticisms such as the possibility of unnoticed sensory cueing, or design faults at the statistical-analysis stage. This early debate will not concern us here and several reviewers agree that by the late 1930s parapsychology experiments were no longer open to obvious criticisms of procedure or statistical analysis.[25] The statistical debate was ended for most parapsychologists (although not for some orthodox scientists —see the arguments of Brown and Bridgman below) by a statement from the Institute of Mathematical Statistics in 1937 endorsing the parapsychologists' procedures. Thus by the 1940s the parapsychologists had obtained one of the hall-marks of scientific legitimacy, endorsement of their statistical methods by one of the most authoritative groups of scientists, the mathematicians.[26]

Subsequently, and to an increasing extent, the parapsychologists (and one may see this as their constitutive strategy) have incorporated into their work the complex experimental techniques available to physicists, biologists or psychologists. For instance, in the modern parapsychology experiment, E.S.P. data are automatically recorded and processed, often by means of a direct computer link-up, thus evading the possibility of unconscious bias at one stage of the experiment at least. The generation of random targets may now be based on, for instance, quantum transitions processed by complex electronic equipment. This kind of target generator can be tested for randomness over millions of trials, and, being capable of producing fresh numbers at almost unlimited speed, can be incorporated with ease for instance, into experiments which may try to measure complex parameters such as speed of psi action, or can be used to test for psi 'learning'.[27] At the same time, there have been a growing number of attempts to discover personality variables related to success at psi tasks, and to develop ideas such as a 'decline effect', responsible for the lack of consistency in subjects' performances over extended periods.[28] Other conceptual tools such as information theory —a powerful heuristic in terms of normal communication systems— are increasingly being incorporated into the analysis of extrasensory communication systems.[29]

All this has been accompanied by an increasing sophistication with statistical analysis and experimental techniques such as 'double blind' judging of results, and the use of independent observers. It seems likely that the best of modern parapsychology comprises some of the most rigorously controlled and methodologically sophisticated work in the sciences.

Since Rhine's work there have been many accounts of good experiments to be found in the literature, and these may appear completely convincing. Indeed many of the most 'hard headed' parapsychological researchers have come into the field as a result of reading this literature though they themselves may never have seen or experienced any type of paranormal effect whatsoever. (The reader is recommended to read Schmidt[30] for what the authors and many parapsychologists consider to be a paradigmatically convincing account). It might be thought that a number of such carefully conducted experiments, competently reported and presented in the constitutive forum, would be sufficient to establish the existence of psi phenomena. (At least one physicist turned parapsychologist to whom we have spoken supposed that this would be the case once he had published his definitive article. Subsequent events proved him wrong.) The situation is, however, far more complicated than this.

The tactics of the critics

(ii) Blank Refusal to Believe

Surprisingly it is not uncommon in this field to find prejudice (in a literal sense) given as the main reason for rejecting parapsychology even in the 'objective' literature of the constitutive forum. For example, the psychologist D. O. Hebb has remarked:

> 'Why do we not accept E.S.P. as a psychological fact? Rhine has offered us enough evidence to have convinced us on almost any other issue . . . I cannot see what other basis my colleagues have for rejecting it . . . My own rejection of [Rhine's] views is in a literal sense prejudice.'[31]

That it should be permissible to make such statements in this forum is a startling breakdown of the normal boundaries.

Such criticisms are not limited to the constitutive forum. For example, in an address to the American Association for the Advancement of Science (A.A.A.S.), delivered in 1958, the Vice President recalled the earlier remarks of the physicist Helmholtz, who said:

> 'I cannot believe it. Neither the testimony of all the Fellows of the Royal Society, nor even the evidence of my own senses would lead me to believe in the transmission of thought from one person to another independently of the recognised channels of sensation. It is clearly impossible.'[32]

The Construction of the Paranormal

(iii) *Using the Symbolic Hardware of Philosophy*

Some critics have hidden their beliefs behind semi-philosophical rhetoric, thus superficially maintaining the boundary between what may, and may not be said in the literature. For instance the psychologist T. R. Willis comments:

> 'The conclusions of modern science are reached by strict logical proof, based on the cumulative results of numerous ad hoc observations and experiments reported in reputable scientific journals and confirmed by other scientific investigators: then and only then, can they be regarded as certain and decisively demonstrated. Once they have been finally established, any conjecture that conflicts with them, as all forms of so-called "extra-sensory perception" plainly must, can be confidently dismissed without more ado.'[33]

This type of criticism although referring to some variant of the 'scientific method', draws its weight from the 'ethnocentricism of now'[34]—nothing is true which conflicts with what is now known. The criticism can be dressed up as the technical 'a priori argument', 'Hume's argument concerning miracles', or 'Occam's Razor'. An example of the a priori argument comes from Hansel, who writes:

> '. . . the a priori argument . . . may even save time and effort in scrutinizing the [E.S.P.] experiments . . . In view of the a priori argument against it we know in advance that telepathy, etc., cannot occur.'[35]

Hume's argument is expressed by Price[36] when he writes:

> 'Now it happens that I myself believed in E.S.P. about fifteen years ago, after reading *Extra-Sensory Perception After Sixty Years,* [a book by Rhine] 'but I changed my mind when I became acquainted with the arguments presented by David Hume in his chapter "Of Miracles" in *An Enquiry concerning Human Understanding.*

> 'Hume's argument runs as follows: "A miracle is a violation of the laws of nature; and as a firm and unalterable experience has established these laws, the proof against a miracle, from the very nature of the fact, is as entire as any argument from experience can possibly be imagined . . .".'

Such arguments too have appeared in the contingent arena. Occam's Razor, for example, is used by Hanlon in his article in the semi-popular journal, *New Scientist*:

> 'By Occam's Razor it is only necessary to show that plausible normal explanations have not been excluded in order to prefer such explanations . . . And their experiments fail the Occam's Razor test . . .' (The experiments referred to are those of the Stanford Research Institute team who investigated Uri Geller and others).[37]

(iv) *Association with Unscientific Beliefs*

Many of the criticisms of parapsychology even in the constitutive forum, rest upon its external basis in spiritualism and its occult associations. For instance, the psychologist Boring has written:

> 'It is quite clear that interest in parapsychology has been maintained by faith. People want to believe in an occult something.'[38]

The commentator Rawcliffe claims:

> 'To view the modern E.S.P. movement in perspective, one must realise that it is basically a cult—a cult of the supernatural in technical dress. The perpetuation of all such cults depends ultimately on irrational beliefs and the ignoring or "explaining away" of rational criticism.'[39]

Szasz also makes the point that the identification of E.S.P. with the occult:

> '. . . is responsible for the obscurantism which pervades this area of inquiry and which makes its companionship unwarranted in the larger field of scientific disciplines.'[40]

That parapsychology's popular associations may be cited in criticism in the constitutive forum displays the flexibility of boundaries that we have referred to.

In the contingent forum this type of criticism has appeared although here the pretence of 'objectivity' has often been dropped. An extreme form has been presented by the psychoanalyst, H. Hitschmann. He described interest in psi as:

> '. . . the narcissistic tendency to ascribe to oneself "supernormal" faculties [corresponding] to the infantile craving to possess omnipotence of thought, a faculty of acting at a distance, and the like, as found . . . in the child, savage and the insane.'[41]

Other critics have associated parapsychology directly with spiritualism and have attempted to imply that the subject matter of parapsychology has been 'overtaken' by science. A case for the historical illegitimacy of psi has been made by the well-known sceptic, Chris Evans.[42] In an article in *New Scientist,* aimed at finally laying parapsychology to rest, Evans wrote:

> 'Most striking, of course, is the way in which, to all but the totally committed, psychical research and its subject matter seems so hopelessly, woefully out of date.'[43]

Other critics acknowledge that parapsychology does bear some of the hallmarks of a modern science, but do not consider that this is enough. As Price puts it:

'In short, parapsychology, although well camouflaged with some of the paraphernalia of science, still bears in abundance the markings of magic.'[44]

The dangers of parapsychology's association with the occult have not gone unnoticed by parapsychologists. For example, Beloff writes:

'Parapsychology has, all through its history suffered from its fatal attraction for persons of unbalanced mind who seek in it their personal salvation . . .'[45]

(v) *Accusations of Triviality*

In contrast to the arguments of those who feel that psi phenomena must be rejected because of their occult associations, are the arguments of those critics who feel that psi phemonena are simply uninteresting. For example, the psychologist Boring[46] has stated that E.S.P. data represent 'an empty correlation' and Stevens[47] claims that 'the signal-to-noise ratio for E.S.P. is simply too low to be interesting'. In an editorial of *Science,* in the context of a discussion of E.S.P., it is claimed that 'unexplained cases are simply unexplained. They can never constitute evidence for any hypothesis'.[48] Similarly the distinguished physicist turned philosopher of science, P. W. Bridgman, has written in an article in *Science* that:

'I am unwilling to accept the genuineness of any phenomenon that leans as heavily as does E.S.P. on probability arguments.'[49]

A. J. Ayer has written in the contingent forum:

'The only thing that is remarkable about the subject who is credited with extra-sensory perception is that he is consistently rather better at guessing cards than the ordinary run of people have shown themselves to be. The fact that he also does "better than chance" proves nothing in itself.'[50]

(vi) *Attacks on Methodological Precepts*

A more startling statistical criticism made against parapsychologists came in the 1950s from the mathematician, Spencer-Brown. Brown[51] accepted the results of the parapsychologists, not as evidence of psi, but as 'the most prominent empirical reason for beginning to doubt the universal applicability of classical frequency probability'. Brown's position is clearly stated in an article in *Nature;* he wrote:

'Though not doubting the validity of some of the experimental work by the accepted standards, I was led to question the validity of one of the accepted standards.'[52]

In other words, if experiments plus statistics equal psi phenomena, Brown was prepared to abandon statistical inference to avoid the necessity of accepting psi. Brown tried to show that statistically significant correlations could be generated between different parts of the tables of random numbers that parapsychologists were using for their controls, so that their results might have no more significance than that of one random series compared to another. The statistical criticisms of Bridgman, and Brown's criticisms in particular show the length to which sceptics are prepared to go, for, were their arguments to be accepted, normal scientific statistical procedures would have to be abandoned over a wide area.

The parapsychologists responded to Brown's arguments by conducting their own experiments with random number tables. For example one investigation, carried out by A. T. Oram[53] claimed to give 'a simple factual reminder that our statistical methods, when tried out in the absence of any possible influence from psi phenomena, do give reliable "chance" results'.

Interestingly, Brown's arguments, as well as being directed towards parapsychologists, can be interpreted as putting forward a hypothesis which is as much a challenge to science as is parapsychology itself. The concept of synchronicity, explicitly put forward by Jung, and implicitly by Brown,[54] is currently in vogue among some parapsychologists, perhaps due to the recent emphasis on such ideas by Koestler.[55] In the light of this current sympathy the initial hasty scepticism towards Brown may seem in need of explanation. One may speculate that, at the time, Brown's work seemed to threaten, not just to withdraw the hallmark of statistical competence from the parapsychologists, but to abolish it altogether.

(vii) *Unfavourable Comparisons with Canonical Versions of Scientific Method*

Another prerequisite of scientific legitimacy which critics claim that parapsychology has failed to satisfy, is the need for a theoretical explanation of the phenomena. This criticism seems to have been levelled in particular in the late 1950s and early 1960s. It was made, for example, by Thomas Szasz when he wrote:

> '. . . in the realm of psychical research, in spite of widespread interest and intensive effort over more than half a century, there is still nothing that would deserve to be called a theory, even by the most enthusiastic

248

proponents of this work. This, in the writer's opinion, constitutes the most decisive factor which casts doubt upon the "reality" of the entire structure of parapsychology.'[56]

Tart, Schmeidler and Beloff,[57] (all parapsychologists) have claimed this to be one of the most important reasons for the rejection of psi by orthodox scientists. Of course, the objection begs the question of what is to comprise a 'theory' in science. Certainly the criticism does not seem to apply to contemporary parapsychology. Most of our present respondents are working with what they regard as 'theories' of parapsychology. Indeed one of the central foci of interest in parapsychology at the moment is the debate between those adhering to the various electromagnetic and quantum-mechanical explanations of psi. In any case, parapsychologists have pointed out that, even if researchers are not committed to a particular theory, 'black boxism' is a legitimate research technique in orthodox science.[58]

Another argument levelled by the critics is that parapsychology has not produced anything like 'a repeatable experiment'. We will not deal in detail with the complexities inherent in this objection for one of us has already considered it at length,[59] but further examples of repeatability cited as the touchstone of scientific legitimacy can be found in the writings of Crumbaugh and Cohen.[60] Crumbaugh, beginning a considered discussion of the problem, writes that repeatability is:

'. . . crucial and must be met before the great bulk of scientists will swing over to accept the E.S.P. hypothesis.'

Such criticisms have also filtered through to the contingent forum, but in a less subtle form. For instance, Cohen, writing in *The Nation* claims:

'Obviously successful E.S.P. experiments are not repeatable and thus do not meet a basic requirement of all scientific experiments.'[61]

What needs to be carefully argued in the constitutive forum is here *'obvious'* in the contingent forum. The authoritative voice of the constitutive forum is borrowed without the caution engendered through bearing ultimate responsibility for the point at issue.

Some of the above criticisms, which comprise the constitutive front of the attack on parapsychology, seem visibly influenced more by the desire to reject psi in particular, than by considerations of universal standards. Thus many of the criticisms would have a devastating effect if turned against parts of orthodox science. Also different critics regard different criteria as crucial, and some criteria are seemingly inconsistent. For example, on the face of it, parapsychology cannot be ruled out both because its results conflict with science, and because they are uninteresting and statistically insignificant.

The fact is that although a group of scientists have dedicated a considerable portion of their lives to the attempt to discredit psi (an interesting phenomenon in itself), they have not succeeded in revealing any universally acceptable criteria to distinguish parapsychology from science. As a result, critics have been forced into bringing into the constitutive forum, arguments usually considered more appropriate in the contingent forum. One or two cases of this process have been discussed above, but the most remarkable critique of parapsychology to enter the 'scientific' literature is the accusation of widespread fraud.

(viii) *The Fraud Hypothesis*

Accusations of fraud against individuals have occurred in other sciences, but this particular criticism is levelled against a whole discipline. Price in his notorious article in *Science* gave a rationale for this:

> '. . . we must recognize that we usually make a certain gross statistical error. When we consider the possibility of fraud, almost invariably we think of particular individuals and ask ourselves whether it is possible that this particular man, this Professor X, could be dishonest. The probability seems small. But the procedure is incorrect. The correct procedure is to consider that we likely would not have heard of Professor X at all except for his psychic findings. Accordingly, the probability of interest to us is, the probability of there having been anywhere in the world, among its more than 2 billion inhabitants, a few people with the desire and the ability artfully to produce false evidence for the supernatural.'[62]

Price then proceeded to show ways in which fraud could have been used in a particular famous experiment. (Later Price[63] retracted his accusation of fraud against Soal and Rhine in a celebrated letter to *Science*.)

This tradition of giving credibility and persuasiveness to the fraud hypothesis by the demonstration of its *possibility* has become a standard procedure in the critique of parapsychological experiments. Professor C. E. M. Hansel[64] made extensive use of this technique in his book *E.S.P. A Scientific Evaluation*. He actually repeated several of the well known experiments obtaining similar results through 'normal' mechanisms, the use of one sort of technical trick or another. More recently, Joseph Hanlon has attempted to discredit the

Stanford experiments on Uri Geller by the invention of a scenario where normal sensory communication was managed through hidden radio transmitters and a receiver embedded in Geller's tooth, in such a way as to deceive the experimenters into thinking they were witnessing E.S.P.[65]

Hansel and Hanlon both make it clear that they are not suggesting that the fraud did actually occur by the mechanisms they suggest. Both use the fraud hypothesis as a soothing addendum to some version of the a priori argument. Though E.S.P. is seen as a priori impossible, the phenomena claimed by the parapsychologists must still be explained away. The fraud hypothesis fills this lacuna.

There can be no defence against this argument if it is pushed to extremes. In formal terms, an E.S.P. experiment requires that the experimenters demonstrate that no sensory channels of communication exist between the subject and the object of perception. Thus to design a criticism-free experiment the experimenters have to think of *every possible* normal means of communication between subject and object before the experiment takes place, so that they may arrange the protocol in such a way as to block every such channel. But it is always possible to find a normal channel of communication by the very nature of the experimental set-up. There always must be some normal channel of communication (however indirect) between the subject and the object of an E.S.P. experiment for it to constitute an experiment. Furthermore available normal channels of communication are potentially infinite in number because they are as *open to innovation* as science itself. Thus the credibility of an experiment depends on the outcome of a kind of race between experimenters and critics. How long can the experiment live before the determined critic can invent a normal means of communication which might have been used? The critic can always win the race if he is sufficiently determined and ingenious, because he is given an unlimited time to reach the finish.

However, even if the critic has any difficulty in inventing a plausible normal means by which the communication could have taken place, he has available the gambit of 'extending the conspiracy'. For instance, if he cannot think of a way in which the subject on his own could cheat the experimenters he can 'extend the conspiracy' to outside helpers. Hanlon,[66] referring to Geller, sets up this scenario between him and his manager, Andrija Puharich:

H. M. Collins and T. J. Pinch

'If Uri came to Puharich and said 'Andrija, I have known you for a year now and never once have I cheated you. Now they are asking me to do things I may not always be able to do, but if I fail no one will believe in Hoova. You are a great inventor—give me something to help me just once in a while".'

Hanlon legitimises this accusation of fraud by his appeal to Puharich's belief in Hoova (extra-terrestrial powers). He claims:

'. . . if Uri's request come via Spectra [the spokesman for Hoova] Puharich would be sure to obey. Thus, Puharich need not be party to a widespread and continuing fraud to have helped Uri in this way.'

If necessary, the critic can next extend the conspiracy further to include the experimenters as well (as Price does), and any observers too, at which point the actual conduct of the experiment ceases to have any relevance at all. The logic of the fraud hypothesis not only appears to remove any need for empirical tests from the scientific decision-making process but can also be put forward without any empirical evidence that fraud actually took place.

The paranoia thus engendered in the parapyschologists is well illustrated by the bizarre research technique adopted by one of our respondents. In an attempt to pre-empt the fraud hypothesis this researcher is having his experimental apparatus for demonstrating E.S.P. (a Schmidt machine) built and designed in modular units, by different scientists (unknown to each other) so that *no individual knows how the whole machine works*. This, he hopes, will prevent the charge of experimental collusion via the experimenters 'doctoring' the apparatus to favour positive results. It will be interesting to see which of the many methods of fraud still available will be cited as responsible should positive results be produced in this case.[67]

Critics using the fraud hypothesis also make great play of parapsychology's historic associations. To be fair, it must be made clear that *there is* a history of unambiguous fraud in the area of psychical research. The subject started out from a basis of cheesecloth apparitions and invisible wires which were the props of fraudulent mediums, but this history may now be used unscrupulously. For instance Price's justification for accusing Soal of fraud appeals to this history of fraudulent mediums. Price writes:

'I would want seven or eight confederates in order to imitate 170 Soal sittings. And the reader who finds that he cannot conceive of the possibility that any leading modern parapsychologist could be fraudulent should compare his attitude with certain earlier judgements concerning the honesty of mediums.'[68]

Although one would not expect criticisms based on the historical associations of a discipline to appear in the constitutive forum (one does not find published criticisms of surgery, because it arose out of barbering, or of chemistry, because it arose out of alchemy), here again is an example where they have percolated through in the case of parapsychology.

The point of the above discussion of the fraud hypothesis is not to ridicule the critics of parapsychology—we must apologise for any unintended sarcasm—but to show its universal applicability and therefore to beg the question of its infrequency of use in the rest of science.

So far the arguments we have looked at have been taken from what we have called the constitutive forum. Most of these arguments, as we have shown above, have also been echoed in the contingent forum. We hope that the picture which is emerging will show further that formal presentations in themselves need never lead to the ultimate acceptance of results by determined critics. We turn now to examine in detail the activities which are found only in the contingent arena.

3. *Tactics of Legitimation and Rejection in the Contingent Forum*
The tactics of the parapsychologists

(ix) *Metamorphosis*

As already mentioned, the strategy of the parapsychologists has been that of metamorphosis,—of 'becoming' scientists. Thus they have acquired university posts (parapsychology courses operate at many American universities), Ph.D. studentships (there are Ph.D. studentships in this area in at least three British universities now), chairs (Surrey University has recently established a new chair with psychical research connections) and government funding for research (still chiefly in the U.S.) and, to a limited extent, they publish in established orthodox journals. On a global scale parapsychology has many of the characteristics of orthodox scientific disciplines.[69]

Recognition of this is evidenced in, for instance, the statement of the executive secretary of the National Institute of Mental Health (an American government agency) on the recent awarding of a grant to a parapsychologist. The secretary, commenting on the parapsychologists. said:

'They are perfectly well trained, respectable scientific investigators. They are sincere and serious and they deserve a chance.'[70]

A statement reflecting similar sentiments about individual work is to be found in the editorial comment explaining *Nature's*[71] publication of a recent parapsychological article (to be discussed below in more detail).

> 'Despite its shortcomings, the paper is presented as a scientific document by two qualified scientists, writing from a major research establishment apparently with the unqualified backing of the research institute itself.'[72]

Further recognition was given in the affiliation of the Parapsychological Association to the American Association for the Advancement of Science, an episode described by Douglas Dean[73] in an emotive document subtitled 'Parapsychology is now a Recognised Science. How it was done'.[74] The first stage in gaining affiliation was to form the Parapsychological Association (P.A.) in 1957; as Dean put it:

> '. . . this was the first step in creating professionalism in the parapsychology area.'

Since then, after waiting the necessary five years the P.A. has applied for affiliation in 1963, 1967 and 1968, being turned down on each occasion. Finally, in 1969, its application was accepted following a rousing speech by the social anthropologist Margaret Mead. The chairman's comments at the crucial meeting indicate the type of criteria considered important in assessing such applications. He said:

> 'The committee on Council Affairs considered the P.A.'s work for a very long time. The Committee came to the conclusion that it is an association investigating controversial or non-existent phenomena; however it is open in membership to critics and agnostics: and they were satisfied that it uses scientific methods of enquiry: thus that investigation can be counted as scientific. Further information has come to us that the number of A.A.A.S. fellows who are also members of the P.A. is not four as on the agenda but nine.'

The value of the affiliation is captured by Dean when he comments:

> 'Now, however, many parapsychologists' positions in Universities would be strengthened. The P.A. membership would rise as many good scientists would be able to join now without forfeiting their jobs or their promotion. Money may be easier too . . . We can rejoice for a time, for many of us have yearned for decades to be regarded as respectable scientists . . .'

(x) *Laundering The Funds*

The question of money draws attention to one ironical facet of this process of transformation into science. 'Becoming' scientists is an expensive business, but parapsychology as a whole has no immediate shortage of funds. The problem is that the source of funding is itself often an embarrassment, coming as it does from wealthy widows and the like, and reminding parapsychologists and others of the science's origins in the murky world of spiritualism.

Until 'scientific' parapsychology can achieve a breakthrough into large-scale government funding it will have to rely on contributors' interest in the 'other side' for a considerable proportion of its resources, and will be unable to escape the 'spiritualist'/'scientist' schism which characterises many of its professional organisations. These occult associations, as we saw above, can be made much of by the critics.[75]

Thus the external basis of parapsychology, as well as providing funding for the parapsychologists' tactics in the contingent forum, is also a weakness to be exploited by the critics. In other ways too the critics have directed their strategy against the parapsychologists' attempts at metamorphosis.

The tactics of the critics[76]

(xi) *Ad Hominem Arguments*

A good example of the critics' approach in action can be found in the recent critiques of the Stanford work on Geller and others. For instance Joseph Hanlon and Martin Gardner[77] when discussing these experiments, consider it legitimate to mention factors concerning the personal history and interests of the researchers. Hanlon writes:

'Targ has worked in the parapsychology area on and off for fifteen years. Puthoff has gone through encounter groups and other West Coast fads, and is now a scientologist (as is Ingo Swann [one of the psychics used in the experiments]).'

The implied criticisms here are first that both experimenters are firm believers in the phenomena and secondly, presumably, that Puthoff is gullible enough to believe in 'fads' such as scientology. Gardner also describes one of the experimenters as a 'physicist and scientologist' and makes the point that 'those who record E.S.P. data are almost always firm believers in E.S.P.' Gardner and Hanlon both make great play of the fact that Targ and Puthoff were laser physicists and were thus not competent to do E.S.P. experiments, which Gardner, for instance, regards to be the province of psychologists.

He comments on the experimental report:

> 'That, of course, is the voice of a physicist familiar with observer effects in quantum mechanics. It is not the voice of a psychologist.'

He also criticises the experimental design, he claims:

> 'It is the design of a physicist trained to investigate physical laws—laws that do not exhibit psychological quirks.'

These criticisms begin to be reminiscent of 'Catch 22'. The experimenters' background in psi makes them suspect as observers, while their background in physics renders their psi-experimental expertise suspect! The personal history of a scientists' involvement in the field is rarely considered a relevant factor in orthodox science, at least not explicitly, but, when orthodoxy is challenged, this type of factor is apparently considered important.[78]

Other personal details of the experimenters are considered to be relevant by Hanlon and he even goes so far as to assess the eyesight of one of them. Similar tactics are used in a recent review of parapsychology by Phillip Morrison[79] who considers it relevant that, in a parapsychology experiment done over a century ago, one of the scientists was 'advanced in age' and another was 'half-blind'. Morrison also introduces another informal factor into the evaluation of experimenters, this is experimental pedigree. He creates the image of the 'clumsy fisted theorist' who, of course, is incapable of doing competent experimental work.

The reviews by Hanlon, Gardner and Morrison all appeared in semi-popular scientific journals (Hanlon's in *New Scientist* and Gardner's and Morrison's in *Scientific American*). However this does not mean that they are unimportant scientific documents in the E.S.P. controversy. Because of the scarcity of papers relating to parapsychology appearing in the 'hard' scientific literature, many scientists form their opinions to some extent through reading the semi-popular journals.[80] This again emphasises the permeability of the boundary between the constitutive and contingent forums in this case. One of the above authors has told us that he regarded his particular article as 'an important scientific contribution'. And again, the special role which the semi-popular journals have played is indicated in the plans (stillborn) of *New Scientist* to organise and fund a series of scientific tests with Uri Geller, most certainly a bid to constitute new knowledge.

(xii) *Magnifying Anecdotal Evidence*

Papers written by the experimenters which were never intended for publication and were, at the most, provisional statements indicating that *prima facie* there was something to investigate have also been used to criticise their authors. Hanlon uses this tactic on two occasions in his review of the Geller experiments. Firstly, he considers it legitimate to make detailed criticisms of the experiments done at Birkbeck College based on an unpublished paper which one of the experimenters had produced for private circulation. Secondly, he attacks Puthoff's capabilities as an observer on the basis of anecdotal evidence (later incorporated in a privately circulated letter) that Puthoff believed a description of the workings of a magnetometer by a psychic (with no scientific training) to be adequate.

(xiii) *Denying Orthodox Publications*

The issue of publication in orthodox journals has played an important part in the tactics of the critics. Despite the considerable amount of experimental evidence for psi phenomena published in the parapsychology journals, there have been comparatively few reports in orthodox journals. The parapsychology journals are read mainly by parapsychologists and are taken by few university libraries, so the main way of attracting the attention of orthodox scientists is via a publication in one of the orthodox interdisciplinary journals such as *Science* or *Nature*. As already mentioned, the little survey work which has been done in this area has indicated a bias against publishing the positive results of parapsychologists in contrast to the space given in these journals to the sceptics such as Bridgman, Brown, Price, and Hansel.

Parapsychologists have long claimed that the refereeing system of orthodox journals is biased against them. For example, among others, the distinguished parapsychologist and psychologist, R. A. McConnell, has written:

> 'On the basis of experience in other fields I am convinced that the refereeing system frequently operates to suppress the publication of new and important material that happens to be personally distasteful to the referees to whom it is referred.'[81]

These comments were made in the context of an incident involving a paper submitted to *Science* by a group of parapsychologists which was rejected after two favourable and two unfavourable referees' reports, was resubmitted, and was again rejected after a further three referees had recommended publication and one had been against it. This evidence together with the comments of the journal editor (above) who admitted that there was little point in sending parapsychology papers out for refereeing, indicate that processes of rejection operate against parapsychology before its knowledge claims are formally presented.

(xiv) *Diluting Orthodox Publication*

The subtlety of certain of the mechanisms limiting parapsychology's metamorphosis is illustrated in a case of which we have slightly more detailed knowledge—the publication in *Nature* of the Stanford Research Institute's (S.R.I.) investigation of Uri Geller and other subjects, and referred to briefly above. This publication was accompanied by comment specially explaining editorial policy. In addition, the editorial included extracts from unfavourable referees' reports, and was written in part by Chris Evans, the author of several articles sceptical of parapsychology. In this way, the triumph of publication in *Nature* was diluted, the seeming stamp of legitimacy emasculated by making it a case of special treatment—at best a kind of tokenism.

Moreover, just in case anyone should mistake the S.R.I. article for real science, the *Nature* editorial went on to draw its readers' attention to the polemically critical article published in *New Scientist* in the same week (mentioned several times in the previous section) thus:

'The *New Scientist* does a service by publishing this week the results of Dr. Joe Hanlon's own investigations into a wide range of phenomena surrounding Geller.'

What the editorial does not state is that the Editors of *New Scientist* and *Nature* had collaborated in publishing their papers, a collaboration which included some discussions and exchanges of documents.

We have been told that Hanlon's critique of Geller could have been published well before the S.R.I. paper appeared in *Nature* but that the *New Scientist* deliberately delayed publication. Any belief in simple publication of positive experimental results in the orthodox literature as a means of establishing the validity of paranormal phenomena is naive indeed.

It should be stressed that we are not suggesting that co-operation between journals constitutes a conscious conspiracy to discredit parapsychology. There can be no doubt that all parties acted in what they honestly believed to be the best interests of scientific truth. Indeed the editorial board of *Nature* have gone out of their way to extend their evaluation process in the case of Geller-type metal-bending by actually accompaning scientists in their visits to the homes of 'mini-Gellers' to see the phenomena for themselves. The point we are making is that the modes of action which are considered legitimate in relation to parapsychology are more extensive than for other 'young' sciences.

Finally, to illustrate the problem of publishing results in parapsychology we will refer to our own limited experience of publishing in this field. One of us (Collins) has been involved in some experiments, carried out in collaboration with colleagues in the physics department at the University of Bath, investigating 'mini-Gellers'. These experiments found no evidence of paranormal metal-bending and, on several occasions, 'normal' methods of bending (cheating) were observed. The results of these experiments were published in the correspondence column of *Nature*.[82] The editor has indicated that if an experimental report of this (correspondence) type had contained positive findings it would not have been accepted.

4. *The Levy Affair—The Machine at Work*

Despite the tactics of the critics the tactics of the parapsycholgists have paid off in the sense that they now appear to be able to invoke many of the internal social processes of legitimate disciplines in handling their affairs. In order to illustrate this we will, in the last part of this paper, focus on the reaction of the parapsychologists to a recent discovery of fraud within their discipline.

In 1974 the director of one of the best known parapsychology research centres was accused by co-workers of faking results. The scientist concerned was Dr. J. Levy, a protege of Rhine and director of the famous research centre at Durham, North Carolina, where Rhine had done most of his early work. Levy had been producing excellent results working on experiments with rodents. Indeed these experiments had caused great excitement in the parapsychological world, and were the basis of the following comment made in a recent review of biological aspects in the paranormal:

'From among the heterogeneous collection of experiments described here there is only one fact which has, in the writer's opinion, been established beyond all reasonable doubt, namely the existence of precognition in rodents. The fully automated experiments with mice and gerbils have been replicated sufficiently often and yielded such clearly significant results that we are now justified in claiming this phenomenon as one of the most firmly established in parapsychology. To the workers in the field the establishment of one fact may not seem very much to justify the large amount of effort expended. To the academic biologist, however, even this one fact must appear revolutionary, since it seems to overthrow many of the present day assumptions of his science.'[83]

However, towards the middle of 1974 (almost simultaneously with the publication of the above comment) Levy began to attract the attention of his co-workers by acting suspiciously in the vicinity of the automatic data-recording devices while experiments were in progress. Technicians made their own secret records of data and, when these were compared with Levy's, his were found to be inaccurate, being positively biased. At first sight, bearing in mind the extravagant claims made for Levy's results, his position of eminence in the foremost research institution, and the perpetual rearguard action against the fraud hypothesis, this scandal seemed to have the potential to finish parapsychology once and for all. How did parapyschologists react?

The most striking part of the way in which parapsychologists dealt with the Levy case was the openness that they exhibited in describing the events. On discovery of the fraud, details were immediately sent to all persons known to be planning to use Levy's work in articles, books or other presentations. Likewise those involved in efforts to repeat his experiments were notified. J. B. Rhine then published a long statement in the *Journal of Parapsychology*[84] in which he announced that all Levy's experimental reports, published or unpublished, authored by him or jointly were to be considered unacceptable. All Levy's work confirmed independently by one or more other experiment should, for the present, be evaluated entirely on the strength of the replicated work itself. But Rhine also pointed out that Levy had been caught by other parapsychologists, so that there was no possible case for collusion. Also, he drew parallels with cases of fraud in orthodox science and claimed that the implication for parapsychology was no greater than the Summerlin affair was for medical research.[85]

In general the parapsychologists have not over-reacted to the Levy affair. They managed to keep it out of the hands of the press until all parapsychologists had been informed, and they managed to avoid any charges of a 'cover up'. Those parapsychologists working in the same area as Levy, to whom we have talked, have stressed that this case of fraud is only a temporary set back and the parapsychologists should concentrate on attempting to replicate Levy's original experiments. In general the motives ascribed to Levy have been similar to those attributed to Summerlin. Levy was, like Summerlin, a 'high powered' young man, sponsored by an older established researcher. He had made a major breakthrough in the field with experimental results, but when they failed to continue, he faked his data so that the experiment should continue. Levy was also subject to extra pressure as the administrative head of a large research laboratory and pressure from his family who wanted him to work in the more orthodox field of medical research, for which he had been trained. The final parallel between Levy and Summerlin is that there have been reported independent replications of both sets of faked results!

The reaction of the parapsychologists to a potentially catastrophic occurrence seems to have been effective. Critics have been disarmed to some extent by its use as an illustration of the effectiveness of parapsychology's internal control mechanisms. Thus Puthoff and Targ[86] use the example of the Levy affair in precisely this way in a paper published in the prestigious orthodox journal *Proceedings of the I.E.E.E.*, they comment:

> 'It should also be noted that parapsychological researchers themselves recently exposed fraud in their own laboratory when they encountered it.'

Rather than seeing the Levy affair as the last nail in the coffin of parapsychology, at least one other parapsychologist now feels confident enough to use the affair as an illustration of parapsychology's legitimacy as a science. McConnell remarks:

> 'The recent uncovering of an intentional falsification of experimental data by a relatively well known parapsychologist has provided a new impetus to consider the problem of fraud. In a sense, this incident is a *cause for congratulation* inasmuch as it was this parapsychologist's close professional associates who discovered and revealed his dishonesty. From this fact the world at large may draw reassurance that in parapsychology, as in any other field of science, professional deception will not be tolerated.' (Our emphasis.)[87]

The handling of the Levy affair certainly appears to us to be on a par with the handling of cases of fraud in orthodox science and is thus an indication that parapsychology has acquired many of the social characteristics of an orthodox science. The tactics of acceptance thus seem to have provided the parapsychologists, if not with legitimacy, at least with a reservoir of credibility which acts as a buffer against some of the criticisms, such as widespread fraud, brought to bear on it by the sceptics.

Conclusion

What we have done in this paper is to look at some aspects of the explicit debate over the acceptance of 'scientific' parapsychology. We have divided the exposition into two halves by reference to the notions of 'constitutive' and 'contingent' forums. These are categories which at one time might have been thought to have epistemological significance, but recent work in the sociology of science has, we believe, dissolved this idea, showing that the constitution of scientific ideas can be seen as a product of contingent actions. Nevertheless, these categories can still be used to distinguish between theorisation, experimentation, professional publication and the other activities of scientists in connection with their work. Also, the two forums embody different expectations of types of visible action. In the constitutive forum actions normally should be seen to be based on universalisable premises and in the contingent forum actions should normally be seen to be incidental to the constitution of knowledge.

In looking at parapsychology, we have found a number of cases of, as it were 'full frontal' breakdown of this norm. In the constitutive forum, we have found prejudice and other particularistic bases of belief openly endorsed. In the contingent forum, we have found items intended as substantive contributions to the constitution of scientific knowledge, rather than commentary and exposition. In themselves, these boundary crossings can be seen to represent a tactic of the orthodox scientists, they expose the fact that parapsychology should not be treated in the same way as a science, i.e. that 'something unscientific is happening', despite its practitioners' attempts to metamorphosise themselves—so that '*nothing* unscientific is happening'.

Throughout, we have intended this paper to be entirely neutral as to the existence of paranormal phenomena. In saying that the constitution of scientific knowledge can be looked at as a product of contingent actions, we are endorsing a relativistic thesis within which consideration of the 'actual existence' of a phenomenon is redundant. It is, we believe, only through this perspective that the full richness of the social processes involved in the construction of scientific know-ledge can be revealed. In addition, from this perspective, a strategy of metamorphosis makes eminent sense, for when 'scientists' turn their attention to something, then 'that really is something'!

University of Bath.

Note Added December 1976. Since writing this paper further examples illustrating the processes discussed on pp. 250-252 have appeared. For instance see Harmon, and Puthoff and Targ.[88] Harmon writes:

'We are asked to believe that no conceivable communication channel existed between "transmitter" and "receiver" other than by some exotic attenuationless seemingly magical information propagation.
'I feel certain that your readers can conceive of many possible alternative conventional channels. Both electronic engineers and magicians, for example, will be at no loss to suggest many.'

Note Added June 1977. By June 1977 this paper was itself being brought into the argument. It is perceived, it seems, as a paper which might favour the parapsychologists' case. Thus, we have received a spleenful letter from a well known professional magician-and-sceptic which attempts to persuade us to change our attitude to research in the paranormal and claims that:

'Seriously, how men of science such as yourselves can make excuses for . . . [Targ's and Puthoff's] incompetence is a matter of astonishment to me . . . [and] . . . I was shocked at your paper; I had expected science rather than selective reporting.'

On the other hand, parapsychologists have been complimentary. An American academic, intending to forward the paper to possible sponsors among others, has commented in a letter to us:

'It is just so accurate and well done and coming from an "outsider", it will carry so much more weight.'

These comments are sociologically interesting in themselves but also give us some cause for concern, lest the paper be generally misconstrued outside the *sociological community*, for which it was intended. The paper *is* neutral regarding the existence of paranormal phenomena—its relativism makes the question of their existence redundant. We are delighted that a discussion of the tactics of scientific legitimisation should be of use to practitioners, but we must point out that it can only be of use to those who have *already* decided whether they want the phenomena to exist or not, and, can only be seen as *pro* parapsychology by those who have decided that the tactics of denying legitimacy to the subject are less honourable than those used to try to gain it. For ourselves, as professional sociologists, we are disinterested in these questions. Thus, we do not condemn the departures from normal scientific practice which we describe, nor laud the tactics of metamorphosis essayed by the parapsychologists.

[1] L. Wittgenstein: *Philosophical Investigations*, Blackwell, Oxford, 1953, and; *Remarks on the Foundations of Mathematics*, Blackwell, Oxford, 1956.

[1a] J. P. Emerson: 'Nothing Unusual is Happening', in T. Shibutani (ed.): *Human Nature and Collective Behavior*, Prentice-Hall, Englewood Cliffs, 1970 pp. 208-222.

[2] P. Feyerabend: *Against Method*, New Left Books, 1974; I. Lakatos and A. Musgrave (eds.): *Criticism and the Growth of Knowledge*, Cambridge University Press, Cambridge, 1970; I. Lakatos: 'Proofs and Refutations', *British Journal for the Philosophy of Science*, Vol. 14, 1963, pp. 1-25, 120-129, 221-245, 296-342; T. S. Kuhn: *Structure of Scientific Revolutions*, Chicago University Press, Chicago, 1970.

[3] B. Barnes: *Scientific Knowledge and Sociological Theory*, Routledge & Kegan Paul, London, 1974; H. M. Collins and G. Cox: 'Recovering Relativity: Did Prophecy Fail?' *Social Studies of Science*, Vol. 6, 1976, pp. 423-445

[4] H. M. Collins: 'The Seven Sexes: A Study in the Sociology of a Phenomenon', *Sociology*, Vol. 9, 1975, pp. 205-224.

[5] H. M. Collins: 'Upon the Replication of Scientific Findings: A Discussion Illuminated by the Experiences of Researchers into Parapsychology', paper read at the S.S.S.S., I.S.A. Conference, Cornell University, 1976.

[6] T. J. Pinch: 'What does a Proof do if it does not Prove?', in E. Mendelsohn, P. Weingart and R. D. Whitley (eds.): *The Social Production of Scientific Knowledge*, Reidel, Dordrecht, 1977.

[7] J. Beloff: *New Directions in Parapsychology*, Elek Science, London, 1974, p. 1. Beloff's quotation continues:
'Such phenomena are variously referred to as "parapychological", "parapsychical", "psychical" or "psychic" but . . . the convention now widely current in the technical literature [is to use] the abbreviation "psi".
Psi phenomena fall into two main categories: psi cognition, better known as ESP (Extrasensory Perception), and psi action, better known as PK (Psychokinesis). Psi cognition or ESP can further be subdivided according to whether it is presumed to depend on another person (the 'agent') whose normal cognitive processes constitute the source of the information, in which case it is referred to as 'telepathy', or whether it is presumed to be independent of any such mediation so that the information comes directly from the target object or event, in which case it is referred to as "clairvoyance".'

[8] C. Evans: 'Parapsychology—what the Questionnaire Revealed!' *New Scientist*, 25 January 1973, p. 209.

[9] The interview data on which this paper is based comes from fieldwork conducted by Collins in 1971-75, and by Collins and Pinch in 1975-76.

[10] C. Honorton, M. Ramsey and C. Cabibbo: 'Experimenter Effects in Extrasensory Perception', *Journal of the American Society for Psychical Research*, Vol. 69, 1975, pp. 135-149, Appendix.

[11] M. Billig: 'Positive and Negative Experimental Psi Results in Psychology and Parapsychology Journals', *Journal of the Society for Psychical Research* Vol. 46, 1972, pp. 136-142.

[12] R. K. Merton: *Social Theory and Social Structure*, Free Press, New York, 1967, pp. 550-561.

[13] R. K. Merton: 'The Matthew Effect in Science: The Reward and Communication System of Science', *Science*, Vol. 199, 1968, pp. 55-63; B. Barber: 'Resistance by Scientists to Scientific Discovery' in B. Barber and W. Hirsch (eds.): *The Sociology of Science*, Free Press, New York, 1962, pp. 539-558.

The Construction of the Paranormal

[14] For example, Collins: op. cit., 1975, 1976; B. Wynne: 'C. G. Barkla and the J. Phenomenon: A Case Study of the Treatment of Deviance in Physics', *Social Studies of Science*, Vol. 6, 1976, pp. 307-348.

[15] We underline *'seen to be'* and *'look as though'* to stress that we are talking only of the expected *appearance of things*.
In a recent unpublished paper (M. J. Mulkay: 'Norms and Ideology in Science', mimeo, York University, 1976), Mulkay treats norms in science as 'vocabularies of justification'. This approach would fit well with the discussion pursued here, and this discussion could be interpreted as exploring the differing vocabularies of public and private communications. Mulkay identifies what we would call different constitutive values and shows how they are used in the contingent forum in order to secure political status for the scientific enterprise as a whole. For more discussion of the language of the constitutive forum, see G. N. Gilbert: 'The Transformation of Research Finding into Scientfic Knowledge', *Social Studies of Science*, Vol. 6, 1976, pp. 281-306. For two other interesting sociological studies of parapsychology see P. D. Allison: 'Social Aspects of Scientific Innovation: the Case of Parapsychology', unpublished Masters Thesis, University of Wisconsin, 1973; and M. D. Gordon: 'The Institutionalisation of Parapsychology: A Study of Innovation in Science', unpublished M.Sc. Dissertation, University of Manchester, 1975.

[16] Pinch: op. cit., found in this study of the reception of Bohm's ideas on the foundation of quantum theory that several heterodox interpretations of quantum mechanics were published but failed to cause any ripples on the surface of physics. For an attempted analysis of why Bohm's ideas were explicitly rejected as opposed to the implict rejection of many ideas in quantum theory, see Pinch: op. cit. The Editor of a well known science journal has also told us that many papers published in his journal are 'wrong' but most pass into the literature uncontested.

[17] ibid.

[18] Wynne: op. cit.

[19] Collins: op. cit., 1975.

[20] R. G. A. Dolby: 'What can we usefully learn from the Velikovsky Affair?', *Social Studies of Science*, Vol. 5, 1975, pp. 165-175; A. De Grazia (ed.): *The Velikovsky Affair*, University Books, New York, 1966.

[21] Many of the cults discussed by C. Evans (*Cults of Unreason*, Panther, St. Albans, 1974) would fit into this box. The idiosyncratic numbering of the boxes is deliberate. Increasing cognitive distance from the cultural centre of modern science (wayoutness) follows the anticlockwise direction indicated.

[22] We are referring here, not to the impact of the content of the material published in constitutive journals, but to the legitimating effect of getting any material into this forum.

[23] It is important to remember that our prime classification division concerns the *places* where actions (arguments) occur. It would therefore, be appropriate but clumsy to give a full inventory of arguments under each heading.

[24] Hence no parapsychology journals are referred to in the central discussion. The parapsychology journals have no place in our forums. Rather the parapsychology establishment has its own parallel constitutive and contingent forums, related, we would expect, as those of orthodox science.

[25] C. Honorton: 'Error Some Place', *Journal of Communication*, Vol. 25, 1975, pp. 103-116.

[26] For a discussion of the relationship between mathematisation and professionalisation, see R. D. Whitley: 'Changes in the Social and Intellectual Organisation of the Sciences: Professionalisation and the Arithmetic Ideal,' Mendelsohn *et al.*: op. cit.

[27] A review of the methodological advantages of this type of instrumentation is to be found in H. Schmidt: 'Instrumentation in the Parapsychological Laboratory', in Beloff (ed.): op. cit., 1974, pp. 12-37.

[28] For a review of some personality correlates with E.S.P. see G. R. Schmeidler: 'Personality Differences in the Effective Use of E.S.P.', *Journal of Communication*, Vol. 25, 1975, pp. 133-141.

[29] See, for example, R. L. Morris: 'Building Experimental Models', *Journal of Communication*, Vol. 25, 1975, pp. 117-125.

[30] H. Schmidt: 'Mental Influences on Random Events', *New Scientist*, 24 June 1971, pp. 757-758.

[31] D. O. Hebb: 'The Role of Neurological Ideas in Psychology', *Journal of Personality*, Vol. 20, 1951, pp. 39-55.

[32] R. T. Birge: 'Science, Pseudo-Science and Parapsychology', A.A.A.S. Vice Presidential Address, Washington D.C., December 1958.

[33] C. Burt: 'Psychology and Parapsychology' in J. R. Smythies (ed.): *Science and E.S.P.*, Routledge and Kegan Paul, London, 1967, p. 62.

[34] Collins: op. cit., 1975, p. 205.

[35] Quoted in Honorton: op. cit., p. 111.

[36] G. R. Price: 'Science and the Supernatural', *Science*, Vol. 122, 1955, pp. 359-367.

[37] J. Hanlon: 'Uri Geller and Science', *New Scientist*, 17 October 1974, pp. 170-185.

[38] E. G. Boring: 'Paranormal Phenomena: Evidence, Specification, and Chance', in the Introduction to C. E. M. Hansel: *E.S.P.: A Scientific Evaluation*, Charles Scribner's Sons, New York, 1966.

[39] D. H. Rawcliffe: *Illusions and Delusions of the Supernatural and the Occult*, Dover, New York, 1959.

[40] T. S. Szasz: 'A Critical Analysis of the Fundamental Concepts of Psychical Research', *Psychiatric Quarterly*, Vol. 31, 1957, pp. 96-107.

[41] Quoted in F. C. Dommeyer: 'Parapsychology: Old Delusion or New Science?', *International Journal of Neuropsychiatry*, Vol. 2, 1966, pp. 539-555.

[42] C. Evans: 'Long Dream Ending', *New Scientist*, 20 March 1969, pp. 638-640.

[43] ibid.

[44] Price: op. cit., 1955.

[45] Beloff: op. cit., 1974.

The Construction of the Paranormal

[46] E. G. Boring: 'The Present Status of Parapsychology', *American Scientist*, Vol. 43, 1955, pp. 108-116.

[47] S. S. Stevens: 'The Market for Miracles', *Contemporary Psychology*, Vol. 12, 1967, pp. 1-3.

[48] H. Hoagland: 'Editorial', *Science*, February 1969, p. 163.

[49] P. W. Bridgman: 'Probability, Logic and E.S.P.', *Science*, Vol. 123, 1956, pp. 15-17.

[50] A. J. Ayer: 'Chance', *Scientific American*, October 1965, pp. 44-54.

[51] G. S. Brown: *Probability and Scientific Inference*, Longman, London, 1957.

[52] G. S. Brown: 'Statistical Significance in Psychical Research', *Nature*, Vol. 172, 1953, pp. 154-156.

[53] A. T. Oram: 'An Experiment with Random Numbers', *Journal of the Society for Psychical Research*, Vol. 37, 1954, pp. 369-377.

[54] C. G. Jung: *Synchronicity*, Routledge & Kegan Paul, London, 1955; G. S. Brown: *Laws of Form*, Allen & Unwin, London, 1969.

[55] A. Koestler: *The Roots of Coincidence*, Hutchinson, London, 1972.

[56] Szasz: op. cit.

[57] C. T. Tart: 'Models for the Explanation of Extrasensory Perception', *International Journal of Neuropsychiatry*, Vol. 2, 1966, pp. 488-505; G. R. Schmeidler: 'The Influence of Attitude on E.S.P. Scores', *International Journal of Neuropsychiatry*, Vol. 2, 1966, pp. 387-397; J. Beloff: 'Parapsychology and its Neighbours', *Journal of Parapsychology*, Vol. 34, 1970, pp. 129-142.

[58] Schmeidler: op. cit., 1966.

[59] Collins: op. cit., 1976.

[60] J. C. Crumbaugh: 'A Scientific Critique of Parapsychology', *International Journal of Neuropsychiatry*, Vol. 2, 1966, pp. 539-555; D. Cohen: 'E.S.P. Science or Delusion?', *The Nation*, 9 May 1966, pp. 550-553.

[61] Cohen: op. cit.

[62] Price: op. cit., 1955.

[63] G. R. Price: 'Apology to Rhine and Soal', *Science*, Vol. 175, 1972, p. 359.

[64] Hansel: op. cit.

[65] Hanlon: op. cit. Although Hanlon's article was in the semi-popular journal *New Scientist*, the permeability of the boundaries between the two forums has meant that this contribution was intended (and has probably succeeded) in constituting scientific knowledge. Hanlon's contribution is discussed in more detail below.

[66] ibid.

[67] It is an interesting exercise to try and 'conjure up' such objections (*Quis Custodiet Custodes?*).

[68] Price: op. cit., 1955.

[69] Of course, it could be argued that there is a crucial 'size' which demarcates a science from a non-science and that parapsychology's still small institutional base does not make it a science. However, it is difficult to determine the 'size' of a science by any abstract criteria. Certainly there are specialist areas in orthodox science which are on a smaller institutional footing than parapsychology. It seems that the appropriate size of a discipline will only be established by a combination of factors such as available resources, cognitive importance in relation to other areas, etc., and in general these factors can only be identified after the discipline has 'taken off'. The problem of finding criteria connected to size is illustrated by at least one physicist turned parapsychologist informing us that the area was already saturated and that there were not many new problems for researchers to take up. This contrasts with the view of most parapsychologists who consider that parapsychology has yet to 'take off'.

[70] Quoted in N. Wade: 'Psychical Research: The Incredible in Search of Credibility', *Science,* Vol. 181, 1973, pp. 138-143.

[71] 'Investigating the Paranormal', *Nature,* Vol. 251, 1974, pp. 559-560.

[72] ibid., p. 560. Evidence of the type of factor which is considered important by parapsychologists in gaining academic acceptance comes from an article by R. A. McConnell. Under a sub-heading. 'Recent Landmarks of Academic Acceptance', McConnell mentions publication of a review of E.S.P. in a major psychology text-book, publication of a paper on E.S.P. in the *American Psychologist* and affiliation to the A.A.A.S. as key events in the acceptance of psi. See R. A. McConnell: 'Parapsychology and the Occult', *Journal of the American Society for Psychical Research,* Vol. 67, 1973, pp. 225-243.

[73] E. D. Dean: 'The Parapsychological Association Becomes Affiliated with the American Association for the Advancement of Science', unpublished informal document, 1969.

[74] At the time Dean was secretary of the Parapsychological Association.

[75] A factor considered relevant by the critics of parapsychology, but not usually mentioned in critiques of other sciences is the origins of the grants received by the parapsychologists. To give one example, M. Gardner ('Concerning an Effort to Demonstrate Extrasensory Perception by Machine', *Scientific American,* October, 1975, pp. 114-118) somewhat gleefully concludes a critical review of the parapsychological research done at the Stanford Research Institute by commenting on the termination of the researchers' (Targ and Puthoff) legitimate source of funding—the North American Space Agency.
The importance of funding to critics is understandable in the context of parapsychology's attempts to gain legitimacy. The acquisition of resources from the normal scientific channels can be seen as an important step in parapsychology's attempted metamorphosis and hence also a 'sensitive' area for critics to focus on. The critics seem to be using the funding issue to add leverage to their other criticisms. Hanlon and Gardner refer to the responsibilities attached to such legitimate funding with the implications that if the parapsychologists don't succeed they will be wasting public money. The parapsychologists' attempts to gain legitimate sources of funding can thus be seen as a 'double edged sword'.

[76] In this section we will be considering those contingent activities which have not emerged into the constitutive forum. For instance, we will not discuss further the attempts to discredit the results of the parapsychologists by

reference to prejudice, philosophical technicalities, occult associations, lack of theory, repeatability and fraud, although all such criticisms are to be found in the contingent forum.

[77] Hanlon: op. cit.; Gardner: op. cit.

[78] Charles Tart has made this point in discussion with us.

[79] P. Morrison: 'Uri Geller: International Pied Piper of the Credulous, and Other Matters', *Scientific American*, February 1976, pp. 134-135.

[80] This suggestion is supported by the result of survey work showing how orthodox scientists got to hear about E.S.P. See Evans: op cit., 1973; L. Warner: 'What the Younger Parapsychologists think about E.S.P.', *Journal of Parapsychology*, 19 December 1955, pp. 228-235. Ransom in an excellent review of criticisms of parapsychology also reached this conclusion. See C. Ransom: 'Recent Criticisms of Parapsychology: A Review', *Journal of American Society for Psychical Research*, Vol. 65, 1970, pp. 289-307.

[81] Honorton *et al.*: op. cit., p. 144.

[82] B. Pamplin and H. M. Collins: 'Spoon Bending: An Experimental Approach', *Nature*, Vol. 257, 1975, p. 8. The correspondence column of *Nature*, as opposed to the Letters section, allows for material which is unlikely to get past a referee and is generally written in a more anecdotal style.

[83] J. L. Randall: 'Biological Aspects of Psi', in Beloff (ed.): op. cit., 1974, p. 92.

[84] J. B. Rhine: 'A New Case of Experimenter Unreliability', *Journal of Parapsychology*, Vol. 38, 1974, pp. 215-225.

[85] B. Culliton: 'The Sloan-Kettering Affair, A Story with a Hero', *Science*, 16 May 1974, pp. 644-650 and 'The Sloan-Kettering Affair (II): An Uneasy Resolution', *Science*, 15 June 1974, pp. 1154-1157.

[86] H. E. Puthoff and R. Targ: 'A Perceptual Channel for Information Transfer over Kilometer Distances: Historical Perspective and Recent Research', *Proceedings of the I.E.E.E.*, Vol. 64, 1976, pp. 329-356; and 'Reply', *Proceedings of the I.E.E.E.*, August 1976, p. 1259.

[87] R. A. McConnell: 'The Motivations of Parapsychologists and Other Scientists', *Journal of the American Society of Psychical Research*, Vol. 69, 1975, pp. 273-280.

[88] L. H. Harmon: 'Comments on "A perceptual channel for information transfer over kilometer distances: historical perspective and recent research",' *Proceedings of the I.E.E.E.*, August 1976, p. 1259; Puthoff and Targ: op. cit.

H. M. Collins and T. J. Pinch

APPENDIX

Main Published Sources of Material Referred to in Forums

CONSTITUTIVE FORUM

International Journal of Neuropsychiatry
Journal of Personality
Nature
Psychiatric Quarterly
Science
J. Beloff (ed): *New Directions in Parapsychology*, Elek Science, London, 1974.
G. S. Brown: *Probability and Scientific Inference*, Longmans, London, 1957.
C. E. M. Hansel: E.S.P.: *A Scientific Evaluation*, Charles Scribner's Sons, New York, 1966.
D. H. Rawcliffe: *Illusions and Delusions of the Supernatural and the Occult*, Dover, New York, 1959.
J. R. Smythies: *Science and E.S.P.*, Routledge and Kegan Paul, London, 1967.

CONTINGENT FORUM

New Scientist
Scientific American

EXPERIMENTAL PARAPSYCHOLOGY AS A REJECTED SCIENCE

Paul D. Allison

A FUNDAMENTAL tenet of Popperian philosophy of science is that ideas should not be judged scientific or unscientific, true or false, on the basis of their origins.[1] Truths may come from sources that are quite unreliable, and false theories may come from the most trustworthy persons applying the most rigorous methods. Rather, 'scientific' ideas are those susceptible to empirical tests. Ideas should be accepted or rejected on the basis of their ability to withstand rigorous tests better or worse than their competitors.

This point of view surely has some value as a canon of scientific practice, and it may even describe how ideas get accepted or rejected as scientific knowledge in the long run. But in the short run, the sources of ideas surely do have effects on their reception by scientific and other communities. Previous studies of the reception of innovations in science have tended to obscure this fact by focusing on innovations proposed within the scientific community. Stephen Cole,[2] for example, found little relationship between physicists' rank in the stratification system and the speed with which their work was recognised. But innovative ideas about the empirical world that are proposed, elaborated and promoted by non-scientists may meet a quite different fate.

One such idea is that organisms can acquire information and affect their environments directly, without the usual intervention of the senses or the muscles. The experimental study of these extrasensori-motor interactions, known as parapsychology, has lately achieved a status approaching that of a legitimate scientific specialism. At the least, it has become a highly professionalised activity performed by men and women with scientific educations, most of whom occupy positions in academic science departments.

In this chapter, I shall examine how this professionalisation came about, paying particular attention to the social conflicts that accompanied it. My sources include both primary and secondary literature from the history of parapsychology, and results from a mail survey of U.S. members of the Parapsychological Association—the only professional organisation for experimental parapsychologists. Conducted in the spring of 1972, the survey produced 120 usable returns for a response rate of 90 percent.

The beginning of academic interest

Although experiences and events interpreted as paranormal or psychic have been reported with great frequency throughout recorded history, the immediate progenitor of parapsychology was the movement known as Spiritualism—the belief that the dead communicate with the living, usually through the intervention of mediums. Sweeping through the U.S. and Great Britain in the second half of the 19th century, interest in Spiritualism was largely concentrated among the lower-middle and working classes. But there was also considerable interest among social elites, for whom it became an exciting leisure activity.[3]

Eventually the movement began to attract serious attention in academia. In 1882 scholars from a variety of fields met at Cambridge to found the Society for Psychical Research (SPR) with the expressed purpose of 'making an organized and systematic attempt to investigate the large group of phenomena designated by such terms as mesmeric, psychical and Spiritualistic'.[4] By 1900 the SPR had nearly 1000 members including many persons of substantial wealth and prestige: former prime ministers, nobility, fellows of the Royal Society, bishops, etc. A similar organisation, the American Society for Psychical Research (ASPR), was founded in 1884 but never quite achieved the reputation of its British counterpart.

The SPR sponsored most of the empirical research into psychic phenomena prior to 1920. Although the vast majority of SPR members were only dabblers and dilettantes, an enormous quantity of sustained, serious investigation was carried out by a handful of men led by Henry Sidgwick and including F. W. H. Myers, Edmund Gurney and Frank Podmore. These men dedicated their lives to psychical research, and reinforced that dedication through close companionship and collaborative investigations.[5] None of them had much training in the natural sciences. Some held academic positions in the humanities, and most had sufficient independent wealth to provide a comfortable living.

Their research generally consisted of careful field investigations of reported phenomena, usually the performances of mediums. Since they often accepted conditions laid down by the mediums themselves, the scientific value of their work was somewhat limited. Nevertheless, the fraudulent tactics of scores of mediums were exposed by this group. Gradually a consensus emerged that some mediumistic feats were legitimate, but that they were accomplished not through the intervention of spirits but by telepathic and psychokinetic powers of the mediums.

There was also some scattered experimental investigation during this period including work done by such notables as Oliver Lodge and William Crookes, two outstanding physicists of the era, and Claude Richet, a Nobelist in physiology. In contrast to the Sidgwick group, however, the experimentalists did not really constitute a social network. For the most part, they failed to build upon the work done by others, and they rarely pursued their investigations beyond a few experiments.

In short, psychical research during the late 19th and early 20th centuries was basically an amateur activity. Even those who spent most of their time investigating mediums pursued this work not as a professional career, but as a personal mission. Moreover, in neither the Sidgwick group nor among the experimentalists do we find 'studentship' or apprenticeship in any meaningful sense of the words. Psychic investigators developed their knowledge, skill and lore independently or in collaboration with peers. Although many investigators had university affiliations, psychic phenomena were not yet regarded by university authorities as an appropriate subject to be taught or studied.

The professionalisation of psychical research

A revolution in psychical research began in 1934 with the publication of *Extra-Sensory Perception* by J. B. Rhine, a professor of psychology at Duke University. Thoroughly familiar with previous research on the paranormal, Rhine came to the field with a degree in biology and an intense commitment to the experimental method. He began his work in 1930 by conducting card guessing trials with several Duke students who seemed to possess substantial clairvoyant ability. Over the next four years, Rhine and his collaborators performed tens of thousands of guessing trials under widely varying conditions, with remarkable results.

These results were first made public in the 167-page monograph

273

Paul D. Allison

whose title (coined by Rhine) has since become a part of everyday language. Although primarily addressed to a scientific audience (it contains 45 tables, 5 graphs, and extensive documentation) *ESP* soon created a popular sensation. Within a year, it began to get favourable reviews in national magazines and newspapers. In 1937 Rhine published the more popularly oriented *New Frontiers of the Mind* which became a Book-of-the-Month Club selection. Media interest reached a peak in late 1937 and 1938 when most magazines and newspapers ran articles on ESP.[6]

Not surprisingly, there was also a highly critical response from the academic community, especially from psychologists. The dimensions of that rather vehement reaction are well documented in this volume by Collins and Pinch. Later I shall consider some of the causes and effects of the orthodox resistance, but first let us continue with Rhine's work and the changes he wrought on parapsychology (Rhine's new term for psychical research, borrowed from the German).

There is a growing consensus that *Extra-Sensory Perception* constituted a paradigm for parapsychological research in the Kuhnian sense (senses?) of the term. Although Rhine's work contained many innovative elements, McVaugh and Mauskopf[7] argue that most of these innovations had precedents in earlier experimental psychical research. In their view, Rhine's contribution was the synthesis of these innovations in a highly successful research project. Some of the more important elements of *ESP* were

(1) the experimental distinction between clairvoyance[8] and telepathy and an emphasis on the percipient as the active agent;

(2) the use of statistical methods to evaluate the probability that results could or could not be accounted for by chance;

(3) the introduction of standard procedures for such operations as the presentation of cards, the elimination of sensory cues, the recording of results, etc., as well as a standard terminology for both procedures and the phenomena under study.

Beyond these innovations, two aspects of Rhine's work were especially influential in establishing parapsychology as a professional activity. First, there was his unprecedented success in finding strong evidence for ESP ability among large numbers of ordinary college students. No previous experimental work had even approached this level of above-chance scoring,[8a] and most researchers believed that

274

psychic ability was an extremely rare occurrence. This enormous success gave later researchers both a model to emulate and the confidence that good results could be obtained. Second, Rhine did not stop with experiments designed merely to demonstrate the existence of psi,[9] but began to study physical, physiological, and psychological conditions which either facilitated or hindered paranormal performance. Although his initial findings on correlates of ESP were based on very limited evidence, they suggested a multitude of further experiments. And that is where their true significance lay. What Rhine had presented, in essence, was a blueprint for a long-term and highly diversified programme of investigation, the sort of programme that could occupy an entire career, or indeed many careers. He had thus laid the groundwork for a community of researchers dedicated solely to sustained, cumulative investigation of paranormal phenomena.

Rhine's contributions to the professionalisation of parapsychology were not merely intellectual. His position at Duke where parapsychological research had the encouragement of the psychology department chairman, William McDougall, provided him with a unique opportunity to continue his investigations with assistance from doctoral students in psychology. Between 1935 and 1947, a total of 21 students worked in his semi-autonomous Duke Parapsychology Laboratory[10] and seven of these co-authored papers with him. A few students wrote dissertations on parapsychological topics and later continued their work as full-time research associates in his laboratory.

Meanwhile, a number of academics throughout the U.S. were sufficiently impressed with Rhine's work to try their hand at it. To report this growing body of research, Rhine founded the *Journal of Parapsychology* in 1938. Most of the major developments continued to come out of Rhine's laboratory. During the '30s and '40s, he and his co-workers claimed to have demonstrated the existence of several new psychic abilities including psychokinesis, the direct influence of the mind on material objects, and precognition, the ability to predict randomly generated events in the future.

Experimental parapsychology today

Rhine and his co-workers dominated the emerging field until the late 1940s. Around that time, however, there emerged several professional parapsychological researchers who worked in the Rhine paradigm but who were completely independent of the Duke Parapsychology Laboratory. Among them were R.A. McConnell at the University of Pittsburgh, Gertrude Schmeidler at City University of New York, and Ian Stevenson at the University of Virginia. This trend continued so that by 1975 'reputable' parapsychological research was being conducted at many locations across the U.S.

In spite of growing geographical and institutional dispersion, the field retains a high degree of intellectual and social cohesion. Many parapsychological researchers work in formally organised research institutes such as the Psychical Research Institute (Durham, N.C.), the Institute for Parapsychology (Durham, N.C.), the American Society for Psychical Research (New York), the Maimonides Dream Laboratory (New York), and the Division of Parapsychology (University of Virginia). The research centers have a pattern of 'interlocking directorates' whereby members of one center sit on the steering committees or boards of directors of other centers.[11] Most of the major research centers also have at least one staff member who received training at Rhine's laboratory.

The key integrating institution is the Parapsychological Association, founded at Durham, N.C., in 1957 to 'advance parapsychology as a science, to disseminate knowledge of the field, and to integrate the findings with those of other branches of science'.[11a] Although membership in the PA is somewhat restricted (a fact to be discussed later), a survey of the literature indicates that the organisation includes almost all the publishing researchers in the field. Only two journals in the U.S. regularly report experimental parapsychological research, the *Journal of Parapsychology* (JP) and the *Journal of the American Society for Psychical Research* (JASPR) Of 205 articles published in a recent ten year period in these two journals, well over 90 percent had at least one PA member as an author. Of 84 American authors listed in *JP* articles, 60 were PA members (most of the remaining 24 appeared to be students). The survey results I shall report apply only to U.S. and Canadian members of the PA.

PA members have fairly high rates of participation in the organisation, with 53 per cent saying they attended at least two of the five previous annual conventions. Respondents were also asked how often they had 'face to face or telephone contact with other parapsychologists in a typical month.' Forty-eight per cent said they were in contact with other parapsychologists at least once a week, and 17 per cent reported daily contact.

PA members are not just dabblers in the field but generally have a high degree of professional commitment. Fifty-one per cent say that parapsychology is their major area of interest, and 78 per cent have done parapsychological research in the previous ten years. They also published an average of 2.9 journal articles reporting original parapsychological research in the preceding five years. Educational standards among parapsychologists are fairly high. Almost 60 per cent of PA members hold a doctorate, while another 27 per cent have a master's degeree. Seventy per cent of the respondents thought that one ought to have at least a master's degree before undertaking 'serious parapsychological research on a continuing basis.' However, 70 per cent also agreed that special training beyond that found in regular academic programmes is 'essential for successful, high quality research in parapsychology.'

Although PA members are employed in a wide variety of settings, 49 per cent work in colleges or universities. Another 17 per cent work in private research institutes. Those in academia are distributed among departments as follows: 30 per cent psychology, 19 per cent psychiatry, 18 per cent physical sciences, 12 per cent biological sciences, 21 per cent other.

In short, professional parapsychologists have many characteristics in common with research workers in most scientific specialisms. A careful reading of the two experimental journals will indicate that parapsychologists also practice a highly technical, rigorous, and quantitative methodology. In fact, if one knew nothing of parapsychological terminology, it would be difficult to distinguish the *Journal of Parapsychology* from, say, the *Journal of Experimental Psychology*.

The quest for legitimacy

It would appear that Rhine and his followers have been remarkably successful in their aim of building a professional scientific specialism devoted to the study of paranormal phenomena. They have recruited a moderately large number of people with doctorates who are devoting their careers to experimental parapsychology. Many hold academic positions. They have formed themselves into a professional association and seem to be able to maintain rigorous standards for published research. They publish two journals in the U.S. Moreover they have been able to maintain this pattern for several decades, and have been successful in transmitting their accumulated knowledge and skill from one intellectual generation to the next. By no means dependent on a single organisation, they now have institutional bases in a variety of locations and settings.

I would be remiss if I failed to note that there is also a much larger number of persons who call themselves parapsychologists but who do not participate in this group to any significant extent. These include individuals who claim psychic abilities and perform paranormal feats; those who claim to be able to train others in extrasensory performance for a fee; those who have formed quasi-religious groups based around psychic phenomena; those who write exclusively for popularly oriented parapsychological books and periodicals; and others without advanced degrees who carry on parapsychological investigations of one sort or another but who do not publish their results in the experimental journals. As I will argue shortly, the existence of this 'lay parapsychology' has an enormous impact on the academic, experimental side of the field. But this hardly negates the existence of a truly professional, scientific parapsychology which has somehow managed to distinguish itself from more popular manifestations of belief in psychic phenomena.

What is particularly surprising about the achievement of parapsychologists is that they have been able to construct and maintain these professional institutions in the face of intense resistance from mainstream scientists. Although some would argue that resistance has been declining in recent years, there can be little doubt that parapsychology had few friends in the scientific community from the time Rhine's work was first published until at least the 1960s. While the published criticism of parapsychological research is well known,[12] the more insidious forms of resistance are less-easily documented, and to an unfortunate degree, we must rely on the claims of parapsychologists that they have often been the victims of unfair practices. Virtually no parapsychological research appeared in orthodox journals in the 1930s and 1940s, and Rhine[13] reports that this was not due to a lack of submissions. A few such publications have appeared in the last 10 years, but most either reported negative results or came out under highly unusual or questionable circumstances (see the chapter by Collins and Pinch). In terms of hiring and promotions, the record is even less clear. One of Rhine's students, J. G. Pratt, claims that he was repeatedly offered a regular academic position at Duke if only he would give up his work in parapsychology. He chose instead to stay on as a research associate in Rhine's laboratory.[14] Surely, other such cases have occurred, but one would hardly expect to find public records of their occurrence. I asked members of the PA if they had experienced discrimination because of their interest in parapsychology and 53 said they had. Of 183 instances of discrimination claimed, 25 per cent had to do with publications, 26 per cent occurred in the area of hiring and promotions, and 29 per cent centred on funding or facilities. Respondents were more likely to have experienced discrimination if they were heavily involved in the field and had an academic affiliation.[15]

The belief that resistance to parapsychology has declined in recent years is based largely on the admission of the PA as a member organisation of AAAS, the awarding of a few federal grants for parapsychological research,[16] and a survey in the *New Scientist* (25 January 1973) which showed somewhat greater belief in the existence of psychic phenomena and greater acceptance of the legitimacy of parapsychological research. While it is probably the case that acceptance of psi has increased somewhat in recent years, this can easily be overstated. The federal grants only supported a tiny fraction of parapsychological research, and there is no evidence that they have increased in number or amount in the last five years. It is still unheard of for a parapsychologist to publish positive results in a major journal. The results in the *New Scientist*, it should be noted, were not based on a representative sample. Consider, moreover, the following statement which appeared in the same year the PA was admitted to the AAAS:

'There used to be spiritualism, there continues to be extrasensory perception, psychokinesis and a host of others . . . Where corruption of children's minds is at stake, I do not believe in freedom of the press or freedom of speech. In my view, publishers who publish or teachers who teach any of the pseudo-sciences as established truth should, on being found guilty, be publicly horsewhipped, and forever banned from further activity in these usually honorable professions.'

This was from E. U. Condon[17] past president of the AAAS and the American Physical Society, and former director of the U.S. Bureau of Standards.

In spite of continuing hostility on the part of many orthodox scientists, parapsychologists have been equally unrelenting in their efforts to break down resistance and persuade scientists that their work is legitimate. Rhine's first publication, *ESP*, set the pattern for this effort by being primarily oriented towards a scientific audience rather than to laymen. The research that followed in the 1930s and 1940s was almost a dialogue with their critics. Every time a possible inadequacy in the experimental design was pointed out, new experiments would be conducted 'to pile safeguard upon safeguard in the effort to stifle all remaining doubt as to the adequacy of the conditions of the ESP experiments'.[18] Such safeguards included duplicate record sheets to avoid recording errors, locked boxes for depositing record sheets, and photographic evidence of the results. Parapsychologists even seemed to go out of their way to solicit criticism from responsible scientists. In 1938, for example, several critical psychologists were invited to serve on a board of review for the *Journal of Parapsychology*, and for two and one-half years their comments were published alongside the experimental reports.

These efforts have often been frustrating to parapsychologists because of the apparent lack of progress in gaining legitimacy, and because the extreme controls required to eliminate all possible sensory cues (even those available through deceit) have made parapsychological research more expensive, more time consuming, and to some degree, less successful. Many parapsychologists argue, in fact, that the high degree of control demanded by critics make the experiments so dull for both researcher and subject that it adversely effects paranormal performance. Psychic ability, they claim, is much more likely to be manifest under highly dramatic and emotional circumstances, which can hardly be produced in experimental situations.

Given these perceived limitations of the experimental method and the extremely slow progress in convincing orthodox scientists, one must ask why parapsychologists have continued to toe the scientific line for some forty years. Aside from ideological commitments to a scientific approach, one explanation is that the potential benefits to parapsychologists of *any* lessening of opposition are well worth the cost. The reason is simply that orthodox scientists control most of the things that are good for the specialism as a whole and for individuals in pursuit of a career. In order for a specialist group to survive and grow, at least three things seem necessary: (1) *Resources*. Specialism members must have regular sources of income that allow them sufficient time for independent research. Furthermore, in empirical disciplines they must have 'irregular' funds to cover the costs of research. (2) *Recruitment*. To keep the specialism from dying out, there must be access to advanced students with high interest and intellectual promise.[19] (3) *Communication*. There must be channels for regular and relatively unrestricted communication among specialism members.

Parapsychologists have been able to manage their own research communication through the two journals, *JP* and *JASPR*. But in the U.S. today, professorships in graduate departments of universities are the usual source of regular income, time for research, and graduate students. Thus the availability of such positions, controlled by scientific elites, is critical for development of the specialism. Most grants for research come from public agencies which are also controlled by disciplinary elites. To those who merely want to study psychic phenomena as a hobby, these things are not terribly important. But to those who want a research career in parapsychology, there is clearly an enormous motivation to do what is necessary to attain these ends.

As we have noted repeatedly, however, the successes have been few and far between. Although half the PA members hold academic positions, only a handful of these are in major graduate departments. As might be expected, these parapsychologists do not supervise many graduate students studying parapsychology. Only 24 of the 120 respondents reported that they had any graduate students under their supervision as advisor or major professor. Furthermore out of 121 students reported, only 39 were thought to have a significant interest in parapsychology. Assuming the usual rates of graduate student attrition, this number seems woefully insufficient to insure any long-term growth for the field.

Given parapsychologists' concerted efforts to win over orthodox scientists, why have they not been more successful? One frequently advanced explanation is that the phenomena are not replicable—individual experiments may be highly persuasive, but they cannot be repeated at will. While the discovery of an easily repeatable experiment might ultimately save parapsychology, the lack thereof surely does little to explain the intensity of those who oppose the field. It certainly hasn't stopped other fields (e.g. psychology) from being accepted as scientifically legitimate. No, the opposition seems to stem most from two closely related features of parapsychology: its threat to basic scientific assumptions and its origins in and continued association with the occult.

Psychic phenomena are, first of all, unexplainable by any current scientific theory. Both parapsychologists and legitimate scientists seem to agree on that point. Although parapsychologists have proposed numerous imaginative theories, none has achieved even a modicum of consensus. Gertrude Schmeidler a parapsychologist, has suggested[19a] that theories of psychic phenomena fall into two classes: the incomprehensible and the unbelievable. Beyond its inexplicability, psi directly contradicts several deeply held assumptions and firmly established laws of physics. Parapsychological research suggests that psi is completely unrestricted by distance or any kind of physical shielding; the size of the material target has no effect; in the form of precognition, psi implies an effect preceding its cause in time.

To make matters worse, many parapsychologists, especially Rhine, seem to exult in the anomalous character of psi. As late as 1972, Rhine was claiming that:

> 'Even now, however, physics cannot be regarded as the logically inclusive term it so long has been assumed to be. It is no longer the basis of *all* natural science and of the *entire* system of reality in the universe. In other words, we can now say the universe is more than physical—and that this is an experimental, not merely a speculative conclusion.'[20]

Gertrude Schmeidler and R. R. McConnell[21] two parapsychologists who have never worked with Rhine, have concluded on the basis of their research that:

> "ESP phenomena, such as telepathy and clairvoyance, are a type that has no place in the physical universe . . . We are forced to conclude that the picture of the universe which present-day physicists have roughed out for us will have to be modified once again.'

McConnell, it should be noted, holds a doctorate in physics. Other parapsychologists seem to be in substantial agreement. To the statement 'A satisfactory explanation of psi will probably require revolutionary changes in a number of disciplines, including physics, biology and psychology', fully 57 per cent of the PA members agreed strongly and another 28 per cent agree 'somewhat'. PA member were also asked why, in their judgment, other scientists had resisted parapsychological work. Sixty-seven per cent rated as very or extremely important, the statement that 'Parapsychology threatens the established mechanistic world view of scientists.' Only 5 per cent saw this as unimportant. Similarly, 58 per cent rated as very or extremely important the explanation that 'Parapsychology conflicts with current physical or biological theories.' In short, parapsychologists view themselves as revolutionaries who are persecuted for daring to question the orthodox creed.

Why should parapsychologists go out of their way to emphasise their differences with mainstream science when it only hurts their efforts to obtain legitimacy? One plausible explanation is that this revolutionary ideology helps maintain internal esprit de corps in the face of an opposition that would resist them in any case. Indeed, Hagstrom[22] argues that emerging disciplines often make utopian claims as to the importance of their field, a point also made by Griffith and Mullins.[23] This makes particular sense in the light of parapsychologists' strong belief in the strength of their experimental evidence of psychical phenomena. Of seven reasons presented to them as possible explanations for the resistance of scientists to parapsychology, the one rated most important was 'Scientists are simply unfamiliar with the present evidence for psi.' Seventy-three per cent saw this as very or extremely important, and another 20 per cent rated it as somewhat important. If, as they believe, the evidence is so strong, it makes good sense to attract as much attention to it as possible.

The appeal to laymen

A second reason why parapsychologists should choose to put a radical interpretation on their work is the obvious appeal to a second audience: laymen. Of crucial importance to the development of parapsychology is the fact that, in the absence of support from the scientific community, there has been and continues to be a heavy reliance on monetary and other forms of support from interested laymen. Although Rhine received some initial support from the psychology department at Duke, from 1935 onward he had to raise his own funds.[24] And there was nowhere else to go but to wealthy laymen, most of whom were primarily interested in the prospect of a scientific demonstration of life after death.[25] Over the years, their contributions to parapsychology have been quite substantial. In 1968, Rhine's Foundation for Resarch on the Nature of Man controlled assets of about two million dollars.[26] In 1966, the American Society for Psychical Research reported stocks and bonds worth $664,000 in addition to a five-story building in New York City.[27] The Parapsychology Foundation was reported to have disbursed more than a million dollars for research grants by 1968. Most of the contributors have preferred to remain anonymous, but a few are well known: Chester Carlson (deceased), inventor of xerography; Eileen Garrett (deceased), wife of a

Paul D. Allison

New York publisher and founder of the Parapsychology Foundation; Frances Payne Bolton (deceased), former Republican representative from Ohio; W. Clement Stone, multimillionaire president of the Combined Insurance Company of America and a heavy contributor to Richard Nixon's presidential campaigns.

To the dismay of many parapsychologists, this money has often come with strings attached. For example, the endowed research professorship at the University of Virgina stipulates that 'the incumbent will devote at least fifty per cent of his time to research into the question of survival of the human personality after death'.[28] The Psychical Research Foundation, an offshoot of Rhine's laboratory, is by charter devoted exclusively to the question of post-mortem survival. Recently, a wealthy Arizona prospector left an estate of almost $300,000 to an unspecified institution that would attempt to find scientific proof of the existence of the human soul. After a long court battle involving many claimants, the money was eventually awarded to the American Society for Psychical Research.[29]

Besides the money, parapsychologists have also relied on laymen as a base for recruitment. Cut off from the scientific journals and from significant numbers of graduate students, it has been difficult for parapsychologists to spread the word about their research to qualified students and researchers. For the most part, they have had to rely on the mass media as a means of attracting potential recruits. Rhine recognised[30] quite early the importance of the mass media in arousing interest among 'psychology students and instructors, men and women who would not have learned of the research through technical journals for many years, if at all.' He seems to have made good use of that fact. A typical pattern of recruitment, at least into the middle 1960s, was for students and researchers to contact Rhine's laboratory after reading popular accounts of his work. If they seemed to hold promise as parapsychological researchers, they were invited to the laboratory for training under a Visiting Research Fellowship programme for periods ranging from three to twelve months.[31] Many of these were mature researchers in other fields. Indeed, over 40 per cent of my respondents said they had decided to become involved in parapsychology after already completing their education and having entered another field.

Parapsychologists also talk frequently with laymen about their research. Seventy-four per cent of my sample report that they discuss

284

parapsychology with laymen other than their family at least once a week, compared with only 43 per cent who discuss parapsychology with other professionals (non-parapsychologists) once a week or oftener. Thirty-seven per cent say they 'frequently' address lay groups on the subject of parapsychology while another 37 per cent do so 'occasionally'. Those who express greater interest in parapsychology also interact more frequently with laymen.[32] A substantial part of this interaction is initiated by laymen. As early as 1937, Rhine complained of being deluged by letters, phone calls and visitors to Duke laboratory. As he put it, 'I had never dreamed there were so many brands and branches of the "occult sciences" as there are in practice in this country . . . Our laboratory must have come in contact with every one of them by this time.'

Important as this lay interest and support has been to parapsychology, it also poses a number of dangers. Chief among these is the hostile reaction it generates among orthodox scientists, the very group that parapsychologists have been trying to win over. As Hagstrom[33] has noted, scientific disputes tend to become much more intense whenever laymen get involved in the debate. Scientists view appeals to unqualified audiences as threats to their own autonomy in deciding questions of experimental evidence often leading them to take 'retaliary action'. (A good example is the case of Velikovsky[34]). Pope and Pratt's[35] survey of early scientific criticism of parapsychology strongly suggests that the intensity of the attack was determined in large part by the degree of attention parapsychology was receiving in the mass media, a fact noted by Rhine himself:

> 'The aggrandizing sensationalism which went on undaunted was a factor in generating the studied coolness to the work with psi. Many said as much. Parapsychology now belonged to the entertainer, the popular writer, the comic strip artists, and even to Broadway.'[36]

The attacks did not start until after *ESP* had begun to capture public attention in 1935; they rose to a peak in 1938, one year after the peak in popular attention, then declined sharply along with mass media notices. Although the initial criticism was 'moderately well tempered', as publicity rose 'there was an increasing irritation conveyed by explicit statements of condemnation'.[37]

The usual tendency of scientists to resist the interference of lay--men has been exacerbated in the case of parapsychology because of the peculiar interests of those laymen who inhabit its fringe: magic, witches, spirits, astrology, mysticism, divination—all the bugaboos of modern empirical science. Indeed, the massive upsurge of interest in the occult over the last decade has become a matter of great concern to parapsychologists for the potential harm it may cause. In an address at a recent convention of the Parapsychological Association, R.A. McConnell warned of the threat posed by the 'occult defilers of scientific parapsychology'. He has argued that 'much of the reluctance of orthodox scientists to endorse extended support for ESP research arises from their failure (and that of the lay press) to make a clear distinction between popular and scientific belief'.[38] Most parapsychologists share that concern. PA respondents were asked to evaluate the statement:

> 'The increasing interest among laymen in various occult practices will probably be harmful to parapsychology. There should be an effort to disassociate the field from such movements'

Seventy-three per cent agreed with this statement, about half of these expressing strong agreement. Only six per cent strongly disagreed.

The reaction of orthodox scientists is not the only basis for this concern. Parapsychologists have come to depend on the support of wealthy laymen, but these same donors are now the target of numerous organisations and enterprises which have sprung up to promote various occult and spiritualistic aims. The increased competition can only hurt.

Most threatening of all is the possibility that experimental parapsychology will itself be corrupted, that it will be infiltrated by persons with low scientific standards and bizarre interests. There is some precedent for that fear. As early as 1947, there was an attempt to found a professional society of parapsychologists—The Society for Parapsychology—but it was soon overrun by followers of L. Ron Hubbard's dianetics movement (now known as scientology). When they captured many of the leadership positions, the group quickly disintegrated.[39]

While this was an extreme case, the maintenance of scientific standards in the midst of an enormous 'pseudo-scientific' fringe has been a continual problem for parapsychologists, and has led to concerted efforts to erect barriers around the field. Consider the membership requirements for the Parapsychological Association. To be a full voting member one must:

(a) hold a doctorate or have a 'professional affiliation with a recognized academic institution or research organization;'
(b) have 'prepared a paper on some aspect of parapyschology which in the opinion of the Council is of high professional calibre, and which has been published in a scientific journal or which merits such publication;'
(c) be nominated by two members of the assocation and elected by a majority vote of the governing Council (consisting of four officers and three councilmen).

To be an associate member, one need only have a bachelor's degree and need not have written a paper, but must still be nominated and elected in the same manner.[40] Even this is not enough for Rhine who argues that the PA should:

> '. . . keep on raising standards as well-trained membership becomes available and to watch admission at the convention too. Rather than admit everyone, it is best to encourage the formation of other groups for those requiring more lenient qualifications. Over-permissiveness within a group endangers the whole value of the organization.'[41]

My survey results suggest that laymen do, in fact, have a 'corrupting' influence on the field. One of the main areas of disagreement in parapsychology today is over the study of spontaneous cases—naturally occurring, usually dramatic instances of psychic ability. Rhine and his supporters have argued repeatedly that while such fieldwork can be useful in generating hypotheses, it is only through experimentation that parapsychology can really advance. Others who have become frustrated by the lack of progress and the extreme technicality of the current literature call for a return to the earlier tradition of field studies. Results from the mail survey indicate that experimentalists predominate in the PA, but their majority is not a large one. Fifty-seven per cent disagreed with the statement 'More than laboratory work, what is most needed at present in parapsychology is a sustained and careful attention to spontaneous cases.' As shown in Table 1, the response varies substantially by the degree of involvement

TABLE I

Percentage of Parapsychological Association members who favour the study of spontaneous cases over experimentation, by interest in the field and frequency of contact with laymen.

Contact with Laymen	Interest in Parapsychology	
	Major	Minor
Frequent	47% (30)[a]	60% (15)
Infrequent	23% (30)	44% (43)

[a] Base of percentage in parentheses.

in the field and by the frequency with which they discuss parapsychology with laymen. Those most involved tend to support experimentation, while those who interact frequently with laymen are more likely to support spontaneous casework. (Both effects were statistically significant in a log-linear analysis). Additional analyses show that those who interact frequently with laymen are less likely to condemn 'fads and borderline areas', more likely to support research on post-mortem survival, and less likely to say that the occult movement will be harmful to parapyschology.[42]

Summary and conclusion

Experimental parapsychology poses a real dilemma for established science by presenting a picture of methodological innocence and theoretical guilt. On the one hand, parapsychologists have done their best to go about their work like hard nosed empiricists, designing and redesigning their experiments to eliminate every possible alternative explanation. On the other hand, they take every opportunity to emphasise the radical implications of their research and the bankruptcy of mainstream science. The response, after the initial burst of criticism in the 1930s, has been largely one of silent resistance, an attempt to ignore the offender wherever possible. Parapsychologists may get such token recognition as membership in the AAAS, but for the most part they cannot get federal grants, they cannot publish their research in prestigious journals, and they have only limited access to students.

Yet, the field has not only survived but prospered. It has done so by turning its most serious liability into an asset. The claims which have made parapsychology so unattractive to scientists have been extremely attractive to large numbers of laymen. They have provided the great bulk of the resources to keep the field going when it would otherwise have disintegrated. Their interest has made it possible to use the mass media as a base of recruitment. And they have undoubtedly reinforced the determination of parapsychologists through their moral support.

This support has hardly been an unmitigated blessing, however. It has increased the hostility and resistance of the scientific community and it has threatened the integrity of parapsychology as a community of professionals. Parapsychologists have been able to control the latter threat by strongly enforcing organisational boundaries and publication standards. This has been possible, in part, because of high geographical concentration and strong leadership. Whether they can continue to do so in the face of increased dispersion and a large, anti-scientific occult movement remains to be seen.

Cornell University.

[1] Karl R. Popper: *Conjectures and Refutations,* Routledge & Kegan Paul, London, 1962.

[2] Stephen Cole: 'Professional Standing and the Reception of Scientific Discoveries', *American Journal of Sociology,* Vol. 76, 1970, pp. 286-307.

[3] Alan Gauld: *The Founders of Psychical Research,* Routledge & Kegan Paul, London, 1968.

[4] Society for Psychical Research: *Proceedings of the Society for Psychical Research,* Vol. 1, 1882, pp. 3-6.

[5] Gauld: op. cit.

[6] J. B. Rhine: *New Frontiers of the Mind,* Farrar and Rinehart, New York, 1937; Dorothy Pope and J. G. Pratt: 'The ESP Controversy', *Journal of Parapsychology,* Vol. 6, 1942, p. 175.

[7] Michael McVaugh and S. H. Mauskopf: 'J. B. Rhine's *Extra-Sensory Perception* and its Background in Psychical Research', *Isis,* Vol. 67, 1976, pp. 161-189.

[8] Clairvoyance is the extrasensory perception of objects or objective events. Telepathy is the extrasensory perception of the mental state or activity of another person.

[8a] McVaugh and Mauskopf: op. cit.

[9] Psi is a general term including both ESP (clairvoyance, telepathy, and precognition), and psychokinesis.

[10] J. B. Rhine: 'Some Guiding Concepts for Parapsychology', *Journal of Parapsychology,* Vol. 32, 1968a, p. 191.

[11] P. D. Allison: 'Social Aspects of Scientific Innovations: The Case of Parapsychology', unpublished master's thesis, University of Wisconsin, 1973.

[11a] Parapsychological Association: *Constitution and By-Laws of the Parapsychological Association,* (Third Edition), 1970.

[12] Pope and Pratt: op. cit.; C. E. M. Hansel: *ESP: A Scientific Evaluation,* Charles Scribner's Sons, New York, 1966.

[13] Personal communication to the author, 1974.

[14] J. G. Pratt: *Parapsychology: An Insider's View of ESP,* Doubleday, New York, 1964.

[15] Allison: op. cit.

[16] Nicholas Wade: 'Psychical Research: The Incredible in Search of Credibility', *Science,* Vol. 181, 1973, pp. 138-143.

[17] E. U. Condon: 'UFOs I have Loved and Lost', *Bulletin of the Atomic Scientists,* 25 December 1969, pp. 6-8.

[18] J. B. Rhine: *The Reach of the Mind*, William Sloane Associates, New York, 1974.

[19] C. S. Fisher: 'The Last of the Invariant Theorists', *European Journal of Sociology*, Vol. 8, 1967, pp. 216-244.

[19a]Gertrude Schmeidler: 'Parapsychology', in David L. Sills (ed.): *International Encyclopedia of the Social Sciences*, Macmillan and Free Press, New York, 1968, pp. 386-399.

[20] J. B. Rhine: 'Parapsychology and Man', *Journal of Parapsychology*, Vol. 36, 1972a, pp. 101-121.

[21] Gertrude Schmeidler and R. A. McConnell: *ESP and Personality Patterns*, Yale University Press, New Haven, 1968.

[22] W. O. Hagstrom: *The Scientific Community*, Basic Books, New York, 1965, pp. 211-215.

[23] B. C. Griffiths and N. C. Mullins: 'Coherent Social Groups in Scientific Change', *Science*, Vol. 177, 1972, pp. 959-964.

[24] N. Freedland: *The Occult Explosion*, Putman, New York, 1972, p. 75.

[25] J. B. Rhine: *Parapsychology: From Duke to FRNM*, The Parapsychology Press, Durham, 1965, p. 7.

[26] John Kobler: 'ESP' *The Saturday Evening Post*, 9 March, 1968, pp. 65-68.

[27] J. G. Fuller: *The Great Soul Trial*, Macmillan, New York, 1969, p. 104.

[28] *FRNM Bulletin*, No. 12, Spring 1969.

[29] Fuller: op. cit.; W. Uphoff and M. J. Uphoff: 'Can U.S. Catch up on Psychic Study?', *The Capital Times*, Madison, Wisconsin, 18 December 1972, p. 42.

[30] J. G. Pratt *et al.*: *Extra-Sensory Perception after Sixty Years*, Bruce Humphries, New York, 1940 (reprinted in 1966), pp. 360-361.

[31] Rhine: op. cit., 1968a.

[32] Allison: op. cit.

[33] Hagstrom: op. cit., pp. 271-272.

[34] A. De Grazia (ed.): 'The Politics of Science and Dr. Velikovsky', *The American Behavioral Scientist*, Vol. 7, 1963 (later published as a book titled *The Velikovsky Affair*).

[35] Pope and Pratt: op. cit.

[36] J. B. Rhine: 'Psi and Psychology: Conflict and Solution', *Journal of Parapsychology*, Vol. 32, 1968b, p. 118.

[37] Pope and Pratt: op. cit.

[38] R. A. McConnell: *ESP: Curriculum Guide*, Simon & Schuster, New York, 1971, p. 84.

[39] J. B. Rhine: 'News and Comments: Is Parapsychology Losing its Way?', *Journal of Parapsychology*, Vol. 36, 1972b, pp. 169-176.

[40] Parapsychological Association: *Constitution and By-Laws of the Parapsychological Association*, 1970, 3rd edn., p. 4.

[41] J. B. Rhine: 'News and Comments', *Journal of Parapsychology*, Vol. 35, 1971, p.247.

[42] Allison: op. cit.

KNOWLEDGE ABOUT SEA-SERPENTS

Ron Westrum

IN recent years Western society has shown a very strong interest in controversial anomalies like UFOs, the Loch Ness Monster, Bigfoot, and so forth. This resurgence of interest in possible 'deviant' phenomena has generated a large literature of varying quality, arguing for, or (in a minority of cases) against, the existence of the anomalies in question.[1] A major concern of this literature has been the quality of the evidence supporting the anomaly's existence in each case. Whether the evidence has been eyewitness testimony, physical 'traces', or instrumental records like photographs, the problem has virtually always been the same: does the evidence provide convincing proof of the anomaly's existence? There is, however, a more basic question: where does the evidence come from in the first place? How is it that we get the 'cases' over which an argument about the anomaly's existence can take place?

Specific cases or 'sightings' are of course not the only basis for deciding that a given hypothetical anomaly exists or does not exist. The state of scientific knowledge, current intellectual or scientific fashions, and cultural traditions in the form of legends or folk-tales also enter into such a decision. But specific sightings or groups of sightings are the focal point for the social negotiation of the reality of a given type of anomalous event. Hence, it is crucial to discover what the sources of these sighting reports are. If reports are indeed used as the decisive pieces of evidence, then knowing *how* reports reach us and *which* reports reach us are of the utmost importance. Elsewhere[2] the author has referred to the sum of channels by which reports reach a given decision-maker as a 'social intelligence system'. How such a system works to transmit reports of anomaly sightings will be our major concern here. The problem of knowledge about sea-serpents will be used as a specific example to illustrate the difficulties of securing information about anomalous events in general. In other papers the author has examined this problem in relation to knowledge about meteorites[3] and Unidentified Flying Objects.[4]

Sea-Serpent Sightings

For the purposes of this paper a 'sea-serpent' will be defined as any large elongate marine creature of an apparently unknown species. The word 'marine' is critical here, since it exempts fresh-water creatures like the Loch Ness Monster (usually placed under the heading of 'lake monsters') from consideration. This distinction will be used for purposes of convenience rather than from any deep philosophical motive, and is a result of the bifurcation of the literature on alleged serpentine animals into fresh- and salt-water categories.[5]

The first collection of specific sea-serpent reports, as opposed to merely legends and folk-tales, was presented as part of Bishop Erich Pontoppidan's *Natural History of Norway*.[6] The controversy began in earnest, however, with the American sightings of 1817-19, off the Massachusetts coast. Repeated sightings led to crowds of observers at the shore and even expeditions to capture the monster. The American sightings led to the first articles in scholarly journals and an official report of the Linnean Society of Boston.[7] The 'American sea-serpent' also began to be observed by the British in 1848 with a well-publicised report of an animal seen from H.M.S. *Daedalus* and by the end of the nineteenth century, when interest in it began to fade, it had long since assumed an international character. A running scientific controversy over the existence of 'the great sea-serpent' continued throughout the nineteenth century. Although sightings continued steadily into the twentieth century, the scientific controversy lost its momentum around 1900. The sea-serpent continued on in popular culture, however, as a symbol of the *canard* or contrived sensational event.

Our concern here is not so much with the scientific controversy *per se*, however, as with the origin of the data which fuelled the controversy. What we will do will be to take the currently available stock of sea-serpent reports and study the way in which these reports have become public. In the process we will gain some insight both as to the nature of the experiences represented by the reports and the channels by which these reports have been transmitted to us. The stock of reports we will use is that represented by Bernard Heuvelmans's definitive work, *In the Wake of the Sea-Serpents*.[8] Heuvelmans's book, which contains reports of 587 sightings, represents the most exhaustive effort to date to collect the scattered reports of sea-serpent sightings from available sources. By examining the sources of the reports that Heuvelmans used, we can begin to form an idea of how scientists become aware of data about anomalous events like sea-serpents. What will emerge from this examination is a picture of a very complex system of data transmission, unorganised and inefficient, but which is nonetheless responsible for our current knowledge of these hypothetical animals.

It would seem from Heuvelmans's data that sea-serpent sightings occur at an average of about three per year, a rate that has remained steady since 1800 (see Table I).[9] An individual year, of course, may have many more reports or none at all. That the average has remained steady is nonetheless remarkable, in view of the enormous growth of population and communications since 1800, both of which could be expected to swell the number of sightings. For reasons which will soon become clear, this statistic is difficult to interpret, and could be due to: 1) a smaller number of experiences of a 'sea-serpent' kind 2) a decreasing propensity to report such experiences 3) fewer of the types of animals which are labelled 'sea-serpents' 4) fewer contacts between such animals and human beings or 5) some combination of these factors.

TABLE I

Number of Sea-Serpent Sightings Per 50-Year Period

Before 1800	1801-1850	1851-1900	1901-1950	1951-1966
32	166	152	190	47

TOTAL: 587
Source: Heuvelmans (1968)

The sightings catalogued by Heuvelmans represent a great diversity of experiences. In many cases, a report was made of a sighting by a single observer, either on land or at sea; in some cases two or more persons on board a vessel participated in the experience; in a minority of cases large crowds on shore witnesed what seemed to be a large serpentine creature. In the American sightings of 1817-19 a strange creature was repeatedly seen off the Massachusetts coast, often by 'hundreds of witnesses'. In some cases the crowds had gathered expressly to see the 'monster'. James Prince, a District Marshal, stated that on one occasion in 1819 he and about two hundred other witnesses watched a sea-serpent off Nahant, Massachusetts for more than three hours.[10] In other cases the sightings were of very brief duration. Thus there is no single 'pattern' which such sightings follow.

How should we regard these sightings? Are they instances of human credulity, the 'will to believe', optical illusions, or veridical experiences with creatures unknown to naturalists? Certainly some of the experiences are difficult to dismiss as the result of simple fraud; many of the early sightings in the United States were sworn before a Justice of the Peace, or in a court of law. In some cases the reputations of the witnesses seem to rule out fraud as a reasonable explanation. But the possibility of optical illusion is present even with witnesses of unimpeachable character. Especially in situations in which the concept 'sea-serpent' was known to the observers, how can we be sure that the witnesses were not the victims of a kind of perceptual contagion?[11] The possibility of perceptual contagion cannot be ruled out in all cases, but certain features of some cases make it seem very unlikely.

The first such feature is the 'escalation of hypotheses' noticed by Hynek[12] and earlier by Carrouges[13] in many Unidentified Flying Object sightings. This term refers to the tendency of the anomaly witness to see the stimulus initially as something non-anomalous. It is not unusual for a sea-serpent sighting to begin with the object being perceived as a log, a rock, or an overturned boat. It is seen as a sea-serpent only after other perceptual hypotheses have been tried and found wanting. The report of a sea-serpent sighting by the Rev. Donald Maclean illustrates this pattern:

> '. . . I saw it in June 1808 not on the coast of Eigg, but on that of Coll. Rowing along that coast, I observed, at the distance of about half a mile, an object to windward, which *gradually excited astonishment*. At first view it appeared like a small rock. Knowing that there was no rock in that situation, I fixed my eyes on it close.
> Then I saw it elevated considerably above the level of the sea, and after a slow movement, distinctly perceived one of its eyes. Alarmed at the unusual appearance and magnitude of the animal, I steered so as to be at no great distance from the shore . . .' (my emphasis).[14]

Bruner states in his well-known essay on perceptual readiness[15] that the facility with which something is perceived is related to its expected probability of occurrence. Since sea-serpents are hardly a common occurrence, we would expect them to be perceived only with difficulty.

In other cases there is no 'escalation' but it is apparent that more than simple perceptual contagion is involved. In the James Prince sighting mentioned earlier, Prince noted that

> 'The first view of the animal occasioned some agitation, and the novelty prevented that precise discrimination which afterwards took place . . . after being accustomed to view him, we became more composed . . .'[16]

Prince claimed that he had at least a dozen distinct views of the animal, and indicated that he had been 'accustomed to see whales, grampuses, porpoises, and other large fishes'[16a] hence was reasonably confident that the animal was of an unknown kind. In regard to the same sighting Samuel Cabot said

> 'I was now satisfied that the *sea-serpent* was before me, and after the first moment of excitement produced by the unexpected sight of so strange a monster, taxed myself to investigate his appearance as accurately as I could.'[17]

Hence even when there is considerable emotion involved in a sea-serpent experience, this does not mean that the perceptions involved have an entirely contagious character.

Another feature of interest is the use of 'critical checks' by the percipient during an anomaly experience. In his study of the public reaction to the Orson Welles 'Invasion from Mars' broadcast of 1938, Cantril found that belief in the reality of the 'invasion' was influenced by lack of what he called 'critical ability'.[18] Briefly, critical ability referred to the use of checks on the validity of one's own perceptions. Many of those who heard the broadcast made checks on its authenticity either by using the internal evidence of the broadcast itself or by checking the social context for counter-indications, such as routine programmes on other channels. Those who did not perform such critical checks, even when they were of a high educational level, believed that the play was indeed a news broadcast and that the Martians were actually landing. The use of critical checks by sea-serpent 'sighters' similarly might result in the unmasking of optical illusions, and in any case are indications that the witness is concerned about the accuracy of his own perceptions.

In 1908, Vice-Admiral R. H. Anstruther observed a strange creature shoot out of the water while he was standing on the bridge of H.M.S. *Caesar*:

> 'I had never seen such a creature before in all my long experience at sea, so I hastily called the navigating officer, who was at the standard compass, to come to my end of the bridge, in case the reptile, or whatever one may call it, should show itself again.'[19]

Calling for additional observers is a common form of perceptual check in many sightings. In another case, F. W. Kemp, an officer of the Provincial Archives of British Columbia, saw what he called a sea-serpent near Chatham Island. To make sure he had correctly perceived the creature's length, he measured some logs against which he had been able to compare the creature, and found that he had been correct.[20] The use of perceptual checks in these and other cases suggests that some sea-serpent witnesses were very much concerned with the accuracy of their own perceptions.

It is quite another matter, however, to argue that there really *are* such large elongate creatures unknown to science, and it is not intended to do so here. Our aim is to establish merely that these cases might possibly be of interest to scientists in the same way that ball lightning cases are of interest to them, even though many scientists are not sure that ball lightning exists.[21] In what follows we will not assume that sea-serpents exist but only that there exists in society a stock of 'sea-serpent' experiences or 'sightings' which naturalists and others might be interested in studying. We must now consider how these experiences travel from percipients to society at large and how some of them come into the hands of scientists.

The Reporting of Sea-Serpent Experiences

It is very important for the collection of anomaly data that individual cases become public at some point. Although there are some cases in which percipients correspond directly with anomaly researchers, as we shall see, it is much more frequently the case that data on anomalies are collected from public, printed sources. How does a percipient's experience get into print? Probably the most common channel is newspaper reporting. A reporter or editor hears of a sighting and prints the report, with or without an interview with the percipient. A less frequently used channel is the scientific periodical. A scientist, usually a naturalist, will hear of a report, investigate it himself, or in some cases will actually be the percipient, and the report will become printed in a channel which is likely to call it to the attention of other scientists. Other major sources are non-scientific periodicals, autobiographies, local history books, and books specifically on the subject of sea-serpents (see Table II).

To enter any of these channels, however, the experience must be made public by the percipient. In some cases the percipient himself goes directly to the channel, but often the report becomes public only when the percipient mentions the sighting to members of his primary group, who then pass it on to a wider public.

TABLE II

Preliminary Channels of Sea-Serpent Reports

Newspapers	... ...	48%	(209)
Scientific Journals	... ...	18%	(80)
Non-Sea-Serpent Book	...	14%	(59)
Book on Sea-Serpents	...	13%	(57)
Magazine	... ...	6%	(28)
Television	... ...	1%	(4)
	TOTAL	100%	(437)

Whether or not the primary group serves as an incubator for the report, however, the percipient must still tell others of his experience. And in some cases the primary group will recommend against making the report public or will agree not to divulge it. There is thus a problem at the very source of the report: the percipient may not wish to make his experience public. He may decide to tell no one else, to avoid even the reactions of his friends; or he may decide that while his friends can be trusted with the experience, a wider public might be less willing to believe his account. As one author has noted[22] certain categories of experience may not be acceptable to others, and a person having such an experience may be subjected to social sanctions if he persists in asserting the reality of his experience. Ridicule is often used to sanction reporters of anomalous experiences, and percipients who wish to avoid ridicule may well decide to keep their experiences to themselves.

Some percipients do decide to publicise their experiences or may find them publicised for them. Sometimes they do so because they naively think they will be believed. It is possible to read in some reports sentences like 'All doubts may now be set at rest about the great sea-serpent'.[23] Yet never is the report so convincing that doubts are in fact set aside. Usually the percipient is considered a hoaxer or a fool. In 1875 Captain George Drevar, from whose ship the *Pauline* a sea-serpent had been sighted, was ridiculed by the press. He complained that

'It is easy for such a paper to make any man, good, great, or interesting, look ridiculous. Little wonder is it that my relations write saying that they would have seen a hundred sea-serpents and never reported it; and a lady also wrote that she pities anyone related to anyone that had seen the sea-serpent.'[24]

Similarly, in a book of reminiscences by Vice-Admiral H. L. Fleet, he states that

'At last we . . . returned to Bermuda. On the passage Moubray and I saw what we considered to be a sea-serpent, but decided to say nothing about it, having due regard to the scepticism of the British public . . .'[25]

The late Commander Rupert Gould indicated in his book on the sea-serpent that he personally knew five naval officers who had seen at one time or another what they considered to be sea-serpents, but who had decided that the best course was to say nothing about them.[26] And indeed such behaviour is very prudent, as many histories of ridiculed witnesses show. How many experiences are supressed due to the fear of ridicule is difficult to estimate, although it seems likely that a great many, probably the majority, are never reported at all.

Nor is there any certainty that a sighting will be published even if a report is made. Newspapers may wish to avoid ridicule themselves and scientists may be even more sensitive about associating themselves with such a 'crackpot' subject. On the other hand, it is often suggested that it is precisely newspapers which are responsible for the spate of sea-serpent reports during the summer, the 'silly season':

'In the dull season of the year, when there is a decided lack of interesting or startling events, and when newspaper editors are at their wits' end for material, three objects derived from the domain of the biologist have been credited with the task of reviving the tide of public interest, and of restoring peace and composure to the editorial mind. It need hardly be said that the three objects alluded to are: "the frog from the solid rock", "the gigantic gooseberry", . . . and the "reappearance of the great sea-serpent." '[27]

Of course, summer may not be the only dull season of the year for newspaper editors, but since it is often believed by the public that summer is such a 'silly season', let us examine what relation sea-serpent sightings have to summer-time.

From the data in Table III (first row) it is obvious that, of the *sightings* contained in Heuvelmans, summer is by far the most heavily charged season—more in this case than the other three seasons combined. Interestingly enough, this is just what one would predict on the basis of old Norwegian tradition: according to Pontoppidan,[28] the great sea-serpent was seen in Norway only on days when the weather was calm in July and August. The 'silly season' theory,

TABLE III

Season of Sightings of and Articles on The Sea-Serpent

	Summer	Fall	Season Winter	Spring	Total
Season of Sea-Serpent Sightings (Northern Hemisphere)	53% (185)	20% (69)	12% (40)	15% (53)	100% (347)
Season of Newspaper and Weekly Magazine Articles on the Sea-Serpent (Northern Hemisphere)	25% (83)	33% (108)	14% (46)	28% (91)	100% (328)

however, argues that it is newspaper *articles* about the sea-serpent which are most likely to appear in summer, not the actual creatures. Looking at the dates of all the newspaper and magazine articles cited in Heuvelmans (Table III, second row), we find that summer is by no means the most popular season for stories on the sea-serpent. The case for harassed editors seems even weaker when we consider Table IV, which shows that sightings tend to be attributed to summer even by those media (like books) which are relatively insensitive to season of publication. So sea-serpent sightings do tend to be a summer phenomenon, but not through the needs of newspaper editors. Of course, if one wishes to consider that editors may have a dull season at other times of the year, then perhaps the 'silly season' theory is still tenable; but this idea is difficult to test.

TABLE IV

Source vs. Season of Sighting

	Winter	Spring	Summer	Fall	TOTAL
Newspapers	14% (25)	18% (33)	44% (79)	23% (42)	99% (179)
Scientific Journals	2% (1)	13% (6)	72% (34)	13% (6)	100% (47)
Non-Sea-Serpent Book	7% (2)	7% (2)	70% (19)	15% (4)	99% (27)
Sea-Serpent Books	10% (4)	12% (5)	67% (27)	10% (4)	99% (40)
Magazine	15% (3)	25% (5)	20% (4)	40% (8)	100% (20)
Television	0	0	50% (1)	50% (1)	100% (2)

Ron Westrum

There is another way in which newspaper and magazine articles *are* very important to sea-serpent reporting: the report release phenomenon. It is not unusual in anomaly reporting to have a delay, often of several years, between the experience and a report of it in some public channel. Often the occasion for the release is the publication of an autobiography or other material of a historical nature; but more commonly, it is the publication of *someone else's* report. This phenomenon, report release, is most strongly evident after the publication of an article on sea-serpents, *e.g.* in a popular magazine. Readers of the article who have had sightings themselves often write to the author of the article, detailing their own experiences. This not only creates a greater store of data in the author's possession, but frequently means that more reports will be published in the same channel. It encourages an individual who has not reported his own sighting to think that others are having the same experiences.

An example of report release is the response to an article by Sanderson in the *Saturday Evening Post*, 'Don't Scoff at Sea Monsters'.[29] As a result of this article, Sanderson received at least nine new reports, the median age of which was twelve years. The oldest was 46 years old.[30] A 1961 television panel discussion in England by the British Broadcasting Corporation elicited seven reports of comparable vintage.[31] An even clearer picture of the delays involved in reporting can be gained from consideration of the more than 30 reports from the Vancouver, British Columbia area.

Although the first sightings from this area date from 1912, the first public recognition of the phenomenon occurred in 1933, when two Canadian government officials indicated that they had seen the creature, which was quickly dubbed 'Cadborosaurus'. These two reports quickly released a flood of older ones, involving around a hundred witnesses. The atmosphere created by this publicity also insured good reporting for the next two decades, for sixteen sightings were reported between 1933 and 1969. Even so, a 1912 sighting did not reach public attention until the 1960s, and a 1928 sighting did not emerge until 1954.[32]

Articles on sea-serpents in scientific journals also tend to release more cases. This release can occur even if the articles which act as releasers indicate a negative attitude towards the reality of the sightings. Persons believing that they have observed sea-serpents may write to those with neutral or negative views either in an attempt to persuade them to change their opinions or from a desire that their sightings be satisfactorily explained. To be sure, authors whose views are negative may be less likely to publish the new cases they get than those with positive views would be, and these cases may not be transmitted any further. In some cases, however, the communications may be addressed to the journal itself rather than the author of the article, and may be printed by the editor. For instance, the British scientific journal *Nature* printed nineteen separate contributions on the sea-serpent from 1872 to 1885.[33] Some of these were sightings sent in to confute articles with negative views. In general, then, writings on the sea-serpent tend to generate new cases, even if the writings are negative.

How many of the reports in our sample were released by the publication of other reports, we do not know. We do know that at least ten percent of the reports were admittedly released only after someone's sighting. But when one considers reports which were released because there had been a recent sighting, or which were released only in conjunction with another sighting, or during 'flaps', one could easily estimate that only a third or less of the sightings were 'independently' released. And very few of these latter would have been released at all if the words 'sea-serpent' did not exist as a convenient label to describe these experiences.[34]

TABLE V

Class Composition* vs. Number of Observers

	Upper-middle or higher	Middle class	Lower class	Totals
No. of Observers 1	64% (25)	8% (3)	28% (11)	100% (39)
2	61% (51)	26% (22)	13% (11)	100% (84)
3	46% (25)	20% (11)	33% (18)	99% (54)
4	33% (14)	19% (8)	49% (21)	101% (43)

*Any assignment of observers to social classes, which was done in this case by occupation, must remain extremely rough. How is one to assess the status of a Tasmanian mining engineer vs. that of a steamer's third officer? Or for that matter, the Grand Huntsman to the King of Sweden? Thus the validity of each identification of a given occupation with a class status is problematic. Overall, however, the general tendencies are clear.

Finally, individual characteristics such as the percipient's social class affect reporting. Higher class individuals are more likely to have access to means of communication and their social position is likely to command more respect.[35] Their superior education is also likely to manifest itself in a greater confidence that they can distinguish a genuinely anomalous stimulus from a non-anomalous one. These three factors are likely to contribute to a disproportionately higher *reporting* rate for the higher classes although the *sighting* rate is probably the same for all classes. In Table V we find that the accuracy of this hypothesis depends on the size of the group involved in the sighting: the smaller the group, the more important higher class position is. A similar finding is indicated in Table VI, where sightings from ships are broken down into categories by status of reporter. In those cases where the reporters are identified, captains and officers are by far overrepresented. The sightings in which only captains and other officers are included is in fact 27 per cent of the total sightings from ships. Even in the most favourable interpretation of the other cases, this suggests a higher reporting rate for officers.[36]

TABLE VI

Sightings From Ships—Status of Reporters

Captain only	...	...	...	...	...	11% (20)
Captain and officers only			...	...	...	16% (29)
Seamen only	...	...	...	...	...	5% (8)
'Ship's crew'		...	...	...	...	57% (100)
Unknown	...	...	...	...	...	11% (19)
					TOTAL	100% (176)

We see, then, that the reporting process is strongly affected by social factors—the fear of ridicule, the publication of the reports of others, and the social position of the percipient. Even if a percipient wishes to make a report there is no guarantee that it will be published—so it may never enter a public channel. It is thus very unlikely that public reports are a random sample of experiences. It is equally unlikely that the temporal pattern of reporting reflects the temporal pattern of sighting. As we have seen, sightings tend to occur in the summer months. From our data on channels it would appear that newspapers, far from concentrating reports in summer, tend to disperse them throughout

the year, although there is a low point in winter. The report release
phenomenon often causes reports to follow one another closely in
time—although the sightings may be temporally far apart. Still, there
are a few periods in which a large number of sightings occur in a
relatively short period of time, as in the Massachusetts sightings of
1817-19.[37] There are thus both waves of sightings and waves of reports: but a wave of reports can occur in the absence of a wave of
sightings, through the report release process.[38]

The Expanding Data Base

The report release process expands the data base of sea-serpent
sightings. As we have seen, released reports may become public directly or they may end up in the hands of authors of sea-serpent articles
and books. As time goes on, more and more cases are available for
study. As the number of cases increases, however, the necessity for
a catalogue of cases, especially a critical catalogue, increases. The two
most ambitious efforts in this direction have been Oudemans[39] and
Heuvelmans.[40] The work of later compilers has been greatly assisted,
of course, by the labours of earlier ones. Heuvelmans has indicated
that he spent six years of uninterrupted labour writing the first (1965)
edition of his work.[41] Without the previous efforts of earlier compilers, especially Oudemans, however, his book would have included
many fewer cases.

TABLE VII

Growth of Data Base

Date of Compilation	Number of Cases Included	Cases previous to date which were available in 1976*
Pontoppidan (1755)	11	(16)
Linnean Society (1817)	31	(62)
Oudemans (1892)	189	(318)
Heuvelmans (1965)	548	(615)
Heuvelmans (1968)	587	(615)
Heuvelmans (1976)	615	

*Based on list given in Heuvelmans 1976.

The growth of the stock of sea-serpent cases is shown in Table VII.
The numbers in parentheses indicate cases prior to the date of the

compilation which were available in 1976. The difference between the number of cases available now and the number of those actually included in a compilation is due to the joint effects of report release and intensive search by researchers. Even the different editions of Heuvelmans's book show the growth of the data base. Between his 1965 and 1976 editions, for instance, his catalogue grew from 548 to 615, a twelve percent increase. And new reports continue to turn up.[42]

One might think that with this expanding number of reports, there would be an increasing inclination on the part of naturalists to investigate them. This is not the case, however. We will now consider why this expansion of data has not led to an expansion of interest.

Scientists' Evaluation of Sea-Serpent Reports

It is ironic that a growing stock of reports of sea-serpent sightings has been accompanied by a declining interest in the subject on the part of naturalists. In the nineteenth century supporters of the sea-serpent's existence included many of the great naturalists of the time: Sir Joseph Banks, Benjamin Silliman, Louis Agassiz, and Thomas Henry Huxley. The sea-serpent also had many well-known detractors, like Richard Owen, William Mitchill, and Sir Charles Lyell.[43] On the whole the intellectual climate was at least one of an interested neutrality, if not actually favouring the existence of the hypothetical monster. In the twentieth century it is hard to find naturalists interested in the problem at all, and very few write about it. Let us speculate on the reasons for this state of affairs.

The increasing data base has had relatively little effect on scientists' interest in sea-serpents. Instead, scientific interest has tended to focus on the Loch Ness Monster, a much more tractable problem.[44] Loch Ness is a relatively small body of water, sightings are frequent, and there are a fair number of photographs of the supposed 'monster'. Because the area of the Loch is relatively limited, one can employ sonar and underwater stroboscopic cameras to detect and record possible passages of the creature.[45] The instrumental records may not be as satisfactory as a carcass, but at least the naturalist does not have to depend completely on eyewitness accounts. With the sea-serpent, on the other hand, none of these advantages exists. With the exception of the probably fraudulent Le Serrec films,[46] there is no extant photograph of a sea-serpent. Sea-serpent sightings are infrequent and unpredictable, and eyewitness accounts are the only source of data. Re-

gardless of the number of cases, the data simply are not very satisfactory. Few of the witnesses have had any training in zoology and
they are almost always caught unprepared (which may account for the
lack of photographs). Many naturalists would probably agree with the
assessment of Richard Owen, one of the nineteenth century's most
eminent anatomists, in regard to the sea-serpent sighting from H.M.S.
Osborne:

> ' . . . remarks thereon by observers not conversant with natural history,
> and so situated, preclude the formation of any opinion worth recording
> of the nature of the object or objects causing the phenomena as
> interpreted by the foregoing witnesses.'[47]

Nor does there seem to be any single common feature which one
could use to distinguish the genuine sea-serpent reports from the
spurious ones. Many reports describe creatures so different from those
in other reports that they simply could not be of the same species.
Heuvelmans,[48] who strongly believes that sea-serpents exist, solves this
problem by positing at least *seven* different types of animal.[49]

Then there is the problem of hoaxes. It seems clear that there have
been a number of reported sightings which were definitely fraudulent;[50] and many others which have been treated as genuine are probably also fraudulent. The perceptual errors and ignorance to which
Owen referred are bad enough, but when the possibility of outright
fraud is added, sea-serpent investigation is not likely to seem promising to naturalists. Samuel Mitchill, one of the founding fathers of
American science, felt that so many sea-serpent hoaxes had been per-
petrated that the subject was scarcely worth consideration.[51] Even in
the cases where the witnesses' characters would seem to preclude a
hoax, there is still the possibility of optical illusion:

> 'Now, after all these mistakes, deceptions and wilful perversions on the
> subject, every person of consideration may admit that the gambols of
> porpoises, the slow motions of basking sharks and the yet different
> appearance of balenoepterous whales, all of which have fins on their
> backs, may have given rise to those parts of the narrations, not already
> herein commented upon.'[52]

The 'data' are thus likely to seem tainted by deception and error, and
difficult to decipher, in any case. If it is so difficult to prove that the
Loch Ness Monster exists, how much more difficult is it to prove the
existence of the 'great unknown' of the seas! Naturalists are not likely
to look at sea-serpents as a soluble puzzle. They are therefore unlikely
to expend their energies in trying to solve it.[53]

Research does not take place in a social vacuum, however. Sea-serpents, like the Loch Ness Monster, are a subject on which the public's motives for desiring scientific research are not likely to make the subject appealing to scientists. Suspicion of two motives in particular is likely to create considerable reluctance on the part of scientists to involve themselves with sea-serpents: the public's romantic interest in their existence and its desire to embarrass 'the experts'. In regard to the first motive, let us consider Richard Owen's remarks on the *Daedalus* case. In commenting on the sighting of an alleged sea-serpent from H.M.S. *Daedalus*, Owen stated that if it could be shown that the animal seen was not a saurian,

> 'It destroys the romance of the incident, and will be anything but acceptable to those who prefer the excitement of the imagination to the satisfaction of the judgement.'[54]

For his work in the debunking of the *Daedalus* sighting Owen was hailed by his colleagues as 'the killer of the sea-serpent'.[55] Scientists rightly suspect that the sensational and mysterious aspects of anomaly sightings are very attractive to the public and detract from the interest which they feel the public should have in more routine 'popular science'. The press's ridicule of witnesses also serves to discourage scientific interest, as scientists hesitate to involve themselves with a subject having such non-serious overtones.

The second motive is no less strong, even if it is characteristic of a much smaller group. Science is the dominant intellectual enterprise of our time and there are few areas of life which it does not affect. In this way, natural science is to the twentieth century what the Church was to the Middle Ages. The limited nature of scientific expertise is often neglected both by persons inside and outside science, and scientists are sometimes regarded as infallible experts on the earth and the cosmos. As Dixon[56] has observed, however, there are many persons in modern society who resent this posture of infallibility, and accordingly welcome occasions upon which scientific expertise is shown to be in error. Since scientists are likely to express negative opinions about deviant phenomena like sea-serpents and UFOs, any indications that reports of these phenomena might be well-founded are welcomed by this group. If scientists could be forced to change their opinion about the reality of sea-serpents or the Loch Ness Monster, this would be seen as a major victory by those who feel that science has become too arrogant in its own authority.[57]

The existence of these motives and related ones means that the existence of sea-serpents is not merely an intellectual question, but an emotional one as well. The prestige of science and the hopes of the public are staked on different outcomes in the controversy. If sea-serpents are accepted by science, this would prove that science has been wrong. It would also mean that the public's romantic belief in the 'great unknown' was justified.[58] These concerns are likely to affect any scientific evaluation of the creature's existence. In addition, as we have seen, the subject is not a very promising one from the standpoint of the data, and a naturalist who invests his time in the area is likely to get little support and encouragement from his colleagues or from the scientific community at large. It is hardly surprising, therefore, that the growth of the data base has not meant a comparable growth of interest on the part of scientists.

This attitude, in turn, is responsible for a continuing scepticism vis à vis sea-serpents by the press, which derives its attitudes (in part) from what it believes the attitude of the scientific community to be. Percipients are unlikely to report sightings because they know what the public reaction to the report is likely to be, and how their sighting is likely to be reported in the press. The system, then, is reflexive to the extent that scientists' attitudes towards sea-serpents influence the rate of reporting of sightings. There is a kind of self-fulfilling prophecy inherent in the pronouncement that 'sea-serpents do not exist', since the pronouncement can inhibit the transmission of information that might indicate otherwise. What we find out about sea-serpents is determined in part by what we already believe to be the case.

Conclusion

In considering the social transmission and accumulation of data about anomalies like sea-serpents, we confront a rather unusual system of knowledge production. Individuals or groups have sightings of what they believe to be large unknown marine creatures. In some cases these sightings are reported, often after a long delay, and are then printed in public sources. Cases from these sources are gradually assembled into catalogues which provide a resource for interested researchers. Not many naturalists become interested in the data, however, since observations have not been gathered systematically, nor do the observers usually have any technical training. In addition, public attitudes towards sea-serpent reports discourage rather than encourage scientific interest. The lack of scientists' acceptance of the reality of sea-serpents in turn tends to inhibit reporting.

Our knowledge of sea-serpents, then, depends upon this diffuse system of social intelligence and especially on the efforts of those few naturalists, like Oudemans and Heuvelmans, who decide that the imperfections of the data are less important than the subject's intrinsic interest. Those who interest themselves in sea-serpents are likely to receive few rewards from the scientific community for their work, unless (like Owen) they seek the data only to debunk it. Yet the information continues to grow, in fits and starts to be sure, but it does grow. Should, by some miracle, a sea-serpent carcass or some significant portion thereof be discovered, a considerable documentation will already be found to exist. Should no such convincing piece of evidence be found, our successors may well conclude that the collection and processing of such 'evidence' was the work of scientific Quixotes.

It is well to consider, though, that many other anomalies may be subject to the same social relations as sea-serpent reports. In my earlier work on UFOs and meteorites[59] I have demonstrated that very similar difficulties are likely to be present in the collection of information about other events which violate current scientific doctrine. These difficulties may be interesting to sociologists, but they are frustrating to scientists who develop an interest in a type of event considered impossible or implausible. In some cases the difficulty may be so severe that even a researcher strongly interested in a given anomaly may not be able to find data on it, because the data have never been collected. Even in the computerised world in which we live it may be hard to retrieve data on events like sea-serpent sightings because the system of social intelligence is so imperfect.[60]

It must also be remembered that the average scientist, in making a decision about an anomalous event, may not engage in any systematic data search at all, but may base his decision on those few cases which come to his attention. The fact that this sample may be unrepresentative and may not contain some of the most interesting cases may seem irrelevant, since the anomaly may be a relatively low priority in his research anyway. He may not even realize that compilations of similar cases exist and might regard them as irrelevant if he were aware of them. This indifference to anomaly information is a major factor in its non-dissemination.

Anomalies share with a number of other types of events the property that reporting is highly responsive to social demand. One thinks immediately, for instance, of crimes,[61] concentration camps,[62] and air safety problems.[63] The marketing of news often takes public demand into consideration[64] and organisational intelligence tends to be strongly influenced by what those higher up in the organisation want to hear.[65] In all these areas, however, the fact that transmission of reports is tied to the demand for them is often forgotten when the reports are being evaluated. This tendency to forget social factors in transmission can result in an incorrect assumption that a paucity or absence of reports indicates that nothing is happening. Likewise, a 'flap' of reports may erroneously indicate that a sudden increase in the rate of the events in question is occurring.

In considering what we know about certain types of events like sea-serpent sightings, it may be well to consider explicitly the social processes responsible for our awareness of these events. There is a natural tendency on our part to assume that reporting is more complete and representative than often is the case.[66] With a more realistic understanding of how information about such events is generated we can make a sounder evaluation of what the data mean, and what kind of evidence they provide for the existence and nature of the events in question.

Eastern Michigan University.

[1] For a partial review of this literature, see Ron Westrum: 'A Note on Monsters', *Journal of Popular Culture*, Vol. 8, No. 4, 1975, pp. 862-70.

[2] Ron Westrum: 'Science and Social Intelligence about Anomalies: The Case of Meteorites', paper presented at the meetings of American Sociological Association, Chicago, Illinois, October 1977a.

[3] ibid.

[4] Ron Westrum: 'Science and Social Intelligence About Anomalies: The Case of UFOs', *Social Studies of Science*, Vol. 7, No. 3, 1977b.

[5] For a review of the literature on sea-serpents, see B. Heuvelmans: *In the Wake of the Sea-Serpents*, Hill and Wang, New York, 1968; for a review of the literature on lake monsters, see Peter Costello: *In Search of Lake Monsters*, Coward McCann and Geoghegan, New York, 1974.

[6] Erich Pontoppidan: *The Natural History of Norway*, A. Linde, London, 1755, 2 vols.

[7] Linnean Society of Boston: *Report of a Committee of the Linnean Society of Boston Relative to a Large Marine Animal Supposed to be a Serpent Seen near Cape Ann, Massachusetts, in August 1817*, Cummings and Hilliard, Boston, 1817.

Ron Westrum

Heuvelmans: op. cit., 1968. Data from the 1968 edition were used for purposes of analysis. Additional data are contained in the 1976 edition, but it arrived too late for the data to be incorporated in the present paper.

9 It is evident from the new cases that are being discovered that this is an underestimate, but it will have to serve for the present.

10 Cornelius A. Oudemans: *The Great Sea-Serpent*, E. J. Brill, Leiden, 1892, pp. 206-209.

11 See Westrum: op. cit., 1977b, for a discussion of perceptual contagion.

12 J. Allen Hynek: *The UFO Experience: A Scientific Enquiry*, Regnery, Chicago, 1972, p. 13.

13 M. Carrouges: *Les Apparitions des Martiens*, Arteme Fayard, Paris, 1963, pp. 188-95.

14 Oudemans: op. cit., p. 151.

15 Jerome Bruner: 'On Perceptual Readiness', *Psychological Review*, Vol. 64, 1957, pp. 123-52.

16 Oudemans: op. cit., p. 207.

16a ibid., p. 208.

17 ibid., p. 210.

18 Hadley Cantril: *The Invasion from Mars*, Harper and Row, New York, 1966, pp. 112-24.

19 Heuvelmans: op. cit., 1968, p. 385.

20 ibid., p. 442.

21 Stanley Singer: *The Nature of Ball Lightening*, Plenum Press, New York, 1971; Eugene Garfield: 'When Content Analysis Strikes Ball Lightening', *Current Contents*, Vol. 8, No. 20, 1976, pp. 5-16.

22 Jeff Coulter: 'Perceptual Accounts and Interpretive Asymmetries', *Sociology*, Vol. 9, No. 3, 1975, pp. 385-96.

23 Oudemans: op. cit., p. 321.

24 Heuvelmans: op. cit., 1968, p. 225.

25 Rupert Gould: *The Case for the Sea-Serpent*, Philip Allan, London, 1930, p. 189.

26 ibid.

27 Andrew Wilson: *Facts and Fiction of Zoology*, Humboldt Library of Popular Science Literature, No. 29, Vol. 2, J. Fitzgerald, New York, 1882, p. 12. It says something for the persistence of interest in the 'great unknown' that it is still familiar to the readers of this article, while most of them will find the other two objects somewhat obscure.

28 Pontoppidan: op. cit., Vol. II, p. 196.

29 Ivan T. Sanderson: 'Don't Scoff at Sea Monsters', *Saturday Evening Post*, 8 March 1947, pp. 22-3, 84-7.

30 Heuvelmans: op. cit., 1968, p. 508.

31 ibid., p. 495.

[32] ibid., pp. 441-5.

[33] References will be supplied by the author on request; they are too numerous to list here.

[34] The author is strongly of the opinion that anomalous experiences which are believed to be unique are seldom reported. It is bad enough for the percipient that the experience is anomalous in the first place. When similar experiences have not been shared by others, however, the percipient is in an even worse situation, since he lacks the cognitive support that others' experiences would provide.

[35] Bentham speaks of 'a witness belonging to a higher class of a condition which presumes a more careful education, a greater responsibility, more sensibility to honour, in a word, a known witness . . .', J. Bentham: *A Treatise on Judicial Evidence*, J. W. Paget, London, 1825, p. 39.

[36] It is true, of course, that officers have duties which more often include surveillance of the ship's environment, and generally have more access to telescopes, binoculars, etc. Even so it is hard to credit the difference in reporting rate entirely to this factor.

[37] Gould: op. cit., pp. 29-72.

[38] 'Crime waves' are also generated as much by changes in the parameters of the reporting process as by actual increases in the amount of crime. For an example, see L. Steffens: *The Autobiography of Lincoln Steffens*, Literary Guild, New York, 1931, pp. 285-91.

[39] Oudemans: op. cit.

[40] B. Heuvelmans: *Le Grand Serpent de Mer*, Plon, Paris, 1965; op. cit., 1968; and, *Le Grand Serpent de Mer*, Plon, Paris, 1976, 2nd edn.

[41] B. Heuvelmans: personal communication, 6 May 1977.

[42] New cases are still being discovered in nineteenth century newspapers by Gary Mangiacopra: 'The Great Unknowns of the Nineteenth Century', *Of Sea and Shore*, 1976-7 (Winter), pp. 201-6, 228.

[43] Heuvelmans: op. cit., 1968, pp. 23-44.

[44] Maurice Burton: *The Elusive Monster*, Rupert Hart-Davis, London, 1961; Roy Mackal: *The Monsters of Loch Ness*, Swallow Press, Chicago, 1976.

[45] Mackal: op. cit.

[46] Heuvelmans: op. cit., 1968, pp. 531-5.

[47] Gould: op. cit., p. 165.

[48] Heuvelmans: op. cit., 1968.

[49] ibid., pp. 537-73.

[50] Oudemans: op. cit., pp. 12-59.

[51] W. L. Mitchill: 'The History of Sea-Serpentism', *American Journal of Science and the Arts*, Vol. 15, 1829, pp. 351-61.

[52] ibid., p. 356.

[53] The scientist is likely to direct his efforts to working on those problems which he feels have a fair chance of being solved, on which he feels he can

make progress. See Peter Medawar: *The Art of the Soluble*, Penguin, Harmondsworth, 1969.

⁵⁴ Heuvelmans: op. cit., 1968, p. 205.

⁵⁵ Richard Owen: *The Life of Richard Owen*, John Murray, London, 1894, 2 vols., Vol. I, p. 334.

⁵⁶ B. Dixon: *What is Science For?* Penguin, Harmondsworth, 1976 pp. 183-199.

⁵⁷ R. Grimshaw and P. Lester: *The Meaning of the Loch Ness Monster*, Centre for Contemporary Cultural Studies, University of Birmingham, 1976, pp. 27-30.

⁵⁸ ibid., pp. 31-6.

⁵⁹ Westrum: op. cit., 1977a and b.

⁶⁰ Fortunately anomalous events of various kinds are rapidly being catalogued by specialised societies and a number of popular periodicals. One such society is the International Fortean Organization, 7317 Baltimore Avenue, College Park, Maryland, 20740, U.S.A. Another excellent resource is the systematically arranged *Sourcebooks* of William Corliss, of which nine have so far been published. For details write to Sourcebook Project, Glen Arm, Maryland, 21057, U.S.A.

⁶¹ Nigel Walker: *Crimes, Courts and Figures*, Penguin, Harmondsworth, 1971.

⁶² E. C. Hughes: 'Good People and Dirty Work', in H. S. Becker (ed.): *The Other Side: Perspectives on Deviance*, Free Press, New York, 1964, pp. 23-36.

⁶³ S. Barlay: *Aircrash Detective: An International Report on the Quest for Air Safety*, Hamish Hamilton, London, 1969, 120-143.

⁶⁴ Anonymous: 'The News Doctors', *Newsweek*, 25 November 1974, p. 87.

⁶⁵ H. Wilensky: *Organizational Intelligence*, Basic Books, New York, 1967.

⁶⁶ Westrum: op. cit., 1977a.

UFOLOGY: THE INTELLECTUAL DEVELOPMENT AND SOCIAL CONTEXT OF THE STUDY OF UNIDENTIFIED FLYING OBJECTS

Joseph A. Blake

The UFO Problem

THIS paper is concerned with ufology. By ufology we mean the study of unidentified flying objects as elements in an independent theoretical-conceptual scheme. This is a roundabout way of referring to ufology as a 'science', necessitated by the fact that its status as a 'science' is questioned. Yet, ufology has developed as a distinct body of data studied by distinctly 'credentialled' investigators, some of them affiliated with organisations devoted to the study of UFOs. Ufology is also in the process of developing distinct theoretical schema appropriate to its data base. The task of this paper will be to explore ufology as a developing science, in comparison with and against the backdrop of conventional or normal science.

The essential problem in regard to unidentified flying objects has always been accountability. There are two general ways of accounting for them. The first is to define them as natural phenomena, thus including them within the bounds of normal science. Indeed, we may say that the definition of UFOs as natural phenomena follows from the acceptance of one or another of the theories of normal science. Those within this category include the debunkers and the hopefuls. The former are convinced that UFOs are 'nothing more than' stars, birds, swamp gas, hoaxes, or 'mass hysteria'.[1] The hopefuls are those who would argue, and hope to demonstrate, that UFOs are secret weapons, extra-terrestrial vehicles or something else subsumable under normal science.[2] Their task is to marshall the evidence. This task appears doomed to frustration by virtue of the non-receptiveness of establishment science.[3]

The second style of accountability has been the attempt to present UFOs as something beyond the confines of normal science. For twenty-five years or more this type of accounting has been monopolised by the cult groups and their leaders.[4] Accountability schemes have been notably idiosyncratic and hopelessly inaccessible to verification procedures of any kind. Such schemes have all fixated one basic fact, however, and that is the essentially experiental nature of UFOs. It is from this point that a second style of accountability emerges. Its proponents adopt what they call a 'macrocosmic approach'[5] and refer to what they do as either 'ufology' or 'paraufology'.

The experience of UFOs extends at least two centuries into the past.[6] Records go that far back with certainty. Equally certain is the fact that such experience occurs in dispersed groups of people, either publics or social networks. The phenomena consist of the reported reactions of the people involved to an event or series of events, first in small numbers, then increasing to a high point, finally decreasing again. If plotted on a graph, the horizontal axis of which is in time units and the vertical axis in numbers of people, the phenomena assume the shape of a curve or wave.[7] Such a wave may occur once or it may recur. If the wave, or one of the waves, is 'caught' at some point in its existence by the organisation of some of those who helped to constitute it, then it becomes an 'arrested' wave. At this point, traditional social science language may refer to a social movement.

The UFO as a category derives from, and specifically refers to, a series of waves following one another more or less continuously since 1947; it is also applied to a number of previous waves which were recognised and interpreted at their times of occurence as observations of 'strange' or 'mysterious' aerial objects. Specifically recognised waves occurred in the late 1890s in the United States, 1909 and 1913 in Great Britain, near the end of World War II in Europe and the southwest Pacific, 1945 and 1946 in Scandinavia and 1947 to date around the world.[8] It is this last set of waves, publicly initiated by the famous Kenneth Arnold sighting, which was 'arrested' or organised. The organisation of devotees and interested people ensured the continued existence of the phenomena by ensuring continually generated data and by providing at least minimal resources for the study of such data. From this basis emerged ufology.

The UFO Experience and Emerging Ufology

F. S. C. Northrop says that, 'Nature . . . as given by natural science, is partly known empirically by immediate intuition and the senses and partly known theoretically by the intellect and the imagination checked indirectly by experimental verification'.[9] He adds, however, that the 'immediately apprehended fact' which is intuited is 'independent of all concepts and theory'.[10] Facticity implies meaning and to endow that which is intuited or sensed with meaning is to bring to bear theoretical presuppositions and conceptualisations. As Hanson puts it, 'every perception involves an aetiology and a prognosis'.[11] As something is immediately apprehended there is a tendency either to ignore it or to integrate it into an already existent socially defined order of things.

Yet some experiences are too jarring. They are strange enough to resist integration and bold enough to defy being overlooked. The social basis of the extension of such phenomena has been referred to. At this point we must address the phenomena. Our perspective suggests that that which is experienced will either be ignored, integrated, or form the basis of a new socially constructed reality. We are studying ufology as part of one of these new realities. To do so will require an examination of the developing *theories* of ufology, in terms of those shared elements called 'ufology'. It also requires addressing the experience and with this we shall begin.

The category 'UFO' includes sightings of 'flying saucers' and other unknown aerial objects, as well as close encounters, physical effects (e.g., illness), and electromagnetic effects (e.g. interference with the operation of automobiles and other machinery). As Flammonde[12] points out in his history of the phenomena, these constitute the body of data to be accounted for. The category also includes abductions,[13] contactee stories, animal mutilations,[14] biblical phenomena,[15] occult phenomena,[16] strange disappearances,[17] including those in the so-called 'Bermuda' or 'Devil's' Triangle.[18] Even more marginally included are accounts of the Yeti, Sasquatch ('Big Foot') and other 'strange animal' sightings.[19]

What we have to deal with here is the UFO as experienced, the translation of these experiences (sightings) into reports and the categorisation of such reports by ufologists. What we begin with is the sighting report. Leaving out all the peripheral phenomena and focusing on unidentified *flying* objects we find reporter conceptualistations differing over time. Reports connected with the first major wave, 1896 to 1897, are phrased in terms of 'mystery airships'. Later waves up through the 1930s are characterised by reports of 'ghost airplanes'. Allied airmen near the end of World War II reported 'foo fighters'.

Swedes, in 1946, reported 'ghost rockets'. In the series of waves beginning in 1947 were to be found reports of 'flying saucers' and many similarly named flying objects.

All these reports offer us labels. These labels were of things familiar applied to things unfamiliar.[20] As Hynek tells us in reference to his interviews with UFO reporters:

> 'The experience had the "reality" of a tangible physical event, on a par with, for example, the perception of an automobile accident or of an elephant performing in a circus, except for one thing; whereas reporters have an adequate vocabulary to describe automobiles and elephants, they are almost always at an embarrassing loss for words to describe their UFO experience.'[21]

A descriptive label 'both classic and original' was provided by one of Fowler's respondents:

> ' "It was like two hamburger buns, one on top of the other, with a sandwiched piece of meat sticking out all around." Here was a genuinely honest attempt to describe an inexplicable but very real event within the context of the witness's common vocabulary and everyday experience.'[22]

The suggestion here is that the UFO experience is uncommon, i.e., not an everyday life experience. Clark and Coleman go even further, suggesting that many UFO experiences are essentially altered states of consciousness. Of one case, for example, they ask (and answer):

> 'Was Johannis's a "real" experience? A question like this is almost impossible to answer . . . because in the UFO myth "objective" and "subjective" elements are often indistinguishable. Perhaps significantly, however, Johannis relates that early in the experience he felt as if he were "dreaming".'[23]

That the UFO experience is labelled, however objective or subjective, is clear. That the labelling represents the application of the familiar to the unfamiliar is also clear. What is not clear is, on the one hand, a consistency of labelling among reports in a wave and, on the other, diversity in labelling among waves.

It is with the development of specific problems that we find the development of a science and, in this regard, ufology is not an exception. The general problem in regard to UFOs is accountability. One of the first theoretical problems to emerge is in relation to the consistency, yet diversity, of reported experiences. Simply stated, the *nature* of UFOs seems to fit the historical time period in which they are sighted. This fact has been commented upon by several ufologists.[24] Related to this is the question: why don't they make themselves known to us? The ways of dealing with these questions correlate highly with different perspectives.

There are three ways of dealing with these questions. Two of these ways treat the UFO phenomena as objective, one treats them as subjective phenomena. The over-all naturalist approach to this problem is to phrase it in terms of perception and misperception and correct or incorrect conceptualisation; the latter assessment is made on the basis of possible conceptual schemes known to the natural scientist rather than those available to the witness. One of the best accounts of this type is by Hartmann,[25] who analysed sighting reports of the re-entry of satellite debris. Of those who tend to define UFOs as objective phenomena, some see the different historical waves as representing essentially different phenomona, or at least see the phenomena of pre-1947 waves as inaccessible. These are generally the same people, debunkers or hopefuls, who tend towards defining UFOs as natural phenomena. Others who define UFOs as objective phenomena suggest the differences over time as due to operator intent. Stringfield, for example, suggests that:

> 'Whatever the reason, or non-reason, for the UFO actions . . . recorded in the more than eighty thousand entries in Dr. David Saunders' data bank, it appears that human kind is at the mercy of a vanguard who, seemingly selfish in purpose, continue to *reconnoiter Earth, in chill contempt,* to fulfil that purpose.'[26]

In reference to humanoid encounters he says:

> 'Research records show again and again, when humanoids are near, so is an odor. Stranger than their odor is their diversity of size and features and behavior. Ted Bloecher and I have frequently discussed these factors. "They seem to be taunting us", I said. "How else can you explain their mischief?" ". . . Or perhaps their demonstrations are staged," offered Bloecher, "concocted for the benefit of the witness. Maybe they monitor our adrenalin . . . ".'[27]

Salisbury[28] tells us that, 'UFOs have specific characteristics that match the time and place of their sightings.' He suggests that, 'the UFOs seemed to be putting on a show, a display *aimed specifically at the witnesses*'.[29] The approach of Salisbury and Stringfield is a natural science approach of hopefuls. One of the more consistent subjective approaches is that of Clark and Coleman[30] and will be dealt with in the next section.

Theoretical Elements of Ufology

Among the theoretical elements of ufology with which we shall deal are conceptualisation, scope and methodology. By conceptualisation, of course, we refer to the language of ufology. Although some

Joseph A. Blake

confusion and ambiguity exists in this regard it is, nonetheless, the area of most agreement among ufologists. By scope we refer to the breadth of phenomena covered by various perspectives in ufology. It is in this regard that we find the most diversity among ufologists as different definitions of scope come to define different and competing theories of UFO. By methodology we refer to those rules of procedure and evidence used by ufologists in guiding their work and determining the credibility of their data. Here we find the greatest collective emphasis among ufologists.

Conceptualisation

We have, inevitably, used certain concepts of ufology already in this paper. An expanded discussion is necessary, however. We have first to note the distinction between a sighting and a report. According to one ufologist:

> 'A "sighting" is any observation of some unexplained aerial phenomenon. A "report" is the oral or written record of a sighting. A "case" refers to a report, plus other elements that are associated with it, such as information about the observer, an account of the investigation, references to the report, or conclusions drawn from the information gathered.'[31]

Such distinctions are simple, common, but necessary. We need only refer to a case in which the distinctions were not made to see why.

The fact is that many UFO sightings are not reported. A Gallup public opinion poll released early in 1966 estimated that a total of 5,000,000 Americans have seen UFOs; 5 per cent of the sample who had heard of UFOs reported a sighting to the Gallup interviewer.[32] This compares to a total of 10,147 reports to the United States Air Force up to January 17, 1966.[33] This is substantiated by Hynek:

> 'Whenever I give a presentation to some group I frequently will ask them, well, how many of you have seen something in the skies you couldn't explain; that is, a UFO . . . I have been surprised to find that 10 to 15 per cent . . . [indicate that they have]. Then I ask the second one, did you report it to the Air Force? And maybe one or two will say that they have.'[34]

Further verification of this fact is provided by an attitude survey done for the *Scientific Study of Unidentified Flying Objects,* which revealed that 87 per cent of those in the sample who had seen a UFO reported it only to family and friends.[35]

Failure to distinguish between a sighting and a report may obscure important differences between those who answer 'yes' to a questionnaire item and those who take the time, trouble and risk of offering a report to an official agency. Warren,[36] for example, overlooks this distinction. He utilised the Gallup poll data referred to above to test his hypothesis that UFO sightings are linked to status frustration and status deprivation. He found a positive relationship. His findings may hold in comparing sighters and non-sighters who responded to the poll. They may even say something about a society that generates such problems. But they constitute a social science debunking and moral put-down of those who *report* UFOs, as well as many of those studying the phenomena. The Gallup sample represented a cross section of the nation's population. Those who actually report sightings constitute a very select group, evidently differing from sighters in terms of occupation, status, education, etc. Findings in relation to the first group cannot be generalised to the second.

That there is some loose usage of the terms among ufologists is also evident when they are used to define other concepts. Bloecher,[37] for example, defines a 'wave' as, 'any sudden and pronounced increase of UFO sightings on a national scale, above what is ordinarily considered an average daily rate.' Flammonde[38] defines a 'concentration' as, 'an unusually high number of sightings in one location, or over a larger geographical area in a very short period of time.' That those authors refer to the temporal and spatial parameters of aggregated reports, rather than sightings, is obvious from their discussion. The basis of confusion here lies in the fact that, in any wave or concentration, different numbers of reports may be made to different agencies. For example, Hall,[39] representing the National Investigations Committee on Aerial Phenomena, lists twenty reports for 1947; the United States Air Force Project Blue Book release[40] lists 122; Bloecher[41] searched 142 newspapers in 93 cities of 49 states, 2 Canadian provinces and the District of Columbia and found 843 reports.[42]

The relationship of 'waves' and 'concentrations' to 'flaps' is apparent. A flap is the result of a wave-concentration. Bloecher[43] gives us the Air Force definition of flap as an 'advanced state of confusion'. Both Flammonde[44] and Stringfield[45] indicate the media generated nature of a 'flap'. According to Flammonde:

> 'The importance of knowing the difference between "concentration" and "flap" lies in the fact that often a single peculiar sighting or alleged landing may stir up the reporters, who rush off, write their stories, and create a "flap", while a considerable number of less sensational sightings may occur in a given region, creating a "concentration", but be almost ignored by the press.'[46]

It is also apparent that there is an affinity between the concepts 'wave' and 'flap' depending upon the looseness or tightness of the conceptual distinction between 'sighting' and 'report'. And, despite some looseness as to what is actually subsumed by the concept 'unidentified flying object',[47] it is coming to be clear that, as Hynek puts it, 'We can define a flying saucer as an aerial phenomena [sic] or sighting that remains unexplained to the viewer at least long enough for him to write a report about it.'[48] This is the conceptual kernel of UFO research although many non-aerial phenomena may become part of a 'case' and, eventually, a theoretical development.

Scope

The second theoretical element to be addressed is scope. The scope of ufology is determined by attempts to define boundaries and subject matter. Since boundary and subject matter varies by investigator, clearly ufology in general is of wide and diverse scope. Nonetheless, there are clearly emerging trends. First, there is what we might call a rigorous naturalist approach. Here, the emphasis is on unidentified flying objects in the strictest sense of that term (see Hynek's definition earlier) and on modern (i.e., post-1947) waves. Other material is included only to the extent of constructing a case for each report. This is ufology as practised by the naturalists. It is characterised by an approach emphasising elementary fact gathering and, in some cases, the propagation of a primary operating hypothesis (e.g., the ETH—Extra-terrestrial hypothesis). Its methodology is borrowed to a large extent from the established sciences.

A second approach differs from the first mainly by including historical experience (mystery airships, ghost rockets, foo fighters) as part of the UFO phenomena. In fact, this is an overlapping category, characterising, on the one hand, all but the most 'rigorous' of the objective and subjective naturalists, on the other hand, most macrocosmic ufologists. The latter are most clearly recognisable by their inclusion into UFO phenomena of all the sorts of material referred to by the naturalists as peripheral or irrelevant.[49] Historically, of course, this was the position of Charles Fort.[50] The most consistent recent attempt at this approach is by Clark and Coleman and deserves further attention.

The work of Clark and Coleman[51] comprises most of the elements of ufology with which we have been dealing so far. Clark and Coleman consider the 'central problem' of UFO to be, 'the absence of really conclusive evidence that the objects are what they appear to be—namely, spaceships from other planets'.[52] This 'central problem', however, is set within the context of modern sightings. In fact, the theory developed by Clark and Coleman is macrocosmic, as revealed in their table of contents and discussion. Their discussion of fairyland, voices from heaven, mystery airships and UFOs—couched in terms of magical, religious, and technological impulses and the 'mystery in the machine'— covers contactee reports, humanoid encounters and abductors, sightings of mystery animals ('Bigfoot'), visions and occult phenomena, and mysterious aerial objects across the centuries and in various cultures. Thus, it is clear that the theoretical problem is, for them, to find consistency amid diversity. To distinguish themselves from what we have called the naturalists they coin a label for what they are about: paraufology. They refer to paraufology as a way of 'understanding the incomprehensible'.[53]

Clark and Coleman discover similarities in stories of fairy contact, religious visions and contacts, encounters and abductions involving UFO operators. All, they claim, have dream elements.[54] The reporter of the experience talks in terms of feelings of floating; all report a kind of dream perception in which few details are visible, and there is a vague scenic description, as of a nebulous realm or area. Many report paralysis or immobility. There is time distortion.

> 'This all tends to suggest that UFO contacts, with their attendant "visits to other planets", arise out of the same mechanism [as fairy visions]; that is, they, too, are hallucinatory trance visions whose accompanying "objective" paranormal manifestations serve to reinforce the notion that these visions are of a real place with real inhabitants.'[55]

The UFO experience, then, is essentially an altered state of consciousness, akin to dreams, trances, hypnagogic and hypnonomic phenomena.[56]

This altered state of consciousness (the 'UFO experience'), according to Clark and Coleman, serves as a way of revealing basic and universal human needs and feelings. These unconscious needs and feelings are expressed through the altered states of consciousness as mythic elements or 'archetypes'. Clark and Coleman discuss some of these mythic elements, borrowing heavily from Jung. They speak, for example, of the element of roundness that continually reappears (e.g., the shape of the UFO), representing psychic wholeness, the ubiquitousness of the number three, the existence of 'hermaphroditic, yet "strangely beautiful" beings', etc.[57] Although they devote a good deal of discussion to these archetypical elements, it seems that they could be eliminated from the theory without serious disjuncture.

Clark and Coleman have made an interesting case for the UFO experience as essentially an altered state of consciousness. They also argue that the 'impulses' listed in their table of contents—magic, and fairies, religion, technology and mysterious machinery—represent conscious rationalisations of the phenomena, each appropriate to its historical-cultural time and place. These rationalisations are conscious, collective attempts to define what Flammonde calls 'undefined sensory experience'.[58]

Yet in another sense it is clear that the Jungian archetypes *are* an essential aspect of the theory. Dropping such a discussion leaves a viable question: what *are* UFOs? Without the Jungian archetypes we are left with a discussion of the relationship of theory and experience; of the *rationalisation* of experience. Such a discussion would, in itself, be valuable by orienting our perspective to an examination of the interworking of sensory experience—phenomena—and collective attempts to structure and organise that experience. It orients us to the social practice of accounting and accountability. But it also leaves open a question as to the *cause* of the phenomena. What precipitates the experience? This allows several kinds of answers. Clark and Coleman provide one. The altered states of consciousness are internally generated by human needs. Clark and Coleman ask, 'Of what can we possibly be certain when liars, lunatics, dreamers, and honest sober citizens all appear to be talking in the same language?'[59] Their answer is:

'If at their core UFO events are subjective, products of unconscious needs, the UFO fact and fiction may be inseparable, for they draw on the same creative source; the human psyche and the archetypes of the collective unconscious.'[60]

Hence, the relationship among altered state of consciousness, archetype and rationalisation.

True to their task of theory-building, Clark and Coleman offer two 'laws' of 'paraufology'. They are:

1. 'The UFO mystery is primarily subjective and its content primarily symbolic.'[61]
2. 'The "objective" manifestations are psychokinetically generated byproducts of those unconscious processes which shape a culture's vision of the other-world. Existing only temporarily, they are at best only quasiphysical.'[62]

This 'otherworld' of which they speak, the symbolic representation of the unconscious, has its dark side as well as its bright side. Not all human needs and feelings, however universal, are deemed good, beneficial or altruistic. In this light they quote Peter Rogerson:

> 'This idea of the UFO and Fortean phenomena [unexplained physical and paraphysical events] as symbolic of the unconscious forces within ourselves allows us to understand some of the fervour behind the scepticism of government and science. The [U.S. Air Force] Project Bluebook and Condon Enquiry [the much-criticised University of Colorado government sponsored UFO study . . . which after two years and half a million dollars concluded that UFOs are not worth studying] can be seen as magical acts, ritual exorcism of the "terrors of the dark", and a magical reaffirmation of the boundaries of the "cultural universe".'[63]

In the process of building their own new science, paraufology, they critically bare a weakness of normal science, by exposing its operations as essentially human.

Methodology

When we speak of methodology we refer to rules for the conduct of inquiry. We can analytically distinguish rules of procedure from rules of evidence. The former refers to ways of generating data, the latter to the evaluation of the data that are generated. The *general* rule of procedure is that only that which is obtained by proceeding according to specifiable rules can be accorded the status 'data'. The *general* rule of evidence is that only those data that meet certain criteria can be accorded the status 'good data', or 'credible data'.

'Methodologies' clearly differ. Those whom we have called the naturalists prefer to follow the canons of normal science. This results in an emphasis on methodology, with perhaps some hypothesis testing but little emphasis on theory building. The 'paraufologists' are more likely to adopt a 'macrocosmic' approach emphasising theory construction and de-emphasising methodology. It becomes, at times, difficult to determine rules of procedure and evidence. Nonetheless, there is a methodology implied by the macrocosmic approach. Clark and Coleman tell us, for instance, that:

> 'If at their core UFO events are subjective, products of unconscious needs, the UFO fact and fiction may be inseparable, for they draw on the same creative source; the human psyche and the archetypes of the collective unconscious.'[64]

Since the approach focuses on the *content* of UFO accounts *as given*, the procedural rule must be that *any story relating to UFOs con-*

stitutes data. Good data, we may assume, are those which have enough points of incredibility to allow comparison among apparently similar cases.

It seems at times that the overriding concern of the naturalists is with developing methods adequately to determine the nature of UFOs. The naturalists themselves provide a strong force for defining ufology as a science. Many have natural science credentials. By bringing themselves and their tools to the study of UFOs they strive to bring respectability to the phenomena. They attempt to do this through an emphasis on methodological rigour.

Among the naturalists we find the expected injunctions of clear definition;[65] preferable acceptance of first hand reports;[66] clear interview strategies;[67] and generally close investigation of each case using the available tools of the social and natural sciences. The author has personal experience in this regard from having heard an investigation reported by a member to the Chicago Area Subcommittee of the National Investigations Committee on Aerial Phenomena. The investigator used a questionnaire, as well as informal interview techniques, scouted and measured the terrain, calculated altitude by use of trigonometry, etc. Whatever else it was, the result was a well conducted investigation. Where appropriate, the naturalists use other techniques, such as photo analysis,[68] and laboratory forensic techniques.

We also find the naturalists prepared to be methodologically creative. The report of the Condon group on the unworthiness of UFOs for study occasioned such creativity. Both Saunders and Harkins and Hynek[69] proceed from a critique of the Condon group. Both claim that the Condon group violated a cardinal rule of procedure by failing to define the problem correctly. Saunders and Harkins note that:

> 'When the University of Colorado Project began, the ETI [Extra-Terrestrial Intelligence] Hypothesis did not look very promising. This was not because ETI couldn't explain a lot of otherwise perplexing "facts", but because it was not established at the more fundamental level that these "facts" were remarkable enough to require any explanation at all.'[70]

According to Hynek:

> 'The history of science has shown that it is the things that don't fit, the apparent exceptions to the rule, that signal potential breakthroughs in our concept of the world about us. And it was these cases that should have been studied from many angles. The committee chose to consider only the problem of whether UFO reports . . . supported the

hypothesis that the earth was being visited by extra-terrestrial intelligences (ETI). UFO=ETI was the defining question. It did not try to establish whether UFOs really constituted a problem for the scientist, whether physical or social. The question of whether puzzling reports of UFOs throughout the world might constitute "genuinely new empirical observations" was not considered.'[71]

He adds that, 'The only hypothesis the committee could have productively tested was: *There exists a phenomenon, described by the content of UFO reports, which presently is not physically explainable.*'[72]

From this point Saunders and Harkins and Hynek take us to the construction of rules of evidence. The test of good data for Saunders and Harkins is their 'remarkability'.

'We may measure the remarkability of any sample of first-class (objective) statistical data about UFOs in order to see if the sample contains enough discrepancies to justify an effort at better explanation. If it doesn't, so be it! If it does, we may wish to say that we have discovered a fact—making careful note of just what the fact is and with what degree of remarkability it has been established . . . No matter what degree of remarkability is achieved, one analysis cannot yield more than one fact.'[73]

These 'remarkables' can then be used to construct hypotheses and theory.

Hynek[74] constructs an S-P diagram, where an index of Strangeness constitutes one axis and a rating of Probability constitutes the other axis. Each is scored one to ten.

'The Strangeness Rating is . . . a measure of how "odd-ball" a report is . . . More precisely, it can be taken as a measure of the number of information bits the report contains, each of which is difficult to explain in common-sense terms.'[75]

Probability refers to the degree of confidence one has as to 'whether the strange event occurred as stated'.[76] Probability has two components, report reliability and witness credibility. The first is 'measured' in terms of internal consistency, consistency among witness statements, as well as judgments of the degree of reporter conviction and 'how it all hangs together'.[77]

Witness credibility is not treated as explicitly, probably because the elements of witness credibility had been worked out by others long before. We can indicate these elements of witness credibility and reasonably assume agreement by Hynek. Richard Hall,[78] in his compendium of NICAP data, argues witness credibility in terms of occupational credentials. Pilots, scientists, engineers and others in occupations demanding professional, scientific or technical expertise, good perception, and observational skills such as familiarity with the sky and/or flight technology are presumed to be good witnesses. To this are added citizens of good standing or 'reputation'. Robert L. Hall[79] suggests as elements of 'credible testimony' reputation in the community, lack of 'motive for prevarication or distortion', familiarity with UFO phenomena (and presumably attitude toward UFO), and several factors already considered as elements of report reliability. Once having determined S-P rating for each case, it is possible to separate the 'signal' from the 'noise'.[80] It is noteworthy that much of the work of the naturalists consists of programmatic statements rather than constructed theories. An exception lies in the work of Vallee, whose four books, as noted by Durant,[81] have proceeded from a naturalist to a macrocosmic perspective similar to that of Clark and Coleman.

The Social Context of Ufology

Any attempt to explore ufology as a developing science must address the social context of that development. It is only then that we will understand the forces that conditioned ufology and those that delay its being fully accorded scientific status. There are three major elements to consider: the journalistic press, the United States Air Force, and the scientific community. It is fitting that we begin with the press, since it was the press that first took note of the phenomena and offered a conceptualisation of importance.

The UFO sighting and report that publicly initiated the modern series of UFO waves was by Kenneth Arnold in early 1947. According to Jacobs:

'The Arnold sighting [1947] was vital for modern UFO history in the United States. As a result of his description of the objects, the newspaper headline writers coined the term *flying saucer,* which rapidly spread around the world as the most popular phrase to describe UFOs. The phrase allowed people to place seemingly inexplicable observations in a new category. Witnesses scanning the sky could now report that they saw something identifiable: a flying saucer. Moreover, the term subtly connoted an artificially constructed piece of hardware; a saucer is not a natural object. Consequently when a witness said at that time that he saw a flying saucer, he implied by the use of the term itself that he had seen something strange and even otherworldly. The term also set a tone of ridicule for the phenomena. The idea of saucers flying on their own volition was absurd. The term allowed people to laugh at the very notion of an unusual object in the sky without having to confront the circumstances behind the event. Saucers do not fly. It was ludicrous for a witness, using the only phrase available to him, to say that he saw one. Therefore, he obviously did not see one. The term itself made the actual event seem invalid.'[82]

This conceptualisation was set in the context of a journalistic 'theory' that 'flying saucers' constituted 'silly season' phenomena. For a scientist to engage the phenomena seriously was to risk damaging his professional reputation.

At the same time, the United States Air Force took an interest, based on the possibility that UFOs might constitute a threat to the nation.[83] The Air Force began investigating reports in 1947, and from 1948 to 1949 and 1951 to 1969 maintained special investigative projects.[84] There were two main perspectives represented in the Air Force in its early years of investigation, those who believed UFOs to be extra-terrestrial and those who believed them to be natural, terrestrial phenomena. The former group maintained a tenuous domination of the early effort. This tenuous domination ceased entirely with the deliberations and recommendations of the Robertson Panel in 1954.

The Robertson Panel, named after its chairman, consisted of a small group of eminent scientists convened by the United States Air Force and the Central Intelligence Agency to consider the UFO problem. Jacobs[85] refers to the Robertson Panel as 'the most influential government-sponsored, non-military UFO investigation of the 1950s.' It 'spent a total of twelve hours studying the UFO phenomenon'. The Robertson Panel was more concerned with public reaction towards UFO phenomena than with the nature of the phenomena themselves. This was quite in line both with the scientific establishment's definition of UFOs as 'mass hysteria', and with an earlier Cold War conditioned Air Force position that an 'enemy' could use the UFO phemenomenon as a 'weapon' in psychological warfare by creating confusion and inducing 'panic' and 'mass hysteria'.[86] The result was the initiation of a long standing Air Force policy of ridicule and silence on the subject.

This policy was fore-shadowed by earlier Air Force treatment of the phenomena. As Larsen[87] documents, the United States Air Force issued a document labelled 'Project Sign', classified 'Secret', in 1949; at the same time, a substantially altered document labelled 'Project Saucer' was released to the press. The documents were different in substance and tone, and the latter utilised (apparently with success) the journalistically constructed concept of ridicule.

Joseph A. Blake

Flammonde[88] alleges the imposition, by the Air Force of a 'canopy of silence' over the media presentation of UFO material. He claims that, 'the periodical index . . . listed no material on the subject from October 1947 to January 9, 1950, although *Time* and the *Saturday Evening Post* did return to the puzzle at least once'.[89] In fact, there *were* listings for that time period in *The Reader's Guide To Periodical Literature* but under the headings 'Illusions and Hallucinations', 'Aeronautics', 'Airplanes', and 'Balloons—use in Research'. This does raise an important question, however, about the role of the media in relation to the UFO phenomenon. Jacobs[90] reports on the serious attention given to UFO phenomena in four major magazine articles in 1952 (one in *Life,* two in *Look,* one in *Time*) and on Air Force fears that such attention would increase the number of reports. He cites Ruppelt[91] to the effect that, upon examination of statistics, no such one way relationship could be found.

On the other hand, both Jacobs[92] and Flammonde[93] suggest a relationship between the Air Force position on UFOs and its policy of ridicule and silence and the amount of attention given the phenomena by the media. We offer a test of this by comparing the number of reports made yearly to Project Blue Book (the Air Force investigative project) from 1947 to 1969 to the number of listings in *The Reader's Guide to Periodical Literature* for the same period of time. This appears as Table 1. We find that the ratio of *Reader's Guide* listings to Blue Book reports fluctuates in the early years, reaching high points of .076 in 1950 and .053 in 1951 (i.e., 5.3 articles for each 100 reports). The ratio drops rather precipitously and remains low until 1966, when it begins climbing to a high in 1969 (the year of the Condon Report). In 1961, for example, the ratio was .000; there were *no* articles in major magazines despite the fact that 591 reports were made to Project Blue Book. The increasing ratio of magazine articles to reports from 1966 to 1969 reflects growing concern about sighting reports and increasingly serious presentations by the major magazines. It also parallels the period of study of UFOs done by the Condon group and funded by the Air Force. It appears that the 'canopy of silence' hypothesis has merit.

Why then, has ufology not been fully accorded scientific status? We suggest that journalistic ridicule, then official silence and ridicule, fostered definitions of UFO phenomena as unsuitable for serious scientific study. The scientific establishment, in turn, supported the

TABLE 1

Major Magazine Articles and UFO Reports

Year			Magazine Articles	UFO Reports	Ratio of Articles to Reports
1947	...	...	5	122	.049
1948	...	...	0	156	.000
1949	...	...	3	186	.016
1950	...	...	16	210	.076
1951	...	...	9	169	.053
1952	...	...	35	1501	.023
1953	...	...	11	509	.021
1954	...	...	7	487	.014
1955	...	...	10	545	.018
1956	...	...	5	670	.007
1957	...	...	9	1006	.009
1958	...	...	3	627	.005
1959	...	...	5	390	.013
1960	...	...	3	557	.005
1961	...	...	0	591	.000
1962	...	...	1	474	.002
1963	...	...	2	399	.005
1964	...	...	0	562	.000
1965	...	...	3	886	.003
1966	...	...	44	1112	.039
1967	...	...	22	937	.023
1968	...	...	10	375	.027
1969	...	...	17	146	.116

Sources:
1. Reports to Project Blue Book in D. M. Jacobs: *The UFO Controversy in America,* Indiana University Press, Bloomington, 1975, p. 304.
2. Magazine articles as counted from *Reader's Guide to Periodical Literature.*

official policy. The Robertson Panel put its stamp of approval on official policy in 1954; the Condon Group, whose findings and methodology were approved by the National Academy of Sciences, did the same thing in 1969.[94] UFOs became intellectually excluded phenomena.

The intellectual exclusion of a topic from scientific study has profound implications. It reduces conceptualisation of the topic from the status of 'knowledge' to that of 'belief', 'ideology', or worse. It stigmatises those who would pursue study of the topic. It also means that those who would pursue its study are likely to be excluded from the means of producing science. This means that data generation and collection will be difficult (the U.S. Air Force, e.g., for years refused to release information on UFO cases); there will be no basis for career construction, recognition and validation (the gates of academia have been largely closed to UFO researchers); and there will be a lack of material resources, i.e., money, equipment and organisation.[95]

It was under these conditions that private individuals began to combine interests and to develop research oriented organisations. The Aerial Phenomena Research Organization (APRO) began in the midwest in 1952, Civilian Saucer Intelligence (CSI) began in New York in 1952, Civilian Research, Interplanetary Flying Objects (CRIFO) existed in Ohio from 1954 to 1957, and the National Investigations Committee on Aerial Phenomena (NICAP) began in Washington, D.C. in 1957. There were, and are, others. Stringfield[96] lists seven major UFO research groups, Flammonde[97] lists five in the United States and thirty-three in fifteen other countries, and Vallee[98] without clearly distinguishing research from other orientations, lists twenty-two 'current' and eight 'defunct' groups. These privately funded research groups provide an organisational basis for ufology.

Through most of the early years of their existence they not only served as data collection points but also battled for respectability. This was particularly true of NICAP, which maintained a many-years-long lobbying effort in Washington, D.C. In the period 1957 to 1969, 'NICAP had become a force as a public pressure and education group that no other UFO organisation could match. Its power and pressure were a major concern to the Air Force, and it had helped keep the UFO issue alive for the public and in Congress.[99] The cardinal goal of these groups was the scientific analysis of UFO phenomena. Through the organisational base began to develop 'specialists', not only in ufology, but in various aspects of it. There are, for example, specialists in photo analysis, physical traces, electro-magnetic effects, encounters, the government role in UFO investigation, and UFO history, including specific 'flaps' (such as the 1890s airship). According to Jacobs:

'The new theory [sic] among UFO investigators was that individual scholars would have to study selected aspects of the phenomenon and come to independent conclusions. The shift was away from asking the "outside" community to consider the origins of UFOs and toward en-

332

The Study of Unidentified Flying Objects

couraging the growing number of individual scientists interested in the subject to conduct their own internal investigations free from the encumbrances of the "scientific establishment".[100]

This came to be most strongly emphasised following the Condon report in 1969. In 1974 the first UFO research organisation was formed that was completely under the direction of scientists (i.e., 'naturalists'); it was called the Center for UFO studies, and directly collected data, as well as getting case information from NICAP, APRO and MUFON (Midwest UFO Network, formed in 1969).[101]

Summary

Ufology is the study of unidentified flying objects. We have argued it to be a science in development, in terms of the coalescing of perspectives on UFOs. These perspectives have been identified as the naturalist and the macroscopic, distinguished in terms of theoretical scope, methodology and emphasis, but similar in problem and conceptualisation. We have also pointed to the essentially moral and power bases of modern science, government and popular thought as represented by the journalistic press and the effect of conceptual exclusion on ufology. Ufology is an intellectual product of social groupings *not* of the intellectual elite. Its social base lies outside the intelligentsia and its organisational arena. Nonetheless, UFO phenomena have been persistent enough and incredible enough to occasion the emergence of social ties among the curious and interested, and through their activities to result in the emergence of ufology.

Wright State University.

[1] H. T. Buckner: 'Flying Saucers are for People', *Trans-Action*, Vol. 3, No. 4, 1966, pp. 10-13; E. Condon: *Scientific Study of Unidentified Flying Objects*, Bantam, New York, 1969; H. Hackett: 'The Flying Saucer: A Manufactured Concept', *Sociology and Social Research*, Vol. 32, 1948, pp. 869-873; L. W. Littig: 'Affiliation Motivation and Belief in Extraterrestrial UFOs', *Journal of Social Psychology*, Vol. 83, 1971, pp. 307-308; C. Sagan and T. Page (eds.): *UFOs—A Scientific Debate*, Cornell University Press, Ithaca, 1972; J. R. Stewart: 'Cattle Mutilations: An Episode of Collective Delusions', paper read at Midwestern Sociological Society Annual Meeting, 1976; D. I. Warren: 'Status Inconsistency Theory and Flying Saucer Sightings', *Science*, 1970, pp. 599-603.

[2] R. H. Hall (ed.): *The UFO Evidence*, National Investigations Committee on Aerial Phenomena, Washington D.C., 1964; R. H. Hall, T. Bloecher and I. Davies: *UFOs: A New Look*, National Investigations Committee on Aerial Phenomena, Washington D.C., 1969; J. A. Hynek: *The UFO Experience: A Scientific Enquiry*, Henry Regnery, Chicago, 1972; G. Lore:

Joseph A. Blake

Strange Effects from UFOs, National Investigations Committee on Aerial Phenomena, Washington D.C., 1969; Sagan and Page: op. cit.; D. R. Saunders and R. R. Harkins: *UFOs? Yes!*, Signet, New York, 1968.

3 Condon: op. cit.

4 See L. E. Catoe: *UFOs and Related Subjects: An Annotated Bibliography*, United States Government Printing Office, Washington D.C., 1969; P. Flammonde: *The Age of Flying Saucers*, Hawthorne, New York, 1971; D. M. Jacobs: *The UFO Controversy in America*, Indiana University Press, Bloomington, 1975.

5 L. H. Stringfield: *Situation Red, the UFO Siege!*, Doubleday, New York, 1977, p. 40. cf. B. Steiger (ed.): *Project Blue Book*, Ballantine, New York, 1976, chapter 13.

6 C. Fort: *The Books of Charles Fort*, Holt, New York, 1941, pp. 216-224, 257-280, 286-290, 507-521, etc.

7 cf. R. L. Morrill: 'Waves of Spatial Diffusion', *Journal of Regional Science*, Vol. 8, 1968, pp. 1-18.

8 J. Clark: 'A Contact Claim', *Flying Saucer Review*, Vol. 11, 1965, pp. 30-32; also, 'The Strange Case of the 1897 Airship', *Flying Saucer Review*, Vol. 12, 1966, pp. 10-17; and 'More on 1897', *Flying Saucer Review*, Vol. 13, 1967, pp. 22-23; Fort: op. cit., pp. 507-521; P. Flammonde: *UFOs Exist!*, Balantine, New York, 1976; C. Grove: 'The Airship Wave of 1909', *Flying Saucer Review*, Vol. 16, 1970, pp. 9-11, and 'The Airship Wave of 1909 —Pt. 2', *Flying Saucer Review*, Vol. 17, 1971, pp. 17-19; D. B. Hanlon: 'Texas Odyssey of 1897', *Flying Saucer Review*, Vol. 12, 1966, pp. 8-11, and 'The Airship . . . Fact and Fiction', *Flying Saucer Review*, Vol. 16, 1970, pp. 20-21; D. B. Hanlon and J. Vallee: 'Airships over Texas', *Flying Saucer Review*, Vol. 13, 1967, pp. 20-25; Mrs. Hinfelaar: 'The New Zealand "Flap" of 1909', *Flying Saucer Review*, Vol. 10, 1964, pp. 32-33; J. A. Keel: 'Mystery Aeroplanes of the 1930s, Part 2', *Flying Saucer Review*, Vol. 16, 1970a, pp. 9-14; J. Vallee: 'Ghost Rockets: A Moment of History', *Flying Saucer Review*, Vol. 10, 1964, pp. 30-32.

9 F. S. C. Northrop: *The Logic of the Sciences and the Humanities*, Meridian, New York, 1967, p. 289.

10 ibid., p. 35.

11 N. R. Hanson: *Patterns of Discovery*, Cambridge University Press, London, 1965, p. 21.

12 Flammonde: op. cit., 1976.

13 J. Fuller: *The Interrupted Journey*, Dial Press, New York, 1966.

14 F. B. Salisbury: *The Utah UFO Display: A Biologists Report*, Devin-Adair, Old Greenwich, Connecticut, 1974; Stewart: op. cit.

15 J. F. Blumrich: *The Spaceships of Ezekiel*, Bantam, New York, 1974; B. H. Downing: *The Bible and Flying Saucers*, Avon, New York, 1968; B. Trench: *The Sky People*, Spearman, London, 1960.

16 J. Weldon and Z. Levitt: *UFOs: What on Earth is Happening?*, Bantam, New York, 1976.

17 D. E. Keyhoe: *The Flying Saucer Conspiracy*, Holt, New York, 1955; B. Steiger: *Flying Saucers are Hostile*, Award Books, New York, 1967.

The Study of Unidentified Flying Objects

Spencer: *Limbo of the Lost,* Bantam, New York, 1973 and *No Earthly Explanation,* Phillips Publishing, Springfield, Massachusetts, 1974.

19 Stringfield: op. cit.

20 R. N. Shepard: 'Some Psychologically Oriented Techniques for the Scientific Investigation of Unidentified Aerial Phenomena', in Committee on Science and Astronautics, United States House: *Symposium on Unidentified Flying Objects,* United States Government Printing Office, Washington D.C.. 1968.

21 Hynek: op. cit., p. 12.

22 R. E. Fowler: *UFOs: Interplanetary Visitors,* Exposition Press, Jericho, New York, 1974, p. 6.

23 J. Clark and L. Coleman: *The Unidentified: Notes Toward Solving the UFO Mystery,* Warner Paperback, New York, 1975, p. 35.

24 ibid.; Salisbury: op. cit., pp. 220-221; Stringfield: op. cit., chapter 5.

25 W. K. Hartman: 'Process of Perception, Conception and Reporting', in Condon: op. cit., pp. 567-590.

26 Stringfield: op. cit., p. 194.

27 ibid., p. 98.

28 Salisbury: op. cit., p. 221.

29 ibid., p. 220.

30 Clark and Coleman: op. cit.

31 T. Bloecher: Report on the UFO Wave of 1947, privately printed, 1967, p. xiv.

32 U.F.O. Investigator, Vol. 3, 1966, p. 7.

33 L. Davidson: *Flying Saucers: An Analysis of the Air Force Project Blue Book Special Report No. 14, Third Edition,* Ramsey-Wallace, New Jersey, 1966, c. 6.

34 Hynek: op. cit., p. 194.

35 A. Lee: 'Public Attitudes Towards UFO Phenomena', in Condon: op. cit., pp. 209-243.

36 Warren: op. cit.

37 Bloecher: op. cit., p. xiv.

38 Flammonde: op. cit., 1976, p. 9.

39 Hall: op. cit., 1964, pp. 129-130.

40 Davidson: op. cit., c. 6.

41 Bloecher: op. cit.

42 Saunders and Harkins: op. cit., suggest, by the way, that reports also differ by the agency to which they are submitted.

43 Bloecher: op. cit., p. xiv.

335

Joseph A. Blake

44 Flammonde: op. cit., 1976, p. 10.

45 Stringfield: op. cit., pp. 124, 133.

46 Flammonde: op. cit., 1976, p 10.

47 cf. ibid., chapter 2.

48 Hynek: op. cit., p. 8.

49 Flammonde: op. cit., 1976.

50 Fort: op. cit.

51 Clark and Coleman: op. cit.; cf. J. Vallee: *Passport to Magonia*, Regnery, Chicago, 1969; J. A. Keel: *Operation Trojan Horse*, Putnam, New York, 1970b.

52 Clark and Coleman: op. cit., p. 181.

53 ibid., p. 225.

54 ibid., pp. 35, 186-187.

55 ibid., pp. 76-77.

56 C. T. Tart (ed.): *Altered States of Consciousness*, Wiley, New York, 1969.

57 Clark and Coleman: op. cit., p. 39.

58 Flammonde: op. cit., 1976, chapter 2.

59 Clark and Coleman: op. cit., p. 196.

60 ibid., p. 201.

61 ibid., p. 236.

62 ibid., p. 242.

63 ibid., p. 238.

64 ibid., p. 201.

65 Bloecher: op. cit; Flammonde: op. cit., 1976; Hynek: op. cit.

66 Flammonde: op. cit., 1976; Stringfield: op. cit., p. 11.

67 Condon: op. cit.,; Stringfield: op. cit., p. 47.

68 S. Nixon: 'Analysis of UFO Photographs', *UFO Quarterly Review*, Vol. 2, No. 1, 1974, pp. 13-20.

69 Saunders and Harkins: op. cit.; Hynek: op. cit.

70 Saunders and Harkins: op. cit., p. 211.

71 Hynek: op. cit., p. 194.

72 ibid., p. 201.

73 Saunders and Harkins: op. cit., p. 210.

74 Hynek: op. cit., chapter 4.

[75] ibid., p. 24.

[76] ibid., p. 25.

[77] ibid.

[78] R. H. Hall: op. cit.

[79] Robert L. Hall: 'Prepared Statement' in *Symposium on Unidentified Flying Objects*, U.S. Government Printing Office, Washington D.C., 1968, p. 109.

[80] J. and J. Vallee: *Challenge to Science: The UFO Enigma*, Ace Books, New York, 1966.

[81] R. J. Durant: 'Book Reviews', *Pursuit*, Vol. 9, No. 2, 1976, pp. 45-47.

[82] Jacobs: op. cit., p. 37.

[83] Condon: op. cit.; Flammonde: op. cit., 1976, especially chapter 20; Jacobs: op. cit.; E. Ruppelt: *The Report on Unidentified Flying Objects*, Ace Books, New York, 1956.

[84] Flammonde: op. cit., 1976, p. 446.

[85] Jacobs: op. cit., p. 93.

[86] Evidently the Russian authorities adopted the same postion towards UFOs in the Soviet Union—see I. Hobara and J. Weverbergh: *UFOs From Behind the Iron Curtain*, Bantam, New York, 1975, p. 33.

[87] S. J. Larsen: 'Documentation: Evidence of Government Concern', in *Proceedings of 1971 Midwest UFO Conference*, the UFO Study Group of Greater St. Louis, 1971.

[88] Flammonde: op. cit., 1976, pp. 249, 352-353.

[89] ibid., p. 249.

[90] Jacobs: op. cit., p. 74.

[91] Ruppelt: op. cit., 1956.

[92] Jacobs: op. cit.

[93] Flammonde: op. cit., 1976.

[94] ibid., p. 413.

[95] cf. R. Collins: *Conflict Sociology*, Academic Press, New York, 1975, chapter 9.

[96] Stringfield: op. cit., pp. 213-214.

[97] Flammonde: op. cit., 1976, pp. 448-454.

[98] Vallee and Vallee: op. cit., pp. 234-243.

[99] Jacobs: op. cit., p. 256.

[100] ibid., pp. 258-259.

[101] Flammonde: op. cit., 1976, pp. 448, 450; Jacobs: op. cit., p. 283.